THE NEW AGE OF NAVAL POWER
IN THE INDO-PACIFIC

THE NEW AGE OF

NAVAL POWER

IN THE

INDO-PACIFIC

STRATEGY, ORDER, AND REGIONAL SECURITY

CATHERINE L. GRANT, ALESSIO PATALANO,
AND JAMES A. RUSSELL, EDITORS

FOREWORD BY VICE ADM. ANN E. RONDEAU, USN (RET.)

GEORGETOWN UNIVERSITY PRESS / WASHINGTON, DC

The publisher is not responsible for third-party websites or their content. URL links were active at time of publication.

Library of Congress Cataloging-in-Publication Data

Names: Grant, Catherine L., editor. | Patalano, Alessio, editor. | Russell, James A. (James Avery), 1958- editor.
Title: The new age of naval power in the Indo-Pacific : strategy, order, and regional security / Catherine L. Grant, Alessio Patalano, James A. Russell, editors ; foreword by Vice Adm. Ann Rondeau (USN ret.).
Description: Washington, DC : Georgetown University Press, [2023] | Includes bibliographical references and index.
Identifiers: LCCN 2022026241 (print) | LCCN 2022026242 (ebook) | ISBN 9781647123383 (hardcover) | ISBN 9781647123390 (paperback) | ISBN 9781647123406 (ebook)
Subjects: LCSH: Sea-power—Indo-Pacific Region. | Naval strategy. | Indo-Pacific Region—Strategic aspects.
Classification: LCC VA643 .N48 2023 (print) | LCC VA643 (ebook) | DDC 359.009164—dc23/eng/20230413
LC record available at https://lccn.loc.gov/2022026241
LC ebook record available at https://lccn.loc.gov/2022026242

♾ This paper meets the requirements of ANSI/NISO Z39.48-1992 (Permanence of Paper).

24 23   9 8 7 6 5 4 3 2 First printing

Printed in the United States of America

Cover design by Jim Keller
Interior design by BookComp, Inc.

Dedicated to James,
who experienced the Indo-Pacific as a sailor,
strengthened ties across its confines as an officer,
and enabled many others to learn about
its strategic significance as a scholar.

CONTENTS

ILLUSTRATIONS

TABLE

FIGURES

FOREWORD

The United States has entered another era—and different kind—of great-power competition, one in which the Navy and maritime issues will figure prominently in our unfolding and dynamic strategic environment. As highlighted in the December 2020 report by the US Navy, the US Coast Guard, and the US Marine Corps, *Advantage at Sea: Prevailing with Integrated, All-Domain Naval Power*, our purposes of preserving freedom of navigation on the high seas, deterring aggression, and winning wars are as important today as they have ever been.

Nowhere are the challenges of these missions as pronounced as they are in the vast Indo-Pacific maritime domain, an area encompassing half the earth's surface that ranges from the West Coast of the United States to the western coast of India, south to the Antarctic, and north to the Arctic. The region is home to thirty-six countries with more than 50 percent of the world's population. Its strategic importance cannot be overstated. As emphasized in the US Department of Defense 2019 report titled *Indo-Pacific Strategy Report: Preparedness, Partnerships, and Promoting a Networked Region,* "the Indo-Pacific is the single most consequential region for America's future."

The US Navy and its partners around the world face myriad challenges in constructively applying naval and maritime power across this maritime domain to preserve the rules-based international order and to ensure the free flow of people and commerce that is so vital for global peace and prosperity. The essays in this volume are intended to help current and future military leaders, political officials, policy professionals, and academics to unpack the different dimensions of applying naval power across this domain. The expert contributors remind us of the complexities and strategic importance of this job that falls to the US Navy and its many partners around the world.

These essays are also intended to spur an intellectual revolution within the ranks of our junior leaders as they think through the difficult and complex problems of applying naval power in the Indo-Pacific that are highlighted in this volume. Indeed, the intellectual capacity of our active-duty leaders is essential to anticipating and effectively maneuvering in this complex maritime environment. Leaders must master intellectual resilience and agility in this new age of great-power competition. The intent of this volume's authors is to nourish the emergence of a future generation of naval strategists with works such as this that follow from the rich history of strategic thought from such great naval strategists as Alfred Thayer Mahan, Julian Corbett, and Bernard Brodie to help guide us in the future.

It is entirely appropriate that the Naval Postgraduate School should assume a leading role in this effort by exposing naval professionals both in the United States and around the world to the complex issues facing their institutions in the Indo-Pacific. The chapters in this volume will encourage our junior leaders to steep themselves in the Indo-Pacific challenges as they grapple with thinking their way through twenty-first-century challenges in the classroom and at sea. In addition to a collection of scholars from the Naval Postgraduate School and the Naval War College, we are also particularly grateful for the inclusion of our partners in the War Studies Department at King's College, the University of London, in this project. This simply emphasizes that as practiced on the high seas, the US Navy continuously operates with coalition partners from around the world—all of whom also need to address the challenges of promoting peace, security, and prosperity in the Indo-Pacific.

Vice Adm. Ann E. Rondeau, USN (Ret.)
President, Naval Postgraduate School

ACKNOWLEDGMENTS

This volume would not have been possible without the support and enthusiasm of Bruce Stubbs, the recently retired director of strategy and concepts (N72S), in the Office of the Chief of Naval Operations in Washington, DC. We greatly appreciate his support and that of his office in encouraging us to unpack the dynamics of naval power in the Indo-Pacific. We also want to express our gratitude for the support of Sadie Hastings, Matt Kline, and Cecelia Davis in the Naval Postgraduate School's Naval Research Program. Last, we want to emphasize that those authors in this volume who are employed by the US Department of Navy and the US government are expressing their own opinions in their respective chapters and not necessarily those of the Navy or the government.

ABBREVIATIONS

ADIZ	air defense identification zone
ASEAN	Association of Southeast Asian Nations
ASW	antisubmarine warfare
A2/AD	antiaccess/area-denial
AU	Australia
AUKUS	Australia, United Kingdom, and United States (security group)
CASD	continuous at-sea deterrence
CCP	Chinese Communist Party
CER	Chinese Eastern Railroad
C4ISR	command, control, communications, computers, intelligence, surveillance, and reconnaissance
CLCS	Commission on the Limits of the Continental Shelf (United Nations)
CMC	Central Military Commission (China)
COMCASA	Communications Compatibility and Security Agreement (US-India)
DMZ	demilitarized zone
ECS	East China Sea
EEZ	exclusive economic zone
ESCS	East and South China Seas
FFA	Pacific Islands Forum Fisheries Agency
FOIP	Free and Open Indo-Pacific
FONOP	freedom-of-navigation operation
FPDA	Five Power Defence Arrangements
ICBM	intercontinental ballistic missile
IEA	International Energy Agency
IOR	Indian Ocean region
IPCC	Intergovernmental Panel on Climate Change
ITLOS	International Tribunal on the Law of the Sea
JDA	joint development area
JMSDF	Japan Maritime Self-Defense Force

KIG	Kalayaan Island Group
KMT	Kuomintang
LCS	littoral combat ship
LDP	Liberal Democratic Party (Japan)
MIRV	multiple independently targetable reentry vehicle
MOU	memorandum of understanding
NATO	North Atlantic Treaty Organization
NLL	Northern Limit Line (South Korea)
NPT	Non-Proliferation Treaty
PIC	Pacific Island country
PLA	People's Liberation Army
PLAN	People's Liberation Army–Navy
PMSP	Pacific Maritime Security Program (Australia)
PNG	Papua New Guinea
PRC	People's Republic of China
PSI	Proliferation Security Initiative
ROC	Republic of China (Taiwan)
ROKN	Republic of Korea Navy
SCS	South China Sea
SEANWFZ	Southeast Asia Nuclear Weapon–Free Zone
SEATO	Southeast Asia Treaty Organization
SIDS	small island developing states (Pacific)
SLBM	submarine-launched ballistic missile
SLOC	sea line of communication
SSBN	nuclear-powered ballistic missile submarine
UNCLOS	United Nations Convention on the Law of the Sea
UNSCR	United Nations Security Council Resolution
USSR	Union of Soviet Socialist Republics
WMD	weapon of mass destruction

1

Naval Power and a Framework for Regional Security in the Indo-Pacific

Alessio Patalano, James A. Russell,
and Catherine L. Grant

After a hiatus of a little more than two decades, competition at sea is back as a central issue of international security.[1] Starting in the 1990s, the United States–led dominance over the world's oceans defined the growth of trade, freedom of navigation, and the post–Cold War engagement in expeditionary operations from Africa to Central Asia. Today this freedom to use the oceans as a vast maneuvering space for civilian or naval purposes stands contested. Senior US military leadership now emphasizes how maritime theaters are no longer places where nations can take for granted the freedom of navigation and movement of goods at sea and the freedom of operational conduct, most notably in the East and South China Seas.[2] Indeed, as a result of the oceans becoming a contested space once more, the very foundations of today's global economic interdependence stand vulnerable to hostile state actions. As a result, the US debate on the strategic value of naval power to national security has shifted away from the concern about how to influence international politics by projecting power ashore back to the need to ensure the capacity to meet actors challenging freedom of navigation or, in case of war, sea control.[3] In a similar fashion, other actors with major stakes in international maritime order, from Japan to the United Kingdom and France, from the North Atlantic Treaty Organization to the European Union, have all expressed concerns about the systemic challenges that states such as Russia and China present to freedom of the seas.

In part, this is the result of strategic exhaustion in the United States brought on by two decades of expensive and inconclusive operations on land in the Middle East and South Asia. These have drained intellectual capacity, affected the availability of resources, and reduced the political capital to sustain a Pax

Americana. More broadly, the return to an emphasis on relative naval power recognizes that the global strategic environment has changed. The last two US National Security Strategy documents, adopted in 2017 and 2022, respectively, and naval documents published throughout this period, indicate a renewed focus on the risks to the stability of the ocean and on the needs of how to gain sea control as a primary condition of retaining operational freedom.[4] Countries such as the United Kingdom, which also has globally postured armed forces, share these assumptions about the importance of being prepared to fight for sea control in more contested maritime theaters.[5] Indeed, the reactivation in 2018 of the US Navy (USN) Second Fleet to deal with a less stable North Atlantic is one of the most recent policy actions that reflects this shift in attitude.[6] Similarly, post–Cold War concerns with maritime security and governance to deal with transnational challenges as enshrined in such concepts as the "thousand ship navy" have now taken a less prominent role.[7]

THE PUZZLE: WHY DOES NAVAL POWER MATTER IN THE INDO-PACIFIC?

Nowhere is the urgency to meet state-on-state competition at sea more strongly felt than in the Indo-Pacific region.[8] In this part of the world, freedom of navigation stands challenged by regional states' continuous investments in military power, including technologies that have reduced the capability gap with the USN, and the renewed political will to use it. This is a particularly troubling issue in the United States, where there is a well-established understanding that Washington's ability to project power globally rests upon naval dominance.[9] In the Indo-Pacific, naval power reflects the use of naval forces (including navies, coast guards, and all the other military and paramilitary organizations capable of operating in the maritime theater) to signal, manage, govern, deter, coerce, and, if necessary, fight a war, in the pursuit of two sets of missions. On one hand, for more than a decade now, the People's Republic of China (PRC) has been leading this transformation to wider uses of naval power as a tool of statecraft to contest American dominance in the region. It is systematically modernizing and expanding its military power, from capabilities to deny access in the East and South China Seas, if not to assert control in these theaters—including across the Strait of Taiwan—to those required for expeditionary missions well beyond their confines on a scale that has no precedent in recent times.[10] China's ability to project power at sea and to contest the control of key maritime areas has become a crucial test for America's continued global leadership.[11]

American concerns over the return of naval competition and the challenge posed to its prominent position in world affairs are not mistaken. The PRC's sustained funding for conventional and nuclear-powered submarines, different types of surface combatants (also encompassing enhanced coast guard cutters and militia fleets), and the expansion of land-based power-projection systems—even the development of artificial military outposts on contested island features—are redefining the military balance across the Indo-Pacific.[12] In fact, as Chinese oceanographic research and naval activities expand farther afield to the Indian Ocean, Africa, the Middle East, and the polar regions, there is ground to consider whether authorities in Beijing nurture global rather than regional ambitions—well beyond East Asia.[13] Although China states that it is pursuing "a national defense policy that is defensive in nature,"[14] in a maritime operational context the distinction between offensive and defensive capabilities is difficult to draw. Depending on the specific scenarios, there is considerable overlap between offensive and defensive capabilities.[15] China shows a desire to become a "maritime power" that is inherently related to their aim of reviewing and upgrading the country's status on the world stage.[16] When such declarations are paired with trends in the country's naval capabilities, it is possible to argue that for Chinese authorities having a defensive posture does not set limits on the geographic boundaries of China's reach.

On the other hand, in the Indo-Pacific, competition stands for more than what Adm. Stansfield Turner defined as a potential struggle for "sea control."[17] The wider expansion in the array of capabilities available to states operating in this region is both the result of, and a propellent for, further expansion of missions. This relates to the widening constabulary and law-enforcement activities aimed at the management of maritime boundary delimitations and territorial disputes resulting from the rights and duties of coastal states brought about by the 1982 United Nations Convention on the Law of the Sea (UNCLOS). Whether to protect national rights or to challenge those set forth by others, the maritime spaces of the Indo-Pacific have today become a national security priority that includes more than major-power competition. In particular, UNCLOS has contributed to the development of new attitudes toward the problem of ocean governance as a state responsibility to be pursued nationally or collaboratively. In turn, this process—accelerated by the US post-9/11 concern with transnational security threats—has enhanced governments' awareness of the need for constabulary and law-enforcement activities to address broader "maritime security" issues.[18] In this respect, maritime order and stability are today understood to encompass issues of governance at sea.

As a result of these trends, regional states have adapted their strategies, pursued new capabilities, and seek to address the challenge of striking a balance between capabilities and missions for sea control (warfare functions) and those required to maintain "good order" at sea (maritime security functions).[19] Indeed, this dilemma is further compounded by the fact that in the conduct of daily activities, issues of maritime governance and security are often difficult to fully disentangle from issues of strategic competition. Naval powers deploy forces across the Indo-Pacific to reinforce or challenge excessive claims—US freedom-of-navigation operations being a case in point.[20] Other regional actors, such as Japan and China, engage their capabilities—coast guards or navies, depending on the specific institutional arrangements and hosting-partner preferences—in capacity-building programs to support coastal states in implementing national jurisdictions at sea.[21] In turn, capacity building empowers less capable states with the means to protect maritime rights and, if needed, to challenge others with competing claims—opening options to strategies described by social scientists as consistent with a "hedging behavior."[22] Similar considerations about the potential political significance of naval power in the Indo-Pacific apply to other forms of maritime security assistance, notably humanitarian assistance and disaster-relief missions.[23]

Whether as a quest for international power and military superiority or as a pursuit for better maritime governance and the safeguarding of national sovereignty, naval power stands at the center of regional order and stability. Indeed, naval competition and maritime governance are inherent manifestations of the centrality of maritime connectivity to regional prosperity and security—as assessments of naval developments in Southeast Asia attest.[24] Within this context, Japan provides one of the most notable examples of a regional actor that has expanded naval activities as a way to reinforce regional order and power balance. The Japan Maritime Self-Defense Force and the Japan Coast Guard stand at the forefront of diplomatic efforts and activities as diverse as capacity building and military exercises stretching from Maldives to throughout the Association of Southeast Asian Nations (ASEAN).[25] Naval forces were the spearhead of Prime Minister Shinzo Abe's signature foreign policy Free and Open Indo-Pacific (FOIP) initiative, which embodies the country's call for stable and secure seas linking Africa and the Middle East to Asia.[26] Similarly, regional governments in the South Pacific emphasize the role of naval forces to manage the potentially devastating impact of climate change and environmental degradation on ocean governance and national prosperity.[27]

Based on the aforementioned considerations, how do naval capabilities influence power balance and regional order in the Indo-Pacific? How do different types of capabilities affect regional security? How does a Sino-American naval competition for maritime dominance affect regional stability? Do current examinations of naval activities in the region adequately capture the relationship seemingly linking naval power to statecraft on matters of both military superiority and maritime governance? Does the nature of digital-age systems integration into regional force structures change the way that states think about applying force on the high seas? Equally significant, if naval capabilities affect the conduct of competition and the maintenance of stability, how is the expansion of regional arsenals affecting the risk of instability and war across the various subregional theaters? These questions are essential to understanding why naval power matters in the Indo-Pacific and are the ones we address in this volume.

THE ARGUMENT: NAVAL POWER
AS STATECRAFT IN THE INDO-PACIFIC

We place at the center of our analysis the role of naval forces (including military and constabulary organizations) as significant tools of statecraft.[28] The argument we set forth is that the Indo-Pacific is a meaningful geopolitical construct that captures the geographic centrality of the sea—the Indian and Pacific Oceans—to regional security and the role of naval power in it. We further argue that the impact of naval power on regional security should be understood as the result of the interplay of competitive and cooperative behaviors, enabled by the "hard" and "soft" uses of naval forces and underscored by five drivers informing how states identify priorities, organize agendas, and articulate ambitions in this maritime regional space. Thus, naval power is a tool of statecraft in which capabilities are deployed to conduct a variety of missions to defend territorial spaces, manage the maritime environment, create and enhance partnerships, and project national power. We argue that a systematic examination of the ensemble of naval interactions occurring across the different missions informs how maritime order is understood and how changes in regional security and stability take place. The enablers behind states' pursuits of naval capabilities directly relate to the uses of the sea as a space of maneuver and a resource and to the means to use it—all of which creates a multilayered complex explaining why naval power is such a central tool of statecraft. It is in this complexity, we argue, that rests the key to understanding problems of power, stability, and security in the Indo-Pacific.

Maritime geography holds a central role in the security of the Indo-Pacific. In this part of the world, the centrality of the sea to regional connectivity and interactions is essential to understanding how state actors seek to exert influence—through both coercive and engagement measures. In this respect, we argue that the diffusion of modern naval capabilities across the region does not make it inherently unstable and prone to the risk of war; rather, we posit that in the Indo-Pacific, naval power offers the opportunity for more frequent interactions, not all of which are destabilizing to regional security. We do so by recognizing that for strategic planners and political authorities across the region, the force structures that support coercive action in no way exclude opportunities for constructive interaction. On the contrary, robust capabilities are consistently and regularly deployed to invite partners, strengthen relations, and reassure allies as much as signal, deter, and coerce adversaries. Chinese coercion at sea, for example, is operationalized by a naval order of battle drawing on the multidomain character of sensors and weapons fielded to perform a variety of missions, not all competitive in nature. A Chinese destroyer essential to a denial posture in the China Seas or a carrier task group within and outside their confines could very well stand at the forefront of cooperation in good governance missions, such as counterpiracy.

By placing maritime geography and naval power at the heart of regional security, we take the ambitions of the naval literature (focused on explaining why and how naval power matters in general) a step further and link them to why and how it matters to the study of international affairs. Our collective aim is not just to provide yet another assessment of how navies produce effects; rather, we argue that because of the effects navies generate, a naval approach is particularly suitable to understanding key security mechanics informing today's Indo-Pacific. In this intellectual journey, we take our cue from earlier work on naval diplomacy and deterrence initially developed during the Cold War and aimed at explaining the link between naval power and political influence.[29] Consistent with this body of literature, the chapters in this volume focus on what aspects of the interactions at sea inform the development of national maritime strategies and the procurement of relevant capabilities.

We draw attention to interactions in the specific regional space of the Indo-Pacific as a way to place the study of the naval dimension of security within the broader methodological approach proposed in the regional security complex literature. We share with this approach the ambition to more fully understand the interplay of national and international security, the link between internal conditions in states and relations among states in the region, and the correlations between regional stability and great-power politics.[30] Unlike this literature, however, this volume argues that because the Indo-Pacific is a maritime region, naval interactions are central to unpacking the complex economic, diplomatic, and military relationships linking warfare to security, competition to cooperation, and stability to war.

Defining the Indo-Pacific

One critical consideration concerns the definition of the region in itself. Among the options to define the wider Asia Pacific as a security space, we adopt the "Indo-Pacific" denomination. From a security perspective, the Indo-Pacific is now an established concept among practitioners and political elites. It reflects a recognition of the centrality of maritime geography to security and links maritime strategy and naval power to the way in which state actors engage with each other. In 2016, specifically pointing to how the sea sits at the intersection of economic prosperity and military stability, the Japanese government launched the aforementioned FOIP.[31] In 2017 the United States, too, adopted an Indo-Pacific framework in its National Security Strategy and reengineered its political and military apparatus accordingly with the renaming of Pacific Command "Indo-Pacific Command." Long before the United States began focusing on it, Indo-Pacific notions had been articulated in countries such as Australia.[32] In 2019 India and ASEAN similarly recognized the importance to politically engage within this spatial framework.[33] Major European powers with overseas territorial, economic, and security interests in the region—notably France, the Netherlands, Germany, and the United Kingdom—have recently developed their own Indo-Pacific strategy or endeavored to adopt the term in their national security outlooks.[34] Indeed, even when authoritative Chinese commentators refer to the reluctance in the PRC to adopt this conceptualization of the region, they understand and recognize its significance as much as they are concerned about its implications.[35]

While this framework is now of common use, its meaning and geographical boundaries vary depending on whether one is in Canberra, Tokyo, Beijing, Colombo, or Washington. This is why we still think it is important to review how we consider its utility. After all, "regional spaces" are always geographic constructs.[36] For the purpose of our study, Rory Medcalf offers a compelling case for the Indo-Pacific as a construct fit for "a 21st century of maritime connectivity and a geopolitics that is many-sided, or as the diplomats say, multipolar."[37] As a unit of analysis for interactions among state actors, the Indo-Pacific meets the four characteristics of classical security complex theory: it involves multiple states, it is a geographically coherent grouping (with two oceans as its connecting fabric), it is marked by security interdependence, and it displays clear and durable patterns of interactions.[38] The map in figure 1.1 showcases the broadest (Japanese) and the narrowest (American) views of the boundaries of what constitutes the Indo-Pacific. The differing conceptions still show a consistent "maritime logic," but the US Department of Defense sets the narrowest Indo-Pacific boundaries due to its other combatant commands. In the expansive Japanese conception of the Indo-Pacific, it is a regional space in which the Indian and Pacific Oceans are the core fabric connecting states from the eastern coast of Africa and the Arabian Sea to the Pacific coastlines of the United States and South America in a coherent fashion. For any conception of the Indo-Pacific, it is a space that is inclusive and porous due to its maritime nature with boundaries that fluctuate.

Five Factors of Influence

How does naval power help to explain the complexity of Indo-Pacific security, then? In this volume, our argument is that in a maritime-centric security complex like the Indo-Pacific, a state's ability to affect dynamics of stability

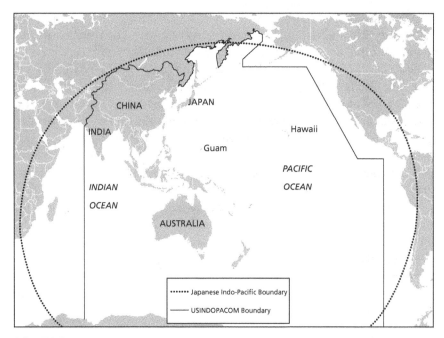

FIGURE 1.1. Map of the Indo-Pacific, showing the maximalist Japanese conception of its boundaries and the narrower boundaries as defined by US Indo-Pacific Command.

and power competition will depend on its capacity to leverage five "factors of influence." These are the capacity to exert control over sea-lanes, the capacity to deploy a nuclear deterrent at sea, the capacity to implement law of the sea in an advantageous way, the ability to control marine resources, and the capacity for technological innovation. These factors unfold directly from the ways in which the sea has impacted human activities. In particular, we build upon Geoffrey Till's work stressing the link between naval power and how and why human beings have chosen throughout history to take to the sea. According to Till, the sea has historically had four uses: a means of transportation, a resource, a means for dominion (the projection of power), and a space for the exchange of information and the spread of ideas.[39] In reviewing Till's approach to the uses of the sea, we believe that these four uses can be reorganized in three categories. The first is related to the sea as a means of transportation for both economic and military reasons. The second use pertains to the notion of the sea as a resource. The third category we identify relates directly to the sea more as a source of innovation to find better ways and means to sail across its expanses (and more recently to fly over them or travel underneath its surface) or indeed project power. Visually, figure 1.2 conveys how the uses of the sea relate to the "factors of influence" of naval power.

Sea Control / Power Projection   Law of the Sea

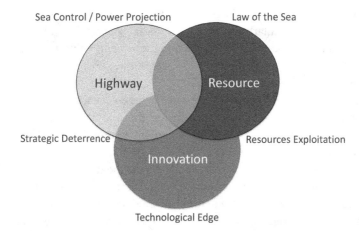

Strategic Deterrence   Resources Exploitation

Technological Edge

FIGURE 1.2. How naval power's five factors of influence relate to the uses of the sea.

The sea's uses as the world's "superhighway" to transport goods that power economies and for military maneuvers are responsible for two factors that are key to the role of naval power in great-power politics and geopolitical competition.[40] The first factor of influence pertains to states' perceptions of their ability (real or perceived) to control sea-lanes to meet national security requirements, whether to protect trade or to project national power and influence. How states consider their ability to access, use, and control sea-lanes informs how they conceptualize the nature of the challenge from peer competitors and their need to prioritize naval capabilities.

The second factor is nuclear deterrence at sea—as a specific type of capability that benefits from the stealth and access that the ocean provides. This gained prominence during the Cold War and today is directly related to the reach and potential of regional strategic arsenals.

The third and fourth factors of influence of naval power's "shaping" capacity in the Indo-Pacific are related to the use of the sea as a resource. The world's oceans remain central to human life, for they contain fish stocks and natural resources invaluable to food and energy requirements.[41] More specifically, the third factor relates to states' capacity to implement the legal frameworks that govern interactions at sea to maximize their positions. These frameworks— most notably UNCLOS—define the rights and duties of state actors, they set boundaries to the application of sovereignty, they protect the freedom of navigation, and, as a result, their application and their enforcement is a defining feature of state actors' interactions.

The fourth factor of influence concerns the ability to exploit natural resources. Their existence, accessibility, and indeed their sustainable use are a crucial factor underpinning efforts toward cooperation and competition. These two enablers are particularly important for understanding the widening of law-enforcement and constabulary activities and the growing value attributed to the legitimacy of operations conducted in respect of the principles and practices of good governance at sea.[42]

The fifth factor of influence is focused on a state's capacity for technological prowess and sophistication—and it relates to the role the sea has in prompting innovation and technological advancement within societies. Navies are technology-intensive organizations, and the ability to nurture innovation and advanced technological know-how directly affects the development of modern capabilities. This, in turn, has implications on national strategy, political ambitions, and, ultimately, how state actors can interact with each other.[43] Access to advanced technology defines the extent to which naval authorities can procure assets to perform a large variety of missions under different circumstances and warships that are tailored to conduct specific types of operations. In turn, access to modern, cutting-edge technology depends on the ever-present need in modern military procurement to control cost escalation, imposing constraints on the number of hulls and types of combat systems. Hence, the technology factor matters in a maritime-centric regional security environment. Within this context, we try in this book to explore how access to (or the lack of) technology affects problems of behavior and, as a result, stability.

Maritime Geography as a Strategic Factor

A main ambition of our argument is to offer a strategic studies alternative to normative explanations about stability in East Asia. Notably, by focusing on maritime geography as a strategic factor in understanding how state actors interact, we propose to overcome the limits of the notion of a traditional "Sino-centric East Asian order and hierarchy" to explain a "pattern of interaction" systematically lacking state actors balancing against China.[44] In particular, such an approach has failed to convincingly explain how the logic of a normative Sinic international system would historically apply to political realities such as Japan or, indeed, Southeast Asia. Relatedly, it has also confused strategies aimed at tailoring military capabilities to emphasize asymmetry—an option open to governments in maritime-centric regional contexts—with a broader reluctance to invest in military power to confront China (based on a quantitative analysis of military procurement in relation to gross domestic product).[45] In the Indo-Pacific, the sea has always mattered strategically in the way in which states interacted with each other. As a result, to borrow David C. Kang's own metaphor, the "size" of the dog in the fight is not as important as the "type" of dog for which one opts.[46] The approach in our volume is set to better explain how state actors specifically choose a dog based on the type of fight—or, indeed, fights—in which they seek to engage.

THE GAP: LINKING THE MARITIME
AND SECURITY LITERATURES

By design, this volume represents an attempt to fill a glaring gap in the field of East Asian security. It has no real equal in the wider literature on this part of the world, which is predominantly divided into maritime strategic works focused on East Asia as a case study or international security scholarship of the region. In this volume, the chapters collectively seek to reconcile this divide by employing a methodology that derives from the latter field of research to engage with themes and issues relevant to the former. Our collective goal is to create an opportunity for a multidisciplinary dialogue in which an understanding of naval matters enriches the study of East Asian security.

Within the realm of maritime strategic thinking, in the volume *International Order at Sea: How It Is Challenged, How It Is Maintained*, Jo Inge Bekkevold and Geoffrey Till led a group of international scholars to offer a review of the comparative nature of maritime issues from the Arctic to Europe and Asia.[47] Their book represents one of the most recent and comprehensive primers in maritime security, introducing one fundamental premise informing our own volume. *International Order at Sea* showcases the importance of "unity" of the ocean in how issues of resource management and exploitation, maritime order and access to sea-lanes, and strategic deterrence are explored in different basins. Bekkevold and Till's crucial contribution is that they provide a strong case for the need to look at maritime security and naval competition as interconnected layers. However, *International Order at Sea* does not specifically link the study of maritime issues to the security dynamics of the Indo-Pacific. In this sense, it shares a methodological approach with our volume, but it does not apply it to examine the region we explore.

On the other hand, other collective works published during the past decade have done much to tackle specific questions pertaining to maritime security and power struggle in the Indo-Pacific. Peter Alan Dutton, Robert Ross, and Øystein Tunsjø focus on the role of legal frameworks in managing maritime security and competition at sea in their study titled *Twenty-First Century Seapower: Cooperation and Conflict at Sea*.[48] In a similar vein, Daniel Moran and James A. Russell have examined in their volume *Maritime Strategy and Global Order: Markets, Resources, Security* how navies have contributed and continue to contribute to maintaining an international maritime order aimed at the circulation of goods and economic growth.[49] By contrast, Geoffrey Till and Jan Chan and also Nicholas Tarling and Xin Chen have focused on the rise of modern maritime forces in

Southeast Asia to explore the growing centrality of maritime issues to regional security debates in *Naval Modernisation in Southeast Asia: Nature, Causes, and Consequences* and *Maritime Security in East and Southeast Asia: Political Challenges in Asian Waters*, respectively.[50] Along not too dissimilar lines, Bernard Cole's *Asian Maritime Strategies* offers a useful review of national approaches to the development of naval power without addressing how such developments relate to the region's changing security dynamics.[51] Till's work on naval arms races in Asia similarly seeks to examine the specific issue of how increased naval capabilities could affect the development of "action-reaction" dynamics, which in turn would exacerbate "security dilemmas" among the region's major naval powers.[52]

In all, the maritime literature has highlighted three key aspects that concern our volume: the increased importance of naval capabilities to national security across the Indo-Pacific, the impact that naval power has on competition and power balance in the region, and the existence of state-on-state gauging considerations as well as concerns over matters of stability, safety, and governance of the region's maritime spaces in the ways in which state actors invest in naval capabilities and assess the role of naval power within the priorities of national security.

These important considerations remain only partly integrated within the security studies literature that is relevant to the Indo-Pacific. In the early 2010s at the Naval War College, Thomas Mahnken and Dan Blumenthal were among the first scholars to bring together a group of distinguished historians and social scientists to debate East Asian security from a strategic studies perspective.[53] Their conversation later became the edited volume *Strategy in Asia*. In it, one of the most insightful conclusions concerns the call for more to be done in mainstream security studies literature to recognize and integrate the impact of geography on the region's historical experience. Specific perceptions of the national security landscape informed the prioritization of the means to address challenges in it.[54] In their volume, geography and strategy were intertwined in shaping how regional actors conceptualized and acted on their security challenges. More recently, Peter Dombrowski and Jonathan Caverley, leading scholars at the Naval War College, have brought together a team of international scholars to specifically address the impact of naval affairs within the wider US-China competition in a special 2020 issue for the journal *Security Studies*. Their groundbreaking work has sought to close the gap between naval studies and the security literature, and our aim with this volume is to continue on the path they started to chart. In particular, we are complementing their work by showcasing how the US-China naval competition is set within a more complicated security complex, which cannot be entirely dissociated from other regional maritime-related issues, notably territorial disputes and subregional power balance.[55]

William Tow's *Security Politics in the Asia-Pacific: A Regional-Global Nexus?* added to this debate over structural influences on regional security by offering a comprehensive review of the links between the global and local dimensions. Global trends in international security have repercussions in specific regions of the world, whether on matters of great-power competition or transnational security. However, in Tow's volume this important point is not fully explored in a maritime context. Instead, the maritime dimension is investigated as a specific subset of issues, somewhat downplaying the importance of the oceans in linking the regional and global dimensions of security.[56] In a similar fashion, Evelyn Goh's *The Struggle for Order: Hegemony, Hierarchy and Transition in Post–Cold War East Asia* raises other crucial issues around the question order and hierarchy as processes negotiated among different stakeholders. In her book, she highlights how in East Asia the security balance is not a question of mere material power. Rather, she points to the role that recognition and legitimacy play in how state actors interact with each other and how specific status is recognized and accepted.[57] Nonetheless, in her case, too, there is no attempt to assess whether and to what extent the fact that the sea is central to how state actors interact remained outside the scope of the analysis.

In our volume, we take stock of this wealth of scholarly work but also push it a step further. By placing the Indo-Pacific as a geographical construct for our analysis, we bring together key themes identified in the East Asian security literature pertaining to the links between geography and strategy, global and regional security, and material and cognitive understanding of security. In so doing, we make a critical original contribution about the mechanics of interactions in the Indo-Pacific. By exploring how naval interplays occur, we showcase how concerns over both naval competition and maritime governance inform state actors' actions. Furthermore, we explain how, depending on the ability to pursue different sets of capabilities, national strategies will naturally seek to strike a balance between the two. In part, this is because, as the maritime literature has long held, the projection of power across the oceans is more complicated to achieve and sustain than on land. As a result, power balance, order, and stability are a negotiated process in which stronger state actors seek to advance their interests through a combination of positive influence and coercion and unilateral and multilateral action. By the same token, weaker state actors will recognize and validate the results of such processes as a way to advance their own agendas.

THE ORIGINALITY: THE GEOPOLITICS OF NAVAL POWER

In reconciling the maritime and East Asian security literatures, this volume makes an original contribution in the current rediscovery of geography and geopolitics in international politics. More than a decade ago, Harvey Starr pointed out how the concept of "space" is one that hardly features in the field of international relations. Indeed, as he pointed out, scholars had predominantly tended to dismiss the relevance of space as deterministic and irrelevant to their analysis.[58] Historians of the discipline would agree with this assessment. Indeed, as they have recently uncovered, leading American scholars tasked with redefining the field's research agenda in the late 1940s and early 1950s made a conscious choice to marginalize geopolitics and geography-informed examinations of international politics.[59]

In the Indo-Pacific, we show that geopolitics is related to the conceptualization of this space. In the realm of security, the recognition of a link between geography and the political dynamics of the Indo-Pacific is not new. Long before Robert Kaplan's "revenge of geography" linked security to maritime affairs, French geopolitician François Joyaux had noted how Asian geography and security were entwined.[60] In particular, Joyaux was among the first scholars to highlight how the maritime expanses of the region connected (and divided) the majority of regional actors.[61] Although not specifically addressed toward the Indo-Pacific, recent scholarship has developed Joyaux's earlier observations. Additionally, authors have articulated how projecting military power across maritime spaces is harder than on land—depending as it is on the capacity to develop and sustain naval capabilities. Scholarship has similarly highlighted how alliances' formation against hegemonic naval powers is less frequent and likely to happen than alliances against continental powers, and, moreover, directly related to these points, scholarship has highlighted that at sea escalation toward war is less likely to take place when compared to escalation on land.[62]

These observations all relate to a key point: hegemony in a maritime space is not—with very few exceptions—related to the conquest of territory.[63] Rather, it is about the ability to retain access to the location of resources and to the ability to freely maneuver along the lines of communication linking them.[64] Our volume makes an original contribution to this wider debate over the specificities of maritime-centric security contexts by exploring how naval power matters well beyond questions of hegemony and military superiority. In the Indo-Pacific, the geopolitics of naval power are also about interactions pertaining to national assertions on, and participation over, matters of maritime governance, access and exploitation of resources, and maritime trade. In so doing, we investigate how these two dimensions are interconnected.

In exploring the geopolitics of the Indo-Pacific, the chapters in the volume seek to explain how naval capabilities—ranging from coast guards to modern and advanced combat forces—can play an important strategic role. In particular, the geopolitics of a maritime region allow us to make better sense of an apparent contradiction in *why* state actors acquire naval capabilities and *how* they use them most of the time. As a general rule, naval capabilities are designed and built to withstand the hardest test: combat. Yet, absent wartime missions, navies (and coast guards) rest at the forefront of foreign and security interactions by means of diplomacy, deterrence, and coercion. A quarter of a century ago, it would have been hard to conceive of a regional environment in which navies (and maritime forces more generally) featured so prominently as instruments of policy. Indeed, for the purpose of this volume, the key intellectual link we seek to articulate is between security dynamics and what is regarded as the cognitive value of naval power in influencing other actors' choice.[65]

THE STRUCTURE OF THE BOOK: AN INTERNATIONAL COLLABORATION FOR DIFFERENT AUDIENCES

Following this introduction, the volume brings together a group of international scholars from relevant disciplines to investigate its main themes. The first part of the volume explores the makeup of the maritime security complex of the Indo-Pacific. Its five chapters examine in detail the enabling factors informing why and how state actors take to the sea as well as set the boundaries of their aspirations in this complex domain. The first three chapters focus on three critical issues. The first focuses on how the sea informs national strategy at the structural level of international security, with Christopher Twomey investigating what the Indo-Pacific means strategically to both the United States and China. As a complement to this perspective, Peter Alan Dutton and Clive Schofield look at how the sea may influence governments' pursuit of maritime capabilities to maximize or protect legal claims and access and exploit marine resources. Both aspects matter considerably across the Indo-Pacific. Nicola Leveringhaus takes the exploration into the realm of nuclear order and stability, providing a much-needed update on how sea-based nuclear deterrents in the Indo-Pacific add a layer of complexity to broader structural dynamics. Against this background, James A. Russell's chapter highlights how technology—and in particular the pursuit of innovation and cutting-edge solutions to strategic problems—is an important consideration for major powers in the Indo-Pacific but one far from being easy to address.

While the first part of the volume seeks to explore the factors informing the region's complexity, the second part attempts to test how their understanding and significance changed over time. We asked its contributors to focus on periods of enhanced competition that affected the Indo-Pacific region, to better highlight what considerations informed the link between naval affairs and security. In particular, Ryan Gingeras seeks to provide greater nuance to the Indian Ocean as a space for competition over trade before the nineteenth century. His chapter explores how the Indian Ocean was a space in which European and

Asian actors converged and in which competition was intertwined with local political dynamics. Gingeras's account stands in contrast with the period covered by Richard Dunley. In Dunley's chapter, it becomes apparent that technological changes taking place at the end of the nineteenth century empowered European powers with a much-enhanced capacity to sustain the projection of power. Moreover, Dunley's chapter engages with how Britain strove to maintain its dominant role in the region in the context of imperial competition with other European powers and the rise of a potential rival in the case of Japan. In another chapter, Daniel Moran reviews the question of naval competition in the interwar period from the perspective of the failure of arms limitations to control the spiraling competition between the United States and Japan. The contribution of Kevin Rowlands on the Cold War is similarly enlightening in exposing how, underneath the bigger umbrella of the systemic competition between East and West, new phenomena such as decolonization and UNCLOS contributed to significantly widen how naval power mattered in the Indo-Pacific. Indeed, the historical journey presented in this part of the book makes it clear how problems of governance and good order at sea as they are understood today started to emerge only toward the end of the Cold War. By contrast, the Dunley and Moran chapters on earlier periods of sustained competition show how interactions in the Indo-Pacific region had been previously managed predominantly through other means, such as diplomacy and coercion. They were more about how material capabilities related to strategic outcomes than about how the uses of the sea related to matters of governance and order.

The final part of this volume takes its framework-setting chapters and historical journey through the Indo-Pacific to the present day. In particular, it focuses on testing the book's framework against the main subtheater of the Indo-Pacific. The key idea in this part of the volume is to examine how main interactions occur across the region and in what ways competition and cooperation can coexist. Indeed, while each chapter could not offer a full assessment of all the different maritime issues in which naval power plays a role, different authors focus on a specific set of issues related to the enablers set out in the first part. The objective in this section is to illustrate how the proposed framework can be applied to provide a more nuanced explanation of regional dynamics. This is why, for example, the chapters by Ian Bowers and Alessio Patalano and Julie Marionneau have a degree of overlap. In his chapter, Bowers examines territorial disputes between North and South Korea, Russia and Japan, and South Korea and China, showing their impact on the subregional dynamics. On the other hand, Patalano and Marionneau look at the dynamics in the East and South China Seas from the perspective of how fairly localized disputes may have an impact on the broader structural level of international security—well beyond the region's boundaries. By contrast, James Goldrick's chapter on the South Pacific is indicative of the opposite: global issues such as climate change may have a particular importance at the theater level in a way that the Sino-American competition has not. James J. Wirtz and Abhijit Singh take yet another perspective on the Indian Ocean and focus on how the wider complexity of issues to tackle can represent an opportunity for enhanced cooperation, in their case between the United States and India. In this section, we also felt that the increasing tensions across the Strait of Taiwan demanded specific attention. Sheryn Lee's chapter seeks to do just that by exploring the different roles naval power plays on the two opposing sides of the strait and links this specific hot spot to both regional and structural security issues.

For all these reasons, we believe the volume's approach and themes make it a valuable addition to key security debates of interest to academics and civilian and military policy stakeholders alike. It offers a new way to think about international security by placing the role of naval power and capabilities at the center of policy action. In particular, we argue how the notion of an Indo-Pacific makes sense from a strategic perspective as it keeps the focus of primary military interaction in the maritime context. We offer the conceptual tools for researchers and academics to further widen the agenda on the study of order and diplomacy and the practice of deterrence and coercion in the Asia Pacific. Additionally, we bring geography back into the understanding of international politics, and with it we offer guidance to policymakers and strategic planners on how competition and cooperation can coexist in a maritime-centric space. We also offer the empirical tools to engage with both in order to maintain stability, control escalation, and limit the risk of war—ranging from a localized affair to a major conflict involving leading regional powers.

NOTES

1. US Department of Defense, *Indo-Pacific Strategy Report: Preparedness, Partnerships, and Promoting a Networked Region* (Washington, DC: Department of Defense, 2019), 8. For an authoritative Chinese perspective on the report and its assumptions, see Shichun Wu, "US-China Competition Will Heat Up in the South China Sea," *The Diplomat*, November 8, 2019.
2. Congressional Research Service, *US-China Strategic Competition in South and East China Seas: Background and Issues for Congress*, CRS Report no. R42784 (Washington, DC: Congressional Research Service, 2019); Office of Secretary of Defense, *Military and Security Developments Involving the People's Republic of China 2019* (Washington, DC: Department of Defense, 2019); Edmund J. Burke et al., *China's Military Activities in the East China Sea: Implication for Japan's Air Self-Defense Force*, Research Report no. RR-2574-AF (Santa Monica, CA: RAND Corp., 2018).
3. For a thorough analysis of the intellectual debate over the changing priorities of American naval strategy in the 1990s and early 2000s, see Gary Anderson, *Beyond*

Mahan: Proposal for US Naval Strategy in the 21st Century (Newport, RI: Naval War College Press, 1993); James Goldrick and John Hattendorf, eds., *Mahan Is Not Enough: The Proceedings of a Conference on the Works of Sir Julian Corbett and Admiral Sir Herbert Richmond* (Newport, RI: Naval War College Press, 1993); John Hattendorf, ed., *US Naval Strategy in the 1990s: Selected Documents* (Newport, RI: Naval War College Press, 2006); and Peter D. Haynes, *Toward a New Maritime Strategy: American Naval Thinking in the Post–Cold War Era* (Annapolis, MD: Naval Institute Press, 2015).

4. White House, *National Security Strategy of the United States* (Washington, DC: 2017); Chief of Naval Operations, *A Design for Maintaining Maritime Superiority 2.0* (Washington, DC: US Navy, 2018); US Department of Defense, *National Defense Strategy of the United States; Including the 2022 Nuclear Posture Review and the 2022 Missile Defense Review* (Washington, DC: 2022), 13; White House, *National Security Strategy of the United States* (Washington, DC: 2022), 45.

5. Ministry of Defence, *Defence in a Competitive Age* (London: Ministry of Defence, 2021), 9.

6. Gary Roughead, *The Trident Returns: Reactivating the US Second Fleet and Revitalizing Anti-submarine Warfare in the Atlantic* (Washington, DC: Center for Strategic and International Studies, 2018); "US Navy Resurrects Second Fleet in Atlantic to Counter Russia," BBC News, May 5, 2018; Mark D. Faram, "Second Fleet Continues to Grow," *Navy Times*, May 30, 2019.

7. Jacob L. Shuford, "President's Forum—A New Maritime Strategy: Admiral Mullen's Challenge," *Naval War College Review* 56, no. 4 (2006): 7–10; Ronald E. Ratcliff, "Building Partners' Capacity: The Thousand-Ship Navy," *Naval War College Review* 60, no. 4 (2007): 45–58. For a formal implementation of the concept in USN strategy, see US Marine Corps, US Navy, and US Coast Guard, *A Cooperative Strategy for 21st Century Seapower* (Washington, DC: Department of Defense, 2007). For a critical analysis of the process that led from the thousand-ship navy to the cooperative strategy, see Haynes, *Toward a New Maritime Strategy*, chaps. 11–12.

8. US Department of Defense, *Indo-Pacific Strategy Report*, 16.

9. For a comprehensive and enlightening treatise on the relationship linking naval power and American security policy, see Simon Reich and Peter Dombrowski, *The End of Grand Strategy: US Maritime Operations in the 21st Century* (Ithaca, NY: Cornell University Press, 2017), chap. 1. For a critical view on the matter of the exercise of American naval hegemony, see Barry R. Posen, *Restraint: A New Foundation for US Grand Strategy* (Ithaca, NY: Cornell University Press, 2014).

10. Geoffrey Till, *Asia's Naval Expansion: An Arms Race in the Making?* (Abingdon, UK: Routledge, 2012); Geoffrey Till and Ristian Atriandi Supriyanto, eds., *Naval Modernisation in Southeast Asia: Problems and Prospects for Small and Medium Navies* (London: Palgrave Macmillan, 2018).

11. An assumption informing, for example, Anders Corr, ed., *Great Powers, Grand Strategies: The New Game in the South China Sea* (Annapolis, MD: Naval Institute Press, 2017).

12. Peter A. Dutton and Ryan D. Martinson, *China's Evolving Surface Fleet*, CMSI Red Books (Newport, RI: Naval War College Press, 2017); Scott N. Romaniuk and Tobia Burgers, "China's Next Phase of Militarization in the South China Sea," *The Diplomat*, March 20, 2019; Steven Stachwick, "China's South China Sea Militarization Has Peaked," *Foreign Policy*, August 19, 2019; Ian Bowers and Collin Koh Swee

Lean, eds., *Grey and White Hulls: An International Analysis of the Navy–Coast Guard Nexus* (London: Palgrave Macmillan, 2019).

13. Peter A. Dutton, Isaac B. Kardon, and Conor M. Kennedy, *Djibouti: China's First Overseas Strategic Strongpoint*, China Maritime Report no. 6 (Newport, RI: China Maritime Studies Institute and US Naval War College, 2020); Ryan D. Martinson and Peter A. Dutton, *China's Distant Ocean Survey Activities: Implications for US National Security*, China Maritime Report no. 3 (Newport, RI: China Maritime Studies Institute and US Naval War College, 2018); Peter A. Dutton, *Beyond the Wall: Chinese Far Seas Operation* (Newport, RI: China Maritime Studies Institute and US Naval War College, 2015).

14. State Council Information Office of the People's Republic of China, *China's National Defense in the New Era* (Beijing: Foreign Language Press, 2019).

15. Alessio Patalano, *Post-war Japan as a Sea Power: Imperial Legacy, Wartime Experience, and the Making of a Navy* (London: Bloomsbury, 2015), chap. 7.

16. In the English language, two volumes that well capture Chinese debates on maritime affairs are Michael McDevitt, *Becoming a Great "Maritime Power": A Chinese Dream* (Arlington, VA: Center for Naval Analyses, 2016), and Hu Bo, *Chinese Maritime Power in the 21st Century: Strategic Planning, Policy, and Predictions* (Abingdon, UK: Routledge, 2019).

17. Stansfield Turner, "Missions of the US Navy," *Naval War College Review* 27, no. 2 (1974): 2–17.

18. Ratcliff, "Building Partners' Capacity," 46–49. Also, a similar approach informed important documents such as European Commission, *European Union Maritime Security Strategy: Responding Together to Global Challenges* (Brussels: European Union's Publications Office, 2014), and Council of the European Union, *Council Conclusions on the Revision of the European Union Maritime Security Strategy (EUMSS) Action Plan* (Brussels: Council of the European Union, 2018). For a critical overview of the different meanings of "maritime security," see Christian Bueger, "What Is Maritime Security?," *Marine Policy* 53 (2015): 159–64, https//doi.org/10.1016/j.marpol.2014.12.005.

19. For a definition of "good order" at sea, see Geoffrey Till, *Seapower: A Guide for the Twenty-First Century* (Abingdon, UK: Routledge, 2009), chap. 11.

20. Eleanor Freud, *Freedom of Navigation in the South China Sea: A Practical Guide* (Cambridge, MA: Belfer Center for Science and International Affairs, 2017). For an informed view on the origins of the US freedom-of-navigation program, see Elliot L. Richardson, "Power, Mobility, and the Law of the Sea," *Foreign Affairs* 58, no. 4 (1980): 902–19.

21. US Department of Defense, *The Asia-Pacific Maritime Security Strategy* (Washington, DC: US Department of Defense), 25–29.

22. Darren J. Lim and Zack Cooper, "Reassessing Hedging: The Logic of Alignment in East Asia," *Security Studies* 24, no. 4 (2015): 696–727, https//doi.org/10.1080/09636412.2015.1103130.

23. Alessio Patalano, "Beyond the Gunboats: Rethinking Naval Diplomacy and Humanitarian Assistance Disaster Relief in East Asia," *RUSI Journal* 160, no. 2 (2015): 32–39, https//doi.org/10.1080/03071847.2015.1031523. For a broader overview of "soft power" and naval activities, see Bruce A. Elleman and S. C. M. Paine, eds., *Navies and Soft Power: Historical Case Studies of Naval Power and the Nonuse of Military Force* (Newport, RI: Naval War College Press, 2015).

24. James Goldrick and Jack McCaffrie, *Navies of Southeast Asia: A Comparative Study* (Abingdon, UK: Routledge, 2013).

25. Alessio Patalano, "Commitment by Presence: Naval Diplomacy and Japanese Defense Engagement in Southeast Asia," in *Japan's Foreign Relations in Asia*, ed. Jeff Kingston and James Brown, 100–113 (New York: Routledge, 2018); Alessio Patalano, "Japan as a Maritime Power: Deterrence, Diplomacy, and Maritime Security," in *The Handbook of Japanese Foreign Policy*, ed. Mary M. McCarthy (New York: Routledge, 2018), 155–72; John Bradford, *Understanding Fifty Years of Japanese Maritime Security Capacity Building Activities in Southeast Asia* (Tokyo: National Institute for Defense Studies, 2018).

26. Alessio Patalano, "Japanese Naval Power," in *The Oxford Handbook of Japanese Politics*, ed. Robert J. Pekkanen and Saadia Pekkanen (New York: Oxford University Press, 2021).

27. Graeme Dobell, "South Pacific Security at Shangri-La," *The Strategist*, June 5, 2019; Jesse Barker Gale, "Competition and Cooperation the South Pacific," National Bureau of Asian Research, August 15, 2019, https://www.nbr.org/publication/competition-and-cooperation-in-the-south-pacific/. See also Sandra Tarte, *Fiji Islands' Security Challenges and Defense Policy Issues*, NIDS Joint Research Series no. 5 (Tokyo: National Institute for Defense Studies, 2010).

28. In this volume, we use the term "naval forces" to capture a state's "architecture" designed to tackle the wider spectrum of security challenges at sea. Bowers and Koh have provided the most comprehensive examination of the diverse ways in which state actors implement national security in a maritime context. Bowers and Koh, *Grey and White Hulls*, 5–11.

29. Notably, see James Cable, *Gunboat Diplomacy 1919–1991: Political Applications of Limited Naval Force*, 3rd ed. (Basingstoke, UK: Palgrave Macmillan, 1994); Jonathan Alford, ed., *Sea Power and Influence: Old Issues and New Challenges* (Westmead, UK: Gower Publishing, 1980); Edward N. Luttwak, *The Political Uses of Sea Power*, Studies in International Affairs, no. 23 (Baltimore: Johns Hopkins University Press, 1974); J. J. Widen, "Naval Diplomacy: A Theoretical Approach," *Diplomacy and Statecraft* 22, no. 4 (2011): 715–33, https//doi.org/10.1080/09592296.2011.625830; and Andrew T. H. Tan, ed., *The Politics of Maritime Power: A Survey*, 2nd ed. (London: Routledge, 2011).

30. Barry Buzan, Ole Wæver, and Jaap de Wilde, *Security: A New Framework for Analysis* (Boulder, CO: Lynne Rienner, 1998), 10–15. For specifics on East Asia, see Barry Buzan, "Security Architecture in Asia: The Interplay of Regional and Global Levels," *Pacific Review* 16, no. 2 (2003): 143–73, https//doi.org/10.1080/0951274032000069660; and Barry Buzan, "The Southeast Asian Security Complex," *Contemporary Southeast Asia* 10, no. 1 (1988): 1–16, https://www.jstor.org/stable/25797984.

31. Kei Koga, "Japan's 'Indo-Pacific' Question: Countering China or Shaping a New Regional Order?," *International Affairs* 96, no. 1 (2020): 49–73, https//doi.org/10.1093/ia/iiz241.

32. Rory Medcalf, "The Indo-Pacific: What's in a Name?," *American Interest* 9, no. 2 (2013): 58–66; Brendan Taylor, "Is Australia's Indo-Pacific Strategy and Illusion?," *International Affairs* 96, no. 1 (2020): 95–110, https//doi.org/10.1093/ia/iiz228.

33. Rahul Roy-Chaudhury, "Modi's Vision for the Indo-Pacific Region," *IISS Analysis*, June 2, 2018, https://www.iiss.org/blogs/analysis/2018/06/modi-vision-indo

-pacific; "ASEAN Outlook on the Indo-Pacific," Association of Southeast Asian Nations, June 23, 2019, https://asean.org/storage/2019/06/ASEAN-Outlook-on -the-Indo-Pacific_FINAL_22062019.pdf; Dewi Fortuna Anwar, "Indonesia and the ASEAN Outlook on the Indo-Pacific," *International Affairs* 96, no. 1 (2020): 111–29, https//doi.org/10.1093/ia/iiz223.

34. "The Indo-Pacific Region: A Priority for France," Ministry for European and Foreign Affairs, updated July 2021, https://www.diplomatie.gouv.fr/en/country-files/asia -and-oceania/the-indo-pacific-region-a-priority-for-france/; Gudrun Wacker, "Europe and the Indo-Pacific: Comparing France, Germany, and the Netherlands: Analysis," *Eurasia Review*, March 10, 2021; HM Government, *Global Britain in a Competitive Age*, CP 403 (London: HM Government, 2021), 66–68.

35. Dingding Chen, "The Indo-Pacific Strategy: A Background Analysis," Italian Institute for International Political Studies, June 4, 2018, https://www.ispionline.it/it /pubblicazione/indo-pacific-strategy-background-analysis-20714; Feng Liu, "The Recalibration of Chinese Assertiveness: China's Responses to the Indo-Pacific Challenge," *International Affairs* 96, no. 1 (2020): 9–27, https//doi.org/10.1093/ia /iiz226.

36. Rory Medcalf, *Indo-Pacific Empire: China, America, and the Contest for the World's Pivotal Region* (Manchester: Manchester University Press, 2020), 5.

37. Medcalf, *Indo-Pacific Empire*, 6.

38. Buzan, Wæver, and de Wilde, *Security*, 15.

39. Till, *Seapower*, 23–33.

40. Chris Parry, *Super Highway: Sea Power in the 21st Century* (London: Elliott & Thompson, 2014), 1–3; Jakub J. Grygiel, *Great Powers and Geopolitical Change* (Baltimore: Johns Hopkins University Press, 2006), 26–27.

41. Till, *Seapower*, 23–33.

42. Andrew Lambert, "The Pax Britannica and the Advent of Globalisation," in *Maritime Strategy and Global Order: Markets, Resources, Security*, ed. Daniel Moran and James A. Russell, 5–19 (Washington, DC: Georgetown University Press, 2016). For an example of a small navy defending a set of wider economic interests, see Deborah Sanders, "Small Navies in the Black Sea: A Case Study of Romania's Maritime Power," in *Small Navies: Strategy and Policy for Small Navies in War and Peace*, ed. Michael Mulqueen, Deborah Sanders, and Ian Speller, 151–67; and Ian Speller, *Understanding Naval Warfare* (New York: Routledge, 2014), 28–32. On the impact of the sea on the nature of naval operations, see Roger Barnett, *Navy Strategic Culture: Why the Navy Thinks Differently* (Annapolis, MD: Naval Institute Press, 2009), 22–31.

43. Till, *Seapower*, 114–44; Speller, *Understanding Naval Warfare*, 170–78; Norman Firedman, "Navies and Technology," in *The Politics of Maritime Power: A Survey*, 2nd ed., ed. Andrew T. H. Tan, 45–61 (London: Routledge, 2011).

44. David C. Kang, *East Asia before the West: Five Centuries of Trade and Tribute* (New York: Columbia University Press, 2010); David C. Kang, "Hierarchy and Legitimacy in International Systems: The Tribute System in Early Modern East Asia," *Security Studies* 19, no. 4 (2010): 591–622, https//doi.org/10.1080/09636412 .2010.524079; David C. Kang, Meredith Shaw, and Ronan Tse-min Fu, "Measuring War in Early Modern East Asia, 1368–1841: Introducing Chinese and Korean Language Sources," *International Studies Quarterly* 60, no. 4 (2016): 766–77, https //doi.org/10.1093/isq/sqw032.

45. David C. Kang, *American Grand Strategy and East Asian Security in the 21st Century* (Cambridge: Cambridge University Press, 2017), 16–17.
46. Kang, "Hierarchy and Legitimacy."
47. Jo Inge Bekkevold and Geoffrey Till, eds., *International Order at Sea: How It Is Challenged, How It Is Maintained* (London: Palgrave Macmillan, 2016).
48. Peter Dutton, Robert Ross, and Øystein Tunsjø, eds., *Twenty-First Century Seapower: Cooperation and Conflict at Sea* (Abingdon, UK: Routledge, 2013).
49. Daniel Moran and James A. Russell, eds., *Maritime Strategy and Global Order: Markets, Resources, Security* (Washington, DC: Georgetown University Press, 2015).
50. Geoffrey Till and Jane Chan, eds., *Naval Modernisation in Southeast Asia, Nature, Causes, and Consequences* (Abingdon, UK: Routledge, 2013); Nicholas Tarling and Xin Chen, eds., *Maritime Security in East and Southeast Asia: Political Challenges in Asian Waters* (London: Palgrave Macmillan, 2018).
51. Bernard D. Cole, *Asian Maritime Strategies: Navigating Troubled Waters* (Annapolis, MD: Naval Institute Press, 2013).
52. Geoffrey Till, *Asia's Naval Expansion: An Arms Race in the Making?* (Abingdon, UK: Routledge, 2012). Also, very closely related to this is Desmond Ball, "Arms Modernization in Asia: An Emerging Complex Arms Race," in *The Global Arms Trade*, ed. Andrew T. H. Tan, 30–52 (London: Routledge, 2010).
53. Thomas G. Mahnken and Dan Blumenthal, eds., *Strategy in Asia: The Past, Present, and Future of Regional Security* (Stanford, CA: Stanford University Press, 2014).
54. Mahnken and Blumenthal, *Strategy in Asia*.
55. Jonathan D. Caverley and Peter Dombrowski, "Too Important to Be Left to the Admirals: The Need to Study Maritime Great-Power Competition," *Security Studies* 29, no. 4 (2020): 579–600, https//doi.org/10.1080/09636412.2020.1811448.
56. For example, see Sam Bateman, "Maritime Security: Regional Concerns and Global Implications," in *Security Politics in the Asia-Pacific: A Regional-Global Nexus?*, ed. William T. Tow, 247–65 (Cambridge: Cambridge University Press, 2009).
57. Evelyn Goh, *The Struggle for Order: Hegemony, Hierarchy, and Transition in Post–Cold War East Asia* (Oxford: Oxford University Press, 2013).
58. Harvey Starr, "On Geopolitics: Spaces and Places," *International Studies Quarterly* 57, no. 3 (2003): 433–39, https//doi.org/10.4324/9781315633152.
59. Or Rosenboim, "Geopolitics and Empire: Visions of Regional Order in the 1940s," *Modern Intellectual History* 12, no. 2 (2015): 353–81, https//doi.org/10.1017/S1479244314000547; Or Rosenboim, "The Value of Space: Geopolitics, Geography, and the American Search for International Relations Theory in the 1950s," *International History Review* 42, no. 3 (2020): 639–55, https//doi.org/10.1080/07075332.2019.1596966.
60. Robert D. Kaplan, *Monsoon: The Indian Ocean and the Future of American Power* (New York: Random House, 2010); Robert D. Kaplan, *The Revenge of Geography: What the Map Tells Us about Coming Conflicts and the Battle against Fate* (New York: Random House, 2017); Robert D. Kaplan, *Asia's Cauldron: The South China Sea and the End of a Stable Pacific* (New York: Random House, 2015).
61. François Joyaux, *Géopolitique de l'Extrême-Orient* [Geopolitics of the Far East], Tome 1: Espaces et Politiques [Vol. 1: Spaces and Policies] (Brussels: Éditions Complexe, 1993).
62. John J. Mearsheimer, *The Tragedy of Great Power Politics* (New York: Norton, 2001), chap. 4; Jack S. Levy and William R. Thompson, "Balancing on Land and at

Sea: Do States Ally against the Leading Global Power?," *International Security* 35, no. 1 (2010): 7–43, https//doi.org/10.1162/ISEC_a_00001; Ian Bowers, "Escalation at Sea: Stability and Instability in Maritime East Asia," *Naval War College Review* 71, no. 4 (2018): 45–65.

63. In the modern history of the Asia Pacific, the Japanese expansion in the 1930s and early 1940s represents the most glaring exception. For a brief summary of changes in Japanese strategy, see Sally C. Paine, *The Japanese Empire: Grand Strategy from the Meiji Restoration to the Pacific War* (Cambridge: Cambridge University Press, 2017).

64. Jakub J. Grygiel, *Great Powers and Geopolitical Change* (Baltimore: Johns Hopkins University Press, 2006).

65. Kevin Rowlands, *Naval Diplomacy in the 21st Century: A Model for the Post–Cold War Global Order* (Abingdon, UK: Routledge, 2019), 11–14.

PART I

The Factors of Influence in Indo-Pacific Security

2

Geopolitics and Strategic Geography in Sino-US Competition

Christopher Twomey

The rise of China is the defining characteristic of international relations in the early twenty-first century. Given its rise occurs in the context of an established pattern of geopolitical affairs dominated by the United States and institutions established in the immediate aftermath of World War II, some degree of Sino-American tension is likely. However, the details of how that tension plays out depend on a variety of structural, ideational, and social factors. Geography is paramount among these, although geography does not provide a static influence on strategic affairs. A reasonable starting point is the following definition by Phil Kelly: "Classical geopolitics is the study of the impact or influence of certain geographic features—these being positions and locations of regions, states, and resources, plus topography, climate, distance, immigration, states' sizes and shapes, demography, and the like—upon states' foreign policies and actions as an aid to statecraft."[1]

Obviously, many of these factors are dynamic, and some mutable. Jakub J. Grygiel focuses a bit more narrowly on the control of "centers of resources and lines of communication."[2] However, as he notes, the influence of technology and—of particular importance in the Chinese case—transportation infrastructure changes across time. Classical theorists in this vein weigh in even more broadly. For instance, Nicholas J. Spykman puts it in figurative terms: "The geography of a country is rather the material for, than the cause of, its policy, and to admit that the garment must ultimately be cut to fit the cloth is not to say that the cloth determines either the garment's style or its adequacy."[3] Or, as Benjamin Schreer summarizes, "Spykman repeatedly emphasised that geopolitics is fundamentally subject to political action and interpretation."[4]

Thus, the core question of this chapter is how does geography, in both its static and evolving forms and in the context of contemporary technology and relevant interests, shape Sino-American competition? To answer this, both countries' regional and global interests have to be assessed. These are themselves also not static and further are contested internally. Nevertheless, their broad contours are fairly clear in both cases. China has a series of territorial disputes that constitute a core interest driving its geostrategic policy. Beyond that, evolving Chinese economic interests throughout the world demand a distinct set of geostrategic choices. For the United States, vital interests center on relations with regional allies and complement a broader strategy aimed at ensuring stability in, and influence over, the global commons.[5]

Although deep historical work is taken up elsewhere in this volume, it is worth noting the elements of continuity and change in both countries' contemporary geopolitical outlook. The ebb and flow of Chinese civilization and its degree of political control over East Asia is fundamentally a story of managing internal crises. Threats to the survival of various dynasties primarily came from within; it is only after significant internal weakening that outside forces preyed on the state. Much of the history of the development of China centers on consolidating control over the expanse of geography populated by populations that had some common element of a Han ethnic identity.[6]

Still, soft, imprecise border regions to the interior were an important source of concern across many dynasties, not least the final Qing reign (1644–1911). The original Silk Road trade networks, traversing territories with unsettled political relations to Beijing, shaped China's exposure (and thus interests) as well. Throughout the past thousand years of Chinese civilization, though, there was also sporadic and relatively limited contact through the seas. Important challenges posed by pirates and bandits along the coast developed tribute relations with Japan, and the important burst of engagement through the Zheng He fleets (what one now might call "military diplomacy") were both significant exceptions to this broader, more dominant trend.[7] Harvard's Robert Ross summarizes this history:

> China's status as a continental power not only reflects geography but also the culture of a land power. For more than 2,000 years, Chinese territorial expansion has been led by peasants seeking arable land, followed by a Confucian culture and the administrative and military power of the Chinese state. During this same period, China never carried out territorial expansion across water. Up to the twentieth century, Chinese development of a navy has been, at best, sporadic and brief. Its maritime tradition has focused on commercial exploration.[8]

However, throughout this more inward-focused period, China nevertheless had a history of viewing East Asia through a geostrategic lens. John King Fairbank and Merle Goldman emphasize that the centrality of China in the tributary system conveyed a sense of Chinese superiority.[9] Although more recent historiography would cast such relations in a less hierarchical sense, China is still seen as having sat at the hub of relevant economic and social/cultural networks.[10]

More recent history, centering on the period since the advent of militarized imperialism by the West in China, also creates an impetus for China to play a sustained role on the seas. Professor Hu Bo, director of the Center for Maritime Strategy Research at China's most prestigious university, Peking University, writes, "From 1840 onward, becoming a maritime power has been the dream and pursuit of generations of Chinese elites."[11] Indeed, as he notes, core territorial disputes that remain central today have their origins across the century of humiliations that followed the First Opium War: "For China, the current situation of the Taiwan Strait, the Diaoyu Islands dispute, and the South China Sea issue are largely related to the loss of control and voice over the East Asian coastal waters since modern times."[12]

For the United States, the historic legacies are similarly lengthy. Although US national history spans only a few hundred years, its culture is intimately linked to a broader Western tradition. America's modern emphasis of ensuring access to the global commons, and the lines of communication they harbor, traces back to Grotian ideals and British naval practices focused on asserting freedom of navigation. The need to deploy military forces to Europe for national security reasons in both world wars and potentially during any eruption of the Cold War reinforced the same interest.

The rest of this chapter examines contemporary manifestations of these legacies. It begins by comparing the interests of each country, given its respective position in the Indo-Pacific geography (and beyond). Next, it turns to an explicit evaluation on the role of geography in shaping policies to pursue those interests. Thereafter, the chapter summarizes each country's geostrategy; that is, how do their interests and geographies shape their preferred concept of military operations? Finally, the chapter concludes with an assessment of the implications for stability in the maritime sphere between the two most powerful countries on the globe today.

NATIONAL INTERESTS IN THE INDO-PACIFIC

Two broad categories of interests are relevant for China and the United States in the Indo-Pacific today: security and economics. The former includes Chinese territorial disputes that enmesh the United States through its alliance commitments. The latter centers on maritime resources in China's littoral but also includes ensuring the security of shipping lanes beyond East Asia. Before discussing each of those in turn, a brief aside on recent maritime interests for both is warranted.

The Legacy of Cold War Interests

The ties to the Cold War are much more direct than centuries-old history. Although there have been changes, both the Chinese and the US militaries continue to field platforms and organizational structures that were optimized to face the geostrategic challenges of the Cold War. For China the central challenge from 1949 through the 1980s was the threat of land invasion. At first Beijing feared an American amphibious invasion. By the late 1960s, if not earlier, the concern had evolved to include a land invasion by the Soviet Union. Common throughout this period was an approach to warfare that focused on using the strategic depth of China to "lure the enemy in deep."[13] This organizational culture deeply imbued the doctrine of the People's Liberation Army (PLA) at the time.[14] It was encapsulated in major "military strategic guidelines" (the broadest strategic framing of threats for the PLA) throughout that period.[15] There was little role for maritime strategy in this period beyond a modest approach to coastal defense.[16] It is worth noting that China's core challenges that remain today (reunification with Taiwan and managing territorial disputes with neighboring countries) also existed during this period. Those are not new security goals. They were just far less salient then, given the existential threats perceived from the United States and the Soviet Union.[17] The evolution in Chinese security interests toward the maritime sphere is thus a major change.

The US perspective has also evolved. However, rather than a single shift, the variation since the Cold War has been in multiple different directions. Ian Speller explains:

> During the Cold War the US Navy maintained a global presence and filled a wide variety of roles but was focused particularly on the challenge posed by the Warsaw Pact. With the dissolution of that alliance, the collapse of the Soviet Union and the disintegration of the Soviet Fleet, the US was without any major rival at sea. In the years that followed, budgets were cut, and Western navies shrank. The US Navy reoriented itself from a force designed to contest sea control with the Soviets to one designed to project power in support of US interests in a variety of crises and limited conflicts overseas. By the beginning of the new century, it had broadened its vision to include an emphasis on maritime security operations and on the need to sustain

partnerships with other navies and agencies in order to police and protect the maritime commons.[18]

Thus, given continued US predominance at sea, the US Navy became primarily a power-projection force for conducting operations against relatively weaker powers (Iraq, Serbia, etc.) through strike operations and delivering and sustained ground forces. It is a radically different kind of challenge that China poses to the US Navy. As this chapter shall chronicle, the evolution by the US Navy and other military branches to face the challenges posed by China's rise has continued.

Conflict over Geographic Features in Sino-American Relations

While the United States and China do not have any directly competing territorial claims, geography is at the heart of their competing interests in the twenty-first century. Taiwan is of paramount importance for geostrategic, political, and cultural reasons. However, island disputes in the South and East China Seas are important drivers of competing geostrategic postures.

Taiwan

It is hard to overstate the importance of Taiwan.[19] As alluded to previously, its separation from the mainland is a constant reminder of China's defeat at the hands of the Japanese imperial military in 1895 and US intervention in the Taiwan Strait in 1950; that is, it serves as a reminder of United States continued intervention in the unfinished Chinese Civil War. As such, its status carries great cultural resonance for the Chinese people. Furthermore, the Chinese Communist Party has staked its legitimacy on reunifying the Chinese territories lost during the "century of humiliations." With Macao and Hong Kong reabsorbed successfully and increasingly comprehensively (if in contravention of Beijing's diplomatic commitments to the United Kingdom), Taiwan is the last outstanding task. Beijing's sensitivity to any aspect of Taiwan's sovereign status is clear from recent events.[20]

Beyond these political and cultural sources, Taiwan is important because of its geostrategic position. The next section discusses the "first island chain" in depth, but suffice it to say that Taiwan serves as *the* keystone of this geographic construct. Alternatively, as a refreshingly frank Chinese scholar of maritime affairs, Hu, puts it, "as for China, Taiwan forms a natural barrier to shield the mainland coastline and is an ideal focal point for the protection of maritime transportation lanes."[21] Most of Chinese commercial shipping docks in ports at or to the north of the Taiwan Strait. While Japan (and South Korea, to a lesser extent) may always pose a threat to the farthest northward hubs, Chinese control of Taiwan (and thus more easily securing the Taiwan Strait in the event of military conflict) would greatly alleviate Beijing's concerns. Moreover, it would also allow Beijing easier access to the deep waters of the Pacific, facilitating power projection and quiet/unmonitored deployment of nuclear-powered attack submarines. (A more detailed discussion of operational implications of this geography is found in a subsequent section.[22])

The US position on Taiwan is literally one of strategic ambiguity. After Washington abrogated its alliance with the Republic of China (as Taiwan was known then and still is now, in the most formal settings) in 1979, the US policy toward Taiwan has been a vague and nonbinding security commitment embodied in the Taiwan Relations Act of the same year.[23] Different leaders might characterize the US policy differently, and private formulations likely deviate from public statements. However, a constant across all of those would be an articulation that any change to the status quo should be decided *peacefully*, with the people of Taiwan having a say in that decision. Anything other than that would risk US military intervention.[24]

For the United States, the interests underlying this vague (but still problematic for Beijing) policy are wide-ranging. Certainly, on human rights grounds, Taiwan's twenty-four million citizens' well-being is of tremendous importance. Thomas J. Christensen emphasizes the exemplary value of Taiwan's flourishing democracy for Chinese citizens.[25] The geopolitical element is also substantial. It is true that formal US military cooperation with Taiwan is highly restricted; there are no US forces permanently deployed to Taiwan, nor are joint exercises held with the Taiwanese military in the region. Although the United States sells advanced weaponry to Taiwan, and there is some training of Taiwanese air force pilots at Luke Air Force Base in the United States, there is little beyond that. Still, the United States benefits militarily from Taiwan remaining outside of Beijing's orbit. The advantages listed earlier for Beijing are disadvantages for the United States in any intense military conflict. Since that prospect is the shadow looming over the contemporary emphasis on great-power competition, it must be considered.

Island Disputes in the South and East China Seas

Taiwan is the most important territorial dispute and piece of strategic geography contested in Sino-American relations, but others exist too. A series of disputed "features" surround continental China. Some are below sea level at high tide, but most are above it, if not fully warranting classification as "islands."[26] The primary sets of contested features are the Spratly and Paracel Islands in the

South China Sea and the Senkaku Islands in the East China Sea.[27] China claims them all.

The Senkakus are not strategically important geography, but they have political and legal importance. They consist of seven miniscule features totaling about six square kilometers, lying as something of an extension of the Ryukyu chain extending to the southwest of Japan. They are uninhabited and unfortified. Japan has administrative control over them, and the United States has overtly stated that its alliance with Japan includes the defense of the Senkakus. Thus, despite their current military irrelevance, they serve as important contested territory in Sino-American relations.

The South China Sea features are a somewhat different story. China claims nearly the entire South China Sea through its "nine-dash line" claim (originally promulgated by the US-supported Kuomintang, who were allies of the United States for more than three decades while they ruled Taiwan). The two main clusters present distinct issues. In the north, China holds all the Paracel Islands. Although fairly modest in size, several are inhabited and fortified. Woody Island, the largest feature, boasts an air base that has regularly hosted PLA–Air Force deployments. Although the island is contested by Vietnam and Taiwan, China has maintained control of it since the 1970s. In addition to controlling the features in this cluster, China has announced straight baselines around them, thus converting the waters between them into "internal waters" akin to a coastal bay in legal terms (according to Beijing).[28]

The second set of features, the Spratlys, are held by five different countries. Vietnam holds most of the main features (twenty-one), the Philippines hold the next most (nine), and Malaysia and Taiwan hold smaller numbers. In the middle with seven features, China has expanded three of those through landfill and major construction, with less pronounced construction on their other held features. The three substantially improved features (Fiery Cross, Subi, and Mischief Reefs) all now have massive runways and major military installations, including radars, defensive fortifications for aircraft and missiles, and basing infrastructure. Although other countries have reinforced and expanded their islands' features, no one has done as much as China has in this regard.

The US position regarding these features is that it takes no stand on who "owns" nearly all of them. Instead, Washington emphasizes that the territorial disputes should be resolved through diplomacy rather than coercive use of force. Additionally, generally highlighting the United Nations Convention for the Law of the Sea (UNCLOS), the United States calls for the disputes about the features and the waters surrounding them to be resolved in accordance with international law. The implications of this latter point are discussed in the following section. However, because the United States is formally allied with the Philippines, has close security relations with Taiwan, and has nascent relations with Vietnam, Malaysia, and Brunei, the United States is not entirely divorced from these issues, even on territorial grounds alone.

The degree of military challenge posed by the recently constructed Chinese facilities varies according to the sort of conflict. In any war between China and its neighbors, the facilities would provide Beijing with tremendous advantages for sustaining and resupplying ships in the far south of the South China Sea as well as the capability (and advantages thereof) of flying combat missions from those airbases. In peacetime, sustaining forces and increasing their time on station is greatly enhanced, regardless of who the potential adversary might be; China's peacetime maritime domain awareness is also much expanded by these features. Their relevance in a high-end, intense conflict with the United States is a bit more debatable. The predominant view is that because they are fixed sites with limited ability for digging down and no ability to disperse assets into nearby complex terrain, they are highly vulnerable to precision-guided munitions.[29] Nevertheless, those effects on peacetime affairs and in shifting the balance with regard to lesser states remain important.

Economic Value of Maritime Regions

There are important territorial disputes that intertwine US and Chinese security interests. Notably, for both sides (and for the US partners in the region), the importance of specific territories is bolstered by the rights to nearby maritime resources that they imply. Moreover, both sides have extremely large maritime claims in the western Pacific. As discussed in Peter Alan Dutton's chapter, under UNCLOS, a zone of up to two hundred nautical miles from "islands" (more in cases of a continental shelf) constitutes a state's exclusive economic zone (EEZ) that can be used for the purposes of fishing, mining, and related economic activities. In the far western Pacific, the US EEZs emanating from Guam, the Northern Mariana Islands, and Palau alone are larger than the area demarcated by China's contentious nine-dash line. Additionally, the US EEZs in the Marshall Islands and surrounding atolls and features (all well west of Hawaii) are larger still. Thus, the United States garners substantial interest in the set of rules under UNCLOS that convey these economic rights.

China's much smaller nine-dash-line zone is different and problematic for (at least) three reasons. First, it is contentious because it presumes Chinese control over features that, as noted previously, are mostly held by others. Although the United States had disputes with Canada and Caribbean states regarding delimitation of its maritime zones, these have been long since resolved, generally without recourse to violence.[30] In China's case, the contested nature of the territorial holdings entices a militarization of the Senkaku and South China Sea disputes (by all sides). Second, in the wake of a 2016 Permanent Court of

Arbitration ruling, none of the features in the Spratlys warrants "island" status, so they would only be permitted much smaller economic zones of significant sovereignty.[31] Third, the nature of China's justification of its nine-dash line relies on "historical claims" to waters rather than the legal principles of UNCLOS and related international law.

China does see the economic value of both sets of its island disputes. As one Chinese analyst, Hu, put it, "the marine economy has already become one of the main means of competing in maritime capability."[32] China's possession of the Senkakus has implications for the veracity of China's extended continental shelf claim to extend its EEZ in that area. Because oil is currently being pumped several hundred kilometers north of the Senkakus, this issue has clear importance. China is currently only drilling on the west side of the median line between Japan and China. However, if extended continental shelf claims by China are allowed (and Beijing's possession of the Senkakus would contribute legal support to that claim), China would have legal rights to the hydrocarbons on the east side as well. The Spratlys and the rest of the South China Sea have traditionally been rich fishing areas and also potentially possess economically viable oil and natural gas deposits. This has been grounds for repeated crises and, to be fair, negotiation between China, Vietnam, Malaysia, and the Philippines.

China's views of the value of these resources, and of the threat posed to them by outsiders, are clear. Toshi Yoshihara and James R. Holmes note, "The claustrophobia many Chinese feel when they glance at the map stems not from inert terrain but from the political, social, historical, and strategic context pervading maritime Asia."[33] Even civilian organizations within China see this threat to economic resources in military terms, as Michael McDevitt explains: "In fall 2013, one official from the State Oceanic Administration (SOA) wrote, 'The most important prerequisite for the building of a maritime power is to . . . protect the nation's maritime rights and interests from being violated. If our nation's core maritime interests and the basic maritime rights and interests cannot be effectively protected, there is no way to talk about building a maritime power.'"[34]

Nature of Sovereignty in Maritime Spaces

Beyond the military relevance of all these contested features and the economic resources their control conveys, China's specific claims regarding the Senkakus and Paracels, and the broader nine-dash line, suggest something else about the way China views the maritime sphere. The nine-dash line and claimed straight baselines in the Paracels and Senkakus suggest a Chinese view about maritime geography that is quite distinct—more akin to rigid sovereignty typically associated with land territories. Straight baselines around the Paracels and Senkakus unambiguously violate the UNCLOS; however, China claims they create internal waters of the oceanic area between those features. This would preclude commercial or military ships from transiting the waters and enhance Chinese economic rights nearby. Although the issue of what China claims within the nine-dash line is a bit vague, most (although, interestingly, not all) claims relying on it are inconsistent with the UNCLOS and the recent finding by the Permanent Court of Arbitration.[35] All of them suggest China sees maritime sovereignty, at least in some cases, as more rigid and unilaterally exercised than do most countries under UNCLOS (which China helped write and ratified).

Experts looking at China come to similar conclusions. For instance, retired US Navy captain Bernard Cole writes, "[Chinese statements] combined with the aggressive actions against foreign fishing craft in the South China Sea during the past decade or more and with actions against US surveillance aircraft and ships, all point toward a view of waters as 'sovereign.'"[36] More broadly, one Chinese academic, Hu, connects this view to a military strategy and calls for China to move beyond its traditional views:

> China's unfavorable geopolitical conditions in the Western Pacific mean that if China's navy is merely confined to activities in the coastal waters of the First Island Chain, through the establishment of an offshore line of defense to protect national security, it would nevertheless be a continuation of the army's strategy. The navy's role and characteristics have far from been fulfilled. China still needs to pursue a defensive national security strategy, but tactically it undoubtedly needs to be more aggressive. Today, the origins and forms of external threats have all undergone major transformation. Building a navy unquestionably cannot be a continuation of an army mentality. Relying solely on coastal defenses and offshore patrols is already inadequate for confronting the modern state of affairs.[37]

While seeing countervailing trends emerging and strengthening, Holmes and Yoshihara concede that "continental ways of thinking are clearly integral to Beijing's worldview."[38]

This point is distinct from the other aspects that drive Chinese interests. Strategic value in some island territories and economic rights to resources are well understood and frequently lead to international tension. However, fundamentally different conceptions about the rights of sovereignty in the maritime space create an entirely different geostrategic challenge.

Freedom of Navigation

The heart of any Mahanian approach to maritime strategy is the importance of freedom of navigation, both for ensuring the free flow of commerce and the ability to flexibly deploy one's own navy. For both China and the United States, freedom of navigation globally is a vital interest. In contrast to the issues raised previously, these interests are not necessarily opposing and, indeed, vary across space.

China and the United States both depend heavily on seaborne commerce for their economies. Indeed, they generally represent the top two trading nations in the world.[39] China became a net oil importer in 1993 and passed the United States as the top importer globally in 2017. While down from what it was a decade ago, China's trade ratio remains remarkably high for a continental-sized economy. Thus, ensuring the free flow of goods, 90 percent of which globally travels by sea, is critical for both nations. Although the Belt and Road Initiative, discussed later, may affect the level of this dependence of China, Peking University's Hu captures this well, remarking, "Undoubtedly, in today's age of high global economic interdependence, freedom of maritime navigation has already become a common interest of every major power."[40] Chinese participation in antipiracy patrols in the Gulf of Aden and Indian Ocean are examples of the kinds of actions Beijing has taken to address this concern. Working alongside the Combined Task Force 151 of the North Atlantic Treaty Organization (NATO), this example displays the overlapping interests both the United States and China have on this issue set. At the generic, global level then, there is little conflicting interest here.

The challenge for the two countries as they face shared interests in global freedom of navigation is that it is not a pure "public good" in economist's terms. That is, capable navies can *selectively* threaten freedom of navigation by a specific adversary's shipping. While this is much more complicated in a globalized era with complex supply chains sourced by multinational contributors, it still poses some challenges. Chinese scholars are well aware of this challenge. For example, Hu notes, "Various points along maritime transportation routes in the Persian Gulf, the Indian Ocean and the South China Sea could all suffer from the threats of potential opponents."[41] Although North Korea has been able to circumvent some United Nations sanctions, the cost of doing so has been high.

The United States has cast its recent regional initiative in defense of this principle of global freedom of navigation. The Free and Open Indo-Pacific initiative aims to ground US involvement in the region in defense of legal norms that support freedom of navigation and generally open trading practices. Although relations with democratic allies and partners are at the center of this diplomatic endeavor, it is framed in broad terms that are not fundamentally opposed to China's geostrategic interests. Thus, for generic challenges to freedom of navigation, such as piracy and distant clogging of choke points (one thinks here of the Strait of Hormuz), the United States and China have broadly aligned interests. However, the closer one gets to China, the more local geography leads to some divergence of interest, as the next section discusses.

Finally, it is worth flagging some convergence about views of freedom of navigation for navies. Historically, there have been somewhat divergent views about the freedom of navigation for military forces. Thus, in the decade of the 2000s, China frequently harassed US Navy reconnaissance outside of China's twelve-mile territorial waters but inside its EEZ. In part, China relied on a minority interpretation of "permissible activities" in other countries' EEZs to justify this behavior. However, in the past five years, China has moved away from this particular legal complaint. While it still complains about such behavior, the logic is grounded in the accusation that such reconnaissance "signals malign intent."[42] In part, the reasoning behind this shift is the growth of Chinese capabilities to engage in precisely the same sort of reconnaissance in waters off Guam, Alaska, Hawaii, and Japan.

Supporting Global Interests

Finally, there is an emerging and broad set of interests for the two countries: defense of their citizens, clients, and investments abroad (particularly in the distant abroad, necessitating naval forces to support). As the dominant player in international affairs since 1945, the United States has long had to defend this interest. It has intervened in Latin America, Africa, Southeast Asia, and the Middle East for a wide variety of reasons but often for something less than geostrategic competition with the Soviet Union. The need for the US Navy (and other services) to be able to support this broader panoply of American interests abroad is ingrained in American strategic thought.

In contrast, for China this is new. Noncombatant evacuation operations in Yemen and Libya in recent years only exemplify future demands on the People's Liberation Army–Navy (PLAN).[43] These missions were served by forces already in the region for the antipiracy mission. As China's economic presence continues to grow globally, there will be additional scenarios where such involvement will be necessary.[44] China has promoted outward-bound foreign direct investment under the "going out" policies that accelerated under Hu Jintao and the Belt and Road Initiative of Xi Jinping. In general, both suggest increased demand for engagement, and the latter has specific geographic implications, as will be discussed later.

In many of these cases, there is no incompatibility between US and Chinese interests. Often, the threat of war (civil or interstate) and natural disasters are the sources of danger. Major powers often work together to address these challenges. However, as China's military capabilities grow, China is likely to have increased interest in the outcomes of such conflicts and, potentially, in involving itself in proxy wars. While it may be anathema to contemporary Chinese declaratory policy, China has a long history of precisely such involvement.[45] Although it is challenging to predict specifics, there is certainly a potential here for con-flicting Sino-American interests. At the very least, the United States chafed as Soviet naval capabilities began more regular "out-of-area" activities in the 1960s and especially 1970s. Similarly, because China increasingly has both the interest in and capability for such interventions, it is likely this will serve as a new source of tension between the two nations.

INFLUENCE OF GEOGRAPHY
ON THOSE MARITIME INTERESTS

Geography obviously has molded the existence of certain interests, as described previously. Certainly the location of the various interests discussed above mat-ters. However, beyond that, a specific feature of geography, the first island chain, plays a major role in the two sides' strategic interaction. Finally, China's situation within Asia affects how China faces its emerging global interests. Each is dis-cussed in turn.

Is Distance Tyrannical?

Since the core areas of contested national interests between the United States and China lie in the western Pacific rather than the eastern Pacific, the role of distance plays a major role in shaping the dynamic between the two. Taiwan lies just seventy-five nautical miles from the Chinese mainland at the narrowest point of the Taiwan Strait. The Senkaku Islands are 180 nautical miles from China's coastline. Farther afield, most of the Spratly archipelago lies some seven hundred nautical miles from Hainan province in southern China. On the other hand, San Diego (home of the US Navy's Third Fleet) is over six thousand nauti-cal miles from China. That distance creates tremendous advantages for the PLA in defending its interests.

That said, the United States has robust alliance relations in the western Pacific as well as several US territories there, mentioned previously. With the Seventh Fleet's home port in Japan and the Fifth and Seventh Air Forces head-quartered in Japan and South Korea, respectively, the United States has tremen-dous forward-deployed capabilities. These forces, plus those afloat, deployed in Guam, or rotating through facilities in partner countries, mitigate the advantage that China's geography offers. It should also be noted that they create a threat to China that is not present in the western Pacific toward the United States: US forward-deployed forces threaten China's homeland.

Allied relationships add complications as well. China must recognize that any conflict over any of these disputed territories and features could well expand to include both the United States and its allies and partners in the region. In contrast, for the United States, managing relations with its allies is diplomatically challenging. According to Schreer, "China's leaders are apparently acutely aware about the challenges posed by geographical distance for the credibility of US extended deterrence in maritime Asia."[46] China recognizes the weakness of its own partnerships within Asia (and beyond).[47]

The First Island Chain:
Land Muddying the Asian Maritime Sphere

The islands running down the East Asian littoral from Japan, through Taiwan, and to the Philippines are the dominant feature facing China's navy as it looks outward from its continental bases. They serve as barriers of some sense for China and choke points for the United States if it wants to limit Chinese scope of maneuver. Although these features are bemoaned by Chinese experts, they are not immutable. Still, the concerns are substantial, as Yoshihara explains:

> When Chinese strategists take stock of their nation's oceanic future, they foresee struggle amid claustrophobic surroundings. To Chinese eyes the string of islands just offshore—the "first island chain" enclosing Eurasia's eastern crest—resembles a Great Wall in reverse where Americans and their Japanese allies guard the sentinel towers. The island chain imprisons China's freedom of oceangoing movement. To them the island chain constitutes not just a physical barrier but also a metaphor for the resistance they expect from the occupants of the first island chain, including such potent maritime competitors as Japan. Consequently, a fitting metaphor for the island chain is a barricade—a line of physical obstacles manned by active defenders to ward off an opposing force.[48]

The sense of containment by both the United States and its allies runs through Chinese views on their strategic position, as one civilian analyst, Hu, from Beijing makes clear:

> The "First Island Chain" and the "Second Island Chain" in the Western Pacific Ocean have become obstacles to the Chinese military forces' access to the oceans from coastal waters. Furthermore, the United States, Japan, and other countries retain the control of almost all key islands on the island chains and important waters in their vicinity with a wary stance on China's construction of a maritime power. In times of war, if the Chinese navy passes through channels in the island chains, it would be directly subject to their control. On a spiritual level, China lacks vital maritime intellectual and cultural reserves.[49]

Indeed, analysts would characterize the situation similarly, although using more benign overtones. For example, according to Schreer, "by employing what Andrew Krepinevich termed an 'archipelagic defense' strategy—a series of linked defences along the 'first island chain'—the United States begun [*sic*] to strengthen its alliances and partnerships with many countries located in the Asia-Pacific 'rimland.'"[50]

Taiwan sits at the center of the first island chain. As previously noted, there is a strategic rationale for its importance beyond its political and cultural status. As one PLAN officer explains, "possessing Taiwan would enable one to effectively control the strategic choke points between the East China Sea and the South China Sea. Possessing Taiwan opens an advantageous waterway to the interior seas of the second island chain while opening a convenient path to the high seas. As such, Taiwan Island serves an important function as the central pivot of the first island chain."[51] The sensitive issue of Taiwan's status is thus reinforced by many factors.

Still, the island chain is not seen as a comprehensive barrier. Rather, it is something to be overcome for Beijing. According to Cole, "the PLAN will not be constrained by lines or Western defensive concepts in defending China's maritime interests. . . . These views reflect the PLAN's recognition of the inherent value of unconstrained, mobile naval power, limited as little as possible by geographic features or the capabilities of statically based weapons."[52]

Similarly, the Chinese scholar Hu notes, "To maintain and defend these interests is not to construct a 'Maritime Great Wall,' but rather to foray beyond these frontiers."[53] The following sections explain those additional interests.

Beyond the Island Chain

As China's maritime capabilities and interests have increased over the past decade in particular, moving through and well beyond the first island chain has been increasingly important and viable. As discussed later in the chapter, this has been coupled with a shift from nearly exclusive emphasis on antiaccess/area-denial (A2/AD) capabilities to more of the trappings of traditional blue-water capabilities. Andrew S. Erickson and Joel Wuthnow note the wide range of views that are visible in the Chinese literature: "Various Chinese authors assert that the island chains are (1) barriers that China must penetrate to achieve freedom of manoeuvre in the maritime domain; (2) springboards for power projection by whomever controls a given island chain; and (3) benchmarks for the advancement of Chinese maritime and air force projection in the Asia-Pacific."[54]

As China looks beyond the first island chain, several key geographies loom. The vast expanse of the Central Pacific is home to deep waters ideal for long-range submarine patrols, and it is also dominated by US forces deploying from

Hawaii and San Diego. The ambiguous tyranny of distance (discussed previously) complicates the Chinese ability to deploy power-projection forces to their east. Additionally, the farther to the east the Chinese look, the closer to major American capabilities they find themselves. Thus, the position in the contested western Pacific is literally reversed. However, the situation for Beijing is exacerbated by the absence of any Chinese allies in the Americas.

More dynamic is the situation toward China's south and southwest. The Indian Ocean is a long way from both China and the United States. For China, projecting power to (or engaging in commerce through) the region requires movement through the Strait of Malacca. During Hu Jintao's reign, discussion of the Malacca dilemma became prominent, highlighting the importance to Beijing of the security of commerce through that vital piece of maritime geography. Although Sino-Singaporean relations benefit from some shared cultural ties and significant shared economic interests, the United States has developed a security partnership of major significance with the city-state. Although not a treaty ally, the United States recently renewed its three-decade-old agreement with Singapore to ensure US military access for the next fifteen years to Singaporean facilities, including a purpose-built dock for large US aircraft carriers.

Beyond that gateway to the Indian Ocean, the United States maintains a number of other relevant strategic relationships. It has a major base on the island of Diego Garcia (owned by the United Kingdom), two bases in Djibouti, and major infrastructure in the Persian Gulf (including a Bahraini base used since World War II). This all greatly facilitates US access to the region and reduces its cost of sustaining forces there, and it also enhances US maritime domain awareness of the region.

The Indian Ocean also brings into the geostrategic picture another major actor, India. The recent resurgence of Sino-Indian tensions brings to the fore latent competitive impulses between the two. While the US-Indian relationship is complex, there are clear signs of continuing improvement in it. At the very least, the presence of another great power's maritime forces is a complicating factor for any PLA deployment to the ocean.

Although it lacks the depth of relationships that the United States has, China is building some strategic depth for its maritime force through its own facility in Djibouti and ambiguous ports in Pakistan and Sri Lanka. Some degree of strategic coherence is often attributed to these moves. As David Brewster states, "some analysts claim that China is following what has become known as a 'String of Pearls' strategy—essentially a Mahanian strategy of building a chain of naval bases across the northern Indian Ocean that would be used by the Chinese navy to protect China's trade routes and potentially dominate the Indian Ocean."[55]

The challenges to achieve this are tremendous.[56] There are nine foreign bases in Djibouti; two are American, and six are held by American allies (France has three, and Japan, Italy, and Britain each have one). China's relations with Pakistan and Sri Lanka are fraught, and both countries deny that the ports China runs in their countries will be used as military facilities. Even if they were, Brewster explicates, "there are considerable doubts about the military value of ports such as Obock, Gwadar or Hambantota to the PLAN in the event of conflict with another major power such as India or the United States. . . . As one Chinese analyst commented, given the distances separating any Chinese interests in the Indian Ocean, these ports would look more like 'sitting ducks' than a String of Pearls."[57]

As China continues to develop relationships with countries in the region, it seems reasonable to expect "dual-use" ports to be available to its navy. However, in most cases, it seems unlikely that these would serve as major assets for projecting power in a high-end conventional conflict. They will nevertheless be valuable in reducing the costs of peacetime engagement in the region.

Molding Geography beyond Asia: Potential of the Belt and Road Initiative

It is useful to consider the ways that China is tailoring its own strategic geography. The Belt and Road Initiative is the primary contemporary manifestation of that effort. The initiative is a massive undertaking to reshape the infrastructure of connectivity between China and points to its west. Its precise focus is elusive,[58] but it certainly includes laying the groundwork to facilitate trade through China's own west (the restive areas of Xinjiang and Tibet) and to enhance China links to Central Asia, the Middle East, Africa, and Europe both over land (initially) and by sea. Since 2014 the Chinese have announced deals valued at approximately $100 billion per year, although executed investment is thought to be considerably lower and has declined in recent years.[59]

To the extent China is successful, this initiative will have important effects on the strategic geography discussed previously. In general, connectivity facing west reduces the maritime challenge from the east—that is, the United States (from Beijing's perspective). Reorienting China to manage relations in South Asia, Central Asia, and beyond deflects attention away from the territorial disputes described previously. Furthermore, development of land routes across Central Asia or through Pakistan to China mitigates the Malacca dilemma and attendant security dilemmas with the United States and India. Thus, as Brewster explains,

> although the OBOR [One Belt, One Road] initiative is principally economic, Chinese officials acknowledge that it has a political and security component

vis-à-vis neighbouring states. Indeed, there can be little doubt that the trans-Myanmar and trans-Pakistan projects, if completed, will have major economic strategic implications for the region, perhaps not all of them yet fully understood—or indeed, intended. The connections could stimulate considerable economic development in the land-locked provinces of Xinjiang, Tibet, and Yunnan, and lead to an expansion of China's economic and political influence in Pakistan and Myanmar and other neighbouring states.[60]

Increased Chinese economic engagement that the Belt and Road Initiative facilitates with the Middle East, Africa, and Europe will certainly drive Chinese attentions to these regions. Those relations will be primarily commercial, and thus their effect on geopolitics is secondary if still tangible. Still, the maritime corridors will increase the importance of the free flow of commerce through the Indian Ocean while the transcontinental corridors reduce its importance. That said, the correlation between projects implemented under the Belt and Road Initiative label do not correlate with the identified "six corridors" of Belt and Road pathways.[61] Scholars Thomas P. Narins and John Agnew conclude, "In fact, one of the key misunderstandings of the Belt and Road Initiative relates to the conceptualisation of the project as comprising well-defined, fixed, and predetermined (maritime and land) routes and transects (as many of the cartographic depictions . . . connote)."[62] So, on balance, none of this is likely to fundamentally restructure the geostrategic situation in the Indian Ocean in the next decade or two. Its major effect should be to modestly reduce Chinese emphasis on the Pacific supply lines.

SECURING INTERESTS IN THE ASIAN GEOGRAPHY: EVOLVING OPERATIONAL CONCEPTS

This final core section asks the question, How have the two countries configured their militaries to secure their interests in the context of the relevant geography? Although both are in flux, there is some interesting (albeit modest) convergence.

China's Military Consolidates Nearby and Ventures Outward

As noted in the introductory section to this chapter, China has historically relied on an "active defense" strategy. The PLA today is focused on "winning informationalized local wars," which require more offensive actions.[63] There is also a sense that such wars will intensify quickly, as reflected by Yves-Heng Lim: "An article published in *China Military Science* argues that because 'the destructive power of high-tech weapons has dramatically increased[,] . . . the first moment of informationalized operations has a decisive impact on the war."[64] This then impels a "need to act offensively and pre-emptively."[65]

The Chinese strategy is usually characterized in the West as A2/AD. China will try to prevent the United States (or others) from accessing nearby waters and deny them operational freedom of maneuver. In practice, this has meant having the means to prevent the United States from operating inside the first island chain in times of conflict and complicating the freedom of operating between the first and second island chains farther out in the Pacific Ocean. A decade ago, China would have relied on large numbers of small, missile-launching patrol boats, diesel submarines with similar weapons, and—mostly—land-based ballistic missiles to hit naval vessels and nearby airfields. This emphasis on relatively cheap and survivable land-based missiles (thus, "using the land to [deny] control [of] the sea"[66]) is a notable departure for China from the practice of other great powers' militaries. Indeed, the fundamental organizational structure of the Chinese military attests to the importance of the missiles: the PLA rocket force is given institutional status equal to that of the other branches, such as the navy and air force. Striking US forces and positions on the first island chain is an important part of this approach. According to Wuthnow, "Chinese strategists view US military presence on the island chains surrounding China as posing two larger strategic challenges: first, they could be used to strike China itself, and second, they could restrict China's access to the Pacific Ocean."[67]

Although Chinese military officials do not use the A2/AD term often, it appears occasionally. Thus, Peking University's Professor Bo writes, "The application and impacts of navies have undergone a great deal of change. With the development of land-based weaponry such as missiles and long-range fighter jets, in addition to acceleration in the construction of space technology, a country with a weaker navy, but with support from mighty land-based 'anti-access' (A2) or 'area denial' (AD), one can self-protect even when faced by a world-class navy and even gain authority over near seas along its homeland."[68] Similarly, the term "counterintervention" appears in Chinese military texts only in narrow operational terms to describe this particular military goal, particularly in Taiwan scenarios.[69]

Until about 2014, this was the central goal guiding Chinese weapons procurement. A fleet of some eighty Houbei Type-22 fast attack patrol boats provided potent "at-sea" capabilities in waters near China. Several score quiet diesel submarines of the *Song* and *Yuan* classes complemented these underwater. Additionally, a panoply of missiles could be launched from land. The DF-21, and more recently the DF-26, could target either land facilities or moving ships at sea, particularly high-value assets such as carriers. A wide range of other missiles, with different ranges, could threaten fixed sites, such as airfields and many radar systems (missile defense or others). Offensive mining also contributed to these capabilities. Finally, most recently, air-launched antiship cruise missiles could be loaded onto long-range bombers to diversify strike packages. These would be used together in what the Chinese refer to as joint firepower strikes, massing fires against vulnerable targets.

Although this Chinese approach would not guarantee success in the invasion of Taiwan, it has served China's other territorial interests well. Certainly, it would raise the cost of US intervention in any regional conflict, whether over Taiwan or in any of the smaller island disputes. (Thus, it serves to deter steps Taiwan might take to further remove itself from ties to the mainland.) Still, limiting Chinese naval capabilities to relatively narrow A2/AD goals is viewed as insufficient. One textbook of the Academy of Military Science (the PLA institution responsible for authoring texts that educate the military) flagged this concern—"the risk that a 'strong adversary' might project 'its comprehensive distant combat superiority in the oceanic direction' to threaten China's interests. Consequently, the PLA has had to 'externally push the strategic forward edge from the home territory to the periphery, from land to sea, from air to space, and from tangible spaces to intangible spaces.'"[70] Certainly, A2/AD would not address those interests beyond the near waters, interests that are growing in importance as China's economy rises in importance in the globalized world.

An important challenge for China's A2/AD approach to securing it maritime interests comes from the inherent range limitations of its component capabilities. According to prominent Western military analysts Stephen Biddle and Ivan Oelrich,

> by 2040 China will not achieve military hegemony over the Western Pacific or anything close to it. . . . A2/AD is giving air and maritime defenders increasing advantages, but those advantages are strongest over controlled landmasses and weaken over distance. . . . This finding derives from the physics of the key technologies coupled with inherent asymmetries in the operating environments of the land, air, and sea surface. . . . The sky and the surface of the sea present much simpler backgrounds than the land.[71]

To address these challenges, around 2014 (although certainly with antecedents before and echoes later) the PLAN began to shift significant emphasis to bluewater capabilities that could patrol sea lines of control far from the local waters.

Political signals of this were apparent in the defense white paper of 2015 that highlighted the mission of "open seas protection."[72] Earlier antecedents of this were apparent, if more muted, in Hu Jintao's call for the PLAN to take on "new historic missions."[73] More tangibly, the Chinese navy began to build larger ships in quantity. Moreover, it commenced serial production of advanced guided-missile destroyers (notably, the Type-52D, displacing some eight thousand tons); the first of these "multirole" destroyers was commissioned in 2014.[74] Also in 2014, China began building its first Type-55 guided-missile cruiser (ten thousand tons) and launched its first Type-75 landing helicopter dock amphibious assault ship (forty thousand tons). Beijing's first carrier began patrolling nearby waters the year before, the same year a more capable Type-903A fast underway replenishment ship was commissioned.

All of these ships are well suited for the distant sea mission set. The Type-52D destroyers and Type-55 cruisers are capable of providing for their own air defense, which has long been a vulnerability for the Chinese navy. Nearly any combination of these ships would pack a powerful payload of offensive missiles. Moreover, many configurations of Chinese surface action groups would have some aircraft, whether rotary or fixed wing, facilitating engagement of a diverse mission set.

That said, these capabilities, which look very much like the American capabilities that China is trying to deter from acting within the first island chain near China, are vulnerable to A2/AD capabilities themselves. Furthermore, while sustainment, air defense, and antisubmarine warfare has improved for these forces, it remains challenging (for any navy but certainly for the PLAN). These forces allow for a "presence" mission, with substantial patrolling capabilities against nontraditional threats, certainly. Even with the limited basing options that China may be developing around the Indian Ocean, these will be vulnerable assets in any great-power competition.

The US Military Rethinks Power Projection and Hunkers Down

The United States also is in the midst of a transformation in how it thinks about naval power in the new era of great-power competition. As noted in the introductory section, freedom of navigation has long been a central tenet for the US Navy. In the post–Cold War era, however, the threat posed to that—and, in particular, to the ability of the United States to securely reinforce Europe in the face of a Soviet attack—has evaporated. Prior to, but amplified during, the wars in Iraq and Afghanistan, the US Navy became a force focused on projecting power directly. The list of ship-launched Tomahawk missile strikes and/or carrier-based air strikes against ground targets smaller powers is long: Iraq (1991, 1998, and 2003 to the present), Yugoslavia/Serbia (1995 and 1999), Afghanistan (2001 to the present), Libya (2011), and Syria (2017), for example.

Doctrinal statements followed this shift in operational emphasis. While still retaining consideration of freedom of navigation, other goals became paramount. Operational concepts such as "from the sea" and "forward . . . from the sea" highlighted this power-projection emphasis in the early 1990s.

Later policy statements encapsulated it as well, as described by Cole: "CS-21 was described as the first maritime strategy to be proclaimed by the United States as a 'joint effort by the Navy, Marine Corps, and Coast Guard.' This strategy unsurprisingly emphasized securing 'the United States from direct attack,' to include ensuring 'secure strategic access and [retaining] global freedom of action.' It is notable also because it named no enemies but emphasized navy roles of ensuring the safety of shipping at sea and preventing unlawful and terrorist activities."[75]

Beyond that, shipbuilding decisions also reflected this emphasis. The expensive *Zumwalt*-class cruisers are literally designed around long-range guns to provide offshore support in relatively uncontested environments. Naval gunfire support was useful in the smaller, brushfire wars that were common in the 1990s and 2000s. However, as the class's costs ballooned and the threat environment shifted, the construction of the class was halted at three hulls (down from early discussions of thirty-two). Similarly, the development of the two variants of the littoral combat ships (LCS) was a different approach to lower threat environments and focused on increasing hull numbers with nimble platforms capable of a wide range of missions in close quarters with an enemy. As the vessel's survivability in an antiaccess environment was called into question (and its costs rose and other issues arose), LCS production was also cut as well. While this is not the place for a detailed discussion of the merits of carriers, it seems fair to note that the US Navy continues to maintain a constant demand for carrier hulls while the threat to them increases.

Still in the past decade, the US military has increasingly focused on adapting to great-power competition. Central to this has been recent innovation to address challenges in the strategic geography of Asia's "contested waters." Doctrinally, these have been encapsulated in loose concepts such as AirSea Battle that first appeared in 2010. This set of ideas focused on extrapolating from late Cold War synergies from joint operations between the US Army and US Air Force (in AirLand Battle) to face the Soviet tank division threat to NATO. Joint Air Force and Navy operations could potentially unwind the A2/AD threat posed by China's modernization. The concept has been widely criticized as being highly escalatory and necessitating large-scale (perhaps unsustainable) air operations over Chinese territory.[76]

By 2015 AirSea Battle had evolved into something called the Joint Concept for Access and Maneuver in the Global Commons. While retaining the emphasis on "jointness," this approach takes a broader view toward how US forces might obtain "access" in contested regions of global commons (e.g., the waters inside and just outside the first island chain). More survivable forces (submarines, for instance) might require less strategic bombing of China.

Most recently the United States is belatedly coming to recognize the "missile revolution" in military affairs. That is, China is not the only country that can take advantage of cheap, land-based missiles to hold at risk power-projection capabilities.[77] This move has been facilitated by the US withdrawal from the Intermediate Range Nuclear Forces Treaty and indeed played a role in precipitating that choice. Within weeks of that withdrawal, the United States tested a land-based launch of a Tomahawk cruise missile, a long-range system that had previously been shown to be effective against ships.[78] The US Army tested a land-based Naval Strike Missile against a ship in Rim of the Pacific Exercise in 2018.[79] Both the US Army and US Marine Corps are innovating with operating concepts that hold Chinese naval vessels at risk from land positions (multi-domain task forces and expeditionary advance base operations, respectively).[80] As yet, the locations where such forces would be positioned are unidentified publicly, but the emphasis on tactical mobility that is required for such forces to be survivable implies that strategic mobility should not be a challenge either. A recent proposal from the Marines' commandant continues this doctrinal evolution.[81]

The US Navy has also adapted to the new environment, although much uncertainty about future plans remains. The LCS has emphasized deployments in Asia with a "hub" system based in Singapore. This includes one armed with the Naval Strike Missile, an upgrade that all LCSs will eventually receive. The Navy has also moved forward with a new frigate development and modestly grown its submarine force. All these capabilities are well suited to the complex terrain near and inside the first island chain. That said, continued emphasis on large multirole surface combatants and power-projection platforms (such as aircraft carriers and amphibious assault ships) maintains continuity with the US Navy's traditional focus.

CONCLUSION

Stepping back from these discussions, it is clear that geography and the two countries' evolving interaction with the region and globe have major effects on the strategic choices they have made and the prospects for conflict between them. The geography of the areas of strategic competition between them will exert a dominant influence on the way that competition plays out. The littoral interests of China fall comfortably inside the range of its A2/AD capabilities. Although the US Navy (and other services) are working to maintain access to defend its interests and those of their allies, major challenges remain.

Beyond the Asian littoral, the situation is quite different. While China has interests spanning the globe today and increased capabilities to defend them, it lacks the robust alliance and basing network that the United States has. The PLAN has certainly developed important power-projection assets that are increasingly capable. It has growing expeditionary experience, although it still falls far, far behind the US Navy in that regard. The challenges posed by long-distance deployments will not easily be met by Beijing.

Although it is beyond the scope of this chapter, some consideration of the potential for Chinese alliance development is warranted, given the importance of that issue for the competition between the two. Another aspect of the Belt and Road Initiative, and of China's economic heft more generally, is to make cooperation with China lucrative for other states. Although this concern is often expressed in the current political dynamic, historical work on alliances generally finds such economic enticements to be a weak form of alliance formation relative to threat perceptions, power dynamics, and a history of predatory behavior.[82] Generally, those factors will complicate China's aspiration in that regard. Furthermore, the United States will likely continue to benefit from expanded geographic reach relative to China because of this. It is useful to differentiate the prospects of unintentional, accidental conflict from those that result from the deliberate pursuit of divergent interests. The strategic geography that China and the United States compete within affects both of these pathways.

The elements of convergence in operational approaches to conflict discussed in the previous section have some positive implications. Widely divergent doctrines can complicate the assessment of the balance of power and the use of military signals to shape potential adversaries' perceptions.[83] Both China and the United States should have a more common view of the balance of power between them and the key capabilities to develop. This will lead to using similar capabilities to send signals between them, giving this some convergence. Both have some degree (or will soon) of capabilities in the A2/AD category and in the traditional power-projection arena. This should reduce uncertainties and play a modest stabilizing effect.

Alternatively, the persistence of some divergence in Beijing's and Washington's views on the nature of sovereignty in the maritime sphere is worrisome. The US position on rights and limitations on sovereignty in different categories of maritime regions has certainly changed across time, and as a country that has not ratified UNCLOS, the United States has some challenges simply proclaiming that "rule of law" is an objective standard. Nevertheless, the Chinese position is distinct from that of the United States and most UNCLOS members. Although it is hard to imagine any major conflict over the possession of a certain reef or a specific rock, the concept of sovereignty over parts of what are generally viewed as global commons does seem to be fodder for more significant conflict. Put more simply, the meaning of "geography" in the maritime sphere differs between the two, and that is dangerous.

Other aspects of the strategic geography and the forces the two sides have developed to compete within it will also be destabilizing. Although there is some commonality of interests over freedom of navigation in general, the potential threats to freedom of navigation are diverse. Antipiracy is certainly a shared interest. General stability near key choke points (the Strait of Hormuz, in particular) is another. Deglobalization, whatever its source, is unlikely to undo the centrality of global trade flows to both economies and the globe, even if some reorientation of specific patterns of trade occurs. Additionally, these aspects of freedom of navigation are indeed common interests and should not be neglected.

In any period of significant Sino-American conflict, the relevant threat would be from each other. As has been stated previously, the United States has significant advantages beyond the geography of the East Asian littoral by virtue of its naval capabilities and location of alliances and bases. However, China is increasingly involved in engaging in maritime domains beyond its nearby waters. The newly competitive domain of global supply-line protection would seem rife for both zero-sum competition and security dilemmas. Both sides will see merit in threatening the other's dependencies, and both sides will take steps to ensure their own security in far-off domains. This geopolitical competition is likely to intensify well into the future.

NOTES

1. Phil Kelly, *Classical Geopolitics: A New Analytical Model* (Stanford, CA: Stanford University Press, 2016), ix.
2. Jakub J. Grygiel, *Great Powers and Geopolitical Change* (Baltimore, MD: Johns Hopkins University Press, 2006), x.
3. Nicholas J. Spykman, "Geography and Foreign Policy, I," *American Political Science Review* 32, no. 1 (1938): 30, https://doi.org/10.2307/1949029.
4. Benjamin Schreer, "Towards Contested 'Spheres of Influence' in the Western Pacific: Rising China, Classical Geopolitics, and Asia-Pacific Stability," *Geopolitics* 24, no. 2 (2019): 503–22, https//doi.org/10.1080/14650045.2017.1364237.
5. Barry R. Posen, "Command of the Commons: The Military Foundation of US Hegemony," *International Security* 28, no. 1 (2003): 5–46, https://doi.org/10.1162 /016228803322427965. Note that for the United States the obvious interest in the security of its population and territory is paramount. However, it is under little direct threat.
6. John King Fairbank and Merle Goldman, *China: A New History* (Cambridge, MA: Belknap Press of Harvard University Press, 1998); David Chan-oong Kang, *East Asia before the West: Five Centuries of Trade and Tribute* (New York: Columbia University Press, 2010).
7. Adm. Zheng He led a series of fleets for the Yongle emperor in the Ming Dynasty that were far larger than anything the Europeans could deploy in the fifteenth century. The fleet explored the Indian Ocean and the coast of eastern Africa,

conducting trade along the way. After several decades of imperial support for such outreach, the far-reaching voyages ceased abruptly in 1433.

8. Robert S. Ross, "The Geography of the Peace: East Asia in the Twenty First Century," *International Security* 23, no. 4 (1999): 103, https://doi.org/10.1162/isec.23.4.81.

9. Fairbank and Goldman, *China*.

10. Kang, *East Asia before the West*.

11. Bo Hu, *Chinese Maritime Power in the 21st Century: Strategic Planning, Policy, and Predictions* (New York: Routledge, 2019), 7.

12. Hu, *Chinese Maritime Power*, 10.

13. Christopher P. Twomey, *The Military Lens: Doctrinal Differences and Deterrence Failure in Sino-American Relations* (Ithaca, NY: Cornell University Press, 2010).

14. Twomey, *Military Lens*.

15. M. Taylor Fravel, "Shifts in Warfare and Party Unity: Explaining China's Changes in Military Strategy," *International Security* 42, no. 3 (2018): 37–83, https://doi.org/10.1162/ISEC_a_00304.

16. Alexander C. Huang, "The PLA Navy at War, 1949–1999: From Coastal Defense to Distant Operations," in *Chinese Warfighting: The PLA Experience since 1949*, ed. Mark A. Ryan, David M. Finkelstein, and Michael A. McDevitt, 241–69 (Armonk, NY: M. E. Sharpe, 2003).

17. Ross, "Geography of the Peace."

18. Ian Speller, *Understanding Naval Warfare* (London: Routledge, 2018), 201, https://doi.org/10.4324/9781315227818.

19. So much so that prominent realists view that as grounds to move the United States away from its relationship with Taiwan as a way to dramatically mitigate Sino-American competition: Charles L. Glaser, "A US-China Grand Bargain? The Hard Choice between Military Competition and Accommodation," *International Security* 39, no. 4 (2015): 49–90, https://doi.org/10.1162/ISEC_a_00199.

20. Jun Tao Yeung, "Why Is Taiwan So Important? The Manipulation of Nationalism in Legitimizing One-Party Rule in China," *Yale Review of International Studies* (blog), October 29, 2019, http://yris.yira.org/essays/3613.

21. Hu, *Chinese Maritime Power*, 10.

22. For focused analysis on this aspect, see Brendan Rittenhouse Green and Caitlin Talmadge, "Then What? Assessing the Military Implications of Chinese Control of Taiwan," *International Security* 47, no. 1 (July 1, 2022): 7–45, https://doi.org/10.1162/isec_a_00437.

23. The best treatment of this period and its policies remains Alan D. Romberg, *Rein in at the Brink of the Precipice: American Policy toward Taiwan and US-PRC Relations* (Washington, DC: Henry L. Stimson Center, 2003).

24. Again, there remains significant ambiguity on the conditions under which this would occur. For a good discussion of this issue, see Gang Lin and Wenxing Zhou, "Does Taiwan Matter to the United States? Policy Debates on Taiwan Abandonment and Beyond," *China Review* 18, no. 3 (2018): 177–206, https://www.jstor.org/stable/26484537.

25. Thomas J. Christensen, "The Contemporary Security Dilemma: Deterring a Taiwan Conflict," *Washington Quarterly* 25, no. 4 (2002): 7–21, https://doi.org/10.1162/016366002760252509.

26. The implications of the Philippines case in front of the Permanent Court of Arbitration regarding the legality of China's South China Sea claims and policy are

substantial for a wide range of Asian and Pacific features. George K. Ndi, "Philippines v China: Assessing the Implications of the South China Sea Arbitration," *Australian Journal of Maritime and Ocean Affairs* 8, no. 4 (2016): 269–85, https://doi.org/10.1080/18366503.2016.1244142.

27. Although referred to as the Diaoyu Islands (or Diaoyutai) by China, this author will refer to them by their Japanese name because they are administered by Japan.

28. It should be noted that China has declared straight baselines around the Senkakus as well, although that is more symbolic, given that China has less administrative or other control over them.

29. One expert, Gregory B. Poling, suggests this sanguine view is overstated, given the large size of these bases. Gregory B. Poling, "The Conventional Wisdom on China's Island Bases Is Dangerously Wrong," War on the Rocks, January 10, 2020, https://warontherocks.com/2020/01/the-conventional-wisdom-on-chinas-island-bases-is-dangerously-wrong/. This author remains relatively optimistic. The munition demands of a sustained operation against these forces is not trivial; many of the most dangerous assets could be struck early with sophisticated munitions, leaving follow-on strikes for less expensive munitions.

30. Indeed, the US-Canadian disputes are cited in the classic study on the restraining effect on conflict of deep interdependence. Robert O. Keohane and Joseph S. Nye, *Power and Interdependence*, 3rd ed. (New York: Longman, 2001).

31. That said, several of the US-administered features in the Western Pacific (e.g., Howland Island, Baker Island, and Kingman Reef) are smaller than the largest Spratly features and so could raise some similar concerns. See Yann-huei Song, "The July 2016 Arbitral Award, Interpretation of Article 121(3) of the UNCLOS, and Selecting Examples of Inconsistent State Practices," *Ocean Development and International Law* 49, no. 3 (July 2018): 247–61, https://doi.org/10.1080/00908320.2018.1479355.

32. Hu, *Chinese Maritime Power*, 19.

33. Toshi Yoshihara and James R. Holmes, *Red Star over the Pacific: China's Rise and the Challenge to US Maritime Strategy*, rev. ed. (Annapolis, MD: Naval Institute Press, 2018), 96.

34. Michael McDevitt, *Becoming a Great "Maritime Power": A Chinese Dream*, IRM-2016-U-013646 (Arlington, VA: Center of Naval Analyses, 2016), 4.

35. Again, see Ndi, "Philippines v China." On the issue of "most, but not all" possible meanings of Chinese claims regarding the nine-dash line are inconsistent with UNCLOS, see Office of Ocean and Polar Affairs, Bureau of Oceans and International Environmental and Scientific Affairs, *China: Maritime Claims in the South China Sea*, Limits in the Seas, no. 143 (Washington, DC: US State Department, 2014). The most official Chinese statement on what the nine-dash line represents is as follows:

China has territorial sovereignty and maritime rights and interests in the South China Sea, including, inter alia: i. China has sovereignty over Nanhai Zhudao [South China Sea features], consisting of Dongsha Qundao [Pratas], Xisha Qundao [Paracels], Zhongsha Qundao [Macclesfield and Scarborough] and Nansha Qundao [Spratlys]; ii. China has internal waters, territorial sea, and contiguous zone, based on Nanhai Zhudao; iii. China has exclusive economic zone and continental shelf, based on Nanhai Zhudao; iv. China has historic rights in the South China Sea.

Although this sounds provocative (and at one level is), it is imprecise as to exactly which "internal waters" are claimed, which features warrant territorial sea, and which specific "historic rights" China is claiming. Ministry of Foreign Affairs, People's Republic of China, "Statement of the Government of the People's Republic of China on China's Territorial Sovereignty and Maritime Rights and Interests in the South China Sea," July 12, 2016, https://www.fmprc.gov.cn/mfa_eng/wjdt_665385/2649_665393/201607/t20160712_679472.html.
36. Bernard Cole, *Asian Maritime Strategies: Navigating Troubled Waters* (Annapolis, MD: Naval Institute Press, 2013), 108.
37. Hu, *Chinese Maritime Power*, 12–13.
38. Yoshihara and Holmes, *Red Star over the Pacific*, 14.
39. Precisely who is first and who is second, China or the United States, depends on precise choice of measure (imports, exports, both, merchandise trade only [since services are less dependent on maritime transport], how should Hong Kong be treated, etc.)
40. Hu, *Chinese Maritime Power*, 12.
41. Hu, 11.
42. Hu, 11.
43. Gabe Collins and Andrew S. Erickson, "Implications of China's Military Evacuation of Citizens from Libya," *China Brief* 11, no. 4 (March 2011), https://jamestown.org/program/implications-of-chinas-military-evacuation-of-citizens-from-libya/.
44. For a thorough assessment of where China finds itself today, see Timothy Heath, *China's Pursuit of Overseas Security*, RR2271 (Santa Monica, CA: RAND Corp., 2018).
45. Chinese support for communist movements in Korea and Vietnam were large-scale. China also provided smaller support to Cambodia and others.
46. Schreer, "Towards Contested 'Spheres,'" 514.
47. Joel Wuthnow, "Asian Security without the United States? Examining China's Security Strategy in Maritime and Continental Asia," *Asian Security* 14, no. 3 (2017): 230–45, https//doi.org/10.1080/14799855.2017.1378181.
48. Toshi Yoshihara, *Dragon against the Sun: Chinese Views of Japanese Seapower* (Washington, DC: Center for Strategic and Budgetary Assessments, 2020), 33–34. For an excellent overview, see Andrew S. Erickson and Joel Wuthnow, "Barriers, Springboards, and Benchmarks: China Conceptualizes the Pacific 'Island Chains,'" *China Quarterly* 225 (March 2016): 1–22, https://doi.org/10.1017/S0305741016000011.
49. Hu, *Chinese Maritime Power*, 16.
50. Schreer, "Towards Contested 'Spheres of Influence,'" 516.
51. Yoshihara and Holmes, *Red Star over the Pacific*, 85.
52. Cole, *Asian Maritime Strategies*, 106.
53. Hu, *Chinese Maritime Power*, 15.
54. Erickson and Wuthnow, "Barriers, Springboards, and Benchmarks," 2.
55. David Brewster, "Silk Roads and Strings of Pearls: The Strategic Geography of China's New Pathways in the Indian Ocean," *Geopolitics* 22, no. 2 (2017): 277, https://doi.org/10.1080/14650045.2016.1223631.
56. For a careful evaluation of possible roles for the Chinese military in the region, see Joshua T. White, "China's Indian Ocean Ambitions: Investment, Infrastructure,

and Military Advantage," *Global China* (June 2020), https://www.brookings.edu/research/chinas-indian-ocean-ambitions/.

57. Brewster, "Silk Roads and Strings of Pearls," 281.
58. Eyck Freymann, "'One Belt One Road' Is Just a Marketing Campaign," *The Atlantic*, August 17, 2019.
59. "The Pandemic Is Hurting China's Belt and Road Initiative," *The Economist*, June 4, 2020.
60. Brewster, "Silk Roads and Strings of Pearls," 284.
61. Jonathan Hillman, *China's Belt and Road Is Full of Holes*, CSIS Briefs (Washington DC: Center for Strategic and International Studies, 2018). For persuasive explanations regarding this lack of coherence, see Min Ye, "Fragmentation and Mobilization: Domestic Politics of the Belt and Road in China," *Journal of Contemporary China* 28, no. 119 (September 2019): 696–711, https://doi.org/10.1080/10670564.2019.1580428; Baogang He, "The Domestic Politics of the Belt and Road Initiative and Its Implications," *Journal of Contemporary China* 28, no. 116 (2018): 180–95, https://doi.org/10.1080/10670564.2018.1511391.
62. Thomas P. Narins, and John Agnew, "Missing from the Map: Chinese Exceptionalism, Sovereignty Regimes and the Belt Road Initiative," *Geopolitics* 25, no. 4 (2020): 809–37, https://doi.org/10.1080/14650045.2019.1601082.
63. Yves-Heng Lim, "Expanding the Dragon's Reach: The Rise of China's Anti-Access Naval Doctrine and Forces," *Journal of Strategic Studies* 40, no. 1/2 (2017): 146–68, https://doi.org/10.1080/01402390.2016.1176563.
64. Lim, "Expanding the Dragon's Reach," 152.
65. Lim, 152.
66. Lim, 160.
67. Wuthnow, "Asian Security," 233.
68. Hu, *Chinese Maritime Power*, 15–16.
69. M. Taylor Fravel, and Christopher P. Twomey, "Projecting Strategy: The Myth of Chinese Counter-Intervention," *Washington Quarterly* 37, no. 4 (2015): 171–87, https://doi.org/10.1080/0163660X.2014.1002164.
70. Passages from the 2013 "Science of Military Strategy," as quoted in Schreer, "Towards Contested 'Spheres,'" 509.
71. Stephen Biddle and Ivan Oelrich, "Future Warfare in the Western Pacific: Chinese Antiaccess/Area Denial, US AirSea Battle, and Command of the Commons in East Asia," *International Security* 41, no. 1 (July 2016): 12, https://doi.org/10.1162/ISEC_a_00249.
72. Zhengyu Wu, "Towards Naval Normalcy: 'Open Seas Protection' and Sino-US Maritime Relations," *Pacific Review* 32, no. 4 (2019): 666–93, https://doi.org/10.1080/09512748.2018.1553890.
73. Cortez A. Cooper, *The PLA Navy's "New Historic Missions": Expanding Capabilities for a Re-emergent Maritime Power*, CT-332 (Santa Monica, CA: RAND Corp., 2009).
74. The Type-52Ds are notable as they are equipped with phased-array radars and vertical launch tubes, making them comparable, at least basically, to cutting-edge destroyers deployed by the United States, Japan, the United Kingdom, and other naval powers. China has commissioned a dozen already, with another dozen (or more) in various stages of construction and outfitting. This is significant because for decades China has built two (or sometimes four) of a particular destroyer design before modifying it and building a few of the next class.

75. Cole, *Asian Maritime Strategies*, 47.
76. Joshua Rovner, "A Long War in the East: Doctrine, Diplomacy, and the Prospects for a Protracted Sino-American Conflict," *Diplomacy and Statecraft* 29, no. 1 (2018): 129–42, https://doi.org/10.1080/09592296.2017.1420535; Eugene Gholz, Benjamin Friedman, and Enea Gjoza, "Defensive Defense: A Better Way to Protect US Allies in Asia," *Washington Quarterly* 42, no. 4 (Winter 2020): 171–89, https://doi.org/10.1080/0163660X.2019.1693103.
77. Michael Beckley, "The Emerging Military Balance in East Asia: How China's Neighbors Can Check Chinese Naval Expansion," *International Security* 42, no. 2 (2017): 78–119, https://doi.org/10.1162/ISEC_a_00294.
78. "US Tests First Ground-Launched Cruise Missile after INF Treaty Exit," Reuters, August 19, 2019.
79. David Larter, "The US Navy's New Anti-Ship Missile Scores a Hit at RIMPAC, but There's a Twist," *Defense News*, August 2, 2018, sec. "Space and Missile Defense."
80. Todd South, "Army to Build at Least Two New Multi-Domain Task Forces," *Army Times*, August 7, 2019; Jim Lacey, "The 'Dumbest Concept Ever' Just Might Win Wars," War on the Rocks, July 29, 2019, https://warontherocks.com/2019/07/the-dumbest-concept-ever-just-might-win-wars/.
81. Nick Childs, "US Marine Corps Raises the Flag—and New Questions—on Future Force Design," Military Balance Blog, International Institute for Strategic Studies, April 3, 2020, https://www.iiss.org/blogs/military-balance/2020/04/united-states-marine-corps-future-force-design.
82. Stephen M. Walt, *The Origins of Alliances* (Ithaca, NY: Cornell University Press, 1987).
83. Twomey, *Military Lens*.

3

Law, Order, and
Maritime (In)Stability

Peter Alan Dutton

One of the critical enablers of a state's ability to sustain naval operations away from its shores is a factor that might be called "normative resonance." Navies operating on extended lines of operation do so with more or less legitimacy in the eyes of local governments in the areas in which they operate—depending on the degree to which their operations conform to local sensibilities about acceptable use of naval power. Legitimacy is a subjective concept, not an objective one, and in a maritime context perceptions of legitimacy are informed by a state's approach to law of the sea, including—but not exclusively—the United Nations Convention on the Law of the Sea (UNCLOS). Thus, legitimacy matters quite a lot for naval power to be effective in fulfilling its political objectives. States that view naval operations by other powers as legitimate are more likely to open ports for logistical support, to see the naval operations as a positive contributor to the regional power dynamics, and to be open to the messages of naval diplomacy. As Colin Powell might have put it, normative resonance is a force multiplier.[1]

It should come as no surprise, therefore, that states—especially those aiming to operate in regional spaces where maritime theaters are central to political interactions—seek to develop and advance their vision of what it is legitimate for navies to do. This chapter's primary aim is to articulate how narratives about norms and law (and approaches to them) relate to matters of perceived legitimacy and, in turn, how this affects maritime stability. In particular, this chapter argues that the Indo-Pacific region is an especially rich area for competing visions of the international laws and norms that should govern the pursuit of national and global security concerns, especially in the maritime commons.

Many regional states have weak capacity to provide maritime governance, let alone to provide for their own security from maritime threats. Many have rich maritime living resources but little capacity to protect them from poaching. Moreover, many were subjected to decades or even centuries of colonialism and, as a result, resent the presence of outside powers. A key contention of this chapter is that all along the extended underbelly of Eurasia, from the Horn of Africa to the Korean Peninsula, these factors have contributed to a specific Indo-Pacific trend since the second half of the twentieth century. This trend sees foreign naval operations in zones of national jurisdiction as illegitimate unless undertaken with coastal state consent and seeks to constrain them through international law.

Trends in international law that favor constrained access for naval operations are, however, at odds with other trends that have emerged since the end of the Cold War. The increase in transnational challenges requires increasing international cooperation to address them. These include terrorism, piracy, poaching, smuggling, and human trafficking. Approaches to international law of the sea that favor maximal access to nonsovereign maritime zones can be an important factor in addressing these challenges. Furthermore, the Indo-Pacific is also the primary locus of a new power competition in response to China's rise and its projection of increasing national power into the maritime domain. Access-oriented approaches to international law of the sea are now also important balancing components in the great-power competition that is gaining steam in the Indo-Pacific today. The resulting maritime competition between China and existing maritime powers—chiefly the United States, Japan, Australia, India, the United Kingdom, and France—has eclipsed transnational challenges as the primary propellant of the strategic dynamics across the region. The Indo-Pacific is feeling China's maritime expansion from the Aleutians to the Bab-el-Mandeb, and no nation in between sits comfortably on the sidelines. In response, naval powers are coming together to combine their strength and to work together to keep maritime Indo-Pacific a free and open space.

One area of particular normative competition is over the right of foreign military forces to exercise the full range of operational freedoms in waters beyond the territorial sea of any coastal state, including in other states' exclusive economic zones (EEZs). History, resource concerns, trading patterns, and local security challenges each play a role in defining the normative preferences of regional states and of those states foreign to the region but present in increasing numbers to promote national, regional, and global security interests. As the strongest global naval power, the United States has played an especially significant role in the evolution of the normative trends and countertrends across the Indo-Pacific region.

A HISTORY OF AMERICAN NORMATIVE
LEADERSHIP AND REGIONAL RESPONSES

American normative leadership in the Indo-Pacific region began in the Pacific Ocean in the aftermath of World War II. American naval power dominated the entire expanse from California to the Chinese coast and from Alaska to Antarctica. This total dominance led easily to normative dominance. Regional stability and freedom of the seas were products of unchallengeable American naval power. Soon, however, vulnerable states began to push back. In 1958, while conflict raged between the Communist and Nationalist forces in the Strait of Taiwan, the People's Republic of China (PRC) declared a twelve-nautical-mile territorial sea in contravention of the three-mile limit supported by the United States and other major maritime stakeholders at the time.[2] China did so in part to seek political leverage against American naval support for the Nationalist forces and to assert a new norm favoring coastal state security interests over navigational freedoms for foreign navies.[3]

China was not alone among coastal Asian states to makes its own declaration. By 1955, in the wake of its own war, North Korea had already declared a twelve-nautical-mile territorial sea with restrictions for foreign warships.[4] In 1977, in the aftermath of its own war in which American sea power played a major factor, Vietnam declared expansive straight baselines, a twelve-nautical-mile territorial sea and restrictions on movement of warships in its sovereign waters.[5] Even some states friendly to America's presence in the Pacific expressed unease with the unbounded US regional naval power and have sought to impose normative limits. In 1961 the Philippines declared a large, box-like expanse of waters around its territory to be its sovereign territorial sea.[6] Malaysia declared a twelve-nautical-mile territorial sea in 1969 with restrictions on nuclear weapons and nuclear-powered vessels.[7] That year, New Zealand also declared its twelve-nautical-mile territorial sea for its islands and for its dependencies the Cook Islands and Tokelau, followed later with exclusionary policies for nuclear-armed or -propelled vessels.[8] Other states friendly to American power chose policies about law of the sea that resonated with the American approach. Australia, Japan, and South Korea, as treaty allies with very close defense links to the United States, have provided consistent support for broad access rights for naval power.

The Indian Ocean region presents a different picture. Concentration of American naval power in the Indian Ocean occurred much later than it did in the Pacific—not until after Britain's retreat "east of Suez" in the early 1970s. Britain had maintained a predominant naval presence in the Middle East and Indian Ocean for nearly two centuries to ensure its lines of communication between Europe and the Indian subcontinent. Financial strain and the independence of many of its former colonies precipitated Britain's retreat, but for most of the 1970s the sum of America's regional naval presence was a token headquarters with irregular ship activity in Bahrain. The preferred American regional strategy during the Richard Nixon, Gerald Ford, and Jimmy Carter administrations employed diplomatic engagement and strengthening of the two "regional pillars," Iran and Saudi Arabia, to assure regional security and stability without undue commitment of American assets.[9]

That posture changed rapidly in the early 1980s after the fall of the shah of Iran led to the formation of a government in Tehran hostile to the United States, and the war between Iraq and Iran disrupted the flow of oil from Kuwait and from Saudi Arabia's eastern ports. The Tanker War in particular, from 1986 through 1988, led to sustained major deployment of American naval power to the region to secure the sea-lanes for the export of oil and gas, to support the interests of regional stability, and to prevent regional encroachment by a peer competitor, which at the time was the Soviet Union. These three objectives have remained the cornerstone of American regional maritime strategy, and since the mid-1980s the United States has concentrated predominant naval power in the region to secure its national interests and objectives.[10]

Until 2001 the United States pursued its regional maritime strategy in the Indo-Pacific with a preference for unilateral predominant power and a focus on bilateral, hub-and-spoke relationships. Even though the administration of President George H. W. Bush pursued an international response to Iraq's invasion of Kuwait in 1990, it was primarily for the purpose of legitimizing the use of dominant American power rather than to muster sufficient international power to adequately respond to Iraqi aggression. After 9/11 American strategic focus shifted considerably to combat transnational terrorist organizations, their state sponsors, and proliferators of weapons of mass destruction (WMDs), largely through a rapid, regional concentration of American ground forces. This meant that the United States shifted its maritime strategy to reflect a preference for collective and cooperative naval activities. This was the case with the establishment by the George W. Bush administration of Combined Task Force 150, with its broad national security missions throughout the greater Indian Ocean region in support of Operation Enduring Freedom in Afghanistan. Similar acts included the administration's creation of the Proliferation Security Initiative to combat WMD proliferation, the promulgation of the 2007 Cooperative Strategy for 21st Century Seapower, and the development of Combined Task Forces 151 and 152 to combat regional piracy.[11] The new reality that these strategies reflected was that although American naval power remained predominant in the Indian Ocean, American ability to compel stability was diluted by a greater need for regional political cooperation in support of American land operations in Iraq and Afghanistan and by the presence of a greater array of international navies in the region than ever before.

China's growing naval presence in the Indian Ocean since December 2008 has begun to complicate the American naval advantages it historically enjoyed in both the Indian and Pacific Oceans. The first overseas base of the People's Liberation Army–Navy (PLAN), located in Djibouti, is evidence of a new maritime dynamic extending across the Indian and Pacific Oceans and unifying them strategically. The People's Liberation Army (PLA) has expressed interest in increasing the number of bases it maintains across the region in Cambodia, Myanmar, Pakistan, Sri Lanka, the United Arab Emirates, and elsewhere.[12] China's power now emanates from the continent into the maritime domain across an expanse from the northern Pacific to the western Indian Ocean. China is a force to be reckoned with in the maritime domain, as elsewhere, and as it projects its national power outward, its national perspectives on the legitimate use of naval power will flow with it.

For decades, American maritime dominance in the Indo-Pacific could ensure American interests without particular regard for regional perspectives on the legitimacy or illegitimacy of its access-oriented norms. However, the American shift of its regional maritime strategy from competitive dominance to cooperative leadership in 2007 required the United States to place greater emphasis on developing a general international consensus on the legitimacy of its access-oriented security norms in the maritime domain. These norms have been under increasing pressure as the Sino-American relationship became increasingly competitive after about 2010. Norms showing preference for unconstrained access for naval power best serve American interests in national security and in ensuring stability in the maritime domain as a key component of the health of the global trading and security system. Accordingly, throughout the Indo-Pacific, but especially in areas in which China is most actively projecting its power from the continent to the sea, American leaders have felt obliged to take more active measures to promote and preserve access-oriented normative interpretations of international law of the sea.[13] This is a major driver of the active Freedom of Navigation Program in the South China Sea, for instance.[14]

CHINA'S EMERGING NORMATIVE APPROACH TO LAW OF THE SEA

In the decades before the PLAN's explosive growth, China's strategic response to the dominance of US naval capacity in the Pacific and Indian Oceans included development of strong antiaccess military capacity and the pursuit of international norms that constrain the use of naval power in the maritime zones under the jurisdiction of coastal states. In the East and South China Seas, China increased its operational activity to challenge US and allied naval operations in and above the waters China claims and used its ability to command regional and global attention as an opportunity to challenge the legitimacy of US military presence in East Asia and American regional leadership more generally.

China launched its first salvo in the normative battle after the EP-3 incident in April 2001.[15] After the collision, a Chinese Foreign Ministry spokesman expressed the view that American aircraft on reconnaissance missions in the airspace above China's EEZ threaten China's security, and the foreign minister demanded that future reconnaissance missions stop.[16] As part of China's overall campaign to delegitimize all foreign military operations in and above its EEZ, the foreign ministry spokesman stated,

> The surveillance flight conducted by the US aircraft overran the scope of "free over-flight" according to international law . . . [in that] any flight in airspace above another nation's exclusive economic zone should respect the rights of the country concerned . . . [and] the US plane's actions posed a serious threat to the national security of China. . . . All countries enjoy the freedom of over-flight in the exclusive economic waters of a nation, [but the EP-3's] reconnaissance acts were targeted at China in the airspace over China's coastal area . . . and thus abused the principle of over-flight freedom.[17]

Additionally, the PRC official news agency, Xinhua, published an analysis of the international law aspects of the collision, which claims reconnaissance flights over the EEZ of another country are threats to "national security and peaceful order of the coastal State" in violation of UNCLOS and customary international law.[18] In light of the large number of such flights conducted by other maritime states—including Russia, the United Kingdom, and Australia—the PRC government's assertion that reconnaissance flights are threats per se reflects its unusually narrow interpretation of international law.[19] Indeed, as part of China's normative campaign to constrain access by foreign naval powers, it engaged its academics to promote the authority of a coastal state to control foreign military activities in its EEZ.[20]

Several Chinese military scholars have argued that the EEZ is an area of Chinese national sovereignty and a zone that serves as "an important strategic protective screen."[21] In a clear reference to American views concerning international law of the sea, these scholars contend that traditional maritime freedoms of all states developed based on an approach to law that links maritime interests with national power and the ability to dominate the oceans. In their view, coastal state sovereignty—including national self-defense interests—should be the overarching interpretive principle of international law of the sea.[22]

The PRC government repeated this theme in March 2009 when five coordinated Chinese ships, including fishing vessels, civilian law-enforcement vessels, and a PLAN vessel, challenged the survey operations of USNS *Impeccable* in

China's EEZ about seventy-five nautical miles off the coast of Hainan Island in the South China Sea.[23] In relation to the incident, a Chinese Foreign Ministry spokesman claimed that the American naval operations in China's EEZ were in violation of both international law and China's domestic laws. The official Chinese perspective on military activities at sea is that

> "freedoms of navigation and overflight" in the EEZ does [sic] not include the freedom to conduct military and reconnaissance activities.... Military activities in the EEZ violate the principle that in exercising their rights and performing their duties [under UNCLOS] States Parties shall refrain from any threat or use of force against [the coastal state]. [Thus] ... "internationally lawful uses of the sea" does not include the freedom to conduct military activities in the EEZ of another state ... [, and] coastal states have the right to restrict or even prohibit the activities of foreign military vessels and aircraft in and over [their] EEZs.[24]

Even as these restrictive Chinese policies concerning international law of the sea have worked well for China in East Asia, they are beginning to present significant problems for China's ability to support and defend its interests in the Indian Ocean. As early as October 2009, for instance, when Somali pirates hijacked the Chinese-flagged merchant ship *De Xin Hai*, with twenty-five Chinese mariners aboard in the central Indian Ocean, 550 nautical miles north of Seychelles and about 700 nautical miles from the Somali coast, the Chinese found themselves operationally hemmed in by their own restrictive policies about norms related to naval activities in the zones of other states.[25]

Nonetheless, China's strict policies regarding the normative approach to international freedoms of the sea have been shaping the activities of the PLAN in the Indian Ocean and will continue to do so. At a United Nations Security Council meeting in 2008, China voted in favor of international military action in the territorial waters of Somalia, as officials acknowledged that Somalia has insufficient capacity to prevent piracy against international shipping in its waters. However, China's statement of support for United Nations Security Council Resolution (UNSCR) 1816 clearly underscored the importance of Somalia's consent for assistance. It is based on this particular understanding that, as of November 2021, China has sent a total of thirty-nine escort flotillas to the Gulf of Aden to conduct antipiracy operations in Somalia's EEZ and elsewhere since its first mission in December 2008.[26] Given China's restrictive views on the authority of the international community to operate in the EEZs of other states, the Somali request to the United Nations was crucial because it specifically invited the international community to help fight piracy in Somalia's territory and waters under Somalia's jurisdiction.

In the ensuing years, despite the increasing tension between China's norma-tive view and its expanding interests and growing naval power, China has not explicitly repudiated its position. But the tensions are mounting. China's expan-sive maritime claims in the South China Sea are based on ambiguous histori-cal rights and interests and directly encroach on the lawfully defined resource zones of China's Southeast Asian neighbors.[27] Furthermore, China continues to enact domestic laws to enforce its claims by expanding the jurisdiction of its maritime law-enforcement agencies, including the Chinese coast guard.[28] These are unusually broad claims for a rising naval power, and the consequences these claims will have on the future direction of international law of the sea remains uncertain.

STATE PRACTICE IN THE INDO-PACIFIC LITTORALS: AN ARC OF ANTIACCESS?

Perhaps in reaction to the presence of British, American, and now Chinese naval power, of all the world's regions, Indian Ocean states have the highest concen-tration of national laws or other identifiable formal acts of state policy that pur-port to limit foreign military activities in EEZs. This trend extends farther east through the Strait of Malacca along the Eurasian continental periphery to the Korean Peninsula. Several possible factors may be behind this trend, including the region's unique geostrategic position as the historical battleground between strong powers on the eastern and western margins of the Eurasian landmass. Second, in the Indian Ocean region, there are only two states that did not fall under colonial rule in the nineteenth and twentieth centuries—Iran and Thai-land. Moreover, the states bordering the South China Sea were also colonized, and China was reduced to semicolonial status. This strong history of colonial-ism by outside maritime powers may explain the backlash against norms that legitimize foreign naval activities off another state's coasts.

Furthermore, Indo-Pacific states have some of the highest rates of popu-lation growth in the world. As these states labor to develop economically and politically, they must make difficult policy choices concerning the application of scarce resources between development and security interests. This has led many states to seek to harness the normative power of international law to express their constrained-access preferences.

In some areas, however, the factor most affecting regional perspectives on norms regarding international access to coastal zones is the unresolved rival-ries and tensions that characterize the current state of regional political affairs. Pakistan and India's fraught relationship is perhaps the single most dominant political force in the Indian Ocean region. Both countries possess nuclear weapons and have a decades-long history of conflict and tension concerning ethnic and religious issues as well as issues with sovereignty over the Kashmir region. A similarly tense dynamic affects the development of Iran's and Saudi Arabia's approaches to freedoms of maritime and aerial navigation. That is also true of the Indonesian and Malaysian approaches and certainly of North Korea's approach as it looks to the south.

The Indian Ocean states have seen great-power competition and colonization, they have regional rivalries of their own, and they have generally weak capacity to defend their resource and security interests in the maritime domain. Not surprisingly, then, given the tensions baked into the broader regional system, there is a general regional preference for constrained-access norms. India, one of the strongest regional powers, stated in its June 1995 declaration upon ratification of UNCLOS that it requires prior consent for "military exercises and maneuvers" in its EEZ.[29] Were it not for the factors mentioned previously, this might seem surprising coming from a state that aspires to be a strong regional naval power.[30] But India's national law goes even further. It asserts authority to prevent or regulate military and hydrographic surveys in its EEZ by equating them with marine scientific research and therefore asserting coastal state jurisdiction under UNCLOS's Article 56. In 2001 India protested to the United States and the United Kingdom for the activities of USNS *Bowditch* and HMS *Scott*, respectively, which had been undertaking military surveys in India's EEZ. India also requires foreign warships to provide notice before entering its territorial sea, a requirement that is not recognized by the United States because it places a limitation on the international right of innocent passage.[31] Additionally, India's government asserts the right to manage jurisdiction over the contiguous zone for security purposes and requires twenty-four-hour notice before a foreign vessel enters its EEZ carrying harmful or dangerous substances, including radioactive materials.[32]

Although this series of limitations is considered unlawful by the United States, which has protested and conducted operational challenges in relation to each, by far the issue of most concern is India's attempt to limit foreign military operations in its EEZ. The term "military exercises and maneuvers" is ill defined and could include only those traditional naval activities related to international security, but it is ambiguous enough that some countries may use it in support of the perspective that constabulary activities to suppress nontraditional threats (e.g., antipiracy operations) in India's EEZ without its consent would be perceived as unlawful. India's agreement to support antipiracy enforcement efforts related to UNSCRs 1816, 1846, 1851, and others does not affect its legal perspective concerning the illegality of military activities in its EEZ because antipiracy operations in and around Somalia are approved by the United Nations Security Council and therefore an internationally approved exception to Somalia's sovereign authority. Thus, like China, India has participated in antipiracy operations in the Gulf of Aden without compromising its legal claims.

Though Iran is not a member of UNCLOS, its 1993 Law on the Marine Areas states that foreign "military activities and practices" in its EEZ are prohibited—a clear outgrowth of its long war with Iraq and its decades-long tensions with the regional operations of the US Navy.[33] Following suit, Pakistan's 1997 declaration upon UNCLOS ratification requires prior permission for foreign warships desiring to "conduct military exercises and maneuvers" in its EEZ and purports to limit aerial navigation above it to only those aircraft that have approved flight plans.[34] Likewise, Bangladesh's 2001 declaration when acceding to UNCLOS prohibits military exercises or operations, especially with weapons or explosives, without its prior consent.[35] In its 2017 Territorial Sea and Maritime Zones Law, neighboring Myanmar claims a security interest in its EEZ and the right to prohibit military aircraft from flying above it without approval.[36]

Two other regional states, Malaysia and Thailand, have acted to limit foreign military activities in their EEZs in whole or in part because of regional political and military tensions. Reflecting the remembrance that during the colonial period British warships used the surrounding seas to disrupt the indigenous independence movement and also reflecting more recent uneasy relations with neighboring Indonesia, in its declaration upon ratification of UNCLOS Malaysia stated that it, too, would require "prior authorization to conduct military exercises or maneuvers in [its] exclusive economic zone."[37] Thailand, a security partner and treaty ally of the United States, acceded to the UNCLOS in 2011 but sided with China and the regional trend toward constrained-access normative interpretations of law of the sea when it did. Its accession statement provides that "in the exclusive economic zone, enjoyment of the freedom of navigation in accordance with relevant provisions of the Convention excludes any non-peaceful use without the consent of the coastal State, in particular, military exercises or other activities which may affect the rights or interests of the coastal State."[38]

The remaining states in the region that claim a sovereign right to exercise control over foreign military activities in the EEZ do so for a variety of unique reasons not related to political or military tensions with another regional power. For instance, in its 1989 Maritime Zones Act, Kenya claims the right to regulate the passage of warships and military exercises in its EEZ although it does not appear to have actually implemented this claim.[39] Mauritius, too, seems to make an unspecified claim of the right to regulate foreign military activities in its EEZ. In a 1984 government notice of maritime zone regulations, Mauritius specifies geographic coordinates within its EEZ where it appears to require warships and submarines to obtain permission before transiting. No attempt to enforce this claim is recorded, and no further regulations appear to have been promulgated.[40]

Finally, Maldives asserts some form of claim to regulate military activities in its EEZ. Its 1996 legislation includes a provision that requires all foreign vessels of any type to obtain permission before entering its EEZ, though this appears to be an effort to use the law to do what Maldives has no physical capacity to accomplish.[41] The island state has a very large EEZ with a fragile ecosystem and rich resources that are susceptible to illegal fishing because it has literally no naval or coast guard capacity. Therefore, Maldives appears to have developed a policy to account for this deficiency by attempting to impose legal restrictions on entry to its EEZ, although it has increasingly partnered with India to provide the necessary forces to accomplish these policing and security functions.[42]

CONCLUSION

The foregoing discussion demonstrates the ambivalence that exists across much of the Indo-Pacific toward the access-oriented norms that major maritime powers prefer and promote. The sovereign states of the region suffered too much under colonialism and now have too many lingering political and capacity challenges to feel fully secure from the possible predations of strong foreign navies. Therefore, they are attracted to normative interpretations of international law that delegitimize the rights of foreign navies to operate freely near their coasts. For decades the United States sought acceptance of its access-oriented approach to international law of the sea, first as a provider of maritime stability, then as a cooperative power leading efforts to provide public goods across the region. Today, however, any progress the United States may have made in achieving normative resonance has been eroded by a new regional concern—the arrival of China as another strong Indo-Pacific naval power.

That said, although the regional normative preference remains one of constrained access, the position appears relatively weakly held. Compared with China's active proselytizing of its constrained-access perspectives, no other Indo-Pacific state appears to have the ambition to make its views universal. The arc of constrained-access sentiment runs along the broad east-west littoral from the Indian Ocean to the Western Pacific, from Kenya and Somalia, to Iran, Pakistan, Maldives, India, Bangladesh, Burma, Thailand, Malaysia, China, and North Korea. But what is its aim? It might seem that the fact some states have expressed formal disapproval of the concept of freedom of the seas for naval forces should be a cause for American strategic concern, given US reliance on open access to secure its national objectives and China's open challenge of this norm. However, China's growing naval power is also a concern in much of the region, giving constrained-access norms new life and new focus. These states may be less concerned about the US-China normative rivalry and more concerned about protecting their maritime security and resource interests from any foreign encroachments.

Still, the observation that the US Navy's critical role in the Indo-Pacific will be as "sea-based balancer" to minimize the risk of interstate conflict may be welcome to some.[43] Even so, the United States will need the cooperation of coastal states to ensure continued regional stability. Cooperation will stem from the perception that American naval operations are undertaken legitimately, which in turn will be reflected in growing normative resonance for the principle of freedom of the seas. However, the cycle begins with an appreciation of, and respect for, the concerns of regional states that make them slow to let down their guard.

NOTES

Byline: The views expressed are the author's own and not meant to represent the views of the US Navy or any agency of the US government.

1. Colin L. Powell, "Remarks to the National Foreign Policy Conference for Leaders of Nongovernmental Organizations," US Department of State, October 26, 2001, https://2001-2009.state.gov/secretary/former/powell/remarks/2001/5762.htm.
2. Thomas Baty, "The Three-Mile Limit," *American Journal of International Law* 22, no. 3 (July 1928): 503–37, https//doi.org/10.2307/2188741; Carol Elizabeth Remy, "US Territorial Sea Extension: Jurisdiction and International Environmental Protection," *Fordham International Law Journal* 16, no. 4 (1992): 1208–52; Ann Hollick, *US Foreign Policy and the Law of the Sea* (Princeton, NJ: Princeton University Press, 1981).
3. "Declaration on China's Territorial Sea," *Peking Review*, September 9, 1958, 21. In addition to the declaration that China would apply a twelve-nautical-mile territorial sea, the issue is full of articles describing PRC outrage at American naval intervention in its civil war against the Nationalist forces.
4. Democratic People's Republic of North Korea Resolution No. 25 (March 1955), https://www.jag.navy.mil/organization/documents/mcrm/KoreaNorth2016.pdf.
5. Socialist Republic of Vietnam, "Statement on the Territorial Sea, the Contiguous Zone, the Exclusive Economic Zone, and the Continental Shelf of May 12, 1977," https://www.un.org/Depts/los/LEGISLATIONANDTREATIES/PDFFILES/VNM_1977_Statement.pdf.
6. "Republic Act No. 3046 of 17 June 1961, An Act to Define the Baselines of the Territorial Sea of the Philippines," United Nations, https://www.un.org/Depts/los/LEGISLATIONANDTREATIES/PDFFILES/PHL_1961_Act.pdf.
7. "Malaysia: Ordinance No. 1 of 1969, Emergency (Essential Powers) Ordinance," National Legislative Bodies / National Authorities (Malaysia), May 15, 1969, https://www.refworld.org/docid/3ae6b5604.html.
8. "Territorial Sea and Exclusive Economic Zone Act 1977," September 1977, New Zealand Legislation, http://www.legislation.govt.nz/act/public/1977/0028/latest/whole.html. Act No. 28 of September 26, 1977, was amended by Act No. 146 of 1980.

9. George K. Walker, ed., *The Tanker War, 1980–1988: Law and Policy*, International Law Studies, vol. 74 (Newport, RI: Naval War College Press, 2000), 33–36.

10. Walker, *Tanker War*, 36–37.

11. US Marine Corps, US Navy, and US Coast Guard, *Cooperative Strategy for 21st Century Seapower* (Washington, DC: US Marine Corps, US Navy, and US Coast Guard, 2007).

12. US Defense Department, *Military and Security Developments Involving the People's Republic of China 2021* (Washington, DC: Office of the Secretary of Defense, 2021), 1, 36, 132.

13. A coastal state's sovereignty extends only to the sea and airspace of the territorial sea, which may extend no more than twelve nautical miles from its baselines. Coastal states exercise limited jurisdiction, not sovereignty, in all other zones beyond twelve nautical miles. These include the contiguous zone, the EEZ, and the continental shelf. Of course, the high seas are areas beyond national jurisdiction in which the fullest measure of freedoms of navigation apply.

14. Jonathan G. Odom, "Maritime Claims in the South China Sea and Freedom of Navigation Operations," in *Building a Normative Order in the South China Sea*, ed. Truong T. Tran, John B. Welfield, and Thuy T. Le, 171–94 (Northampton, MA: Edward Elgar, 2019).

15. On April 1, 2001, a US Navy EP-3 reconnaissance plane collided with a Chinese F-8 fighter, which crashed. The US plane made an emergency landing on China's Hainan Island, and the crew was held until the standoff was resolved eleven days later.

16. "Chinese Spokesman Gives Full Account on US-China Air Collision," Xinhua News Agency, April 3, 2001; "FM Tang Jiaxuan Receives US Letter; PRC Decides to Allow Crew to Leave," Xinhua News Agency, April 11, 2001.

17. Xinhua News Agency, "Chinese Spokesman Gives Full Account."

18. "US Seriously Violates International Law: Signed Article," Xinhua News Agency, April 16, 2001.

19. For a more detailed discussion on state practice and international law related to aerial intercepts, see Nicholas M. Poulantzas, *The Right of Hot Pursuit in International Law*, 2nd ed. (Leiden: Martinus Nijhof, 2002), 343–45.

20. For example, see Xue Guifang and Xiong Xuyuan, "A Legal Analysis of the Establishment of Air Defense Identification Zones," *Journal of Oceans University of China* 6 (June 2007): 36–39. In an apparent reference to Taiwan and the United States, the authors opine that a Chinese air defense identification zone is necessary to prevent foreign attempts "to pilfer Chinese military intelligence in the service of shameful objectives of interfering in Chinese domestic politics and undermining Chinese territorial sovereignty."

21. Wang Shumei, Shi Jiazhu, and Xu Mingshun, "Carry Out the Historic Mission of the Army and Establish the Scientific Concept of Sea Rights," *Beijing Zhongguo Junshi Kexue* [Quarterly journal of the PLA Academy of Military Science and the China Military Science Association] (February 2007): 139–46. Indeed, even before China joined the law of the sea convention, it saw development of the EEZ as a strategy to end "superpower maritime hegemonism and imperialism." Yann-huei Billy Song, "China's Ocean Policy: EEZ and Marine Fisheries," *Asian Survey* 29, no. 10 (October 1989): 983–84, https//doi.org/10.2307/2644793.

22. PLA law of the sea experts allow that an international right to "maneuver" through another state's EEZ might be allowed in a manner reflective of the "innocent

passage" regime in territorial waters, "but even this must not be abused." Presumably, from this perspective any international military activities other than mere passage would be prohibited in and above the EEZ. Such restrictions, of course were never intended by UNCLOS negotiators. Bernard Oxman, "The Regime of Warships under the United Nations Convention on the Law of the Sea," *Virginia Journal of International Law* 24, no. 80 (1984), https//doi.org/10.1163/15718085-bja10066.

23. Peter Dutton and John Garofano, "China Undermines Maritime Laws," *Far Eastern Economic Review* 172, no. 3 (April 2009).

24. Ren Xiaofeng and Cheng Xizhong, "A Chinese Perspective," *Marine Policy* 29, no. 2 (2005): 139–46, https//doi.org/10.1016/j.marpol.2004.08.007.

25. Gregory Viscusi and Hamsa Omar, "Somali Pirates Seize Chinese Bulk Carrier," Bloomberg, October 19, 2009; "China Mulls Military Rescue of Hijacked Sailors," Reuters, October 22, 2009; "China General Says Freeing Hijacked Ship Will Be Difficult, Urges International Co-operation," Associated Press, October 22, 2009.

26. "China Sends New Fleet on Gulf of Aden Escort Mission," Xinhua News Agency, September 26, 2021.

27. Robert Williams, "Tribunal Issues Landmark Ruling in South China Sea Arbitration," Lawfare (blog), July 12, 2016, https://www.lawfareblog.com/tribunal-issues-landmark-ruling-south-china-sea-arbitration.

28. Raul (Pete) Pedrozo, "Maritime Police Law of the People's Republic of China," *International Law Studies* 97, no. 465 (2020).

29. India's declaration upon ratification of UNCLOS states that "the Government of the Republic of India understands that the provisions of the Convention do not authorize other States to carry out in the exclusive economic zone and on the continental shelf military exercises or manoeuvres, in particular those involving the use of weapons or explosives without the consent of the coastal State." United Nations, "Chapter 6 Law of the Sea," United Nations Treaty Collection, 1982, https://treaties.un.org/Pages/ViewDetailsIII.aspx?src=TREATY&mtdsg_no=XXI-6&chapter=21&Temp=mtdsg3&clang=_en#EndDec.

30. Aditi Malhotra, "India Sees a New Regional Role for Its Navy," *Foreign Policy*, June 10, 2016.

31. Act No. 80, Territorial Waters, Continental Shelf, Exclusive Economic Zone and Other Maritime Zones Act, August 1976, quoted in US Department of Defense, *Maritime Claims Reference Manual*, Publication 2500.1-M (Washington, DC: US Department of Defense, 1997).

32. Act No. 80, Territorial Waters, Continental Shelf, Exclusive Economic Zone and Other Maritime Zones Act; Indian Naval Headquarters NAVAREA Notice, January 1998, as cited in US Department of Defense, *Maritime Claims Reference Manual*.

33. US Navy JAG Corps, "Act on the Marine Areas of the Islamic Republic of Iran, May 1993," in *Maritime Claims Reference Manual* (Washington, DC: US Navy JAG Corps, 2014).

34. "Pakistan's Declaration upon Ratification of UNCLOS," United Nations Treaty Collection, February 26, 1997, https://treaties.un.org/Pages/ViewDetailsIII.aspx?src=TREATY&mtdsg_no=XXI-6&chapter=21&Temp=mtdsg3&clang=_en#EndDec.

35. "Bangladesh Declaration upon Ratification of UNCLOS," United Nations Treaty Collection, July 27, 2001, https://treaties.un.org/Pages/ViewDetailsIII.aspx?src=TREATY&mtdsg_no=XXI-6&chapter=21&Temp=mtdsg3&clang=_en#EndDec.

36. "Myanmar Territorial Sea and Maritime Zones Law (The Pyidaungsu Hluttaw Law No. 14, 2017) The 9th Waning of Waso, 1379 M.E. (17 July 2017)," United Nations, 2017, https://www.un.org/Depts/los/LEGISLATIONANDTREATIES/PDFFILES /Myanmar_MZL_2017.pdf.
37. "Exclusive Economic Zone Act, 1984, Act No. 311: An Act Pertaining to the Exclusive Economic Zone and Certain Aspects of the Continental Shelf of Malaysia and to Provide for the Regulations of Activities in the Zone and on the Continental Shelf and for Matters Connected Therewith," United Nations, 1984, https://www .un.org/Depts/los/legislationandtreaties/pdffiles/mys_1984_Act.pdf.
38. US Navy JAG Corps, "Thailand's Declaration upon Accession to UNCLOS, May 15, 2011," in *Maritime Claims Reference Manual* (Washington, DC: US Navy JAG Corps, 2014).
39. Though Kenya is technically outside the Indo-Pacific theater, it borders the Indian Ocean, and therefore its laws are relevant to a broader understanding of the regional trends. "Chapter 371, Maritime Zones Act of Kenya (1989)," United Nations, 1989, https://www.un.org/Depts/los/legislationandtreaties/pdffiles/ken _1989_Maritime.pdf.
40. Paragraph (9)(b)(vii) of the Maritime Zones Act of 1977 claims the right to limit freedom of navigation in the EEZ of Mauritius "ensur[es] freedom of navigation which is not prejudicial to the interest of Mauritius." "Maritime Zones Act 1977 (Act No. 13 of 3 June 1977)," United Nations, 1977, https://www.un.org/Depts/los /LEGISLATIONANDTREATIES/PDFFILES/MUS_1977_Act.pdf.
41. Maritime Zones of Maldives Act No. 6/96, paragraph 14, states, "No foreign vessel shall enter the exclusive economic zone of Maldives except with prior authorization from the Government of Maldives in accordance with the laws of Maldives." "Maritime Zones of Maldives Act No. 6/96," United Nations, 1996, https://www.un.org /depts/los/LEGISLATIONANDTREATIES/PDFFILES/MDV_1996_Act.pdf.
42. "India Gives Maldives Defence Help," BBC, August 21, 2009, http://news.bbc.co .uk/2/hi/south_asia/8213862.stm; "Joint Exclusive Economic Zone Surveillance of Maldives," press release, Indian Navy, February 26, 2019, https://www.indiannavy .nic.in/content/joint-exclusive-economic-zone-surveillance-maldives-0.
43. Robert D. Kaplan, "Center Stage for the 21st Century: Power Plays in the Indian Ocean," *Foreign Affairs*, March/April 2009.

4

Marine Resources and Regional Competition

Clive Schofield

This chapter explores the marine resource dimension to regional competition in the Indo-Pacific region. There is a long-standing resource dimension to the extension of coastal state maritime claims offshore. Rights over marine resources are also a frequent driver, or at the least an undercurrent, to the multiple maritime disputes in the Indo-Pacific region, which are often primarily rooted in sovereignty disputes over islands and their associated waters. These maritime disputes are also themselves a focus for regional competition in the Indo-Pacific as marine resource activities provide an opportunity for claimant states to assert their jurisdiction either by undertaking marine resource exploration or exploitation themselves or by seeking to regulate or prevent the efforts of other claimants to do likewise.

This chapter first appraises what marine resources are provided by the global ocean and are at stake in the Indo-Pacific region. Discussion then turns to the role of marine resources in the development of maritime claims and includes an examination of maritime claims in the Indo-Pacific. Finally, this chapter offers some concluding observations.

WHAT'S AT STAKE?
MARINE RESOURCES IN THE INDO-PACIFIC

The Indo-Pacific region is broadly conceived here as the maritime spaces of the Indian Ocean and the western and central Pacific Ocean, inclusive of the series of semi-enclosed seas located between the East and Southeast Asian continental mainland and islands offshore, which serve to connect the two oceans.

Biodiversity and Essential Ecosystem Services

The vast ocean spaces of the Indo-Pacific offer a cornucopia of marine resources. Arguably the most significant, though often not fully acknowledged, of these resources is that of the marine environment within these waters, their associated biodiversity, and the ecosystems services they offer. In short, the oceans are fundamental to life on planet Earth because they produce 50 to 80 percent of the planet's oxygen and play an essential role in driving the global atmospheric system.[1] Simultaneously, the declining state of the oceans is increasingly well recognized.[2] In part, this is caused by the increasing pressure that ocean environments and marine resources are under because of more diverse and intense activities and uses. That the marine spaces also serve as the primary sink for excess carbon dioxide and heat in the global climate system is a further critical consideration. Indeed, the global ocean absorbs an estimated 20 to 30 percent of anthropogenic carbon dioxide emissions and more than 90 percent of the excess heat produced over the past two hundred years.[3]

Given the vast geographical scale and climatic range of the Indo-Pacific region, it is unsurprising that the region is a hugely diverse and important repository and supporter of global biodiversity. Moreover, it is home to complex and highly productive coastal and marine ecosystems, such as coral reefs, mangroves, and seagrass meadows, all of which offer notable ecosystem services, such as natural coastal protection. This is something that is of increasingly value in the context of accelerating sea level rise. Indeed, the Intergovernmental Panel on Climate Change has indicated that global mean sea level rise in the period 2006–15 has been two and a half times the rate for the period 1901–90, a rate stated with high confidence to be "unprecedented over the last century."[4] These findings are underscored by the panel's report on the physical science basis for its sixth assessment report, which found that the average rate of sea level rise had increased almost threefold from 1.3 millimeters per year in the period 1901–71 to 3.7 millimeters per year in 2006–18, with human influence considered "very likely" to be the main driver for these changes.[5]

Indo-Pacific ocean areas are also increasingly the focus for offshore renewable energy production through wave and, particularly, wind power. Here it can be observed that the International Energy Agency (IEA) has asserted that cost reductions coupled with experience mean that "offshore wind has the technical capacity to meet today's electricity demand many times over."[6] Additionally, following notable success in European waters, there is rising interest in offshore wind development in the Indo-Pacific, notably among India, South Korea, Japan, and Taiwan and especially in China, which added more capacity than any other country in 2018.[7] Moreover, despite the economic contractions associated with the COVID-19 global pandemic, renewable sources of energy, including offshore wind, have continued to grow rapidly—a development that is viewed as an essential component of the path toward net-zero emissions.[8]

These tremendous environmental resources and ecosystem services are, however, increasingly under threat. Coastal environments are under pressure from population shifts toward the coast and related development pressures, something encapsulated by the term "coastal squeeze," as well as pressures induced by climate change such as sea level rise, as noted previously. Indeed, the growing diversity and intensity of ocean uses has meant that marine environments are similarly under greater stress. Benjamin S. Halpern et alia estimated over a decade ago that over 40 percent of oceans already are strongly affected by humans.[9] The effects have only increased since then.[10]

Arteries for Global Trade

The Indian and Pacific Oceans also provide an essential resource in the sense that these maritime spaces facilitate and are fundamental to regional and global trade. It can be noted that many of the Indo-Pacific region's economies—for instance, those of East and Southeast Asia—are raw material and energy poor and thus dependent on imports of these commodities while simultaneously being highly reliant on exports. The ongoing trends of globalization and interdependence of economies means that every economy in the region is linked to the global trading system. In turn this system is overwhelmingly reliant on access to the sea and the shipping it carries. Prior to the COVID-19 pandemic, over 80 percent of global trade by volume and over 70 percent by value was carried by sea.[11] During the pandemic crisis, the global shipping industry and seafarers have proved vital to maintaining global supply chains and are likely to remain so as global trade patterns normalize.[12] Furthermore, over 95 percent of international telephone and Internet traffic is transmitted through submarine fiber-optic telecommunication cables, and those on the Indo-Pacific seabed form an essential part of this global network.[13]

More traditional conceptions of marine resources have, however, tended to center on fisheries and seabed hydrocarbons. The Indo-Pacific ocean spaces support abundant fisheries and aquaculture production. Globally fish production was estimated to have reached approximately 179 million metric tons in 2018, worth an estimated $401 billion.[14] Of that, 156 million metric tons (87 percent) went to human consumption, which means that fisheries and aquaculture continue to play a crucial role in global food security.[15] The significance of Indo-Pacific fisheries to regional and global food security is underscored by the fact that China is both the biggest fisheries producer and consumer globally.[16] This is not, however, to discount the role of other regional countries. For example, while China accounted for 35 percent of global fisheries production in

2018, including greater production from aquaculture than the rest of the world combined, the rest of Asia contributed a further 34 percent.[17]

The oceans are also an important present and likely future source of seabed energy resources. On a global scale in the IEA's "stated policies" and "announced pledges" scenarios, demand for oil continues to grow, albeit at different rates and only beginning to fall toward 2030 in the latter one.[18] Only in the IEA's "net-zero missions" scenario, which envisages no investment in new fields from 2021 onward, is a steep decline in global oil demand anticipated.[19] Meanwhile, there has been a strong postpandemic recovery with respect to demand for natural gas, and this is anticipated to continue to grow, such that China's demand for gas is anticipated to be 40 percent higher in 2030 versus 2020 in the IEA's stated policies scenario.[20] This points to the "enduring importance" of hydrocarbons, including offshore oil and gas fields, in the global and regional energy mix.[21] This is the case unless radical steps toward net-zero emissions eventuate— something that seems far from certain in the aftermath of the twenty-sixth gathering of the Conference of the Parties to the United Nations Framework Convention on Climate Change (COP26) in Glasgow in 2021.[22] Compounding this situation is the reality that the economies of multiple Indo-Pacific states are characterized by high oil-intensity measures and heavy reliance on imported oil. Indeed, as of 2020, the world's top five oil-importing states were China, the United States, India, South Korea, and Japan, thus placing four of the five within the Indo-Pacific region.[23] These factors point to high import dependency for fossil fuels in the Indo-Pacific region for the foreseeable future. In turn, this suggests that the lure of rights over and access to offshore hydrocarbons in nearby maritime areas are likely to remain a potent motivation in maritime disputes and thus for regional competition across the Indo-Pacific region.

EXPANDING MARITIME CLAIMS AND MARINE RESOURCES

The drive toward the advance of maritime zones offshore is largely related to coastal states' desire to gain access to and control over valuable marine resources in "their" waters (and seabed) near their coastlines. A salient example is provided by US Presidential Proclamation No. 2667 from September 28, 1945, otherwise known the Truman Proclamation (after the US president at the time). It asserts the United States has "jurisdiction and control" over "the natural resources of the subsoil and seabed of the continental shelf beneath the high seas but contiguous to the coasts of the United States."[24] An additional, yet less well known, presidential proclamation, also from 1945, asserts US rights to fisheries resources beyond US territorial sea limits.[25]

These explicitly resource-oriented claims on the part of the United States provided an important catalyst for what has been termed "creeping coastal State jurisdiction"—that is, the expansion of coastal state claims beyond their previously generally narrow territorial sea limits to broad areas of seabed and waters farther and farther offshore.[26] Increasing global reliance on oil as a source of energy coupled with technological developments allowing for the exploration for and exploitation of oil reserves from the seabed have also been crucial drivers for states' expansive claims to areas of their continental shelves.

Against this context it is unsurprising that resource-related considerations also strongly informed the drafting of the United Nations Convention on the Law of the Sea (UNCLOS).[27] UNCLOS established a system of maritime zones, the outer limits of which are predominantly delineated on the basis of distance measurements from baselines along the coast. Thus, the limits of the territorial seas, contiguous zones, and exclusive economic zones (EEZs) are all defined by reference to distance measurements. That is, they extend to maximum distances of twelve, twenty-four, and two hundred nautical miles, respectively, from their coastal baselines.[28] The delineation of the outer limits of the continental shelf where it exceeds the two-hundred-nautical-mile EEZ limits are determined in accordance with a complex series of criteria as well as distance measurements from baselines.[29]

UNCLOS has gained widespread international recognition, with 168 parties to it, including the vast majority of states in the Indo-Pacific region.[30] The general international acceptance of the concept of the EEZ and its codification in UNCLOS has had a dramatic impact on the maritime spaces subject to the maritime claims of coastal states. In this context it is notable that the EEZ concept was in large part motivated by the resource interests of developing coastal states that wanted to secure rights over and access to marine resources off their coasts. The result was a compromise whereby coastal states hold rights over marine resources, but freedom of navigation and overflight for vessels and aircraft belonging to other states are maintained, together with the rights for such states to lay submarine pipelines and cables.[31]

CONFLICTING CLAIMS AND DISPUTED WATERS IN THE INDO-PACIFIC

In keeping with practice worldwide, the coastal states of the Indo-Pacific region have proved to be enthusiastic claimants to the maritime zones provided for under UNCLOS. The inevitable consequence of this enormous expansion in national claims to maritime space seaward, coupled with the proximity of the Indo-Pacific states to one another, has been a proliferation in overlapping maritime claims, potential maritime boundaries, and, just as inevitably, maritime boundary disputes in the region. For instance, because EEZ claims are now commonplace, states with coasts up to four hundred nautical miles distant from one another have overlapping maritime entitlements and thus share a potential maritime boundary or the potential to be locked in a maritime dispute. Moreover, as continental shelf rights may extend well beyond the two-hundred-nautical-mile limits of the EEZ from baselines, states even farther removed from one another may require a seabed boundary to be delimited. Here it can be observed that the delineation of outer continental shelf limits is far from complete. At the time of this writing, submissions to the United Nations' Commission on the Limits of the Continental Shelf (CLCS) encompassed in excess of thirty-seven million square kilometers, and less than one-third of the eighty-eight full submissions made to the CLCS have received recommendations from the commission.[32]

The clear linkage between maritime claims and marine resources means that overlapping maritime claims areas (i.e., disputed waters) are fertile spaces for regional competition, both for control over and access to the resources themselves but also as a means to pursue competitive practices against other players within the region. Perhaps contrary to the perception of parts of the maritime spaces of the Indo-Pacific states as being arenas for competition and conflict, many of the coastal states involved have agreed maritime boundaries between them. Alternatively, where conflicting maritime claims have proved to be intractable, provisional arrangements of a practical nature—that is, maritime joint development zones—have been instituted instead of the delimitation of a boundary line. There are, however, numerous maritime disputes in the Indo-Pacific region. Although it can be observed that not all of them are directly resource-related, they nonetheless often do have resource dimensions.

DISPUTED ISLANDS

Disputes involving islands are a particularly troublesome aspect of the Indo-Pacific. Indeed, the region features numerous sovereignty disputes over islands, such that a survey of overlapping maritime claims and resource-related disputes of the Indo-Pacific region in fact becomes a tour of disputes over islands, given that such disputes are necessarily intimately connected to the rights over marine resources within the maritime zones associated with insular features. It is notable that many of these disputes over possession of islands concern tiny, scarcely populated or unpopulated, barren, remote, and largely forgotten features. Such territorial disputes over small islets, rocks, and reefs are therefore, arguably, more to do with the potential maritime entitlements of features (and thus access to valuable marine resources within their waters and seabed) than their land territories themselves. Additionally, even where sovereignty disputes over islands are absent, disputes can arise over whether islands are "fully entitled" and capable of generating extended maritime claims, particularly continental shelf and EEZ rights, or whether they should be classified as mere "rocks," which are unable to do so.[33] Such a classification would be consistent with Article 121(3) of UNCLOS, which stipulates that because such features "cannot sustain human habitation or economic life of their own," they "shall have no exclusive economic zone or continental shelf."[34] Here it can be noted that the award of the Arbitration Tribunal in the South China Sea case between China and the Philippines provided the first international judicial interpretation of the Regime of Islands under UNCLOS (see below).

THE INDIAN OCEAN

Both the eastern and western parts of the Indian Ocean feature one major island (Sri Lanka and Madagascar, respectively) as well as numerous smaller islands, including major archipelagos, most notably that of Indonesia. There are also the Andaman and Nicobar Islands in the east, the Comoro Islands group and islands scattered through the Mozambique Channel, and Seychelles, Maldives, Réunion, and Mauritius to the west. There is, however, a marked contrast between the two "halves" of the Indian Ocean in terms of progress in maritime dispute settlement through the delimitation of maritime boundaries, as considerably more progress has been achieved in the eastern as opposed to the western Indian Ocean.[35]

Part of the explanation for this disparity is that the number of contentious sovereignty disputes over islands complicate maritime jurisdictional claims and efforts toward the delimitation of maritime boundaries in the western Indian Ocean. These disputes include the sovereignty disputes between France and Madagascar over the so-called scattered islands of the Mozambique Channel. France retained control over these small island features—namely, Bassas da India, Europa Island, the Glorioso Islands, and Juan de Nova Island—subsequent to Madagascar gaining its independence in 1960. Although Bassas da India appears to be a low-tide elevation—that is, a feature exposed at low tide but covered at high tide—the other disputed features are small islands possessing points above water at high tide. Thus, they may well be capable of generating claims to territorial seas, at least.[36] Farther to the north, the island of Mayotte is disputed between France and the Comoro Islands (see figure 4.1). This dispute arose in 1974, when the population of Mayotte voted in favor of remaining part of France rather than becoming independent along with the rest of the islands making up the Comoros archipelago. Located around 280 nautical miles to the east of Madagascar, Tromelin Island is disputed between France and Mauritius, some 340 nautical miles to the south.[37]

There are further long-standing island sovereignty disputes in the eastern Persian Gulf between Iran and the United Arab Emirates over Abu Musa Island

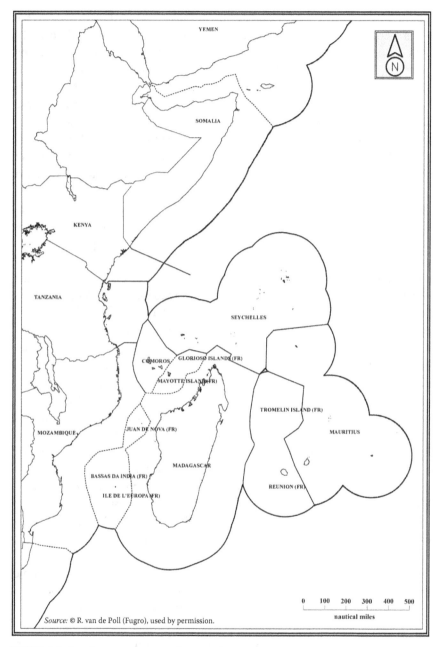

YEMEN

SOMALIA

KENYA

TANZANIA

SEYCHELLES

COMOROS GLORIOSO ISLANDS (FR)

MAYOTTE ISLAND (FR)

TROMELIN ISLAND (FR)

MAURITIUS

MOZAMBIQUE

JUAN DE NOVA (FR)

MADAGASCAR

BASSAS DA INDIA (FR)

ILE DE L'EUROPA (FR)

REUNION (FR)

0   100   200   300   400   500

nautical miles

FIGURE 4.1. Overlapping maritime claims in the southwestern Indian Ocean. *Note:* All undelimited maritime boundaries (dashed lines) are hypothetical strict-equidistance lines as computed in the Fugro Global Law of the Sea database.

and the Greater and Lesser Tunb Islands. The proximity of these islands to the western end of the Strait of Hormuz, one of the world's key maritime choke points, especially for shipments of oil, arguably goes a long way to explaining the strategic significance attached to their possession. Additionally, in the central Indian Ocean, approximately one thousand nautical miles south of India, two thousand nautical miles southeast of the Arabian Peninsula, and twelve hundred nautical miles northeast of Mauritius, the United Kingdom retains administration of the Chagos Archipelago, including a major military base leased to the United States located on Diego Garcia. Mauritius also claims sovereignty over the Chagos group, but despite a 2019 advisory opinion of the International Court of Justice that "the process of decolonization of Mauritius was not lawfully completed when the country acceded to independence" and that "the United Kingdom is under an obligation to bring an end to its administration of the Chagos Archipelago as rapidly as possible," there is no sign of this taking place.[38] These island sovereignty disputes would appear to inevitably also give rise to broad areas of overlapping maritime claims. However, it is questionable whether at least some of these small features are capable of generating broad maritime claims in light of developments in the definition of islands under UNCLOS (discussed later).

Despite progress in terms of maritime boundary delimitation, the western Indian Ocean has, however, not been free from marine resource disputes. Indeed, the catalyst for the recent near completion of the maritime delimitation picture in the eastern Indian Ocean were disputes over seabed resource rights. Speculation that the disputed waters in the Bay of Bengal, one of the world's least explored offshore energy provinces, holds trillions of cubic feet of natural gas, coupled with both advances in offshore drilling technology and increasing demand on the part of the coastal states involved, drive interest in this region.[39] More specifically, oil exploration activities on the part of a South Korean company, Daewoo, under license by Myanmar but in waters also claimed by Bangladesh, led to a naval standoff in 2008.[40] This, in turn, led Daewoo to suspend its exploration operations, and the resulting deadlock over the dispute eventually led to the first maritime boundary case before the International Tribunal on the Law of the Sea (ITLOS).

ITLOS delivered its ruling on March 14, 2012, thereby creating a maritime boundary applicable to territorial sea, EEZ, and continental shelf areas between the two states in the Bay of Bengal.[41] A subsequent arbitration case in 2014 between Bangladesh and India likewise delimited a maritime boundary in the Bay of Bengal.[42] As a result of these cases and the maritime boundaries that they have delimited, substantial clarity over maritime jurisdiction in the Bay of Bengal, and thus concerning rights over its marine resources, has been delivered.

An important caveat in this context is that both of these judicial decisions created so-called gray areas. A key geographical circumstance in both cases was

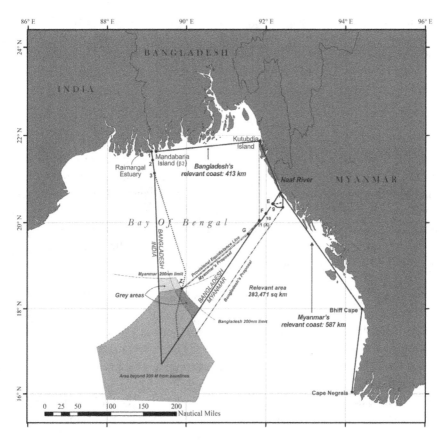

FIGURE 4.2. Maritime claims and boundaries in the Bay of Bengal.

Bangladesh's position on a concave coastline. The consequence of this is that if equidistance lines are constructed, then Bangladesh's maritime entitlements would be substantially squeezed or "cut off" to the advantage of the flanking states to the east and west, Myanmar and India, respectively. Both the 2012 and 2014 tribunals recognized that applying equidistance as a method of delimitation would lead to an inequitable result and therefore opted to adjust the final delimitation lines away from strict equidistance lines. A direct consequence of these adjustments was the creation of two areas where, although continental shelf rights are accorded to Bangladesh as part of its "extended" or "outer" continental shelf over two hundred nautical miles seaward from its baselines, jurisdiction over the superjacent water column rests with either Myanmar or India by virtue of still being within two hundred nautical miles of their baselines (see figure 4.2). While innovative, the definition of the gray area arguably leaves the parties with potentially contentious issues to resolve in the future, especially with respect to ocean governance arrangements in such a complex multi-jurisdictional maritime space.[43] As noted previously, the Bay of Bengal cases were prompted by disputes over rights and access to seabed energy resources. Consequently, it is far from inconceivable that these analogous problems may reoccur within these two overlapping gray areas.

East and Southeast Asia

The maritime spaces of East and Southeast Asia include a series of semi-enclosed seas located between the East Asian continental mainland and islands offshore. The relatively limited extent of the waters involved, allied to the semi-enclosed character of these maritime spaces, leads to the maritime claims of littoral states converging and overlapping. This is compounded by complex coastlines, including the presence of numerous islands—the sovereignty over many of which is subject to dispute.

The South China Sea

Sovereignty disputes over islands, notably the Paracel Islands, Pratas Island, Scarborough Reef (or Shoal), and the Spratly Islands, remain at the core of the South China Sea disputes. These conflicting sovereignty claims have led to overlapping maritime claims that are further complicated by ambiguous, apparently historically based claims, notably China's nine-dash line claim (see figure 4.3). However, there are also clearly marine resource dimensions to the South China Sea disputes.[44]

In particular, there have been long-standing perceptions that the Spratly Islands area is "oil rich" and even "China's Persian Gulf."[45] Numerous incidents involving oil and gas surveying and exploration activities, and their interruption, tend to reinforce the view that access to valuable oil and gas resources underlying contested waters is an important contributing factor to the South China Sea disputes. However, it can also be observed that South China Sea resource estimates regarding hydrocarbons vary hugely and are necessarily speculative with respect to potential oil and gas resources underlying disputed waters because exploration for these resources is impossible precisely because of the existence of the competing claims.[46] In this context it can be noted that claimant states in the South China Sea have routinely used oil and gas exploration activities as proxy means to bolster their maritime jurisdictional and sovereignty claims, leading to numerous protests, counterprotests, and incidents at sea.

The semi-enclosed, tropical environments of the South China Sea and the Gulf of Thailand host marine environments of globally significant biological diversity and are home to reef habitats that help support at least 3,365

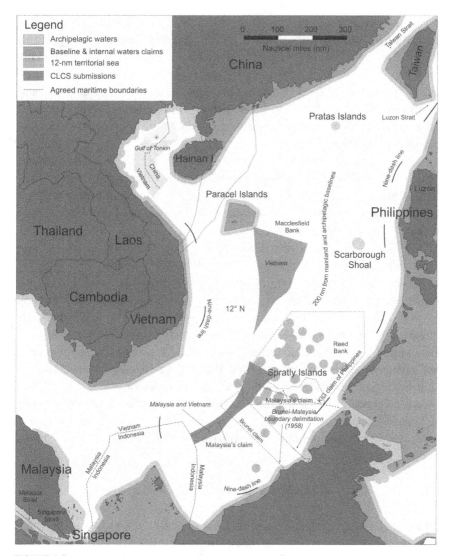

FIGURE 4.3. Maritime claims in the South China Sea.

known species of marine fish.[47] This explains why, for a relatively small part of the oceans, the South China Sea delivers an astonishing abundance of fish—estimated at 12 percent of the global catch and worth over $21 billion per year.[48] Moreover, these marine living resources are fundamental to the food security of regional populations numbered in the hundreds of millions.

Access to the waters of the South China Sea and the Gulf of Thailand to exploit these abundant living resources represents an enduring maritime concern of the littoral states. It follows that the preservation and protection of the marine environment supporting these crucial living resources should be of similar national and international concern. Unfortunately, this does not appear to be the case, given that the marine environment, biological diversity, and living resources of the South China Sea are widely acknowledged to be under serious pressure from threats, including unregulated and often competitive and destructive fishing practices, together with rapid and coastal development and related marine pollution and habitat destruction.[49] Indeed, according to Rashid Sumalia and William Cheung, it has been suggested that reefs were declining at a rate of 16 percent per year.[50] Moreover, they also report 70 percent of mangrove cover has been lost in the past seventy years, and at current rates of habitat loss the remainder will be lost by 2030. Finally, 20 to 60 percent of seagrass beds have similarly disappeared over the past fifty years, and those still in existence are also threatened with destruction.[51]

Although access to the fisheries resources of the South China Sea is clearly a driver for maritime disputes and competition in the South China Sea, it is also clear that fishers and fisheries issues have been used as a means to engage in competition with neighboring states and to assert and underpin overlapping maritime claims. China's denial of Philippine fishers' access to Scarborough Shoal is a prominent example of this type of practice. More recently, the presence of hundreds of Chinese fishing vessels under escort by Chinese maritime enforcement vessels in waters around the Natuna Islands, which Indonesia claimed as part of its EEZ in early 2020, has led to diplomatic exchanges and escalating incidents on the water.[52] This type of activity whereby fishers are used to help assert maritime jurisdictional claims is in keeping with what is known as "gray zone" tactics, particularly on the part of what has been termed China's "fisheries militia."[53]

A Landmark but Contested Decision

Of particular significance to the South China Sea disputes, as well as maritime disputes throughout the Indo-Pacific and beyond, is the landmark ruling on July 12, 2016, of the South China Sea Arbitral Tribunal in the case between the Philippines and China.[54] This award addresses not only South China Sea issues but also key uncertainties in the existing law of the sea, notably issues of historical rights to parts of the ocean and island-related issues. From the outset, China refused to participate in the case, but the tribunal nevertheless found that it had the right to proceed.

As the tribunal resulted from UNCLOS, consequently it could only address issues related to law of the sea; therefore, it could not deal with the core sovereignty issue in the South China Sea—that is, sovereignty over disputed islands. However, in what was a sweeping legal victory for the Philippines, the tribunal dismissed China's nine-dash line historical claim and defined all of the Spratly Islands legally as "rocks" unable to sustain human habitation or economic life of their own and therefore incapable of serving as the basis for maritime claims beyond a twelve-nautical-mile territorial sea.[55]

Additionally, the tribunal found that China had violated the rights of the Philippines in waters off its coasts by interfering with Philippine fishing and petroleum exploration activities, constructing artificial islands, and failing to prevent Chinese fishermen from fishing there. The tribunal also ruled that China had caused severe harm to the coral reef environment and violated its obligation to preserve and protect fragile ecosystems and the habitat of depleted, threatened, or endangered species through its recent large-scale land reclamation and construction of artificial islands.[56] Finally, the tribunal concluded that China had made the dispute worse by permanently destroying evidence of the natural condition of disputed features through its extensive artificial-island building and construction activities.[57]

Gulf of Thailand

The Gulf of Thailand is a semi-enclosed arm of the South China Sea bounded by Malaysia, Thailand, Cambodia, and Vietnam. The gulf's restricted size means that no coastal state can claim a full two-hundred-nautical-mile EEZ entitlement. The presence of numerous islands, islets, and rocks, some of which have been subject to sovereignty disputes—coupled with excessive straight-baseline claims, dubious treaty interpretations, and differing, self-serving applications of equidistance as a method of constructing unilateral claim lines—have complicated the jurisdictional picture. As a result, the delimitation of maritime boundaries in the Gulf of Thailand has proved to be particularly problematic.

Nonetheless, the Gulf of Thailand has proved to be a fertile area for practically oriented alternatives to the delimitation of maritime boundary lines— maritime joint development zones that are predominantly oriented toward the development of seabed oil and gas resources. Indeed, there are joint maritime zones between Cambodia and Vietnam (established in 1982), Malaysia and Thailand (1979 and 1990), and Malaysia and Vietnam (1992) (see figure 4.4). Additionally, in 2001 Cambodia and Thailand entered into a memorandum of understanding (MOU) applicable to their area of overlapping maritime claims, with the objective of seeking the delimitation of a maritime boundary in the overlapping claims area to the north of the 11° north parallel and a maritime joint development arrangement for the overlapping claims area to the south of that line. Such joint zones are consistent with Articles 74(3) and 83(3) of UNCLOS, which provide in identical terms that pending agreement being reached on the delimitation of the continental shelf or EEZ, respectively, "the

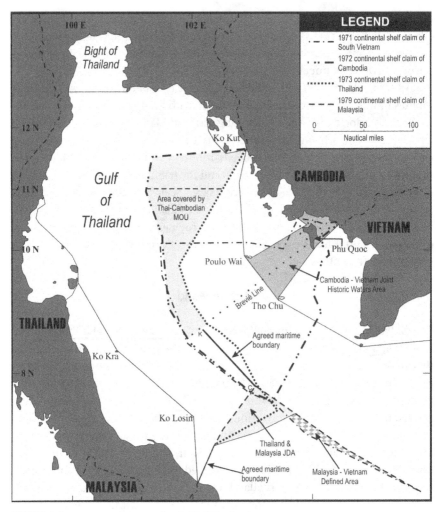

FIGURE 4.4. Maritime claims in the Gulf of Thailand.

States concerned, in a spirit of understanding and cooperation, shall make every effort to enter into provisional arrangements of a practical nature."[58] These joint initiatives provide evidence that competing claims to marine resources can lead to cooperative outcomes. However, it should be recalled that such joint governance mechanisms do not guarantee that seabed hydrocarbons will be found and involve an element of sharing, compromising, and ensuring close bilateral relations that may be geopolitically challenging to maintain over the long term.[59]

East China Sea

Long-standing disputes over Taiwan, coupled with island sovereignty disputes over a group of small and uninhabited islands in its southern part, as well as fundamentally opposing approaches to maritime entitlements, have led to broad areas of overlapping maritime claims in the East China Sea. The disputed features are known as the Senkaku Islands to the state presently administering them, Japan. To the other claimant states of China and Taiwan, they are known as the Diaoyu and Tiao Yu T'ai, respectively. Additionally, Japan is understood to favor the use of equidistance or median lines for maritime delimitation in the East China Sea. In contrast, both China and South Korea argue that the majority of the continental shelf underlying the East China Sea should fall to them under the analogous "natural prolongation" principles. According to this argument, Japan's Ryukyu Islands (on the eastern fringe of the East China Sea) are considered to be geophysically separated from the broad continental shelf area extending from the Chinese mainland and the Korean Peninsula (see figure 4.5).[60]

Nonetheless, marine resources have played an important underlying role in the East China Sea disputes. Suspicions that the seabed of the East China Sea might yield abundant oil and gas resources have led the East China Sea coastal states to grant multiple and, on occasion, overlapping seabed hydrocarbon-exploration concession areas since the late 1970s. Additionally, the relatively geographically restricted semi-enclosed character of the East China Sea means that all of the littoral states are reliant on the same "common pool" fisheries resources, which has led to competition and conflict between them.

To an extent, these marine resource issues have been dealt with through joint zone approaches similar to those adopted in the Gulf of Thailand. Indeed, Japan and South Korea established a joint zone oriented toward oil and gas exploration in 1974, though without subsequent success in exploration.[61] A distinction concerning the East China Sea more recently has been the definition of multiple, and partially overlapping, joint fishing agreements between China and Japan (in 1997), Japan and South Korea (2000), China and South Korea (2001), and Japan and Taiwan (2013).[62] While these joint fishing arrangements arguably represent positive steps toward adopting cooperative management approaches to shared marine resource challenges, they also have a number of drawbacks and have not forestalled ongoing fisheries-related incidents and competition.

In particular, all three joint fishing arrangements are bilateral in nature rather than providing for the sort of multilateral cooperation required to adequately safeguard the fish stocks in question on an ecosystem-wide basis. Problematically, the Sino-Japanese and Sino–South Korean joint fishing zones overlap with one another, creating a complex patchwork of joint zones.[63] Additionally, these

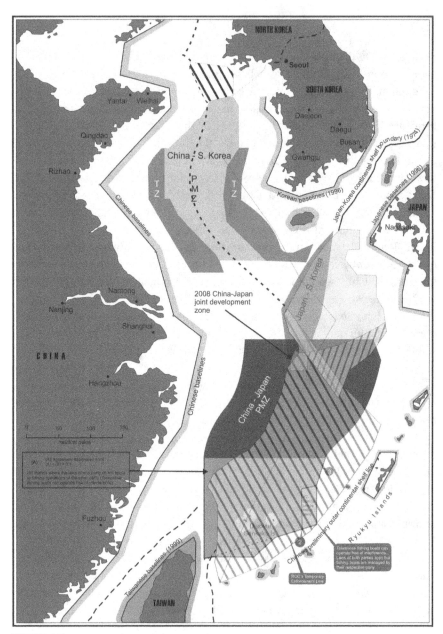

FIGURE 4.5. Maritime claims in the East China Sea.

mechanisms are limited to flag-state-basis enforcement, with minimal joint enforcement envisaged, and include no provisions for joint enforcement efforts against third parties. Moreover, these joint fisheries zones have also not pre-vented ongoing fisheries disputes, especially between China and South Korea.[64]

NORTHEAST ASIA

South Korea and Japan dispute the sovereignty of the Liancourt Rocks, called Dok-do by the South Koreans and the Takeshima Islands by the Japanese. Administered by South Korea since 1951, the disputed features consist of a pair of small islets, approximately two hundred meters apart, and a number of associated rocks, with a total area of just 250 square meters. They are located in the central Sea of Japan or East Sea, to Japan and South Korea, respectively, approximately midway between the two states' mainland coasts. If the islands were to be given full effect on a maritime boundary delimitation between Japan and South Korea based on equidistance, the disputed features would have a dramatic impact on the division of maritime space between the two sides. This is a significant factor, given the area's proven fisheries resources and the unre-alized and, indeed, uncertain potential for oil and gas reserves in the disputed zone (see figure 4.6). The two states did agree to define a joint fishing zone in the vicinity of the islands in 2000, though it is notable that the agreement does not apply to the territorial waters surrounding the disputed features themselves.

Farther north, Japan and Russia dispute sovereignty over the southern Kuril Islands (referred to as the Northern Territories by Japan). The disputed islands are located at the southern end of the Kuril Islands chain and immediately north of Japan's Hokkaido Island. They consist of three main islands, Etorofu, Kunashiri, and Shikotan, together with a cluster of smaller features, the Habo-mai group, and have a combined area of just under five thousand square kilo-meters (see figure 4.6).

Historically the islands were confirmed as Japanese under treaties dating from 1855 and 1875. Under the terms of the Yalta Agreement between the World War II Allies, however, the islands were to be allocated to the Soviet Union, which duly seized them late in the war and thereafter maintained that the matter was settled. Not a party to the Yalta Agreement, Japan considers their acquisition by the Soviet Union (now the Russian Federation) to be illegitimate.

The Kuril Islands are substantial in terms of their territorial area, and they lie in the midst of some of the most productive fishing grounds in the world. This has led to numerous incidents, including shootings and detentions of Japanese fishing boats and crew, and to what Russia terms "illegal" fishing by Japanese trawlers in territorial waters Russia claims as its own. Nevertheless, the two have concluded a number of fishing agreements under which Russia receives

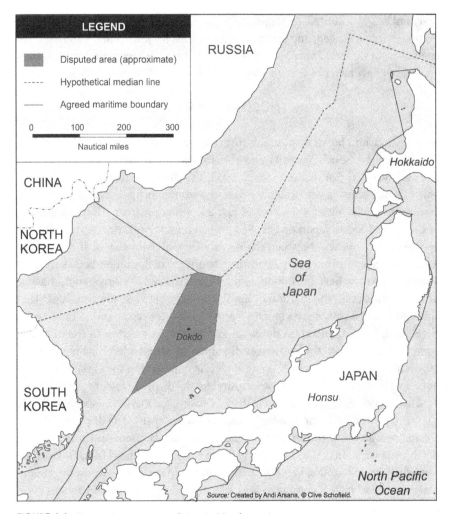

FIGURE 4.6. Competing maritime claims in Northeast Asia.

substantial fees in exchange for granting Japanese fishermen the right to catch specific quotas of certain types of fish within the Russian EEZ.

WESTERN AND CENTRAL PACIFIC OCEAN

In contrast to other parts of the Indo-Pacific region wherein marine resources arguably play a more subsidiary or underlying role in regional competition, among the Pacific small island developing states (SIDS) and territories, marine resources, especially fisheries, are central considerations. Indeed, it is difficult to overemphasize the importance of these EEZ claims to the Pacific SIDS. This is because the rights that these maritime zones provide regarding the fish stocks within them represent the Pacific SIDS's primary economic and development opportunities. These fishery resources not only play an essential role as a traditional and important source of food but they also serve as a critical form of government revenue through fishing access fees paid for by distant fishing states such as China, Taiwan, Japan, South Korea, and the United States.

For example, in 2019 the tuna catch in the western and central Pacific Ocean was estimated at 2.96 million metric tons, the highest on record and valued at $5.8 billion.[65] The Pacific SIDS have in large part achieved substantial return from their fisheries resources by negotiating on a collective basis through the Western and Central Pacific Fisheries Commission, created through the Western and Central Pacific Fisheries Convention, which came into force in 1994.[66] The significance of the revenues derived from tuna is underscored by estimates, both from licensing and fishing, that they constitute 36 percent of gross domestic product in Tuvalu and 32 percent in Kiribati in 2017.[67] As a result, the revenues from tuna fisheries are the dominant source of government revenues—over 60 percent of the public budget for Kiribati, for example.[68] It is also notable that the Pacific Island states have made substantial progress in terms of clarifying the extent of their maritime jurisdictions, doubling the number of maritime boundary agreements in the region in just a decade (2005–15) to thirty-four of a potential forty-nine maritime boundaries.[69]

THE TIMOR SEA

Access to the abundant oil and natural gas resources of the continental shelf underlying the Timor Sea has proved to be the dominant consideration between Australia, Timor-Leste, and Indonesia. Agreements in the early 1970s between Australia and Indonesia placed continental shelf boundaries through the Timor and Arafura Seas, which were advantageous to Australia largely due to the presence of a deep declivity in the sea floor between them, the Timor Trough.[70] However, there was a gap in the line caused by the existence of then Portuguese Timor, which became popularly known as the "Timor Gap" (see figure 4.7). In 1975 Indonesia occupied and subsequently annexed East Timor. Despite international criticism, Australia subsequently accepted Indonesia's sovereignty over East Timor and moved to "complete the line," as it were, in the Timor Sea. Due to significant evolutions in the law of the sea, Indonesia refused to accept a continuation of the line skewed to Australia's advantage. This deadlock was resolved with a joint zone solution, the Timor Gap zone of cooperation.[71]

Following the independence of Timor-Leste from Indonesia on May 20, 2002, a succession of joint zone arrangements was instituted in place of the defunct Australia-Indonesia zone of cooperation.[72] However, as a result of an innovative and cooperative process of conciliation under UNCLOS, on March 6, 2018, Australia and Timor-Leste signed a maritime boundary agreement.[73]

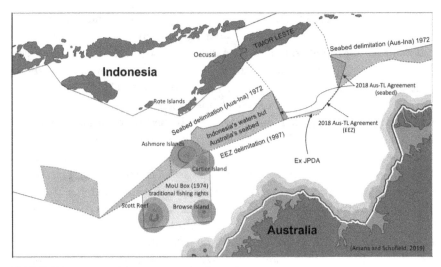

FIGURE 4.7. Maritime delimitation in the Timor Sea.

This represents landmark progress toward resolving what had become a long-standing irritant in relations between the two countries.

However, although the agreement does provide for the establishment of a "special regime" for the Greater Sunrise complex of natural gas fields, which represents the main resource at stake in the dispute, the decision on the development of these reserves has yet to occur. The treaty links the revenue sharing relating to Greater Sunrise to the issue of the destination for the pipeline from the fields onshore to reflect the economic benefits associated with downstream processing activities. Whereas the government of Timor-Leste has been steadfast in preferring Timor as the destination for the pipeline, the consortium of oil and gas companies holding commercial rights over the fields has preferred the option of bringing the resources onshore in Australia, not least to take advantage of existing infrastructure and processing capacity.[74] At the time of this writing, the impasse over the final destination of the pipeline has yet to be resolved, which jeopardizes the development of Greater Sunrise.[75] This dispute serves to illustrate that the downstream processing of marine resources can be just as subject to politicization and competition as access to and sharing of the resources themselves.

CONCLUSION

There seems little doubt that access to and control over ocean spaces and the marine resources that these areas of the Indo-Pacific region contain are of long-standing and abiding significance to the region's coastal states. Whether marine resource issues represent a symptom of wider geopolitical competition in the Indo-Pacific or are drivers for that competition in the first place is rather more difficult to discern with clarity. Access to marine resources certainly touches on national interests; however, at the same time, resource issues can serve as pressure points and opportunities to channel for existing regional competition. Of note here is that maritime disputes are frequently complex, featuring multiple dimensions of which marine resources are but one.

One commonality that can be drawn from most of the subregions of the Indo-Pacific explored in this chapter is the presence of sovereignty disputes over islands. Sovereignty disputes, especially over territory (that is, islands), are often the most contentious and challenging types of disputes to resolve and of greater concern than disputes over maritime rights and associated resources. However, where such disputes are found, inevitably disputes over maritime rights occur also. Moreover, even where island sovereignty is not at issue, disputes will occur over whether insular features can generate broad zones of maritime jurisdiction, namely the continental shelf and EEZ.

A further similarity across the Indo-Pacific region is that seemingly whenever there is an area of overlapping maritime claims, countries and corporations alike claim that the area is rich in resources, particularly oil. Even where such claims are speculative, the concern that disputed waters may be of high resource value underscores the importance of marine resources to national interests. Ultimately, this perception of real or imagined offshore resource riches at stake can itself act as both a major driver and opportunity to pursue competition. That said, the experiences of the Indo-Pacific states also demonstrate that competition over marine resources can serve as an enabler for cooperative maritime governance, illustrated by the numerous maritime joint development zones across the region oriented to seabed energy development or joint fisheries management.

Given the increasing threats to the marine and coastal environments of the Indo-Pacific, compounded by the impacts of climate change, it is to be hoped that marine resource issues will yield further cooperative ocean governance efforts in the future. The Indo-Pacific's valuable yet vulnerable ocean environment is what is really at stake, and it is abundantly clear from the region's experience that no one state on a series of semi-enclosed sea spaces along the littoral of the Indo-Pacific can deal with ocean governance and marine resource management challenges alone.

NOTES

1. National Oceanic and Atmospheric Administration, "How Much Oxygen Comes from the Ocean?," National Ocean Service, https://oceanservice.noaa.gov/facts/ocean-oxygen.html.

2. United Nations, *The Second World Ocean Assessment: World Ocean Assessment II (WOA II)*, vol. 1 (New York: United Nations, 2021), 6.

3. Intergovernmental Panel on Climate Change (IPCC), *Special Report on the Ocean and Cryosphere in a Changing Climate* (Geneva: IPCC, 2019), https://www.ipcc.ch/srocc/home/, "Summary for Policy Makers," 8–9.

4. IPCC, *Special Report*, "Summary for Policy Makers," 10.

5. IPCC, *Climate Change 2021: The Physical Science Basis* (Cambridge: Cambridge University Press, 2021).

6. International Energy Agency (IEA), *World Energy Outlook, 2019* (Paris: Organization for Economic Co-operation and Development, 2019), https://doi.org/10.1787/caf32f3b-en.

7. IEA, *World Energy Outlook, 2019*.

8. IEA, *World Energy Outlook, 2021* (Paris: Organization for Economic Co-operation and Development, 2021); IEA, *Net Zero by 2050: A Roadmap for the Global Energy Sector* (Paris: IEA, 2021).

9. Benjamin S. Halpern et al., "A Global Map of Human Impact on Marine Ecosystems," *Science* 319, no. 5865 (2008): 948–52, https://doi.org/10.1126/science.1149345.

10. United Nations, *Second World Ocean Assessment*.

11. United Nations Conference on Trade and Development, *Review of Maritime Transport 2018* (New York: United Nations, 2018), https://doi.org/10.18356/cd4440fc-en.

12. United Nations Conference on Trade and Development, *Review of Maritime Transport 2021* (New York: United Nations, 2021).

13. Lionel Carter et al., *Submarine Cables and the Oceans: Connecting the World*, UNEP-WCMC Biodiversity Series no. 31 (Lavenham, UK: Lavenham Press, 2019).

14. Food and Agriculture Organization of the United Nations, *The State of World Fisheries and Aquaculture 2020: Sustainability in Action* (Rome: Food and Agriculture Organization of the United Nations, 2020).

15. Food and Agriculture Organization, *The State of World Fisheries*.

16. Food and Agriculture Organization.

17. Food and Agriculture Organization.

18. IEA, *World Energy Outlook, 2021*.

19. IEA.

20. IEA.

21. IEA.

22. UN Climate Change Conference UK 2021, accessed November 5, 2021, https://ukcop26.org/.

23. Daniel Workman, "Crude Oil Imports by Country," World's Top Exports, accessed November 17, 2021, https://www.worldstopexports.com/crude-oil-imports-by-country/.

24. Proclamation No. 2667, 10 Fed. Reg. 12,305 (Sept. 28, 1945).

25. Proclamation No. 2668, 10 Fed. Reg. 12,304 (Sept. 28, 1945).

26. J. Ashley Roach and Robert W. Smith, *Excessive Maritime Claims*, 3rd ed. (Leiden: Martinus Nijhoff, 2012).

27. UNCLOS opened for signature on December 10, 1982, and entered into force November 16, 1994.

28. UNCLOS, Articles 3 and 57 (1994).

29. The outer limits of a continental shelf may be determined in partnership with a scientific and technical body established through the CLCS. Article 76 of UNCLOS provides two formulas according to which coastal states can establish the existence of a continental margin beyond the two-hundred-nautical-mile limit (frequently referred to as the Gardiner Line), based on reference to depth or thickness of sedimentary rocks overlying the continental crust (or the Hedberg Line), consisting of sixty nautical miles from the foot of the continental slope. Two maximum constraints or "cut-off" lines are then applied, either a distance of 350 nautical miles from relevant baselines or a distance of 100 nautical miles from the twenty-five-hundred-meter isobath. Coastal states are required to formulate a submission of information to the CLCS regarding the delineation of continental shelf limits seaward of two hundred nautical miles comprising information related to the morphology of the continental margin in question as well as its geological characteristics. The CLCS examines submissions and then provides recommendations to the coastal state, based on which it delineates the outer limit of its continental shelf. UNCLOS, Article 76.

30. There are 167 state parties to UNCLOS, plus the European Union. Cambodia is the only country in Southeast Asia remaining a nonparty. Additionally, the Republic of China (Taiwan) is a non-party to UNCLOS because it is not a United Nations member state. "Status of the United Nations Convention on the Law of the Sea, of the Agreement Relating to the Implementation of Part XI of the Convention and of the Agreement for the Implementation of the Convention Relating to the Conservation and Management of Straddling Fish Stocks and Highly Migratory Fish Stocks as at 31 March 2018," United Nations, March 31, 2018, http://www.un.org/Depts/los/reference_files/status2018.pdf.

31. UNCLOS, Articles 56 and 58.

32. Leonardo Bernard and Clive H. Schofield, "Disputes Concerning the Delimitation of the Continental Shelf beyond 200 M," in *New Knowledge and Changing Circumstances in the Law of the Sea*, ed. Thomas Heidar, 157–82 (Leiden: Brill, 2020); "Commission on the Limits of the Continental Shelf (CLCS)," Oceans and Law of the Sea, United Nations, updated July 6, 2021, http://www.un.org/Depts/los/clcs_new/clcs_home.htm.

33. The Arbitral Tribunal in the South China Sea case referred to islands not classified as "rocks" within the meaning of Article 121(3) of UNCLOS as "fully entitled islands." See "The South China Sea Arbitration (Republic of Philippines v. The People's Republic of China)," Case No. 2013-19, Permanent Court of Arbitration, https://pcacases.com/web/view/7, para. 280. The award was issued July 12, 2016.

34. UNCLOS, Article 121(3).

35. J. R. Victor Prescott and Clive H. Schofield, *The Maritime Political Boundaries of the World* (Leiden: Martinus Nijhoff, 2005).

36. Prescott and Schofield, *Maritime Political Boundaries*, 468, 470–71.

37. Prescott and Schofield, 282; Clive H. Schofield, "The Trouble with Islands," *Jane's Intelligence Review* 15, no. 9 (September 2003): 42–45.

38. "Legal Consequences of the Separation of the Chagos Archipelago from Mauritius in 1965," International Court of Justice, accessed August 8, 2020, https://www.icj-cij.org/en/case/169. It can also be observed that based on the International Court of Justice's advisory opinion, the International Tribunal on the Law of the Sea (ITLOS) found, in January 2021, that it had jurisdiction to adjudicate on the dispute concerning maritime delimitation between Maldives and Mauritius—a

finding that depends on Mauritius holding sovereignty over the Chagos Islands. See ITLOS, *Dispute Concerning Delimitation of the Maritime Boundary between Mauritius and Maldives in the Indian Ocean (Mauritius/Maldives), Preliminary Objections, Judgment*, ITLOS Case no. 28, January 28, 2021, https://www.itlos .org/fileadmin/itlos/documents/cases/28/preliminary_objections/C28_Judgment _prelimobj_28.01.2021_orig.pdf.

39. Jared Bissinger, "The Maritime Boundary Dispute between Bangladesh and Myanmar: Motivations, Potential Solutions and Implications," *Asia Policy* 10, no. 1 (July 2010): 103–42, https://doi.org/10.1353/asp.2010.0032.

40. Eric Watkins, "Daewoo Suspends Exploration in the Bay of Bengal," *Oil and Gas Journal*, November 2008.

41. ITLOS, *Dispute Concerning Delimitation of the Maritime Boundary between Bangladesh and Myanmar in the Bay of Bengal (Bangladesh/Myanmar)* (judgment), case no. 16, March 14, 2012; Clive H. Schofield, Anastasia Telesetsky, and Seokwoo Lee, "A Tribunal Navigating Complex Waters Implications of the Bay of Bengal Case," *Ocean Development and International Law* 44, no. 4 (2013): 363–88, https://doi.org/10.1080/00908320.2013.808939.

42. "Bay of Bengal Maritime Boundary Arbitration between Bangladesh and India," Permanent Court of Arbitration, accessed November 18, 2021, https://pca-cpa.org /en/cases/18/.

43. Schofield, Telesetsky, and Lee, "Tribunal Navigating."

44. Clive H. Schofield, "Adrift on Complex Waters: Geographical, Geopolitical, and Legal Dimensions to the South China Sea Disputes," in *The South China Sea and Australia's Regional Security Environment*, ed. Leszek Buszynski and Christopher B. Roberts (London: Routledge, 2014), 24–45.

45. Chen, Xiao, "Naihai de ziyuan shijie [The world of resources in the South China Sea]," *Sanlian shenghuo zhoukan* [Sanlian life weekly] no. 46 (2010): 62–67.

46. Nick O. Owen and Clive H. Schofield, "Disputed South China Sea Hydrocarbons in Perspective," *Marine Policy* 36, no. 3 (2012): 809–22, https://doi.org/10.1016/j .marpol.2011.11.010.

47. Rashid Sumaila and William Cheung, *Boom or Bust: The Future of Fish in the South China Sea* (Vancouver: University of British Columbia, 2016).

48. Clive H. Schofield, Rashid Sumaila, and William Cheung, "Fishing Not Oil Is at the Heart of the South China Sea Disputes," *Conversation*, August 16, 2016.

49. Sumaila and Cheung, *Boom or Bust*.

50. Sumaila and Cheung; Schofield, Sumaila, and Cheung, "Fishing Not Oil."

51. Sumaila and Cheung, *Boom or Bust*; Schofield, Sumaila, and Cheung, "Fishing Not Oil."

52. Robert Beckman, "US Joins 'Lawfare' by Diplomatic Notes over Chinese Claims in the S. China Sea," *Straits Times*, June 10, 2020.

53. Jonathan G. Odom, "Guerrillas in the Sea Mist," *Asia-Pacific Journal of Ocean Law and Policy* 3, no. 1 (2018): 31–94, https://doi.org/10.1163/24519391-00301003.

54. "South China Sea Arbitration."

55. "South China Sea Arbitration," para. 646. See also Clive H. Schofield, "The Regime of Islands Reframed: Developments in the Definition of Islands and Their Role in the Delimitation of Maritime Boundaries under the International Law of the Sea," *Brill Research Perspectives in the Law of the Sea* 3, no. 1/2 (2021): 1–126.

56. "South China Sea Arbitration," paras. 950–75, 992.

57. "South China Sea Arbitration," paras. 976–91, 993.
58. UNCLOS, Articles 74(3) and 83(3).
59. Clive H. Schofield, "No Panacea? Challenges in the Application of Provisional Arrangements of a Practical Nature," in *Maritime Border Diplomacy*, ed. Myron H. Nordquist and John N. Moore, 151–69 (Boston: Martinus Nijhoff, 2012).
60. Clive H. Schofield and Ian Townsend-Gault, "Choppy Waters Ahead in a 'Sea of Peace, Cooperation and Friendship'? Slow Progress towards the Application of Maritime Joint Development to the East China Sea," *Marine Policy* 35, no. 1 (2011): 25–33, https://doi.org/10.1016/j.marpol.2010.07.004; Clive H. Schofield, "An Incomplete Maritime Map: Progress and Challenges in the Delimitation of Maritime Boundaries in South East Asia," *Law of the Sea in South East Asia: Environmental, Navigational and Security Challenges*, ed. Donald Rothwell and David Letts, 33–62 (London: Routledge, 2019), 51–54.
61. "Agreement between Japan and the Republic of Korea Concerning Joint Development of the Southern Part of the Continental Shelf Adjacent to the Two Countries," *United Nations Treaty Series* 1225 (1981): 114–36, https://www.marineregions.org/documents/volume-1225-I-19778-English.pdf. The agreement entered into force on June 22, 1978. See also US Department of State, Bureau of Intelligence and Research, "Continental Shelf Boundary and Joint Development Zone: Japan-Republic of Korea," *Limits in the Seas*, no. 75 (September 1977), https://www.state.gov/wp-content/uploads/2019/11/LIS-75.pdf.
62. Clive H. Schofield, "Blurring the Lines: Maritime Joint Development and the Cooperative Management of Ocean Resources," *Issues in Legal Scholarship* 8, no. 1 (2009), https://doi.org/10.2202/1539-8323.1103. See also *Frontier Issues in Ocean Law: Marine Resources, Maritime Boundaries, and the Law of the Sea* 7, no. 1 (2008); and Dustin Kuan-Hsiung Wang, "Taiwan-Japan Fisheries Agreement: Light at the End of a Dark Tunnel," *Asia-Pacific Journal of Ocean Law and Policy* 1, no. 1 (2016): 127–30, https://doi.org/10.1163/24519391-00101009.
63. Seokwoo Lee, Young Kil Park, and Hansan Park, "The Complex Legal Status of the Current Fishing Pattern Zone in the East China Sea," *Marine Policy* 81 (2017): 219–28, https://doi.org/10.1016/j.marpol.2017.03.021.
64. Suk Kyoon Kim, *Maritime Disputes in Northeast Asia: Regional Challenges and Cooperation* (Boston: Brill, 2017).
65. Peter Williams and Thomas Ruaia, "Overview of Tuna Fisheries in the Western and Central Pacific Ocean, Including Economic Conditions—2019" (presented at 16th Regular Session of the Scientific Committee of the Western and Central Pacific Fisheries Commission, August 11–20, 2020, online meeting).
66. See, for example, Quentin Hanich and Martin Tsamenyi, eds., *Navigating Pacific Fisheries: Legal and Policy Trends in the Implementation of International Fisheries Instruments in the Western and Central Pacific Region* (Wollongong, Australia: Ocean Publications, 2009).
67. International Labour Organization, *A Study on the Future of Work in the Pacific* (Geneva: International Labour Organization, Office for Pacific Island Countries, 2017), viii.
68. World Bank, *Tuna Fisheries*, Pacific Possible Series 3 (Washington, DC: World Bank, 2016), Summary for Policy-Makers, 7.
69. Robyn Frost et al., "Redrawing the Map of the Pacific," *Marine Policy* 95, no. 306 (2018): 302–10, https://doi.org/10.1016/j.marpol.2016.06.003.

70. Agreement between the Government of the Commonwealth of Australia and the Government of the Republic of Indonesia Establishing Certain Seabed Boundaries (1971), https://www.un.org/Depts/los/LEGISLATIONANDTREATIES/PDFFILES/TREATIES/AUS-IDN1972TA.pdf; Agreement between the Government of the Commonwealth of Australia and the Government of the Republic of Indonesia Establishing Certain Seabed Boundaries in the Area of the Timor and Arafura Seas, Supplementary to the Agreement of 18 May 1971 (1972), https://www.un.org/Depts/los/LEGISLATIONANDTREATIES/PDFFILES/TREATIES/AUS-IDN1972TA.pdf.

71. 1989 Treaty between Australia and the Republic of Indonesia on the Zone of Cooperation in an Area between the Indonesian Province of East Timor and Northern Australia (1989), http://containeronline.ca/databasecil/1989-treaty-between-australia-and-the-republic-of-indonesia-on-the-zone-of-cooperation-in-an-area-between-the-indonesian-province-of-east-timor-and-northern-australia/.

72. Timor Sea Treaty (2002), United Nations, www.un.org/Depts/los/LEGISLATIONANDTREATIES/PDFFILES/TREATIES/AUS-TLS2002TST.PDF; Treaty between Australia and the Democratic Republic of Timor-Leste on Certain Maritime Arrangements in the Timor Sea (2006), Australian Treaty Series, http://www.austlii.edu.au/au/other/dfat/treaties/2007/12.html (treaty in force February 23, 2007).

73. Treaty between Australia and the Democratic Republic of Timor-Leste Establishing Their Maritime Boundaries in the Timor Sea (2018), https://www.dfat.gov.au/sites/default/files/treaty-maritime-arrangements-australia-timor-leste.pdf.

74. Bec Strating and Clive H. Schofield, "A New Path to Dispute Settlement," Interpreter (blog, Loy Institute), June 12, 2018, https://www.lowyinstitute.org/the-interpreter/new-path-dispute-settlement.

75. Rick Wilkinson, "East Timor Approves Use of Petroleum Fund for Sunrise Acquisition," *Oil and Gas Journal*, January 2019; Vivian Louis Forbes, *Timor-Leste Pipe Dreams: After Compulsory Conciliation, What Comes Next?* (Perth: Future Directions International, 2021).

5

Nuclear Order at Sea

Nicola Leveringhaus

In the past two decades, nuclear order has become a popular concept. Yet, for all the buzz and scholarship, little if anything has been written about nuclear order in the regional or maritime context. This is lamentable, given that the two largest nuclear-armed states, the United States and Russia, have vast nuclear navies and two major regional powers, China and India, are each actively pursuing a sea-based nuclear deterrent. Indeed, at present, there are an estimated 3,890 naval nuclear forces worldwide.[1] This chapter considers nuclear ordering at sea, specifically in the Indo-Pacific, an area encompassing various waters, including the Indian Ocean, the South China Sea, and much of the Pacific Ocean. These are politically tense waters and crowded ones too—with a mix of nuclear and advanced conventional navies and involving Chinese maritime actors, the Indian navy, and US Indo-Pacific Command. The chapter starts with a discussion of nuclear ordering in the Indo-Pacific and the importance of the sea. Its second part sketches out the nuclear navies of the Indo-Pacific and notes their current and likely near-future capabilities. The last section turns to strategic stability and potential for nuclear escalation in the Indo-Pacific. The aim of the chapter is threefold: first, to apply the concept of nuclear order in a maritime context; second, to apply the concept of nuclear order in a maritime context specifically to the Indo-Pacific; and third, to consider the current dynamics of nuclear deterrence at sea as well as the potential for nuclear escalation in the Indo-Pacific.

NUCLEAR ORDER AT SEA

In conceptualizing nuclear order, I will build on my own work published since 2015, which posits that the basic purpose of nuclear order is the attainment of strategic stability.[2] Strategic stability rests on the prevention of arms races and major war, especially escalation to nuclear war.[3] The process of nuclear ordering involves several actors, of which the most important tend to be nuclear-armed states, but nonnuclear states and nonstate actors matter hugely too, as do norms, treaties, legal obligations, confidence-building measures, and organizations.[4] In picturing nuclear order, it is perhaps easier to consider it a messy and unpredictable process, rather than an orderly one, and one that, as William Walker argues, changes over time.[5] Irrespective of the passage of time, this chapter argues that nuclear order can be understood in terms of four enduring pillars: nuclear deterrence, arms control, nonproliferation, and disarmament.[6] These four elements can complement and contradict each other, with implications for the strength or weakness of nuclear ordering in any given context. That said, their relative influence fluctuates over time, reflecting the priorities of national security agendas of the actors involved. Crucially, these pillars share a common principle: to work toward strategic stability. This author agrees with Walker's and Brad Roberts's respective work that, of these four pillars, nuclear deterrence remains "king" because it is intrinsically woven into the history of nuclear order as well as wider global order.[7] Put differently, despite discussion in the 2000s of a nuclear weapons–free world, nuclear deterrence remains a cornerstone of national security policies in major nuclear weapons states.

Walker's work on nuclear order deserves fuller appreciation here. More than any other scholar's, his work has led to a deeper understanding of nuclear order. One of Walker's earliest definitions of nuclear order refers to a balance of two systems: "managed deterrence" and "abstinence."[8] The first system is based on power politics and consists of strategic doctrines and arms control. The second system contains three dimensions: the Non-Proliferation Treaty (NPT), extended deterrence, and security assurances. Here, order is regime-based, maintained via the perceived legitimacy of the nonproliferation norm, the sharing of civilian nuclear energy, security assurances, and safeguards.[9] In this nuclear order, there is an unspoken reliance on nuclear deterrence and a promise, however weakly implemented, of nuclear disarmament by the nuclear weapons states party to the NPT. In other work, Walker suggests there are three "logics" driving nuclear order: armament, disarmament, and restraint.[10] These logics operate in the context of two systems: a managed system of military engagement with nuclear technology (defined as deterrence plus) and a managed system of military/civil abstinence from nuclear technology (nonproliferation plus).[11] One of the great merits of Walker's approach is that it builds civilian as well as military technologies into the nuclear ordering process. This can be analytically useful, especially in the Indo-Pacific context, where seas and oceans act as major shipping routes for transporting spent waste and repro-cessed nuclear fuel from countries such as Japan. Nuclear safety and security at sea are thus integral parts of nuclear ordering within the Indo-Pacific.[12]

Unfortunately, none of the previous literature, my work included, fully accounts for regional space in nuclear ordering.[13] Recent accounts of nuclear order offer excellent country-by-country analysis but do not focus on regions.[14] Yet regions may be viewed as important subsets of global nuclear order.[15] One of the few to mention regions in nuclear ordering, Brad Roberts distinguishes between regional nuclear subsets and subsystems within regions.[16] In my earlier work, I identified, at a very basic level, four nuclear ordering subsystems within the Asian region: Central Asia (Russia and former Soviet republics), South Asia (India and Pakistan as the major states), Southeast Asia (Association of South-east Asian Nations [ASEAN] states), and Northeast Asia (China, Taiwan, South Korea, North Korea, and Japan). At the time of writing my book in the mid-2010s, I did not include the Indo-Pacific as a nuclear subset.[17] Yet today the term "Indo-Pacific" has gained significant traction, particularly in the United States, India, Japan, and Australia. So, what does nuclear ordering look like in the Indo-Pacific, and is it a useful unit of analysis?

NUCLEAR ORDERING IN THE INDO-PACIFIC

A subset of nuclear ordering, the Indo-Pacific inevitably prioritizes the sea over land. This is a refreshing and distinct approach to nuclear ordering since geo-graphical units of analysis tend to be defined around continental, rather than maritime, borders. Before I explore the unique features of the Indo-Pacific, it is useful to point out the common ground it shares with more continental forms of nuclear ordering in Asia. For instance, it shares enduring concerns over North Korean nuclear and missile proliferation, fears over nuclear security and safety in the wake of natural disasters like Fukushima, and the deployment of missile defense systems with both stabilizing and destabilizing effects on deterrence in the region. Institutional aspects, such as the Council for Security Cooperation in the Asia Pacific and the Northeast Asian Security Cooperation Dialogue, also remain relevant in the Indo-Pacific and might be useful platforms for confidence-building measures in the future. Proposals like Asiatom (made in 1995) and ad hoc agreements reached during the now defunct six-party talks can also be understood as methods of building nuclear order within the Indo-Pacific, just as they would be in a more continentally focused Asian nuclear order.[18]

However, the Indo-Pacific as a space for nuclear ordering has four unique features. The first is the status of the United States within this nuclear order.

Unlike other subsets of nuclear order in Asia, where the United States can justify its military presence along alliance lines, in the Indo-Pacific the United States can claim to be not only a security guarantor for allies and regional security but also, crucially, a Pacific power acting on its own national interests. This deepening of status affords the United States both greater legitimacy and influence. Politically, it bypasses a criticism often used to sideline the US role in the region by certain states, such as China—namely, that Asia should be governed solely by "Asian" powers.

Second, the Indo-Pacific is a diverse patchwork of institutional compliance of global-level nuclear treaties and norms. It contains three nuclear-armed states that are not members of the NPT—namely, India, Pakistan, and North Korea. This represents the largest grouping of non-NPT members in any regional setting for nuclear ordering. The region is also home to a diverse set of positions on the Treaty on the Prohibition of Nuclear Weapons, with strong proponents such as the ASEAN states[19] and Pacific Islands[20] but also vocal opponents such as the United States and Russia.[21] To complicate matters, there are no strategic-level treaties regulating the buildup (or reduction) of naval nuclear forces either in the Indo-Pacific or worldwide. The global Seabed Treaty, which entered into force in 1972, is focused on prohibiting only the placement of nuclear weapons on the seabed and ocean floor.[22] The treaty counts with over ninety member parties. Burma, Japan, Malaysia, Singapore, and South Korea joined the Seabed Treaty in 1971, Vietnam joined in 1980, China in 1991, and the Philippines in 1992. In terms of disarmament and nonproliferation arrangements, the Indo-Pacific is home to the Southeast Asia Nuclear Weapon–Free Zone (SEANWFZ) Treaty (or Bangkok Treaty), which opened for signature in 1995 and entered into force in 1997. It has ten member states from ASEAN.[23] The SEANWFZ Treaty can be traced to 1971 and the ASEAN declaration for a zone of peace, freedom, and neutrality. It is different from other nuclear weapon–free zone treaties in that it covers EEZs and provides negative security assurances. This is potentially problematic for the South China Sea, where there are undefined EEZs and continental shelves. Unfortunately, China, France, the United States, and Russia have not yet ratified the protocol.

Third, counterproliferation, nuclear safety, and nuclear security are especially relevant to the Indo-Pacific space.[24] This is largely because the South China Sea has been used to transport illicit dual-use materials from and to North Korea as part of the Pakistani nuclear-smuggling group known as the A. Q. Khan network. US initiatives such as the Proliferation Security Initiative (PSI) and the Container Security Initiative were established under US president George W. Bush to counter such activities. Of the two, the PSI has become a more controversial tool that China rejects but that has significant support from countries such as Singapore, which conducted a PSI exercise in August 2005 in the South China Sea (known as Deep Sabre). Broadly speaking, the PSI has had some success. In May 2011 a North Korean ship (M/V *Light*) bound for the Strait of Malacca, toward Myanmar, was intercepted by a US carrier.[25] North Korea stated the ship contained chemicals and was destined for Bangladesh, but it was suspected of carrying missiles and parts. Ultimately, the United States applied pressure on Singapore and Malaysia to turn the ship away.

Fourth, where the Indo-Pacific is most distinctive is in the elevation of the sea over the land and what this means for strategic deterrence.[26] By putting maritime concerns first, the Indo-Pacific as the referent point for nuclear ordering starts with a focus on nuclear-powered ballistic missile submarines (SSBNs) armed with submarine-launched ballistic missiles (SLBMs) as the cornerstone of nuclear deterrence rather than intercontinental ballistic missiles (ICBMs) based on the land. Typically nuclear navies, where they exist, have tended to serve a secondary (though still strategically vital) role in an overall strategic-level nuclear deterrent by securing a second-strike rather than first-strike capability, based on submarines as the delivery/launch mechanism. A second-strike capability implies an ability to initially absorb and survive a first nuclear strike (a strike that may be expected or a strategic shock) and then, after this first attack, still possess sufficient capabilities to retaliate (however quickly or slowly) in an unacceptable fashion against the enemy. In practice, absorbing and surviving a first strike is likely to be no easy feat. Land-based (especially fixed, siloed) missiles would be particularly vulnerable to a first nuclear strike, whereas sea-based missiles in submarines would, in theory (if quiet, stealthy, and far out at sea), be harder to locate and destroy in the first instance. Hence, the survivability of sea-based nuclear forces for the purposes of a retaliatory second strike seems more likely than for land-based forces. The survivability would be even greater, in theory, if a nuclear-armed state maintains continuous at-sea deterrence (CASD). CASD affords a nuclear-armed state the ability to deploy nuclear forces at sea undetected and on constant alert all year round. Strategic deterrence at sea is not without risks, however. As Desmond Ball argued in the early 1980s in relation to the United States and Soviet Union, stable deterrence at sea is hard to achieve and maintain.[27] This remains even more salient in the Indo-Pacific, where deterrence at sea involves many more actors, as the next section of this chapter demonstrates.

NUCLEAR NAVIES IN THE INDO-PACIFIC

Counting the nuclear navies navigating the waters of the Indo-Pacific is not straightforward. The region is arguably home to at least six "resident" nuclear navies. These are classified as resident if part, or all, of their territory is located around the seas of the Indo-Pacific. By this measure, the six resident nuclear navies belong to the United States, Russia, China, India, Pakistan, and North Korea. Although physically located outside the Indo-Pacific and therefore technically "nonresident," the United Kingdom has the capability (and potentially the political will) to play a role in this theater too.[28] Unusual for a nuclear-armed state, the United Kingdom relies wholly on naval nuclear forces (four SSBNs on CASD) for its strategic deterrent.[29] Defending its role in the area on various grounds, it has deployed conventional naval forces in the Indo-Pacific on several occasions in the past few years for purposes ranging from exercising freedom of navigation to the safeguarding of shipping routes for trade, particularly through the Strait of Malacca. Beyond nuclear naval forces, the Indo-Pacific is home to many advanced conventional naval capabilities, of which China has one of the highest numbers in Indo-Pacific waters. The conventional navies of states allied to resident nuclear-armed Indo-Pacific states, such as the United States, could also be counted too. Japan, South Korea, and Australia are particularly relevant and have clear strategic maritime interests and advanced conventional capabilities, including missile defense, with implications for the stability of nuclear ordering in the Indo-Pacific.[30] However, a strict approach is taken in this section, one outlining the nuclear capabilities of the six resident nuclear navies in the Indo-Pacific.

United States

The United States operates the most established nuclear navy in the Indo-Pacific. During the Cold War, the United States and the then Soviet Union built up vast nuclear navies, which means that both these states have considerable experience of operating nuclear forces at sea. At present, the United States operates eight SSBNs (the aging *Ohio*-class) in the Pacific. The cost of twelve new *Columbia*-class submarines to replace the *Ohio*-class will likely be high but ultimately necessary. Currently, each *Ohio*-class submarine can carry up to twenty Trident II D5 ballistic missiles, and each Trident SLBM can carry up to eight nuclear warheads, but as Hans M. Kristensen and Matt Korda point out, these normally carry an average of four or five warheads, for an average load-out of approximately ninety warheads per submarine.[31] The United States has a CASD capability, which means that four or five SSBNs are thought to be on constant "hard alert" in patrol areas. Today, more than 60 percent of US sea-deterrent patrols take place in the Pacific, reflecting increased nuclear war planning against China and North Korea.[32] Indeed, in the mid-2000s the United States changed bases to improve its targeting of China and North Korea.[33] Since 2016, US SSBN visits have also been made to Guam (the first since 1988), signaling a clear warning to North Korea. The United States has thus reorientated its nuclear navy squarely away from the former Soviet Union to the Indo-Pacific.

In terms of geography the United States enjoys dominance in the Philippine Sea and has conducted intense antisubmarine warfare (ASW) operations with Japan. Although not a claimant state in the South China Sea, it has partnerships and relationships with several states involved in the dispute and recently labeled China's actions in the sea illegal. Since at least the 1990s, the United States has also been developing sophisticated theater missile defense systems in cooperation with its allies in the region, in large part to counter the emerging nuclear and missile threat from North Korea, and some of these systems, whether intentionally or not, may have an effect on the credibility of China's nuclear deterrent too.[34]

Russia

Like the United States, Russia is an established naval nuclear power; it operates ten SSBNs of three classes: six Delta IV, one Delta III, and three Borei. Each submarine can carry sixteen SLBMs, and each SLBM can carry several multiple independently targetable reentry vehicles (MIRVs) (multiple warheads), for a combined maximum loading of approximately 720 warheads. Yet only some of these submarines are operational. Unlike the United States, Russia has significantly less influence in the Indo-Pacific, in part because it does not have any military allies in the region.[35] Indeed, Russia has traditionally placed less emphasis on its Pacific SSBN fleet, though some new Borei-class SSBNs (eventually five) have been moved to the Pacific to replace the aging Delta-III SSBNs.[36]

China

Since 1958 China has long sought a nuclear navy, but the development of this capability has been dogged by substantial domestic and technical challenges over the years. As a consequence, in the past nuclear naval forces have had little impact in shaping China's overall strategic thinking on nuclear deterrence.[37] Only in 2015 did China finally succeed in deploying its first SSBN (a Jin-class 094) on a deterrent patrol in the South China Sea. At present, China operates four 094 SSBNs based at the Longposan Naval Base near Yulin on Hainan Island. Each Jin-class SSBN can carry up to twelve JL-2 SLBMs, all with single warheads and, possibly, penetration aids. This affords China a total of around forty-eight SLBMs. According to US defense sources, two additional Jin-class SSBNs are currently under construction.[38] A third-generation SSBN (Type-096, with JL-3 SLBMs) is expected to begin construction in the early 2020s. The People's Liberation Army–Navy reportedly conducted a first test of the JL-3 in November 2018, with a possible range of nine thousand kilometers. Ultimately it remains unclear how many SSBNs China intends to build, but most external estimates go no higher than ten. Despite the deterrent patrol in 2015, China faces continuing technical hurdles to its emerging sea-based nuclear deterrent, especially related to the noise of its SSBNs and the limited range of its missiles. By comparison, China's land-based, three-stage, MIRV, solid-fueled DF-41 ICBM has a range of twelve to fifteen thousand kilometers, which brings the continental United States within range. As a result, and as Fiona Cunningham has argued, China's strategic deterrent currently remains reliant on its land-based rather than sea-based missiles.[39]

India

In November 2018 India completed the first deterrent patrol of its first SSBN, INS *Arihant*. Soon afterward, Indian leader Narendra Modi declared that India had finally achieved a complete triad of nuclear forces.[40] While declaring a triad so early is premature, it nonetheless emphasizes the importance that India attaches to its embryonic nuclear navy; it matters strategically, not just symbolically. The *Arihant* is strategically important in deterring Pakistan rather than China (India's land-based deterrent being better suited to deterring China).[41] However, it matters symbolically to India in this context because China is also developing the same capability in Indo-Pacific waters. According to Kristensen and Korda, India has plans to build three or four SSBNs,[42] so it remains an open question whether India is seeking a CASD capability in the long run, since four SSBNs cuts it fine for CASD. To arm these SSBNs, India is developing the K-15 SLBM, with a range of seven hundred kilometers, and the K-4 SLBM, with a range of about thirty-five hundred kilometers.

Pakistan

Pakistan has not yet deployed an SSBN on a deterrent patrol, nor does it have any nuclear-powered submarines. However, Pakistan is pursuing a sea-launched version of the Babur missile, but this still requires more testing. If successful, it will have a range of 450 kilometers. Pakistan has been clear about its intentions with a sea platform: it seeks to match India's pursuit of a triad and secure a second-strike capability. Pakistan also defends its sea-based developments as in line with a wider "nuclearization of [the] Indian Ocean Region" and as an attempt to counter regional missile defense.[43] Beyond SSBNs, in January 2017, after India launched its Agni-V ICBM, Pakistan test-fired its first nuclear-capable submarine-launched cruise missile.[44]

North Korea

Like Pakistan, North Korea has presently only an aspirational nuclear navy. However, it is further along the development path than Pakistan.[45] In October

2019 North Korea successfully test launched a Pukguksong-3 SLBM, possibly from a submersible barge rather than a submarine. If it had been tested from a submarine, it would bring within range all of Japan and South Korea.[46] As Michael Elleman argues, North Korea will likely need to build up to five submarines if it wants a CASD capability.[47] This may take at least six years or more to develop. Ankit Panda, of *The Diplomat*, also reported on this test launch and noted that North Korea still has one other ballistic missile submarine, the *Gorae*, berthed at the Sinpo South Shipyard.[48] Another submarine, apparently based on a modification of one of Pyongyang's older *Romeo*-class diesel-electric submarines, was revealed in 2019 to be undergoing refurbishment and modification to serve a ballistic missile launch role.[49] On April 20, 2018, North Korean leader Kim Jong-un declared a moratorium on ballistic missile and nuclear weapons testing, but this did not include SLBMs.

In summary, the United States and Russia operate the most developed nuclear navies. Of the two, the United States is the more dominant nuclear force, with nearly two thirds of its SSBNs located in the Pacific. China has long-standing (but unclear) ambitions for its nuclear navy, perhaps to match the size of the United States in the Indo-Pacific. India, too, is beginning to build a credible SSBN fleet that will be homeported in the Indian Ocean. Yet, for now, India and China have only emerging nuclear navies. As such, neither can maintain CASD, and the ranges and stealth of their respective SSBNs are limited. Finally, Pakistan and North Korea remain aspirational in the development of their own nuclear navies.

STABILITY AND ESCALATION IN THE INDO-PACIFIC

The high level of asymmetry in SSBN capabilities and operational experience among the nuclear navies in the Indo-Pacific raises important questions for strategic stability. To complicate matters, many actors in the Indo-Pacific, especially China,[50] have considerable conventional naval capabilities that may be difficult to distinguish from SSBNs. The Indo-Pacific in the 2020s is thus fundamentally different from, and more complicated than, the Cold War nuclear naval dynamics between the Soviet Union and the United States.[51] Compounding this are the many geopolitical tensions within the region, where India and Pakistan are developing their nuclear navies with each other in mind and the United States and China, two of the largest naval forces in the Indo-Pacific, are at loggerheads in the East and South China Seas.[52] Thus, there is huge potential for escalation and instability in the Indo-Pacific. This section highlights three drivers of concern: the strategic role of SSBNs and their relationship to nuclear deterrence in the Indo-Pacific, the impact of geography on nuclear deterrence in the Indo-Pacific, and military communication (or lack thereof) among nuclear navies in the region.

Strategic Role of SSBNs

Nuclear navies have typically been considered a stabilizing force for deterrence because, in theory, they offer a secure and assured second-strike capability.[53] The so-called stabilizing deterrent effect of SSBNs depends on several interrelated conditions that are not currently met in the Indo-Pacific. The first of these conditions is that naval nuclear forces be survivable. Yet survivability demands stealth qualities (in particular, a quiet SSBN) that most emerging nuclear navies, including China and India, lack. Both countries operate SSBNs that are Cold War–era loud. Survivability also requires either dominance at sea for ease of navigation or the ability to control the seas against enemy forces that may employ ASW. In the Indo-Pacific, no one nuclear navy, whether established or emerging, has full dominance or control. This may be a general feature of all nuclear maritime environments—certainly during the Cold War, neither the United States nor Soviet Union may have felt in control of the waters in which they deployed SSBNs.[54] Yet ASW strategies, such as those employed by the United States in the Indo-Pacific, as well as unmanned underwater vehicles and new technologies for detection, can undermine the survivability of SSBN capabilities, potentially pushing navies to consider an escalatory "use-or-lose" approach in a crisis.[55] Building and deploying a high number of SSBNs might compensate for doubts over survivability. Yet, as Wu Riqiang notes, this is no solution; a massive buildup would likely be counterproductive and unnecessarily escalatory.[56]

Credibility, a second condition, rests on the ability to successfully deter the enemy. If the known or estimated range of the SSBNs does not extend to enemy territory, their use may not be a credible deterrent. At present, the ranges of Chinese SSBNs fail to reach the continental United States, just as the ranges of Indian SSBNs fail to reach China (unless they travel into the South China Sea). Their credibility as a strategic deterrent is thus impaired. This may change in the future as both states develop longer-range SLBMs. An additional factor in credibility relates to alert levels, and a CASD capability might enhance deterrence. As Tong Zhao notes, most naval nuclear forces arm their nuclear weapons when on patrol, even in peacetime.[57] Would this be the same for China and India? Both China and India maintain a no-first-use pledge and, in the Chinese case, dealert their land-based nuclear missiles. Would this be the case for SLBMs as well?[58]

Effective command-and-control measures represent a third condition for stable deterrence. Without clear command-and-control structures, the risk of accidental launch is high. There is, for instance, no information as to whether China employs permissive action links on its SSBNs to prevent unauthorized launch. This would be particularly worrying if, during a crisis, communications between Chinese SSBNs and the Central Military Commission (CMC) are (whether intentionally or not) disrupted by the enemy. This matters since the CMC is mandated to make decisions regarding nuclear use.[59] One way around this is to predelegate launch authority (and alert SLBMs even in peacetime), but, again, these options are not ideal, given risks of overreaction and accidental launch.

Altogether, satisfying the three conditions is not without risk. In the short term, emerging nuclear navies are, as Brendan Thomas-Noone and Rory Medcalf argue, less likely to be stabilizing in terms of nuclear deterrence. In the long term, if the three conditions examined above are met, SSBNs may become a stabilizing force for nuclear deterrence in the Indo-Pacific.[60]

Beyond conditions for deterrence is a broader question of what role SSBNs serve. Stephan Fruehling argues SSBNs could do more than retaliation—they could be used in a first attack.[61] Kristensen and Korda reinforce this point further: modern SSBNs can now strike a target twice as fast as an ICBM, and tactical cruise missiles armed with nuclear weapons would be able to fly low, undetected by theater missile defense systems.[62] According to Kristensen and Korda, in the Indo-Pacific several nuclear navies seem to be developing ultra-accurate missiles that do more than serve a retaliatory function. They point to India's K-15 SLBM and the follow-on to China's JL-2 SLBM and whether the latter may eventually have MIRVs.[63] If this is the case, these SLBMs may no longer be stabilizing as a retaliatory force but instead destabilizing as first-strike weapons in the Indo-Pacific.

As Avery Goldstein and Tong Zhao respectively argue, SSBNs may also perform another role for certain emerging nuclear navies—namely, as a hedge against US missile defenses in the Indo-Pacific.[64] Missiles launched underwater from an unknown location, as opposed to those from a fixed (or defined) area of land, have less predictable trajectories, making it much harder to intercept and destroy through missile defense. Indeed, Pakistan has been clear that it is developing SSBNs with this counter to missile defense in mind, and China and North Korea might also share this view.

The relationship between SSBNs and conventional naval forces in the Indo-Pacific would also matter for escalation to nuclear war in the region. In the past decade, there has been a serious academic debate among US scholars concerning inadvertent escalation, whereby a conventional conflict between the United States and China accidentally crosses the nuclear threshold.[65] A key concern is that the United States might accidentally destroy a Chinese SSBN, forcing China to use nuclear weapons and violate its no-first-use pledge. For some, like Thomas J. Christensen and Avery Goldstein, this danger has exponentially increased as China develops its maritime capabilities (conventional and nuclear), and it may become overconfident in a crisis.[66] More recent work by Caitlin Talmadge progresses through these concerns in a hypothetical yet terrifying scenario of a conflict over Taiwan.[67] The potential for nuclear escalation is made clear. Talmadge shows how inadvertent confusion in US targeting because of the commingling of Chinese missiles could lead to the deliberate disruption of Chinese communications in coastal areas.[68] More concretely, the United States would end up destroying Chinese ports, rendering Chinese SSBNs adrift and unprotected.[69] Yet perhaps comfortingly, Talmadge makes the point that these US conventional operations would not likely undermine China's ICBM force, which remains the cornerstone of its strategic deterrent, despite its emerging nuclear naval forces. Beijing should therefore have "reasonable confidence" that entering conventional conflict with the US would not automatically lead to nuclear escalation. This view is supported by recent work by Cunningham and M. Taylor Fravel, who argue that China is confident a conventional conflict would remain conventional.[70] Elsewhere in the escalation debate, there has been a more technical focus, with work by James Acton highlighting how certain conventional and nuclear technologies are difficult to distinguish from one another.[71] Yet these concerns are not yet shared by all, including China, as Tong Zhao and Li Bin have shown.[72]

Nuclear Bottlenecks: The Role of Geography

The geography of the Indo-Pacific presents unique challenges for the nuclear navies of the region to exercise stable nuclear deterrence. For emerging nuclear navies, the limited range of their SLBMs means that if deployed in littoral waters, their SSBNs have only tactical, not strategic, value in terms of deterrence. For a Chinese Jin SSBN (even next-generation versions) to have strategic value in deterring the continental United States, for example, it would have to sail across the East China Sea and into the Pacific Ocean. This involves traveling through various bottleneck points where it would draw attention and be vulnerable to the hostile antisubmarine warfare of navies that control these narrow entry points into the ocean. If the Chinese opt to not go through these maritime routes, the alternative is to stay within coastal waters, where, as Goldstein has argued, SSBNs are harder for enemy ASW to detect than the open seas.[73] Yet this does not make complete strategic sense. The current Chinese SLBM, the JL-2, is thought to have a range of seventy-two hundred kilometers. If the JL-2 is stationed in the South China Sea, it brings within range Japan, Guam, and parts of India and Russia as well as Hawaii and Alaska but not the continental United States. The projected JL-3 brings some of the continental United States within range but not Washington, DC. In a crisis with the United States, China could be effectively embargoed into the South China Sea. One way out of this is to either develop longer-range missiles—a destabilizing move in terms of modernization—or, alternatively, employ a bastion strategy, as the Soviet Union once did in the Cold War. Under a bastion approach, China would deploy attack submarines as cover for its SSBNs as they travel through the South China Sea. Yet this is potentially destabilizing too and poses a potential high cost for the Chinese in diverting conventional capabilities to this role during a crisis in which its conventional naval forces would likely be used in offensive operations against enemy navies in the Indo-Pacific.[74]

India faces a similar geographical dilemma for strategic deterrence against China. The K-15 SLBM, with a range of seven hundred kilometers, and the K-4 SLBM, with a range of about thirty-five hundred kilometers, are very limited, which suggests that India's SSBNs are primarily there to target Pakistan rather than China. In order to target China, the Indian SSBNs would need to pass the Strait of Singapore and enter the South China Sea, where China has a dominant maritime and territorial presence (through the construction of artificial islands in recent years).

Strategic Silence: No Rules of the Road

None of the emerging nuclear navies in the Indo-Pacific directly talk to one another through military-to-military dialogues. Indeed, the United States and China have so far failed to hold any bilateral nuclear talks at a military-to-military level, despite sincere attempts during the Barack Obama administration.[75] Worryingly, there are no agreements like the 1971 Agreement on Measures to Reduce the Risk of Outbreak of Nuclear War or the 1971 Prevention of Incidents on and over the High Seas that existed during the Cold War to regulate superpower behavior at sea. As Zhao argues, although the United States and China have signed the Convention on the International Regulations for Preventing Collisions at Sea, it is unclear whether it applies to the South China Sea.[76] Yet collisions are not impossible. In 1984 a Soviet submarine became entangled in the nets of a Norwegian fishing trawler. Incidents between established nuclear navies can also occur, as in 2009 when two SSBNs, the British HMS *Vanguard* and the French *Le Triomphant*, collided in the Atlantic Ocean. In 2019 it was reported that a Chinese SSBN had to surface in the South China Sea near a Vietnamese fishing boat, just off the Paracel Islands.[77]

More broadly, there is little appreciation of what each side thinks about nuclear escalation and the potential for inadvertent use of nuclear forces at sea. For instance, there is no shared view among the nuclear navies as to what types of conventional attacks, if any, would elicit a nuclear response. Nor are there shared views on how deterrent patrols should be conducted and communicated and on ways to reduce escalatory signaling during military exercises (especially joint exercises) among the nuclear and conventional navies of the Indo-Pacific. How emerging nuclear navies develop their forces at sea could also be communicated better. As Zhao legitimately asks in his excellent report *Tides of Change*, do all emerging nuclear navies really need CASD to bolster deterrence? He suggests it may enhance stability in the Indo-Pacific if China forgoes such a capability.[78] In any event, without any communication, the potential for misunderstanding under these circumstances is high.

CONCLUSION

The Indo-Pacific offers an excellent lens through which to consider nuclear ordering. Above all, it refreshingly elevates analysis of the role of nuclear forces at sea above traditional concerns around land-based nuclear forces. The Indo-Pacific also has unique characteristics in the nuclear context, with the largest number of non-NPT nuclear-armed states, together with contrasting positions on disarmament and nonproliferation among nuclear and nonnuclear states in the region. Another distinctive ordering principle in the Indo-Pacific is asymmetry between established and emerging naval nuclear powers, with implications for stable nuclear deterrence in the region. While the established naval nuclear powers have clearer doctrinal places for their capabilities, it is not clear this is the case for emerging naval nuclear powers.

This chapter has identified three potential areas of concern for nuclear escalation: the shifting role of SSBNs in strategic deterrence, the role of geography in the region, and the lack of communication among nuclear navies. The first of these concerns reflects a change among emerging powers; the stabilizing effect of SSBNs is in doubt, at least for the short term. Moreover, SSBNs, traditionally known for their second-strike role, are increasingly developed in the Indo-Pacific with what seems like a potential first-strike mission. Geography is another important aspect distinctive to the Indo-Pacific. Emerging nuclear navies in China and India are particularly limited by the geography preventing their SSBNs from truly having a strategic-level effect. Last, the nuclear navies in the Indo-Pacific do not talk to one another. Many of the concerns regarding escalation, from accidental launch to inadvertent escalation from conventional to nuclear thresholds, should be discussed in dialogues between the emerging and established nuclear navies of the Indo-Pacific. The Indo-Pacific as a nuclear order in and of itself is complex and highly evolving. As with all nuclear orders, deterrence is "king," but more needs to be done before nuclear deterrence at sea can be considered stable in the Indo-Pacific.

NOTES

1. Hans M. Kristensen and Matt Korda, "Arms Control and Sea-Launched Nuclear Weapons," in *The Future of the Undersea Deterrent: A Global Survey*, ed. Rory Medcalf et al. (Acton, Australia: Australia National University National Security College, 2020), 11.

2. Nicola Horsburgh, *China and Global Nuclear Order: From Estrangement to Active Engagement* (Oxford: Oxford University Press, 2015).
3. Patrick M. Cronin and Audrey Kurth Cronin, *Challenging Deterrence: Strategic Stability in the 21st Century* (Oxford: International Institute for Strategic Studies and Oxford University Changing Character of War Programme, 2007).
4. See Horsburgh, *China and Global Nuclear Order*, chap. 1.
5. William Walker, *A Perpetual Menace: Nuclear Weapons and International Order* (New York: Routledge, 2011), 20–28.
6. Horsburgh, *China and Global Nuclear Order*.
7. William Walker, "Nuclear Order and Disorder," *International Affairs* 76, no. 4 (2000): 703–24, https://doi.org/10.1111/1468-2346.00160; William Walker, *Weapons of Mass Destruction and International Order*, Adelphi Paper no. 370 (Oxford: Oxford University Press, 2004); William Walker, "Nuclear Enlightenment and Counter-enlightenment," *International Affairs* 83, no. 3 (2007): 431–53, https://doi .org/10.1111/j.1468-2346.2007.00630.x; William Walker, "International Nuclear Order: A Rejoinder," *International Affairs* 83, no. 4 (2007): 747–56, https://doi.org /10.1111/j.1468-2346.2007.00650.x; Brad Roberts, "All the King's Men? Refashioning Global Nuclear Order," *International Affairs* 83, no. 3 (2007): 528, https://doi .org/10.1111/j.1468-2346.2007.00636.x.
8. Walker, "Nuclear Enlightenment," 435–36; Walker, *Weapons of Mass Destruction*, 25.
9. Walker, *Weapons of Mass Destruction*, 28.
10. Walker, *Perpetual Menace*, 5–6.
11. Walker, 24; see figure 1.1.
12. "Safety" refers to a duty of care to one's own nuclear facilities and materials. "Security" refers to an external threat—for instance, of nuclear theft from nonstate actors (e.g., terrorists or smugglers).
13. Walker recognizes and laments this in "Nuclear Order and Disorder," 723n46. Regional nuclear ordering was the subject of Francesca Giovannini's PhD thesis. Francesca Giovannini, "Cooperating to Compete: The Role of Regional Powers in Global Nuclear Governance" (PhD diss., University of Oxford, 2015).
14. Sara Z. Kutchesfahani, *Global Nuclear Order* (New York: Routledge, 2018), offers a succinct primer on the literature on nuclear order, but it, too, is focused on the global over the regional, as is the excellent country-by-country study edited by Toby Dalton, Togzhan Kassenova, and Lauryn Williams, *Perspectives on the Evolving Nuclear Order* (Washington, DC: Carnegie Endowment for International Peace, 2016), and Thomas Maddux and Diane Labrosse, eds., "Forum on 'Global Nuclear Order,'" *Diplomacy and Statecraft* 29, no. 1 (March 2018), https://issforum .org/ISSF/PDF/ISSF-Forum-21.pdf.
15. This section reflects wider analysis on regional security complexity theory in Barry Buzan and Ole Wæver, *Regions and Powers: The Structure of International Society* (New York: Columbia University Press, 2003).
16. Brad Roberts, *East Asia's Nuclear Future: A Long-term View of Threat Reduction*, IDA Paper P-3641 (Alexandria, VA: Institute for Defense Analyses, 2001).
17. Horsburgh, *China and Global Nuclear Order*.
18. Muthiah Alagappa, ed., *The Long Shadow: Nuclear Weapons and Security in 21st Century Asia* (Stanford, CA: Stanford University Press, 2008).
19. "Statement by H. E. Ambassador Dang Dinh Quy, Permanent Representative of Viet Nam to the United Nations on Behalf of the Members of the Association of

the Southeast Asian Nations at the Thematic Discussion on Nuclear Weapons of the First Committee of the 74th Session of United Nations General Assembly," October 21, 2019, United Nations, https://www.un.org/disarmament/wp-content/uploads/2019/10/statement-by-vietnam-on-behalf-of-asean-nw-oct-21-19.pdf.

20. "Open-Ended Working Group Taking Forward Multilateral Nuclear Disarmament Negotiations," A/AC.286/WP.14, United Nations General Assembly, March 3, 2016, submitted by Fiji, Nauru, Palau, Samoa, and Tuvalu, https://www.reaching criticalwill.org/images/documents/Disarmament-fora/OEWG/2016/Documents /WP14.pdf.

21. Andy Weber and Christine Parthemore, "The Future of Arms Control Is Global: Reconsidering Nuclear Issues in the Indo-Pacific," War on the Rocks, February 8, 2019, https://warontherocks.com/2019/02/the-future-of-arms-control-is-global -reconsidering-nuclear-issues-in-the-indo-pacific.

22. For the full text of the treaty, see "Treaty on the Prohibition of the Emplacement of Nuclear Weapons and Other Weapons of Mass Destruction on the Seabed and Ocean Floor and in the Subsoil Thereof (Seabed Treaty)," Nuclear Threat Initiative, updated October 26, 2011, http://www.nti.org/treaties-and-regimes /treaty-prohibition-emplacement-nuclear-weapons-and-other-weapons-mass -destruction-seabed-and-ocean-floor-and-subsoil-thereof-seabed-treaty/.

23. On these states, see "Treaty on the Southeast Asia Nuclear Weapon-Free Zone," United Nations Office for Disarmament Affairs, accessed November 5, 2020, http://disarmament.un.org/treaties/t/bangkok.

24. Kristensen and Korda, "Arms Control and Sea-Launched Nuclear Weapons."

25. "US Navy Intercepted North Korean Ship: Report," Reuters, June 12, 2011, https:// www.reuters.com/article/us-korea-north-usa-ship/u-s-navy-intercepted-north -korean-ship-report-idUSTRE75C0PD20110613.

26. The Australia National University has conducted an extensive project on nuclear deterrence in the Indo-Pacific. See "Indo-Pacific Strategy: Undersea Deterrence Project," Australian National University, updated October 11, 2022, https://nsc .crawford.anu.edu.au/research/impact/15168/indo-pacific-strategy-undersea -deterrence-project.

27. Desmond Ball, "Nuclear War at Sea," *International Security* 10, no. 3 (Winter 1985/86): 3–31, https://doi.org/10.2307/2538940.

28. The United Kingdom has vied for a stake in the Indo-Pacific. See George Zambellas, "Strategic Responsibilities of Navies" (speech, RUSI Seapower Conference, September 14, 2015), https://www.gov.uk/government/speeches/strategic -responsibilities-of-navies. See also Alessio Patalano, *UK Defence from the "Far East" to the "Indo-Pacific"* (London: Policy Exchange, 2019).

29. Ministry of Defense, "The UK's Nuclear Deterrent: What You Need to Know," updated November 9, 2021, https://www.gov.uk/government/publications/uk -nuclear-deterrence-factsheet/uk-nuclear-deterrence-what-you-need-to-know.

30. James Goldrick, "Nuclear-Armed Submarines and the Balance of Power in the Indo-Pacific," The Strategist (Australian Strategic Policy Institute, blog), May 14, 2020, https://www.aspistrategist.org.au/nuclear-armed-submarines-and-the-balance-of -power-in-the-indo-pacific/.

31. Kristensen and Korda, "Arms Control."

32. Tong Zhao, *Tides of Change, China's Nuclear Ballistic Missile Submarines and Strategic Stability* (Washington, DC: Carnegie Endowment for International Peace, 2018), 53.
33. Hans M. Kristensen and Matt Korda "United States Nuclear Forces," *Bulletin of the Atomic Scientists* 76, no. 1 (2020): 46–60, https://doi.org/10.1080/00963402.2019.1701286.
34. Horsburgh, *China and Global Nuclear Order*, chap. 3.
35. Alexey D. Muraviev, "Understanding Russia's Strategic Engagement with the Indo-Asia-Pacific," *Asia Pacific Bulletin*, no. 475 (May 2019).
36. Hans M. Kristensen and Matt Korda, "Russian Nuclear Forces," *Bulletin of the Atomic Scientists* 76, no. 2 (2020): 102–17, https://doi.org/10.1080/00963402.2020.1728985.
37. Toshi Yoshihara and James R. Holmes, "China's New Undersea Nuclear Deterrent: Strategy, Doctrine, and Capabilities," *Joint Force Quarterly*, no. 50 (2008).
38. Hans M. Kristensen and Matt Korda, "Chinese Nuclear Forces," *Bulletin of the Atomic Scientists* 75, no. 4 (2019): 171–78, https://doi.org/10.1080/00963402.2019.1628511.
39. Fiona Cunningham, "The Role of Nuclear Weapons in China's National Defence," in Medcalf et al., *Future of the Undersea Deterrent*.
40. Yogesh Joshi, "Angles and Dangles: Arihant and the Dilemma of India's Undersea Nuclear Weapons," War on the Rocks, January 14, 2019, https://warontherocks.com/2019/01/angles-and-dangles-arihant-and-the-dilemma-of-indias-undersea-nuclear-weapons/.
41. Ayesha Siddiqa-Agha, "Nuclear Navies?," *Bulletin of Atomic Scientists* 56, no. 5 (2000): 12–14, https://doi.org/10.2968/056005005.
42. Hans M. Kristensen and Matt Korda, "Indian Nuclear Forces," *Bulletin of the Atomic Scientists* 74, no. 6 (2018): 361–66, https://doi.org/10.1080/00963402.2018.1533162, 365.
43. Hans M. Kristensen, Robert S. Norris, and Julia Diamond, "Pakistani Nuclear Forces," *Bulletin of the Atomic Scientists* 74, no. 5 (2018): 348–58, https://doi.org/10.1080/00963402.2018.1507796.
44. Zia Mian, M. V. Ramana, and A. H. Nayyar, "Nuclear Submarines in South Asia: New Risks and Dangers," *Journal for Peace and Nuclear Disarmament* 2, no. 1 (2020): 184–202, https://doi.org/10.1080/25751654.2019.1621425.
45. Hans M. Kristensen and Robert S. Norris, "North Korean Nuclear Capabilities," *Bulletin of the Atomic Scientists* 74, no. 1 (2018): 41–51, https://doi.org/10.1080/00963402.2017.1413062.
46. "North Korea Tests Submarine-Capable Missile Fired from Sea," BBC, October 3, 2019, https://www.bbc.co.uk/news/world-asia-49915224; Michael Ellemann, "North Korea's New Pukguksong-3 Submarine-Launched Ballistic Missile," 38 North, October 3, 2019, https://www.38north.org/2019/10/melleman100319/#:~:text=On%20October%202%2C%20North%20Korea,km%20from%20the%20launch%20point.
47. Ellemann, "North Korea's New Pukguksong-3."
48. Ankit Panda, "North Korea Finally Unveils the Pukguksong-3 SLBM: First Take-aways," *The Diplomat*, October 3, 2019, https://thediplomat.com/2019/10/north-korea-finally-unveils-the-pukguksong-3-slbm-first-takeaways/.

49. Panda, "North Korea Finally Unveils."
50. "China's Maritime Ambitions, Implications for US Regional Interests, Statement before the House Foreign Affairs Committee Subcommittee on Asia, the Pacific, and Non-Proliferation on Chinese Maritime Ambitions," June 30, 2020 (statement of Oriana Skylar Mastro, resident scholar, American Enterprise Institute, and assistant professor of security studies, Georgetown University), https://docs.house.gov/meetings/FA/FA05/20200630/110841/HHRG-116-FA05-Wstate-MastroO-20200630.pdf.
51. Ball's "Nuclear War at Sea" remains a classic on escalation in this domain between the superpowers during the Cold War.
52. Mian, Ramana, and Nayyar, "Nuclear Submarines"; "Nuclear Navies in South Asia," Arms Control Wonk, podcast, November 12, 2018, https://www.armscontrolwonk.com/archive/1206292/nuclear-navies-in-south-asia/; Iskander Rehman, *Murky Waters: Naval Nuclear Dynamics in the Indian Ocean* (Washington, DC: Carnegie Endowment for International Peace, 2015), https://carnegieendowment.org/2015/03/09/murky-waters-naval-nuclear-dynamics-in-indian-ocean-pub-59279.
53. However, new research suggests that this claim has been oversold and does not hold up fully to historical scrutiny. See Austin Long and Brendan Rittenhouse Green, "Stalking the Security Second Strike: Intelligence, Counterforce, and Nuclear Strategy," *Journal of Strategic Studies* 38, no. 1/2 (2014): 38–73, https://doi.org/10.1080/01402390.2014.958150.
54. This argument draws on Ball's "Nuclear War at Sea," which suggests great concern for escalation between both superpowers in the 1980s.
55. This scenario is well laid out in Zhao, *Tides of Change*; in Brendan Thomas-Noone and Rory Medcalf, *Nuclear-Armed Submarines in Indo-Pacific Asia: Stabiliser or Menace?* (Sydney: Lowy Institute, 2015), https://www.lowyinstitute.org/publications/nuclear-armed-submarines-indo-pacific-asia-stabiliser-or-menace; and in Wu Riqiang, "Survivability of China's Sea-Based Nuclear Forces," *Science and Global Security* 19, no. 2 (2011): 113.
56. Wu Riqiang "Certainty of Uncertainty: Nuclear Strategy with Chinese Characteristics," *Journal of Strategic Studies* 13, no. 4 (2013): 584, https://doi.org/10.1080/01402390.2013.772510.
57. Zhao, *Tides of Change*, 16.
58. On these positions, see Nicola Leveringhaus and Kate Sullivan de Estrada, "Between Conformity and Innovation: China's and India's Quest for Status as Responsible Nuclear Powers," *Review of International Studies* 44, no. 3 (2018): 482–503, https://doi.org/10.1017/S0260210518000013.
59. On this issue, see Fiona Cunningham, *Nuclear Command, Control, and Communications Systems of the People's Republic of China*, NAPSNet Special Report (Berkeley, CA: Nautilus Institute, 2019), https://nautilus.org/napsnet/napsnet-special-reports/nuclear-command-control-and-communications-systems-of-the-peoples-republic-of-china/.
60. Thomas-Noone and Medcalf, *Nuclear-Armed Submarines*.
61. Stephan Fruehling, "Nuclear-Armed Submarines and Strategic Stability in the Indo-Pacific," The Strategist (Australian Strategic Policy Institute, blog), June 4, 2020, https://www.aspistrategist.org.au/nuclear-armed-submarines-and-strategic-stability-in-the-indo-pacific/.
62. Kristensen and Korda, "Arms Control," 12.

63. Kristensen and Korda, 12, 23.
64. Avery Goldstein, "First Things First: The Pressing Danger of Crisis Instability in U.S.-China Relations," *International Security* 37, no. 4 (Spring 2013): 49–89, https://doi.org/10.1162/isec_a_00114; Zhao, *Tides of Change*.
65. Earlier discussions around inadvertent escalation include Ball, "Nuclear War at Sea," and Barry Posen, *Inadvertent Escalation: Conventional War and Nuclear Risks* (Ithaca, NY: Cornell University Press, 1991). In the case of China, see Andrew S. Erickson and Lyle J. Goldstein, "China's Future Nuclear Submarine Force," *Naval War College Review* 60, no. 1 (Winter 2007): 65–66; and Paul Dodge, "China's Naval Strategy and Nuclear Weapons: The Risks of Intentional and Inadvertent Nuclear Escalation," *Comparative Strategy* 24, no. 5 (2005): 415–30, https://doi.org /10.1080/01495930500448947.
66. Thomas J. Christensen, "The Meaning of the Nuclear Evolution: China's Strategic Modernization and US-China Security Relations," *Journal of Strategic Studies* 35, no. 4 (2012): 447–87, https://doi.org/10.1080/01402390.2012.714710; Goldstein, "First Things."
67. Caitlin Talmadge, "Would China Go Nuclear? Assessing the Risk of Chinese Nuclear Escalation in a Conventional War with the United States," *International Security* 41, no. 4 (2017): 50–92, https://doi.org/10.1162/isec_a_00274.
68. Talmadge, "Would China Go Nuclear?"
69. For a detailed discussion of Talmadge's argument, see Nicola Leveringhaus, "ISSF Article Review 85" on "Would China Go Nuclear?," H-Diplo, ISSF, October 5, 2017, https://issforum.org/ISSF/PDF/ISSF-AR85.pdf.
70. Fiona S. Cunningham and M. Taylor Fravel, "Dangerous Confidence? Chinese Views on Nuclear Escalation," *International Security* 44, no. 2 (2019): 61–109, https://doi.org/10.1162/isec_a_00359.
71. James M. Acton, "Escalation through Entanglement: How the Vulnerability of Command-and-Control Systems Raises the Risks of an Inadvertent Nuclear War," *International Security* 43, no. 1 (2018): 56–99, https://doi.org/10.1162/isec_a _00320.
72. Tong Zhao and Li Bin, "The Underappreciated Risks of Entanglement: A Chinese Perspective," in *Entanglement: Chinese and Russian Perspectives on Non-nuclear Weapons and Nuclear Risks*, ed. James M. Acton, 47–76 (Washington, DC: Carnegie Endowment for International Peace, 2017).
73. Goldstein, "First Things First," 69.
74. The best discussion on a Chinese bastion strategy and what it means for strategic stability is in Zhao, *Tides of Change*, 31.
75. Horsburgh, *China and Global Nuclear Order*.
76. Zhao, *Tides of Change*, 55.
77. H. I. Sutton, "Chinese Nuclear Submarine May Have Been Involved in Incident in South China Sea," *Forbes*, October 16, 2019.
78. Zhao, *Tides of Change*, 55.

6

Technology, Escalation, and War in the Indo-Pacific

James A. Russell

This chapter addresses the intersection of politics, evolving maritime strategies, naval power, and technological change, which are combining to reshape the means through which states in the Indo-Pacific region can exercise power at sea through their navies. Bernard Brodie once remarked that "there is nothing automatic about the influence of weaponry on warfare. That influence lies to be exerted initially through the minds of men, who make judgments, first, about the utility of weaponry and other devices and, second, about the tactical and strategic implications of the general adoption of these new weapons or devices. These judgments can be exceedingly stubborn and may long fly in the face of what to succeeding generations will look like the most overwhelming contrary evidence."[1] Echoing the timeless themes as highlighted by Brodie, the chapter argues that the region's complex geopolitical dynamics are colliding with technological changes in navies that promise to profoundly affect political strategies pursued by regional states up to and including the use of force at sea. The intersection of these phenomena promises to shape political strategies of deterrence, diplomacy, and coercion as practiced by regional states and their decision-makers through their navies. As noted by Brodie, the insertion of humans into this mix is perhaps the decisive wildcard in unpacking the future prospects for naval power and the associated political strategies they enable. How will leaders weigh the considerations for preserving peace and/or using naval power to achieve important political objectives? How will the nature of the naval capabilities at their disposal affect their decision-making? These are some of the questions at play in this chapter.

As observed by Geoffrey Till, navies are in the midst of evolving strategic circumstances in the Indo-Pacific that, in turn, are driving choices by governments to structure the kinds of navies that address their varied needs. As suggested by Till and others, navies find themselves simultaneously asked to function as instruments of competition and influence with other states while also being directed to perform naval missions aimed at promoting the freedom of movement on the high seas to enable interactions in the era of globalization.[2] These competing requirements (cooperation versus competition) come as the US Navy (the world's largest) has been directed to prioritize near-peer competition with Russia and China as part of reorientation of US defense strategy away from irregular wars against jihadists in the Middle East and East and West Africa. The tension between these competing demands also is shaping the decisions by political leaders in building the navies they think they need.

The weight of evidence compiled in this chapter suggests that political trends, in combination with newly fielded digital-age naval systems, will undoubtedly shape pressures on political leaders as they face the prospect of conflict escalation at sea, thus undermining deterrence that has helped keep political disputes at sea from manifesting themselves in a wider war. On land, there is no question that the developed states have become more trigger-happy in the twenty-first century as they have sought to police restive parts of the globe as part of the so-called war on terror across Africa, the Middle East, East Africa, West Africa, and South Asia. Most of these actions have been directed at violent nonstate actors, although in the Middle East various states are exchanging fire through proxy forces.

The use of force on land has been indelibly shaped by the digital capabilities of these forces deployed by the United States—for example, under operational schemes known as effects-based operations and/or "shock and awe." Political and military leaders have found themselves attracted by the capabilities of their digital-age strike systems and the advertised advantages of precision, low collateral damage, low monetary costs, and, just as important, low political risk.[3] As suggested by the capabilities inherent in these systems, warfare is conceived by the developed states as an engineering problem in which the objective of the strike systems is to destroy critical targets at great distances. In Iraq and Afghanistan, for example, this strike warfare theory found its expression at the tactical level with an emphasis on social network–driven analysis. As a result, strikes by missiles, guided bombs, or special operations forces became preferred methodologies of killing Islamic militants. Regrettably, this conception of war as practiced over the first decades of the twenty-first century has not produced strategic effects favorable to those states capable of fighting with these systems.

So far, this violence thankfully has not spilled over into direct and protracted interstate armed confrontations on the high seas, although there have been a number of threatening maritime standoffs involving various states in the Indo-Pacific. Deterrence and escalation have been controlled in places such as the South China Sea and the Senkaku Islands, both sites of confrontations on the high seas. However, this chapter argues that the character of naval weapon technologies will invariably exert greater influence on the heretofore high bar observed by civilian decision-makers on using force at sea that has so far seen the world's oceans remain free from war. With the Indo-Pacific entering a dangerous new era of political friction and maritime competition, political leaders will face increasing pressure on the decision-making calculus that has preserved peace on the high seas—a hallmark of the global order in the post–World War II era. The same arguments that seduced decision-makers to go to war on land in the first twenty-two years of the twenty-first century invariably will find their form in considerations on whether to escalate in the use of force on the high seas.

A principal reason why issues surrounding the potential use of force at sea are at the core of this chapter's purpose is that the Indo-Pacific features numerous maritime disputes over national borders, maritime boundaries, and fisheries as well as important choke points that are vital to the peaceful movement of global trade. These points of friction at sea range in geographic scope across the expanse of the Indo Pacific from the Bab-el-Mandeb in the Red Sea, the Strait of Hormuz at the entry to the Persian Gulf, and the Strait of Malacca, to the Spratly Islands, the Parcel Islands, the Macclesfield Bank, the Scarborough Shoal, the Senkaku Islands, and the exclusive economic zones of the Sea of Japan / East Sea. In the vast Indo-Pacific region, it is not an exaggeration to say that some of the most dangerous disputes between regional states principally exist either at sea or, in certain cases, would involve projecting force across the region's oceans to address competing maritime claims and wider political confrontations.

The chapter first addresses the reaction of states to changing geopolitical dynamics that are manifesting themselves in the form of newer and more capable navies. Second, it addresses the naval technologies and capabilities being bought by states. Third, the chapter analyzes the intersection of the phenomenon described in the first two sections with the political strategies pursued by states with these newer, more capable navies. The third section of the chapter draws on the arms race and offense-defense literature in political science to identify elements of the naval buildup that potentially create escalation instability. This section does not seek to prove or disprove competing points of view surrounding these theories but instead draws on the theories to highlight problematic aspects of the Indo-Pacific's complex strategic environment as manifested in the region's many maritime rivalries.

REGIONAL DYNAMICS AND STATE BEHAVIOR

The potential for war at sea is not lost on the states throughout the Indo-Pacific. The region is fraught with numerous dangerous political disputes. The Indian Ocean features the Iran–Sunni states–US rivalry on display in the Persian Gulf and the Red Sea as well as the enduring India-Pakistan rivalry. China, a historical rival of India, is also increasingly expanding its maritime presence in the Indian Ocean, supported by a growing network of bases in places such as Djibouti on the east coast of Africa and Gwadar in Pakistan. For its part, the United States has maintained a strong naval presence in and around the Arabian Peninsula and the Persian Gulf for the past fifty years, a presence facilitated by a number of important bases, such as the Fifth Fleet's headquarters in Bahrain, now being supplemented by access to the Omani ports of Duqm and Salalah that lie outside the Strait of Hormuz.[4] American sea power has been an instrumental element in the US strategy of pursuing geopolitical stability in the gulf, both during the era of containment in the 1990s and the war following the US invasion of Iraq in 2003.

In the South China Sea and Northeast Asia, the economic and military rise of China is reordering the strategic landscape of the region—one that, like the Persian Gulf, features a series of cross-cutting regional rivalries along with a historical US presence dating to the end of World War II. China has laid territorial claim to large portions of the South China Sea and is operationalizing these claims with poured-concrete quays and airstrips across the Spratly and Paracel chains. China also claims areas in the East China Sea in the Senkaku Islands, which Japan considers part of its territorial waters. However, not all the states in the region present a unified front to the rise of China. Japan is the most powerful and politically important counterweight to China, but its twentieth-century history stands in the way of more constructive relationships with countries such as South Korea, Australia, and Vietnam. The Japanese–South Korean relationship is particularly problematic in that it prevents a more regionally unified response to China's aggressive maritime posture.

Also sitting in the midst of the region's complex political environment is the persistent China-Taiwan dispute—a constant of the post–World War II regional dynamic. There was a time when the United States considered defending Taiwan a core Cold War–era defense planning scenario. Today that commitment is more ambiguous but cannot be completely discounted. In 2019 the US Navy transited the Taiwan Strait at least nine times as part of a region-wide demonstration of the right of freedom-of-navigation operations that seek to challenge China's maritime claims.[5] The prospect of a Chinese attack across the strait perhaps constitutes the most dangerous of the region's long list of maritime friction points.

These maritime disputes and fractious political relations form part of the backdrop of the strategic environment, which, in turn, is driving military spending. Scholars disagree whether the Indo-Pacific region is engaged in a classical arms race—an adapt-react cycle driven by a security dilemma in which states arm themselves in response to the actions of rivals to also arm themselves.[6] In turn, these actions create an arms race spiral. Arms races are nested in realist international relations theory, which regards the international system as one of self-help in which states must rely upon themselves to ensure their protection and security. In turn, that system induces a rational decision-making process in which states analyze external threats to their security and take corresponding steps to protect themselves by building their military capabilities. Another important step they can take is to build political relationships to help address the external threat. Importantly, arms races need not be solely bilateral in nature. Arms races can be a multipolar phenomenon in which the action-reaction cycle can involve many different states. For example, the period between the world wars is regarded as witnessing a multistate naval arms race that states sought to control through the Washington Naval Treaty. Another, more recent example was the interactions between the United States and the Soviet Union in the Cold War.[7] Regardless of whether the region rises to the standards of what international relations theorists would regard as an arms race, virtually all the states in the Indo-Pacific are spending more money than they did in the past on naval armaments of varying types: ships, submarines, airplanes, drones, missiles and munitions, information surveillance and reconnaissance networks, and advanced cyber capabilities.[8]

Navies are gradually being modernized and transformed throughout the Indo-Pacific, a process enabled by growing economies that support steady increases in defense spending stretching back to the late 1980s. According to the Stockholm International Peace and Research Institute, Asia and Oceania are the only regions of the world that have continuously increased defense spending since 1988. Spending rose by 46 percent from 2009 to 2018, by far the largest increase of any region in the world. In 2018 the region accounted for $507 billion in defense spending and boasted five of the world's top fifteen spenders: China (second), India (fourth), Japan (ninth), South Korea (tenth), and Australia (thirteenth).[9] To be sure, this increase in spending is driven mainly by China, which accounted for 49 percent of all regional defense spending, up from 31 percent in 2009. The other states have steadily increased their spending as their gross domestic products have grown. Most states in the Indo-Pacific have kept their spending increases relatively consistent with their overall economic growth rates and have more funds available for defense spending due to the region's rapid economic growth over the past quarter-century.[10] Citing data compiled by Jane's, the accounting firm Deloitte Touche forecasts that naval budgets could grow by as much as 60 percent over the next decade.[11]

Forecasts of global naval spending highlight the degree to which the Indo-Pacific region constitutes the fastest-growing market for naval spending in the world. A 2018 projection by the naval market research firm AMI International predicts that the region will be adding over one thousand naval vessels of all types through 2037—more than twice as many as any other region.[12] Of particular significance is that the countries in the Indo-Pacific are projected to be acquiring as many as 112 new submarines over the period, accounting for more than 30 percent of global forecast.[13] In terms of surface combatants, other market data suggest the Indo-Pacific region will spending $270 billion on new ships through 2029, nearly 28 percent of the global market.[14]

Most observers agree that China's military buildup, accompanied by an aggressive region-wide maritime posture, is driving the regional increase in spending on navies. China has identified a series of island chains, the defense of which it deems important for mainland security. The most important of these, known as the first island chain, runs from the Japanese islands past the Philippines and around the tip of Southeast Asia. Some analysts suggest that the potential number of these island chains spanning the Indo-Pacific will keep moving out into the Pacific and Indian Oceans as China expands its maritime capabilities.[15] The maritime geography of these areas is important if for no other reason than China is asserting its importance. Within the first island chain, China is actively taking military steps to deny the US Navy access.[16]

THE NAVAL TRANSFORMATION

As noted by Richard Bitzinger and others, Indo-Pacific navies are indeed in the midst of a general transformation as they determine how to best integrate digital-age technologies and the alluring capabilities afforded by them.[17] While it is true that the states also are investing in modernization for their land forces, it is clear that the "transformation process" has a particular maritime character in which the states are envisioning a future where they will need to defend themselves and, potentially, project power in, over, and under the Indo-Pacific's vast waters.

Regional states recognize the need for their navies to counter the maritime capabilities of their neighbors—most notably China. Those navies with the funding—China, Taiwan, Japan, South Korea, Malaysia, and Australia, for example—are all aggressively modernizing their navies to take advantage of twenty-first-century digital-age capabilities. To varying degrees, their naval modernizations are seeking to integrate advances in long-range, accurate missiles, missile defense systems, advanced fighter aircraft, communication and cyber networks, and sensors to improve situational awareness and targeting for long-range strikes. A pattern of the buildup in these systems is that they are intended to function as antiaccess/area-denial (A2/AD) systems that are designed to prevent an opponent from achieving freedom of movement in contested geographic areas.[18] A regional trend is that most states are focused on sea-denial as opposed to sea-control systems due to cost. Missiles and radars are cheaper than ships. Only those states with sufficient funds (Japan, China, South Korea, and India) can still seek platforms to perform more traditional sea-control missions.

Nowhere is this phenomenon more evident than in regional states' aggressive moves to add ever more capable submarines to their force structures.[19] As is the case in all naval systems being fielded in the region, China is leading the way in aggressively developing new nuclear-powered submarines—notably the Type-093 *Shang*-class attack boat and the Type-094 *Jin*-class ballistic missile submarine. China's submarine force consists of four nuclear-powered ballistic missile submarines, six nuclear-powered attack boats, and as many as fifty diesel-electric submarines; it is projected to have sixty-five to seventy submarines by the end of 2022.[20] The indigenously produced nuclear-powered boats represent new departures from China's Cold War–era Soviet reengineered systems. The Shang and its follow-on variants are rumored to have achieved stealth levels similar to or better than the improved US *Los Angeles*–class attack submarine.[21] China is believed to have greatly expanded its submarine production infrastructure so that it may be capable of building as many as four nuclear attack boats simultaneously.[22]

Other regional states boast formidable submarine forces. Topping this list is the Japan Maritime Self-Defense Force, which maintains a fleet of twenty submarines, regarded as the world's most advanced diesel-electric boats. In 2019 Japan previewed its latest attack submarine, the 29SS *Tagei* class, which incorporates an air-independent propulsion system with lithium batteries to allow longer, higher-speed submerged operations.[23] In October 2022 Mitsubishi Heavy Industries launched the third boat in the *Tagei* class as part of a $480 million project that eventually will deliver five boats to the Japanese Maritime Self-Defense Force. Following in Japan's footsteps, in December 2016 Australia launched the largest defense effort in the country's history: a $50 billion program to build twelve conventionally powered versions of the French Barracuda nuclear attack submarine to replace six aging *Collins*-class submarines by the mid-2030s. In September 2021 the United States and Australia announced that the aforementioned French program had been canceled. Instead, Australia, the United Kingdom, and the United States will cooperate to help Australia build nuclear-powered attack submarines based either on the US *Virginia*-class or the United Kingdom's *Astute*-class boat. South Korea, Vietnam, Indonesia, the Philippines, Malaysia, and Singapore also are developing their submarine forces.[24] Last but not least, India also is engaged in a dramatic expansion of its current submarine force of fourteen diesel and two nuclear-powered submarines. It is now building its own nuclear-powered ballistic missile submarines and has signed contracts with Russian and German companies to upgrade existing diesel-electric platforms.

By the middle of the century, nearly a dozen navies will be jostling for position in the Indo-Pacific's vast undersea domains—creating a new, dynamic, and dangerous maritime theater. Regional states can expect that these platforms will probe their defenses in ways already being seen on the surface. Most of the stealthy, undersea platforms that will be patrolling the waters of the Indo-Pacific over the rest of the century will have long-range weapons capable of striking targets both on shore and on land, long-range torpedoes to strike ships, and mines to disrupt shipping lanes. These platforms will be capable of striking targets with little warning—holding sea-lanes as well as land-based targets at risk. All these factors create additional friction points and disquieting circumstances for political decision-makers as these fleets inevitably interact with one another.

Another of the technologies being applied to the maritime domain are long-range precision-strike missiles based on land, at sea, and under the waves. These long-range strike weapons are increasingly supported by shore- and space-based strike-sensor complexes. The predicted global proliferation of these systems has become a geopolitical and military reality, perhaps permanently altering the balance between sea- and land-based strike systems.[25] Whereas the United States and its allies once had a monopoly on long-range munitions and their associated strike-sensor complexes, these systems are inexorably spreading around the world to the West's friends and foes alike.

The poster child for land-based strike systems is the family of DF land-based, medium-range ballistic missiles being fielded by the People's Liberation Army. The DF-21D is a mobile missile with a range of approximately one thousand miles that is allegedly capable of hitting targets at sea with nuclear and conventional payloads. Also, the road-mobile DF-26 extends the strike range of these missiles to approximately two thousand miles. Some observers believe these missiles are "game-changing" systems that fundamentally challenge the ability of the US Navy and its coalition partners to operate in maritime areas off the Chinese mainland. These ballistic missiles are further buttressed by an extensive inventory of antiship cruise missiles, notably the YJ-18. During its October 2019 military parade, China unveiled two new ship-killing missiles, the DF-17 hypersonic cruise missile and the DF-100 cruise missile. The US Department of Defense assesses that China's missile inventory consists of 750 to 1,500 short-range ballistic missiles, 150 to 400 medium-range ballistic missiles, and 270 to 540 cruise missile variants.[26] China is developing and has deployed associated satellites and over-the-horizon radar systems to provide targeting support for the missile force.[27]

Like all weapon technologies, missile technology continues its inexorable evolution and diffusion around the globe. Some observers suggest that the world is on the cusp of yet another strike revolution, this time produced by the introduction of hypersonic missiles.[28] This new family of missiles that can maneuver in flight at speeds of at least five times that of sound theoretically offers the capability to hit targets anywhere in the world in thirty minutes or less with conventional or nuclear warheads.[29] The speed and maneuverability of these missiles greatly complicate countermeasures employed by ballistic missile defense systems. In December 2019 Russia announced that it had deployed its first regiment of Avangard hypersonic missiles capable of flying at ten times the speed of sound.[30] Both the United States and China are aggressively seeking these systems. In the fiscal year 2021 defense budget, the US Navy indicated that it will be spending $1 billion to develop and deploy its "conventional prompt strike" hypersonic missile on the new *Virginia*-class submarine later in the decade.[31] As previously noted, China has been pursuing these weapons and may have already fielded a land-based mobile version. In addition to fielding its own systems, Russia has been working on a joint program with India, though it remains unclear whether and when the BrahMos II will be fielded by India.[32]

Ballistic missiles and land-based cruise missiles already are widely available in the Indo-Pacific. In addition to Russia, China, and the United States, missile systems are being deployed in such countries as India, Pakistan, South Korea, Vietnam, Iran, North Korea, and Taiwan. Like the region-wide buildup of undersea platforms, smaller regional states will slowly but surely get access not only to advanced ballistic missile technology but also to the next generation of hypersonic missiles that will enter arsenals in China, Russia, and the United States on a more widespread basis by the end of the 2020s. The spread of these systems into the Indo-Pacific is unconstrained by arms control agreements, assuring that regional states will face the inexorable arms race logic of the need to keep pace with their neighbors. Those states that maintain active security relationships with Russia, China, and the United States are likely to be the first in line to receive the newer, more advanced systems.

In addition to undersea weapons and missiles, regional naval arsenals will also integrate digital-age capabilities in the realm of command, control, communications, computers, intelligence, surveillance, and reconnaissance systems (C4ISR). Regional navies are entering the era of network-centric operations—a trend that will only gather momentum over the rest of the century. Some believe that by 2025 Asia will be spending more on C4ISR than the United States.[33] Warnings in a January 2020 report about a "brittle" US C4ISR network (among other things) in the face of Chinese advances in long-range strike systems, cyber capabilities, and electronic warfare apply throughout the region.[34] These networks constitute a new series of targets as states consider how best to counter the strengths of their regional rivals. For example, in early 2020 analysts at the Center for a New American Security warned that America's C4ISR network needed to be completely redesigned due to vulnerabilities to China's "systems destruction warfare."[35]

The last piece of the regional naval transformation is new ships—platforms that will integrate the families of new, longer-range strike weapons that are integrated into land-based C4ISR systems. China is leading the way with the development of several new ship classes of varying sizes to replace aging ships. The new, multimission ships such as the Renhai guided-missile cruiser may see China's navy boast the most modern capabilities in the world—and certainly within the region.[36] China's second aircraft carrier, the *Shandong*, was in sea trials in late 2019, and a third carrier is under construction, moving China toward a force that may eventually total six carriers. While China may be leading the way, as noted by Geoffrey Till, the first two decades of the twenty-first century have seen a region-wide expansion of naval ship tonnage, with states adding advanced multimission platforms to their navies.[37] Those states with money— Japan, India, South Korea, and Australia—are investing in a variety of newer, more capable surface ships and aircraft.

The United States also has announced aggressive plans to increase the size of its surface fleet from 321 vessels to 372 by 2030, although the final mix of ships within these totals that will include unmanned vessels is unclear.[38] Several recent ship-acquisition programs, such as the littoral combat ship and the DDG-1000 guided-missile cruiser, have been significantly scaled back due to excessive cost and problematic design issues. Similar problems have plagued the new *Ford*-class aircraft carrier program. The US Navy is actively investigating the prospect of integrating networked, unmanned vessels of various sizes and types over the rest of the century. Like the Chinese and Russian navies, it is also investing in hypersonic missiles to bolster strike options from submarines, ships, and land.

ESCALATION AND NAVAL ARMS

The offense-defense literature provides a framework through which to view the intersection of politics and armaments. It is nested in and is an outgrowth of realist international relations theory. In the anarchical, self-help international system, states can choose either offensive or defensive capabilities (or a mix of both) to protect themselves. The offense-defense literature argues that the balance between offensive and defensive capabilities obviously can affect the pursuit of states' offensive or defensive strategies. A state with offensive systems is naturally more likely to fight offensively, whereas the converse also is true that states with defensive systems are more likely to fight defensively. The mix of these capabilities depends on a state's rational consideration of which systems best protect or promote its security. Those states that seek to alter the status quo through force are more likely to pursue offensive military doctrines, and status quo states more likely to pursues defensive ones. The theory posits that war is more likely in situations where offense has the advantage, whereas peace and stability are more likely in situations where the defense has the advantage.[39] Nuclear weapons are widely believed to have tilted the offense-defense balance toward the defense and helped preserve and enable deterrence. For example, an invulnerable nuclear strike force makes it too costly for states to consider attacking another state with this capability.[40] In addition, scholars have drawn upon the theory, among other things, to analyze escalation dynamics of states considering the use of force.[41] The theory has been used to analyze many situations—a favorite being Germany's decision to go to war in the world wars. In both cases, Germany mistakenly believed that its offensive military advantages over its adversaries would result in a short, victorious war.

The theory offers insights into the cost-benefit calculations that could affect escalation dynamics facing decision-makers in the Indo-Pacific. A feature of offense-defense theory is applicable here as multiple states simultaneously seek offensively oriented systems. A particular characteristic of digital-age platforms is their steep cost. Ships, submarines, and airplanes cost a lot of money and strain the resources of most states, which limits the numbers of expensive platforms that can be fielded. For example, the United States provides the twenty-first-century poster that illustrates the follow-on consequences of building multi-billion-dollar platforms such as the DDG-1000, the littoral combat ship, the *Ford*-class carrier, and the *Columbia*-class submarine. The costs of these platforms were prohibitive, even for the United States. One undeniable result is that the US simply will not field many of these platforms. Cost growth undoubtedly played a role in the reduced sizes of both the littoral combat ship and the DDG-1000 programs. Other states face the same logic. It is unclear whether China and its command economy has cracked the code on controlling costs on these complex platforms. However, the net effect of expensive platforms is that states simply will not be able to buy many of them. Moreover, perhaps with the exception of China, they cannot easily regenerate in a war due to industrial base- and cost limitations. This is an incongruity of the Indo-Pacific naval armaments acquisitions—states are buying offensive capabilities in which the overwhelming calculus is to strike first but with limited means for reload—particularly over extended periods. The situation creates a built-in incentive for first use, with the inescapable logic of "use it or lose it" in situations but with the associated problem that if a state does shoot first to avoid losing its bolt, its capacity to fire again is limited. The smaller states are left with the prospect of the one-shot battle since they are not capable of a longer, attritional war.

Another second-order consequence—also on display in the Indo-Pacific—is the rush to deploy precision, long-range missiles and their associated strike-sensor complexes as a low-cost alternative to expensive platforms, as referenced previously. Mobile missile launchers are all the rage these days, and they can be easily moved and are sufficiently cheap to flood missile defense systems where they are employed. The advent of short-, medium-, and long-range land-based missiles is altering the balance between sea- and shore-based systems. In the first two decades of the twenty-first century, that pendulum of advantage clearly has moved toward land-based systems. Missiles also are first-use, offensive weapons in which the advantages to striking first in a coordinated salvo are inescapable. The involvement of land-based strike complexes in the maritime domain also further broadens the battlefield in that planning for use of these systems involves striking targets not just on land but also at sea. In such an environment, a confrontation on the high seas could quickly turn into a multi-domain operation at sea, below the waves, in the air, in space, and, perhaps most significantly, on land. This scheme of operations is perhaps most clearly reflected in a series of documents that began appearing in 2010, first known as the Navy's AirSea Battle, then subsequently as a US joint concept for access and maneuver in the global commons, and more recently as a series of operating concepts such as distributed operations, advanced expeditionary logistics, and other ideas sketched out in official US Navy reports. These included *Advantage at Sea: Prevailing with All-Domain Naval Power* of December 2020, which was followed by the release of *NAVPLAN 2020* in January 2021 by the chief of naval operations.[42] In short, any escalation to using force at sea can quickly escalate to exchanges of fire, not just at sea but in all the domains: land, air, sea, and space.

While not necessarily new, the third disturbing feature of the maritime environment is the timeless truism of any war at sea: the side that strikes first is the side that carries the overwhelming advantage. As emphasized by pre-eminent naval tactician Wayne Hughes in his book *Fleet Tactics and Naval Operations*, success in a confrontation at sea invariably tilts the scale in favor of taking the first shot. As eloquently noted by Hughes, "the great naval maxim of tactics—'attack effectively first'—should be thought of as more than the principle of the offensive; it should be considered the very essence of tactical action for success in naval combat."[43] Myriad additional factors, such as maneuver, concentration of force at the point of attack, technology, leadership, and overall capability in the operating force also frame the strategic importance of his tactical maxim.

When folded under the rubric of the offense-defense literature, these characteristics suggest a military balance that contains a number of inherent instabilities: (1) the nature of the force structures that features expensive, boutique platforms that raise the use-it-or-lose-it dilemma for decision-makers, particularly in a crisis situation; (2) the prevalence of precision-strike complexes that are offensively postured and suggest a multidomain encounter in the event of escalation that stems from a violent confrontation at sea; and (3) the tactical and strategic advantages of striking first. To this list, and as emphasized by Bernard Brodie at the outset of this chapter, must be added the critical wildcard of human or leadership interactions in the strategic environment.[44] Actor rationality in the bargaining framework cannot be assumed. The critical uncertainty is whether one or multiple actors in the framework believe that the opponent(s) cannot or will not respond in kind if an attack is launched due to their own realization of the futility of responding in an unwinnable war. In the Indo-Pacific theater, this circumstance applies most directly to China's perceptions of the correlation of forces and its assessments of whether its adversaries would elect to return fire in the event of war. For example, researchers at the United States Studies Centre in Sydney reached such a troubling conclusion in their August 2019 report *Averting Crisis: American Strategy, Military Spending, and Collective Defense in the Indo-Pacific*. Researchers opined that the perceptions of American military weakness and lack of preparedness throughout the Indo-Pacific may have already led China to conclude that the United States would not respond to a dramatic show of force by the Chinese in one of the many maritime dispute zones. The report noted,

> Having studied the American way of war—premised on power projection and all-domain military dominance—China has deployed a formidable array of precision missiles and other counter-intervention systems to undercut America's military primacy. By making it difficult for US forces to operate within range of these weapons, Beijing could quickly use limited force to achieve a *fait accompli* victory—particularly around Taiwan, the Japanese archipelago or maritime Southeast Asia—before America can respond, sowing doubt about Washington's security guarantees in the process.[45]

Whether or not the researchers accurately reflect the thinking of the Chinese political and military leaders, the quote illustrates that the perceptions of political leaders represent a critical and unknowable feature of the political and military bargaining framework. It is the participation and perceptions of these leaders that is the ultimate and most unstable wildcard considering the prospects for conflict escalation.

In addition to these aspects of the military balance, there is another over-riding consideration in unpacking the political and military dimensions of the geopolitical environment. As emphasized in the offense-defense literature, arms race balances are possibly most dangerously affected by what the political scientist Charles L. Glaser identifies as the "greedy state."[46] Glaser emphasizes that greedy states view arms races as competitive endeavors in which arming is seen as a means to basic security, protection from rivals, and accumulating power. The greedy state also can be seen as a revisionist state—an actor that seeks to fundamentally alter the balance of power in its favor through offensive military advantage. Its motivational framework for acquiring arms thus differs from status quo powers, who may engage in arms buildups as part of a quest to seek security through deterrence.[47] This motivational asymmetry in the regional bargaining framework undermines stability. In the Indo-Pacific, China appears as Glaser's quintessential greedy state—one that is pursuing a military buildup that stems from a desire to establish regional hegemony and influence over any combination of regional rivals. China's overriding objectives of regional ascendancy are being operationalized with its aggressive and illegal territorial seizures of atolls in the South China Sea, not to mention its aggressive maritime posture vis-à-vis Japan and other regional states.

CONCLUSION

Naval arms acquisitions throughout the Indo Pacific are being driven by underlying and long-standing political dynamics that show no indication of abating. Arms-acquisition patterns will thus continue along the lines outlined in the chapter as states seek a mix of expensive boutique-type platforms in combination with cheaper A2/AD weapons. These digital-age weapons are mostly offensive in nature, which in itself creates an escalation of instability as political leaders analyze how best to apply their maritime power in pursuit of political strategies that secure their interests. States face a series of disquieting considerations in maritime confrontations—the tactical necessity of attacking first in combination with the prospect that their systems could be destroyed if they do not shoot first. The use-it-or-lose-it logic is an inherently unstable feature of the regional escalation dynamics. This logic is further reinforced by the boutique nature of advanced naval systems, such as ships that cannot be easily regenerated due to cost and industrial base limitations.

These acquisition patterns might not be considered threatening if the regional states were all simply security seekers that want to prevent war via deterrence to preserve the status quo. As highlighted here, however, the principal regional hegemon, China, almost certainly is a revisionist power that seeks to impose its political will on regional rivals through its buildup that features a robust mix of offensive and defensive systems. This asymmetry in motivational framework is inherently unstable and, as argued here, is exacerbated by the nature of the offensive systems entering the arsenals of all parties.

Another piece of this puzzle is the conception of a potential war at sea that is suggested by the naval weapons and technologies entering regional arsenals. If we are to assess the steps underway to expand the navies of this vast region, a picture emerges in this chapter of what the Germans would refer to as *kriegsbild*, or the "war picture," which has profound implications for political strategies enabled with naval power. The ongoing naval expansion means that the application of naval power at sea will be shaped by the characteristics of the region's new navies, just as the application of force on land by armies has been shaped by the lure of modern digital-age systems. One observation from this chapter is that regional states have a far clearer idea of what a naval battle might look like with their expensive new hardware but a far less clear idea of how such a battle might fit into a larger war and, perhaps more important, what kind of *kriegsbild* they envision should they find themselves in a wider war. Like the wars on land, digital-age systems suggest great tactical possibilities that can be misidentified by political leaders as potential strategic solutions. This intellectual and strategic confusion will affect the exercise of political strategies as practiced by navies on the high seas that are the subject of this volume: diplomacy, deterrence, and coercion. The nature of the region-wide naval transformation may in fact undermine political strategies of states that are meant to prevent the outbreak of war or limit the prospects of escalation in maritime-related crises.

The future, of course, is not predetermined and may not be as bleak as this analysis would suggest. There is a good reason why the world's oceans have been almost completely free of political violence in the post–World War II era. States have so far demonstrated that it is not in their interests to disturb that peace at sea on which their own economic health and political survival depends. The bar for aggressive action or war on the high seas is thankfully a high one. Nevertheless, it would be a mistake to conclude that this calculus will continue unchallenged, for all the reasons cited by Bernard Brodie at the outset of the chapter.[48] Once political and military decision-makers enter the mix of whether or when to escalate to war, unpredictability will become a troubling and undeniable feature of the unfolding confrontation.

NOTES

1. Bernard Brodie, "Technological Changes, Strategic Doctrine, and Political Outcomes," in *Historical Dimensions of National Security Problems*, ed. Klaus Knorr (Lawrence: University Press of Kansas, 1976).

2. Geoffrey Till, "Maritime Strategy in a Globalizing World," *Orbis* 51, no. 4 (June 2007): 569–75, https://doi.org/10.1016/j.orbis.2007.08.002; Sam J. Tangredi, ed., *Globalization and Maritime Power* (Washington, DC: National Defense University Press, 2002).

3. Realizing the advantages of strategic bombardment as first suggested by Guilio Douhet, *Command of the Air* (New York: Cowan-McCann, 1942).

4. Sune Engel Rasmussen and Gordon Lubold, "Omani Ports Give US Navy Greater Control over Strategic Waterway Near Iran," *Wall Street Journal*, March 24, 2019.

5. Jesse Johnson, "US Sends Warship through Taiwan Strait as Top American Military Officer Visits Japan," *Japan Times*, November 13, 2019.

6. Adam P. Liff and G. John Ikenberry, "Racing toward Tragedy: China's Rise, Military Competition in the Asia Pacific, and the Security Dilemma," *International Security* 39, no. 2 (Fall 2014): 52–91, https://doi.org/10.1162/ISEC_a_00176; Andrew T. H. Tan, *The Arms Race in Asia: Trends, Causes, and Implications* (London: Routledge, 2013); Geoffrey Till, *Asia's Naval Expansion: An Arms Race in the Making* (London: Routledge, 2012); Richard A. Bitzinger, "A New Arms Race? Explaining Recent Southeast Asian Military Acquisitions," *Contemporary Southeast Asia* 32, no. 1 (2010): 50–69, https://doi.org/10.1355/cs-32-1c; Christian Le Mière, "The Spectre of an Asian Arms Race," *Survival* 50, no. 1 (February/March 2014): 139–56, https://doi.org/10.1080/00396338.2014.882472. Foundational works on the security dilemma are Robert Jervis, "Cooperation under the Security Dilemma," *World Politics* 30, no. 2 (January 1978): 167–214, https://doi.org/10.2307/2009958; and John H. Herz, "Idealist Internationalism and the Security Dilemma," *World Politics* 2, no. 2 (January 1950): 157–80, https://doi.org/10.2307/2009187. For a summary of literature on arms races, see Charles L. Glaser, "The Causes and Consequences of Arms Races," in *Annual Review of Political Science* 3 (2000): 251–76, https://doi.org/10.1146/annurev.polisci.3.1.251.

7. Captured in Owen Cote, *The Third Battle: Innovation in the US Navy's Silent Cold War Struggle with the Soviet Union*, Newport Paper no. 16 (Newport, RI: Naval War College, 2003).

8. For a good summary, see Jamie Smyth, "Battle Stations: Asian Arms Race Hots Up," *Financial Times*, August 28, 2018.

9. Nan Tian et al., *Trends in World Military Expenditures, 2018*, SIPRI Fact Sheet (Stockholm: Stockholm International Peace Research Institute, 2019).

10. As highlighted in Tim Huxley, "Why Asia's Arms Race Is Not Quite What It Seems," World Economic Forum, September 12, 2018, https://www.weforum.org/agenda/2018/09/asias-arms-race-and-why-it-doesnt-matter/; Lucie Beraud-Sudreau, "Asia's Defence Budgets Dispel 'Arms Race' Myth," International Institute of Strategic Studies, May 30, 2018, https://www.iiss.org/blogs/analysis/2018/05/asian-defence-budgets.

11. This does not imply that all countries will be spending more on their navies. For example, many of the states in Southeast Asia are dominated institutionally by their land forces. See Gregory Vincent Raymond, "Naval Modernization in Southeast Asia: Under the Shadow of Army Dominance," *Contemporary Southeast Asia* 39, no. 1 (April 2017): 149–77, https://doi.org/10.1355/cs39-1e. Raymond argues that institutionalized land-force dominance in certain states may slow the increase in naval spending in states such as Thailand, Indonesia, Myanmar, the Philippines, and Vietnam.

12. AMI International, "Global Submarine Overview: Naval Market Perspectives" (slide presentation at UDT 2018, Glasgow, June 28, 2018), https://cdn.asp.events /CLIENT_Clarion__96F66098_5056_B733_492B7F3A0E159DC7/sites/UDT -2020/media/libraries/2018-presentation/Day-3---Auditorium---Guy_Stitt.pdf.

13. AMI International, "Global Submarine Overview."

14. Citing figures drawn from Deloite, Janes, and Strategic Defence Intelligence in the sales brochure for the arms show IMDEX Asia 2019, May 14–16, 2019. See also Matt Smith, "D&S 2019: $270 Billion to Be Spent on Naval Vessels in Asia-Pacific over the Next Decade," Shephard, November 21, 2019.

15. Wilson Vorndick, "China's Reach Has Grown: So Should the Island Chains," Asia Maritime Transparency Initiative, October 22, 2018, https://amti.csis.org/chinas -reach-grown-island-chains/.

16. Summarized in Toshi Yoshihara and James R. Holmes, *Red Star over the Pacific: China's Rise and the Challenge to U.S. Maritime Strategy* (Annapolis, MD: Naval Institute Press, 2012).

17. Richard A. Bitzinger, "Come the Revolution: Transforming the Asia-Pacific's Militaries," *Naval War College Review* 58, no. 4 (Autumn 2005): 39–60.

18. Le Mière, "Spectre."

19. Yoshi Toshihara and James R. Holmes, "The Next Arms Race," APAC 2020: The Decade Ahead, *The Diplomat*, https://apac2020.thediplomat.com/feature/the -next-arms-race/. Also highlighted in H. I. Sutton, "The 2020s Will Change the World's Submarine Balance," *Forbes*, January 5, 2020.

20. US Department of Defense, *Military and Security Developments Involving the People's Republic of China 2019* (Washington, DC: US Department of Defense), 35–36.

21. H. I. Sutton, "China's Submarines May Be Catching Up to U.S. Navy," *Forbes*, November 24, 2019.

22. Jeffrey Lin and P. W. Singer, "China Is Building the World's Largest Submarine Facility," *Popular Science*, April 19, 2017; Rick Joe, "Pondering China's Future Nuclear Submarine Production," *The Diplomat*, January 23, 2019.

23. Kyle Mizokami, "Taking a Closer Look at Japan's Futuristic Submarine," *Popular Mechanics*, June 25, 2019.

24. Summarized in Yoshihara and Holmes, *Red Star*. Details also provided in Felix K. Chang, "Comparative Southeast Asia Military Modernization III: Maritime Balance in the South China Sea: Submarines in Southeast Asia," Asan Forum, January 16, 2015, https://theasanforum.org/comparative-southeast-asian-military -modernization-3, and Christopher Woody, "China's Growing Sub Force Is 'Armed to the Teeth' and the Rest of Asia Is Racing to Keep Up," *Business Insider*, March 20, 2018.

25. Commission on Integrated Long-Term Strategy, *Discriminate Deterrence: Report of the Commission on Integrated Long-Term Strategy* (Washington, DC: Government Printing Office 1988). See also Dennis Gormley, *Missile Contagion: Cruise Missile Proliferation and the Threat to International Security* (Annapolis, MD: Naval Institute Press, 2010).

26. Office of the Secretary of Defense, *Military and Security Developments Involving the People's Republic of China 2019* (Washington, DC: US Department of Defense, 2019), 36.

27. Eric Heginbotham et al., *Chinese Threats to US Surface Ships, 1976–2017*, RB-9858/4-AF (Santa Monica, CA: RAND Corp., 2015). RAND analysts assess that China's submarines may represent a greater threat to US and coalition shipping than its missile forces.

28. Steven Simon, "Hypersonic Missiles Are a Game Changer," *New York Times*, January 2, 2020.

29. Details of these systems are summarized in "Hypersonic Weapons Basics," Missile Defense Advocacy Alliance, updated May 30, 2018, https://missiledefenseadvocacy .org/missile-threat-and-proliferation/missile-basics/hypersonic-missiles/.

30. "Russia Deploys Avangard Hypersonic Missile System," BBC News, December 27, 2019.

31. Megan Eckstein, "Navy Confirms Global Strike Hypersonic Weapon Will First Deploy on Virginia Attack Subs," USNI News, February 18, 2020.

32. Charles Gao, "Meet BrahMos II: The Super Hypersonic Missile Russia and India May Never Build," *National Interest*, March 2, 2019.

33. George Leopold, "Asia Will Surpass the US in C4ISR by 2025," *Defense Systems Journal*, April 19, 2017.

34. Eli Ratner et al., *Rising to the China Challenge: Renewing American Competitiveness in the Indo-Pacific* (Washington, DC: Center for a New American Security, 2020).

35. Ratner et al., *Rising to the China Challenge*. This CNAS report echoes findings of US vulnerabilities identified in Bryan Clark and Timothy A. Walton, *Taking Back the Seas: Transforming the Surface Fleet for Decision-Centric Warfare* (Washington, DC: Center for Strategic and Budgetary Assessments, 2019).

36. Detailed in Defense Intelligence Agency, *China Military Power: Modernizing a Force to Fight and Win* (Washington, DC: Defense Intelligence Agency, 2019).

37. Till, *Asia's Naval Expansion*. See also Richard Bitzinger, "Come the Revolution: Transforming Asia-Pacific's Militaries," *Naval War College Review* 58, no. 4 (2005): article 6.

38. Megan Eckstein, "Navy Releases Long Range Shipbuilding Plan That Drops on 355 Ships, Lays Out Fleet Design Priorities," *Defense News*, June 17, 2021.

39. There is a vast literature on the offense-defense theory. A few of the foundational works are Jervis, "Cooperation under the Security Dilemma"; and Stephen Van Evera, *Causes of War: Power and the Roots of Conflict* (Ithaca, NY: Cornell University Press, 1999). For a summary of literature, see Sean M. Lynn-Jones, "Offense-Defense Theory and Its Critics," *Security Studies* 4, no. 4 (Summer 1995): 660–91, https://doi.org/10.1080/09636419509347600.

40. For a summary of the issue, see Lynn-Jones, "Offense-Defense Theory," 667.

41. George Quester, *Offense and Defense in the International System* (New York: Wiley, 1977).

42. Michael E. Hutchens et al., "Joint Concept for Access and Maneuver in the Global Commons: A New Joint Operational Concept," *Joint Forces Quarterly* 84 (January 2017); US Marine Corps, US Navy, and US Coast Guard, *Advantage at Sea: Prevailing with All-Domain Naval Power* (Washington, DC: Department of the Navy, 2020); *NAVPLAN 2021* (Washington, DC: US Department of the Navy, 2021).

43. Wayne P. Hughes, *Fleet Tactics and Naval Operations*, 3rd ed. (Annapolis, MD: Naval Institute Press, 2018).

44. Brodie, "Technological Changes."

45. Ashley Townsend, Brendan Thomas-Noone, and Matilda Steward, *Averting Crisis: American Strategy, Military Spending and Collective Defense in the Indo-Pacific* (Sydney: United States Studies Centre, University of Sydney, 2019), 6.

46. Charles L. Glaser, *Rational Theory of International Politics* (Princeton, NJ: Princeton University Press, 2010); Charles L. Glaser, "When Are Arms Races Dangerous? Rational vs. Suboptimal Arming," *International Security* 28, no. 4 (Spring 2004): 44–84, 10.1162/0162288041588313.

47. Glaser, "When Are Arms Races Dangerous?," 58.

48. Brodie, "Technological Changes."

PART II

Naval Power in the Indo-Pacific as History

7

Asian States and Early Imperial Competition in the Indian Ocean

Ryan Gingeras

The genesis of maritime competition in the Indian Ocean is often told as an extension of European history. It is a story that most often begins with the voyage of Vasco da Gama and his fateful arrival in Calcutta in 1498. As Portugal took hold over key ports, such as Goa, Malindi, and Malacca, trading patterns began to shift across the Indian Ocean. The Portuguese shippers exercised greater control over the flow of spices and other commodities, a trend that adversely affected merchants hailing from the Red Sea and the Persian Gulf. Lisbon's successes in Asia inspired greater European interest, prompting a flood of French, Dutch, and British prospectors to seek their own fortune across the Indian Ocean. Within this traditional narrative, local states are often depicted as either hapless bystanders or victims. Paul Kennedy's *The Rise and Fall of the Great Powers* best exemplifies this tendency. In his appraisal of what he terms "the European miracle," Kennedy reduces Europe's competitors in the Indian Ocean to flimsy "Arab dhows," the vessels that often opposed them.[1] To read Portuguese accounts of their victories outside the Straits of Hormuz or Malacca, as he puts it, "is to gain the impression that an extraterrestrial, superhuman force had descended upon their unfortunate opponents."[2]

Kennedy's global survey echoes an often-used explanation for why Asian competitors failed to resist the arrival of European actors. It would seem disparities in technology were the most critical factor in deciding this early contest over the Indian Ocean. Military historians, particularly those who championed the importance of Europe's early modern "military revolution," cite a number of critical European advances, particularly those in gunpower weaponry, shipbuilding, and tactics. Indeed, many navies native to the Indian Ocean were not equipped with cannons at the time da Gama rounded the Cape of Good Hope. Even though states in South Asia and the Indonesian archipelago did eventually field vessels armed with gunpowder weapons, it later proved difficult for some local actors to sustain or equip such navies beyond a short period. Geoffrey Parker, a foremost proponent of the "military revolution" thesis, similarly adds that European advances in fortifications amplified the ability of Portugal's initial efforts to maintain its hold over vital ports.[3] Although there were signs of a South Asian military revolution in the sixteenth century, a study by Peter Lorge poses that the slow dissolution of the Mughal Empire hobbled Indian efforts to resist European intervention into local politics. Rather than assume the mantle of the Mughals, the empire's principal successors, particularly the Maratha, lacked the resources to challenge British hegemony.[4]

The sum implication of this narrative, intentionally or not, does more than offer fodder for the notion of European exceptionalism. It implies that non-European deficiencies in capacity or, worse still, curiosity and flexibility lay behind the eventual triumph of Portugal, Holland, and Britain in the Indian Ocean. More pointedly, one may presuppose that the story of Europe's ascendency in the Indian Ocean implies that Asian states lacked a global strategic vision at this critical juncture in history.

THE INDIAN OCEAN BEYOND EUROPEAN NARRATIVES

New approaches in several historical fields have gone a long way in challenging these intrinsic biases. These new approaches reveal that rather than a space awaiting European capture, the early modern Indian Ocean was an area of intense contestation between several Asian and Middle Eastern states. In this new light, Europe's mastery over the region cannot be explained primarily as the result of the failure of native inquisitiveness, technology, and adaptation. Instead, recent scholarship shows that several important actors, most notably the Ottoman Empire, understood competition in the Indian Ocean in geostrategic terms. Rather than ambivalently ceding the riches of the Orient to European empires, the Ottomans and other states were mindful of their own imperial interests and capabilities in selectively engaging in this escalating maritime contest.

A deeper appreciation of the agency and interests of non-European actors in the early modern Indian Ocean is not simply a matter of historical posterity. It is increasingly clear that the Indian Ocean is becoming a site of intense interregional competition. For several contemporary regional actors, including Turkey, India, and China, the early modern era represents the end of a golden age free of Western influence. To some extent, the research conducted by present-day historians has helped inspire a popular reimagining of this time and its significance. For at least some local actors, today's great-power struggle in the region bears some resemblance to the struggles of the early modern period. From this standpoint, acknowledgment of this early history is to conceive of the present as a new period of reckoning, a moment that may yet see the emergence of an Asian power as preeminent in the region.

Recent discussion of a "return to great-power competition" naturally begs the question of historical precedent. But to talk of an early modern "Indo-Pacific" theater of competition, at least from the perspective of non-European actors, would be misguided. As seen in the following sections, most Asian states before 1800 viewed maritime strategy and trade politics in provincial terms. To some extent this tendency toward limited engagement was due to the lack of capacity. Despite certain noted exceptions, the warships and trading vessels operated by Asian states possessed a limited range. As a result, most trade routes constituted relatively short distances that hugged the Asian and East African coastlines. Above all, the major powers of the early modern era, be they the Mughal Empire, the Ottoman Empire, or the Qing Empire of China, tended to prioritize affairs on land far above events at sea. In this sense, modern attempts at drawing parallels between the past and present remain somewhat daunting.

PRE-EUROPEAN TRENDS ON THE INDIAN OCEAN

Broad-brush historical studies of the Indian Ocean are a relatively recent development in the field of history. Given the diversity of lands encompassing the Indian Ocean region, scholars have long tended to see the history of the basin in a more fractured light. Provincial differences in language and religion, as well as the variety of states found on all sides of the sea, have tended to push scholars to undertake a more compartmentalized approach to the crafting of histories in the region. However, recent generations of historians have been far more inclined to buck this trend. Over the past several decades, there has been an increased drive to craft a broader, more inclusive history of the Indian Ocean. Tracing the evolution of trade and cross-cultural contact has been at the heart of this new approach.

Like the making of the "Atlantic world," the Indian Ocean is increasingly depicted as a singular space that fused cultures together. In this regard, the historical movement of peoples and goods across the sea is critical to this new approach. Scholars often argue several historical continuities endowed the region with a surprising amount of cultural and social coherency. From the late seventh century forward, the Indian Ocean was transformed into a veritable "Islamic sea." By the end of the early modern period (or to around 1750–1800), large numbers of predominantly Muslim states lined the ocean's shores or periphery. Preachers and merchants, as opposed to empires and navies, have long ranked as the most important actors in the making of this epoch. In spite of the diversity of languages and cultures, the spread of Islam created a number of shared traits, as seen in matters of law, belief, and idiom, that allowed for a variety of peoples to travel and conduct business with greater ease and confidence. Remarkably, no state sought to monopolize or influence the broader tempo of trade on the Indian Ocean until the arrival of the Portuguese. Maritime competition remained, by extension, relatively limited until the sixteenth century.[5]

The sudden, and exceptionally brief, appearance of the Chinese navy in the Indian Ocean represents an important exception to this pattern of history. During the famed voyages of Zheng He from 1405 to 1433, Chinese ships traversed the Indian Ocean on seven separate occasions. During the latter stages of this campaign, Zheng's "treasure ships" made port calls as far west as Mogadishu, Jeddah, and Hormuz.[6] The impressive breadth of these voyages alone has inspired both interest and celebration, with several works appealing to the "what if" possibility of a Chinese-dominated age of discovery. An equally provocative element of Zheng's voyages is found in the technological sophistication and scale of the Chinese fleets themselves. At various times during the early 1400s, the Chinese formations dispatched westward numbered in the hundreds of ships (with as many as thirty thousand soldiers and sailors manning the fleet as a whole).[7] The largest craft to set sail, the "treasure ships" (*bao chuan*), were reported to have been immense, with the largest estimated to have been as long as four hundred feet (thus utterly dwarfing European vessels of the era).[8]

Given the more modest means that enabled the Portuguese to assert themselves within the Indian Ocean, the question of why Ming China did not emerge as a great maritime power does seem difficult to avoid. To some degree, historians have posed that the abrupt end of Chinese interest in the Indian Ocean was an expression of long-standing idiosyncrasies (be it Chinese aversion to foreigners or the empire's insecure hold over its western border with Mongolia). Yet it is also clear that the voyages of Zheng He represented more general challenges that plagued would-be hegemons in the Indian Ocean. Each voyage undertaken by Zheng was financed by the imperial treasury, thus representing a massive expense replete with political and financial risks. The state's oversize role in supporting the campaign also reflected how Chinese actors conceived of the goal of the campaign. Rather than private interest or abstract economic concerns, Zheng's patrons saw his voyages west as a fundamentally political exercise. Demonstration of China's strength and largesse (especially in the wake of the Yuan Dynasty's overthrow) proved to be an especially important factor in influencing the initial Chinese decision to engage in this kind of long-range reconnaissance. The potential economic rewards of the voyages were certainly a matter Beijing took into consideration since senior leaders continued to value trade primarily as a source of revenue. Yet unlike the European expeditions that followed, access to commodities for popular or elite consumption did not weigh as heavily on the minds of imperial officials.

Interestingly, in the years that immediately followed Vasco da Gama's entrance into Calcutta's harbor, several young Asian empires would begin to take shape on the periphery of the Indian Ocean. Traditionally historians have depicted the three largest of these states—the Ottoman Empire, Safavid Iran, and the Mughal Sultanate—as relatively uninterested in maritime affairs in the Indian Ocean. Recent scholarship indicates, however, that all three did extend attention to maritime trade and competition in the region. This new scholarly trend dramatically revises contemporary understanding of the beginning of European influence in the region from the sixteenth to the eighteenth centuries. Rather than perceiving a decisive shift away from traditional patterns of trade and power, historians have unearthed a great deal of evidence of continuity within the evolution of the Indian Ocean during this period. More important, there are strong signs that local actors did gradually adapt to the presence of European competitors. As late as the mid-eighteenth century, resistance on the part of local competitors continued to limit the ambitions of Portuguese, Dutch, French, and British merchants and raiders. Rather than disparities in technology or capability, it is clear that events on the land had a greater impact in securing European dominance on the high seas.

STRATEGIC COMPETITION AND WAR-MAKING IN THE EARLY MODERN INDIAN OCEAN

Portugal's arrival to the Indian Ocean was marked by numerous acts of violence and brutality. During his first voyage in 1498, da Gama's flotilla wantonly seized ships and cargo along the East African coast. Four years later his men bombarded the city of Calcutta for two days and massacred hundreds of unarmed Muslim pilgrims bound for Mecca. Other acts of sheer cruelty by the Portuguese followed over the course of the next several decades. For historians of the greater Indian Ocean, detailing the scale and depravity of the Portuguese assault on coastal communities is by no means a trivial matter. Instead, it is presented as a critical factor in explaining the early success of the Estado da Índia. Portugal's way of war "was a violation of the agreed conventions" of trade and competition in the region at large, as one scholar, Kirti N. Chaudhuri, has put it.[9]

Disparities in technology and engineering were an equally important element in Lisbon's first victories. Amply armed with cannons, the Portuguese carrack proved decisive in multiple engagements during the first half of the sixteenth century. In addition, distinctively European-style fortifications, such as Fort Jesus overlooking Mombasa, helped maintain Portuguese influence in various locations well into the seventeenth century. In short, violence was central to Lisbon's approach to trade, be it through wiping out local competition or forcing native merchants to pay customs duties and for safe passage.

More contemporary scholarship tends to highlight the limits to which Europeans enjoyed a military advantage over their Asian opponents. By the mid-sixteenth century both small states and emerging regional powers had begun to adapt to European innovations in technology. For example, the Aceh Sultanate rose and even thrived through the adaptation of more advanced gunpowder weaponry, including cannons, during the early half of the century. Aceh's ability to break Portugal's attempted monopoly in the eastern Indian Ocean was not undertaken alone. Gujarati merchants and Ottoman corsairs were vital in supplying the sultanate with both the design and means to produce both ships and guns capable of keeping the Portuguese at bay. Local competitors also demonstrated the ability to overcome differences in shipbuilding and tactics. Furthermore, Mughal conquests along the coasts of Bengal and Gujarat by the end of the sixteenth century prompted a rapid expansion and modernization of local fleets. In addition to the adaptation of iron nails (as opposed to twine) in ship construction, Mughal ship design often mimicked the galley and caravel shapes found in European and Ottoman models (which led to the building of craft as large as fifteen hundred tons).[10] Other aspiring European powers in the Indian Ocean contended with similarly adept states capable of deploying comparable ships and weaponry. As late as the mid-eighteenth century, ships belonging to the British East India Company labored to suppress attacks staged by pirates and warriors based in the powerful Deccan states of Maratha and Mysore.

Focus on the question of whether military technology was vital to the ascendency of major European powers in the Indian Ocean often comes at the expense of the history of cooperation and coordination in the region. Portugal's ability to anchor itself on Africa's east coast was at first enabled by an alliance forged with the rulers of Malindi in contemporary Kenya. Over time Portuguese adventurers integrated into their surroundings, marrying local women and establishing strong creole communities in Goa, Diu, and Mombasa. British and Dutch voyagers discovered similarly that cooperation with locals was essential to the survival of their trading interests. British merchants and diplomats forged close military and commercial ties with Safavid Iran, an alliance that resulted in Portugal's retreat from the Strait of Hormuz and the Persian Gulf. As late as 1750, Dutch and British merchants and sailors remained dependent on the goodwill and support of native allies, be it in the Moluccas (i.e., the Maluku Islands) or the Coromandel Coast. Though not averse to using violence, the Dutch East India Company actively placated local customs and relationships. In accepting Dutch military support, provincial Javanese leaders equated the newcomers with a mythic "stranger king" of local lore.[11]

Evidence of parity and cooperation among European and local actors in the Indian Ocean underscores a key revision of how contemporary scholars understand the nature of state competition during the early modern era. Though the arrival of Europeans may have led to an increased use of violence in regional trade, historical trading networks were able to endure or overcome these new challenges. More important, native merchants remained essential to commerce on the Indian Ocean. While Europeans certainly damaged the interests of some established networks, new trading groups, such as those composed of Iranian Armenians, often arose in their place.

However, taking these continuities into account does not do away with an essential question: Why did European states, most notably Britain, eventually come to monopolize trade and political power on the Indian Ocean by the turn of the nineteenth century? To answer this, scholars have focused on a variety of possible factors. Though advances in naval technology may have aided the likes of Holland and Great Britain in engaging a variety of regional actors, some scholars have underscored the flexibility and varied resources of the two East India Companies.[12] Direct state actors involved in regional competition, a group that included Portugal's Estado da Índia, lacked the financial wherewithal to sustain expansive activities. In contrast, while distributing risk among private investors, British and Dutch traders could still count on their respective governments to provide diplomatic and military support in times of need. An even more essential element to consider is the degree to which events outside the maritime domain influenced power dynamics on the Indian Ocean.

Perhaps the most essential factor in tilting the balance of power in the region was the slow devolution of the Mughal Empire, beginning in the eighteenth century. Though the breakup of Mughal hegemony did give way to the establishment of relative strong successor states (particularly Mysore and Maratha), the power struggle that ensued in South Asia allowed for the British East India Company to establish a more permanent foothold in Bengal. As scholars such as Christopher Bayly have well documented, the secret to London's success in South Asia did not lie solely in its maritime dominance. Rather, as Bayly notes, it was on the basis of the company's ability to profit from its alliances with local competitors, which led to its acquisition of taxation rights in Bengal in 1765, that gave the British East India Company a competitive edge in both commerce and profitability.[13]

Underscoring the relative degree of parity during the early modern period also serves as a basis to ask other meaningful questions. Despite demonstrating degrees of ingenuity and responsiveness, why did a non-European power pose a more direct challenge to European dominance in the Indian Ocean by the end of the eighteenth century? What prevented comparably sophisticated states in Asia from asserting similar claims of hegemony on the Indian Ocean as a whole? Rather than entertain counterfactual scenarios, it is perhaps best to address these questions through a closer survey of one of the larger non-European competitors of the early modern era: the Ottoman Empire. In looking at Istanbul's entrance in the maritime domain, one gets a more general sense of the kinds of challenges confronted by other competitors from Asia.

OTTOMAN ATTEMPTS AT ASIAN HEGEMONY: A BRIEF SURVEY OF THE SIXTEENTH CENTURY

The Ottoman Empire's ascendance as a naval power on the Indian Ocean came by way of its conquests on land. At the opening of the sixteenth century, Istanbul claimed no territory with direct access to the sea routes to Asia. Yet, with acquisition of Mamluk Egypt in 1517, followed by taking Baghdad and Basra in the 1530s, Ottoman imperial administrators were compelled to see their maritime interests in broader terms. Istanbul quickly became aware of the entrenched commercial interests that emanated from Egypt and Iraq (given that Asian spices had long streamed westward via the Persian Gulf and the Red Sea). Having accounted for the fiscal advantages of controlling important trade routes, the Ottomans' attention focused on the potential profits of the spice trade (largely in the form of import duties) and grew more engaged in dealing with other states along the Indian Ocean littoral.

Like the impact of Portuguese or British self-fashioned explorers, Istanbul's exposure to the peoples and politics of maritime Asia had a dramatic effect upon the intellectual development of elites of the capital. It is through direct contact with Muslims along the east coast of Africa, South Asia, and Java that Ottoman leaders came to conceive of themselves as leaders of a much-expanded Islamic world. Ottoman campaigns off the Gujarati coast and aid to fighters in Aceh nurtured and fortified a similar sense of "discovery" and superiority among observers in faraway Istanbul. Like European conquistadors, Ottoman adventurers boasted of their exotic findings. After journeying down through East Africa, one imperial magistrate swore that the conquest of Abyssinia was only a matter of time, given that local troops consisted of "barefooted and weak footmen with wooden bows and shields made of elephant hides."[14]

The development of a much more globalized perspective on Ottoman imperial interests sharpened how Istanbul conceived of the question of competition within this larger geographic area. The acquisition of lands adjacent to the Red Sea and the Persian Gulf occurred amid the consolidation of Portugal's hold over Goa and the Swahili coast. From 1538 to 1588 the Ottomans launched several massive campaigns, each totaling dozens of ships, to contest Lisbon's hegemony on the Indian Ocean. The result of these efforts was a mix at best. Ottoman land and sea forces did prove successful in maintaining control of the

Red Sea and holding the strategic choke point at Bab-el-Mandeb. Meanwhile, Ottoman diplomatic and military efforts along the Indian Ocean littoral yielded decisive alliances with naval powers, such as the Aceh and Mughal Sultanates. However, all attempts to evict Portugal from the region failed. The empire sustained heavy casualties, in several cases to the point of annihilation, during several grand campaigns off the coasts of Gujurat, Surat, Hormuz, and Zimbabwe. However, disparities in military capabilities do not fully account for Istanbul's failure to project power beyond the Persian Gulf or the Red Sea. To the contrary, recent documentary evidence underscores a surprising degree of parity between the two states (both fleets, it seems, fielded oared galleys *and* tall ships during various clashes).[15] Other factors, such as lack of tactical coordination with allies and sheer misfortune, played critical roles in limiting the Ottoman influence in the Indian Ocean.

Reversals at sea were not the only factors that weighed against Ottoman efforts in the Indian Ocean. Conflicting views in the capital, particularly with respect to grand strategy, influenced how the empire approached questions of power politics in Asia as well. Istanbul's push into the Arabian Sea was largely the product of both internal interest within the Ottoman court (what Giancarlo Casale has referred to as "the Indian Ocean Faction") and provincial pressure (i.e., influence deriving from regional governors).[16] Over the course of the sixteenth century, officials in the Ottoman central government regularly weighed potential gains in the Indian Ocean against the costs and prerogatives of the empire's interest in the Balkans, the Mediterranean, and North Africa.

Among the perceived costs was the degree to which campaigns in Asia strengthened the authority of provincial governors (particularly in Egypt) at the expense of the central government. Port officials, military officers, and regional administrators in Basra and Cairo, for example, tended to be the greatest beneficiaries of the tax revenue from the spice trade.[17] Moreover, although viziers in Istanbul saw competition in the Asian theater as an extension of the larger struggle against their rivals in the Central and Western Europe, other imperatives closer to home drew as much or more attention. In the midst of Ottoman efforts to aid Aceh in its war against Portugal in the 1560s and 1570s, imperial ministers also concerned themselves with major campaigns in Yemen, Russia, and Cyprus. Istanbul's ability to balance between these various areas of concern, as well as recover from dramatic setbacks, are well documented (the total reconstitution of the entire Mediterranean fleet after the disaster at Lepanto standing as testament to this fact).[18] Yet, by the turn of the seventeenth century, it is clear that Istanbul was no longer willing to bear such burdens.

Comparatively speaking, the rise and abrupt decline of Ottoman influence in the Indian Ocean underscores a critical feature that defined the general evolution of power politics in the region during the early modern period. The state carried virtually all the pains of Istanbul's expenditure in maritime affairs in Asia. It appears that merchants in the capital and in the provinces played a relatively limited role in the formation of imperial policy during the sixteenth century. Although the empire was keen to protect allied traders as late as the mid-1600s, private interests were marginal to the financing or deliberations that went into Ottoman efforts in the Indian Ocean. Istanbul was not alone in its increased unwillingness or inability to pay the immense costs for further imperial adventures in the region.

By the mid-seventeenth century, Lisbon also faced increased competition from the Dutch East India Company. Unable to call upon private capital and hard pressed to maintain control portions of its empire in the Americas, Portuguese ministers, too, decided "to give up in Asia as much as" they needed to.[19] Though elements of the Estado da Índia survived well into the twentieth century, Lisbon's receding role within the Indian Ocean paved the way for both the British and Dutch to assume greater influence in the region.

CONCLUSION: THE PAST AS PREMONITIONS FOR THE FUTURE?

It is hard to determine the impact recent research has had on popular perceptions of global competition and power politics during the early modern period. Judging from the popularity of contemporary publications, such as Niall Ferguson's *Civilization: The West and the Rest*, it is clear that at least some scholars and students are resistant to the changing consensus among contemporary historians.[20] What is most telling, perhaps, is the degree to which policymakers and commentators in Asia and the Middle East have grown more conscious of non-European imperial history during the early modern period.

In China, rising global ambitions have given new significance to Zheng He's voyages across the Indian Ocean. Speaking in 2017, President Xi Jinping declared that China's presence in the Indian Ocean would serve as a model for Beijing's current maritime policies. Unlike Europeans, Xi asserted that China's place in the early modern world was not achieved "with warships, guns or swords" but rather as "friendly emissaries" to neighboring states in Asia.[21] Turkish policymakers have recently made similar claims with respect to both the past and present. One of the principal architects of Ankara's current foreign policy, Ahmet Davutoğlu, maintains that Ankara is obliged to reclaim the Ottoman mantle as a naval power. He argues that the Ottoman Empire was "a key state" in the Indian Ocean, a legacy he believed Turkey must carry forward.[22]

Musings such as these may be dismissed as expressions of nationalist fantasies. To do so, however, comes with the risk of ignoring important insights into present and future aspirations among emerging powers in Asia today. It is relatively clear that historical revisionism at least partially influences the perceptions of critical leaders such as Narendra Modi, Xi Jinping, and Recep Tayyip Erdoğan. For them, the early modern ascendency of European powers along the Pacific Rim and in the Indian Ocean was a disaster for the great states of Asia. Many current policies seen in China, India, Iran, and Turkey are often touted as reversing this historical balance of power.

In this light, a greater appreciation of early modern power politics in the Indian Ocean offers certain practical advantages. A closer reading of this period suggests there were no clear determinative factors in deciding which states succeeded as hegemons in the region. Disparities in technology, and even culture, have proven less than decisive than previously thought. One lesson that contemporary observers may draw from the past is the degree to which emerging powers continued to depend on local actors, which led to both new power relationships and the maintenance of the status quo. All in all, no single power, past or present, has ever possessed the resources, know-how, or political will to impose their will on the region alone. This fact should give pause to those who predict the emergence of an "Asian Indo-Pacific" hegemon. Even with the improved capacity of contemporary states such as China, India, or Turkey, the resources needed to operate and coordinate maritime activities across both oceans remains prohibitively high. Moreover, as seen in both the past and present, the ability to maintain large-scale deployments across the Pacific and Indian Oceans depends greatly on political will. It is possible, despite the revisionist impulses seen today, that Beijing or other presumptive powers will eventually lose their taste for naval competition across the whole of the Indo-Pacific domain.

NOTES

1. Paul Kennedy, *The Rise and Fall of the Great Powers: Economic Change and Military Conflict from 1500 to 2000* (New York: Vintage, 1989).
2. Kennedy, *Rise and Fall*.
3. Geoffrey Parker, *The Military Revolution: Military Innovation and the Rise of the West* (Cambridge: Cambridge University Press, 2009), 122.
4. Peter Lorge, *The Asian Military Revolution from Gunpowder to the Bomb* (Cambridge: Cambridge University Press, 2008), 150.
5. Edward Alpers, *The Indian Ocean in World History* (Oxford: Oxford University Press, 2013), 42–68.
6. Louise Levathes, *When China Ruled the Seas: The Treasure Fleet of the Dragon Throne, 1405–1433* (Oxford: Oxford University Press).
7. Lincoln Paine, *The Sea and Civilization: A Maritime History of the World* (New York: Vintage Books, 2013), 374.
8. Levathes, *When China Ruled*, 21.
9. Kirti N. Chaudhuri, *Trade and Civilization in the Indian Ocean: An Economic History from the Rise of Islam to 1750* (Cambridge: Cambridge University Press, 1985), 64.

10. Andrew De la Garza, *The Mughal Empire at War: Babur, Akbar, and the Indian Military Revolution, 1500–1605* (New York: Routledge, 2016), 79.
11. Andrew Philips and J. C. Sharman, *International Order in Diversity: War, Trade, and Rule in the Indian Ocean* (Cambridge: Cambridge University Press, 2015), 162.
12. See, for example, James D. Tracy, ed., *The Political Economy of Merchant Empires: State Power and World Trade, 1350–1750* (Cambridge: Cambridge University Press, 1991); and Niels Steensgaard, *Carracks, Caravans, and Companies: The Structural Crisis in the European-Asian Trade in the Early 17th Century* (Copenhagen: Studentlitteratur, 1973).
13. Christopher Bayly, *Indian Society and the Making of the British Empire* (Cambridge: Cambridge University Press, 1987), 51.
14. Giancarlo Casale, *The Ottoman Age of Exploration* (Oxford: Oxford University Press, 2010), 39.
15. Giancarlo Casale, "Ottoman Warships in the Indian Ocean Armada of 1538: A Qualitative and Statistical Analysis," in *Seapower, Technology, and Trade: Studies in Turkish Maritime History*, ed. Dejanirah Couto, Feza Günergün, and Maria Pia Pedani (Istanbul: Piri Reis University, 2014), 101.
16. Casale, *Ottoman Age*, 88.
17. Salih Özbaran, "Rivalries and Collaborations: Ottoman and Portuguese Empires in a Comparative Historiography," in Couto, Günergün, and Pedani, *Seapower, Technology, and Trade*, 87–88.
18. Daniel Goffman, *The Ottoman Empire and Early Modern Europe* (Cambridge: Cambridge University Press, 2002), 194.
19. Philips and Sharman, *International Order*, 121.
20. According to Ferguson, European success in empire building was rooted in six culturally determined "killer apps": competition, science, private property, medicine, consumption, and work ethic. See Niall Ferguson, *Civilization: The West and the Rest* (London: Penguin, 2011).
21. Max Walden, "Peaceful Explorer or War Criminal: Who Was Zheng He, China's Muslim Symbol of Diplomacy?," ABC News (Australia), November 13, 2019, https://www.abc.net.au/news/2019-09-22/zheng-he-chinese-islam-explorer-belt -and-road/11471758.
22. Ahmet Davutoğlu, *Stratejik Derinlik: Türkiye'nin Uluslararası Konumu* [Strategic depth: Turkey's international position] (Istanbul: Küre Yayınları, 2001), 206.

8

The "Problem of Asia" and Imperial Competition before World War I

Richard Dunley

In 1900, in the words of Alfred Thayer Mahan, there was a "problem of Asia."[1] In its most basic form, this problem could be summed up in one word: China. As he saw it, the "accentuating rivalry between the states of our civilization arising from the unstable condition of China" could no longer be ignored.[2] China had traditionally been the largest and most powerful state in East Asia; however, by the late nineteenth century, it was weak and riven by internal divisions. This created a power vacuum in the region. At the same time, changes in technology were helping to facilitate a new era of globalization. This was marked out not only by a growth in trade but also by the greatly increased ability of Western states to exert power with global reach. Together these factors ensured the area would be the focus of intense imperial competition.

It was this competition that was the subject of Mahan's *The Problem of Asia*. In the preface he gave a rather sobering warning, describing the process of applying historical lessons to contemporary events as "a matter of no slight difficulty." And so it proved. Much of Mahan's specific analysis was incorrect, and his focus on race now seems deeply problematic. However, the way Mahan approached the problem offers real insight into the structures of the region, which helped shape events at the time and arguably continue to influence them today. The book opens with a bold and deeply Mahanian statement: "The onward movement of the world is largely determined, both in rate and in direction, by geographical and physical conditions. Add to them racial characteristics, and we probably have the chief constituents of the raw material, which, under varying impulses from within and without, is gradually worked up into history."[3]

The focus on race is clearly misguided, and the statement has a deterministic and teleological edge that leaves the modern reader uncomfortable. However, this statement, and the rest of Mahan's analysis, firmly locates geography, particularly maritime geography, as central to any understanding of the strategic situation in East Asia. He argues that the coming period of imperial competition in the region will fundamentally boil down into a conflict between land power and sea power and their two greatest protagonists, Russia and Britain. This contest, while primarily over the situation in East Asia, would in Mahan's opinion be fought out on a global scale. Russia's dominance of the Eurasian heartland would be balanced by Britain's control of the sea and, in particular, of the broad Indo-Pacific basin. Russian advances into East Asia, facilitated by Russia's occupation of the "central position," could be checked by the exploitation of Britain's exterior lines and bases, "the action of which is susceptible of unification only by means of a supreme sea power."[4]

In Mahan's eyes, Britain and Russia were fundamentally different, not simply in their relative strengths but also in the aims they sought to pursue and the ways they used military and naval power to pursue them. Perhaps unsurprisingly, Mahan felt the maritime British approach was superior, and he believed that this should, and would, win out. His confidence in British success rested on a perception of the superiority of naval power over land power and, ultimately, his belief that the center of gravity of the region lay at sea.[5] It is easy to pick apart Mahan's specific contentions, but events down to the eve of World War I suggest that his framework of analysis had considerable merit. Maritime geography did shape the strategic situation, and the powers that controlled the sea were able to reassert their dominance in the face of a challenge from the land power. This period also demonstrates the successful application of naval power as a flexible tool of statecraft. This power enabled the maritime states, most notably Britain, to develop a calibrated response to the challenge posed by Russia. This included engagement in diplomacy and alliance building as well as coercion, deterrence, and more than a whiff of cordite. The effective harnessing of naval power and its integration with other tools, such as diplomatic influence and economic power, would allow these states to reaffirm their dominance of the region and in doing so to establish a pattern that would remain true throughout the twentieth century.

THE RISE OF IMPERIAL COMPETITION

Mahan's basic premise, that East Asia would be dominated by the power that was supreme at sea, did not seem hugely revelatory at the turn of the twentieth century but was, in fact, the product of a comparatively recent set of developments. Since the late eighteenth century, Britain had been generally accepted as being the dominant power in East Asian waters. Throughout most of the nineteenth century, this broad concept of "command of the sea" was achieved by potential strength as opposed to real strength in theater, but few doubted the ability of Britain to exert decisive control over these waters if and when needed.[6] In the early period, however, British naval superiority was not easily translated into effects on land. Britain's ability to impact events, even on the East Asian littoral, was limited. The East Asian states, most obviously imperial China, were large and extremely powerful, and the tools of sea power had limited impact. British efforts to improve their trading and strategic position in the region, most notably in the Macartney Mission of 1793, were brusquely rebuffed by the Chinese, confident in the political leverage of their own continental dominance.

This changed dramatically in the period from 1830 to 1860. In part, this was a product of domestic changes in China, which weakened the dominant state in the region and reduced its ability to resist foreign interference. However, of equal significance were technological changes that both incentivized and facilitated far greater Western encroachment in the region. The increasing globalization of trade on the back of industrialized manufacturing and new communication technologies ensured that East Asian, European, and American economies were ever more interconnected. This acted as a pull factor, drawing Western powers into the region and raising perceptions of its importance. At the same time, new military and naval capabilities greatly enhanced the ability of Western powers to coerce Asian ones and in doing so shifted the balance of power between land and sea. Developments in steam, artillery, and armor greatly increased the existing gap in capabilities between European navies and Asian ones, something symbolized by the famous British East India Company iron frigate *Nemesis*. These new technologies allowed Western nations to exercise command of the sea more efficiently and sustainably in the region and project power from the sea. A crucial aspect of this was the vastly increased capability for naval power projection to reach deep inside a country and exploit major river systems often hundreds of miles inland. When combined with other technological developments, such as in small arms, and wider scientific progress in areas, such as navigation, this greatly increased the strength of European maritime powers at the expense of East Asian land-based ones. As Rebecca Matzke has written of the First Anglo-Chinese War (1839–42), Britain used "its naval forces—and the military forces the British navy could project—to coerce the Chinese into a settlement on British terms."[7] This pattern was replicated across Asia, resulting in the infamous "unequal treaties." Britain, in particular, was able to exploit these circumstances and reduce China to an almost semicolonial state and in doing so developed an extraordinary level of power in the region. This meant that the center of gravity of any contest for supremacy in the East Asian region shifted away from the land and firmly into the maritime sphere.

British control of this sphere ensured that in 1880 there was no problem of Asia. Naval power buttressed British dominance across the Indo-Pacific region, and there was little meaningful imperial competition. The Royal Navy instead focused on what would now be described as the maintenance of good order at sea, in the expectation that British trade would benefit most from the provision of this common good.[8] Over the following two decades, the British near monopoly on both naval force and maritime commerce in East Asian waters was slowly eroded. China had long been recognized as a huge potential market, and this began to draw newly industrializing nations into the region, taking advantage of the security provided by Pax Britannica. Additionally, the period saw a return of American trade to East Asia following a midcentury hiatus driven largely by the American Civil War. Trade, as so often is the case, was soon followed by government, and although the American military presence in East Asia remained small, it became something of a diplomatic priority. This was best symbolized by Secretary of State John Hay's Open Door Policy demanding free access for all states to Chinese markets. While this step was viewed by the British as somewhat presumptuous coming from a power with little in the way of military force to back it up, the idea gained widespread support as a way of avoiding escalating tensions. The American return to East Asian markets was mirrored by a growth in German and to a lesser extent French trade, something that again led to an increase in state interest in the region.

These shifts posed certain problems to the British but were relatively easy to anticipate and did not really disrupt the overall balance of power. Two other developments proved far more challenging to the imperial system in East Asia. The first of these was the rapid progress made by Asian states. Following the humiliations of the midcentury, both the Japanese and the Chinese had worked hard to catch up militarily and technologically with the main European powers of the time. The First Sino-Japanese War (1894–95) demonstrated this progress.[9] The Battle of the Yalu River and the Battle of Weihaiwei saw the Japanese fleet destroy the Chinese Beiyang Fleet in some of the first large actions between ironclad warships. The wider conflict highlighted the continuing fragility of the Chinese state and served to increase the sense of there being a relative power vacuum at the heart of East Asia, drawing imperial competitors in. On the other hand, it also established Japan as a major power in the region with considerable naval forces backed up by a modernizing military. This signaled the rise of a regional competitor seeking to play its part in filling the existing power vacuum.

A crucial aspect of this development was that for the first time in almost a century, East Asia was the primary theater for one of the imperial competitors.

Previously the dominance of the British in the Indo-Pacific was underwritten by their control of European waters, allowing them to station comparatively limited forces in theater. Although the Japanese as yet posed little threat to the British, their focused military strength in theater signified a major shift and one that would continue to cause problems for Britain through 1941. Other European powers proved more concerned about the rise of Japan and in particular their territorial demands in northeast China. In the peace treaty at the end of the First Sino-Japanese War, China ceded to Japan the Liaodong Peninsula, including the harbor at Port Arthur. Russia objected to what it saw as interference in its sphere of influence and, together with France and Germany, mounted the Triple Intervention to force the Japanese to abandon their demands. A coercive measure backed by the superior naval forces of the three European powers, the Triple Intervention represented a major escalation in imperial competition in the region and had long-term implications, especially in Tokyo. The perceived high-handed action by the European powers consolidated the position of those among the Japanese elites who called for the country to take action to mitigate such military and diplomatic weakness in the future.

The final development that created Mahan's "problem of Asia" was the tying together of the Russian Empire into a single strategic entity. Russia had long had Far Eastern possessions, but these had been isolated from the western heart of the country. The most effective way to move material from Moscow or St. Petersburg to the Russian Far East had been by sea, which left the possessions highly vulnerable to a naval power. Infrastructure developments at the end of the nineteenth century, most notably the Trans-Siberian Railway, began to change this and established Russia as a first-rate East Asian land power. To buttress this, Russia began to rapidly build a Pacific fleet of considerable strength. Russia soon leveraged its new position to secure major concessions from China in terms of both land and economic rights, which culminated in 1898 with securing a lease on the Liaodong Peninsula, of which the Triple Intervention had recently deprived the Japanese.

The growth of Russian power in the region created major problems for the British and set up the period of intense imperial competition that followed.[10] The reasons for this are multiple but are related to the contrasting natures of British and Russian power. The first and most essential point is that this was a rivalry between a whale and a bear—a sea power against a land power. This rivalry was being contested at numerous locations on the edges of the broad Asian landmass, including the Ottoman Empire, Persia, and Afghanistan. However, up until this point, geography had determined that the only way a developed Western power could intervene in East Asia was by sea. This had ensured British dominance of the region and meant that Russia had been a relatively minor player. The shifts in technology and infrastructure upset that balance.

Furthermore, the very nature of Russian power was different; it was a power *of* the region in a way that none of the other European powers were. Russia had territory in the region that was neither a colony nor a base, and it viewed territory, as opposed to trade, as its primary purpose. This difference fed through into the way Russia sought to exercise power. The Russian Pacific Fleet was built up because it was apparent to all that the maritime sphere was essential to controlling the region. However, at heart, this was a force designed for territorial defense, not the protection of trade and broader maritime security. It was, after all, the navy of a continental power, not a trading nation.[11] It was to describe this force that Mahan coined the term "fortress fleet," something that sums up the different conception of sea power that lay behind its construction. On a more direct level, the development of Russian power in the region challenged British supremacy, and the Russian Pacific Fleet even began to call into question Britain's immediate maritime supremacy. Worse still, it sparked off an arms race with the Japanese, who were determined to maintain a force that could challenge the Russians.

The gradual intrusion of Western powers into East Asia from 1880 to 1900, when combined with the rise of Japan, propelled the region into a new phase of rivalry. In less than two decades, military and political developments had eroded Britain's position as East Asian hegemon. In particular, the strategic advantage bestowed by British naval strength, one that in previous decades had allowed it to secure considerable strategic effect with limited material power, was now under threat. In the emerging regional competition, sea power was perceived to be of vital importance; therefore, states worked hard to shape the environment in which that power was exercised. This took two major forms. The first was shaping maritime geography through the development of bases. These were crucial signaling tools within peacetime naval diplomacy, embodying and facilitating presence. At the same time, they would provide a crucial capability in supporting naval forces during a conflict. The second, interrelated way in which states sought to shape the environment was through diplomacy. All the competing powers sought to use statecraft to improve their strategic position, with naval strength, basing, and maritime geography being the central considerations. This intense competition to shape the maritime strategic environment took place across the decade from 1894 and would prove crucial in determining how competition for power in the region played out from 1904 onward.

BASES SHAPING THE MARITIME GEOGRAPHY

Over the course of the nineteenth century, naval forces had proved to be the vital tool in exercising control in East Asia, underpinning the dominance of European states, especially Britain. However, this military advantage was absolutely reliant on a complex network of overseas bases. The waters of the Indo-Pacific were vast and a very long way from the home ports and industry for most of the imperial competitors. Thus, to maintain a force on station required major infrastructure for coaling, docking, and repairs. This requirement grew considerably toward the end of the nineteenth century, when developments in naval technology, notably triple-expansion steam engines, made warships more complex and fragile pieces of equipment.

As the established power, Britain had a broad network of existing bases providing essential support for its naval presence and a grounding for its ability to exert power in the region. Adm. Sir John Fisher, the first sea lord from 1904 to 1910, talked of the five keys that locked up the world, and in his eyes Singapore was the key to the Indo-Pacific.[12] In truth, it might be better to describe Singapore as the pivot around which British control of the wider region revolved. In this respect, it was supported by India and Australia, which provided larger bases in the Indian Ocean and the southwest Pacific. India, of course, was more than just a base—it acted as almost a secondary metropole, an arsenal in eastern waters providing a pool of resources in the region that no other power could even begin to match. This network of bases ensured that competition in this period was less about the Indo-Pacific and more narrowly focused on East Asia. Here Britain once again held an established position, with Hong Kong acting as both a trading entrepôt and a vital base for the Royal Navy. By the early twentieth century, both the French and the Americans had also established bases in the South China Sea in Indochina and the Philippines, respectively. The British monitored these developments; however, the limited naval presence of these powers and the proximity of Hong Kong ensured they were not of major concern.

The true battle for strategic position took place farther north. It was sparked off by Japan's success in the war against China and its attempt to retain Port Arthur and the Liaodong Peninsula in the resultant peace treaty. The Triple Intervention forced the Japanese to abandon these demands, but in doing so it brought competition in the region into the open. The Germans were the first to move. They had been hoping to establish a base in the region for a number of years, and toward the end of 1897 they exploited the murder of two German missionaries in order to seize the port at Tsingtao.[13] This was formalized the following year with an agreement for Germany to lease the port and establish a de facto colony in the Shandong Peninsula. The Russians almost immediately followed by securing similar arrangements in Liaodong and rapidly building up a major naval base at Port Arthur.

These developments posed a serious problem for the British and the Japanese. In particular, the British position in the region was founded on their naval supremacy, and while there was limited overall challenge to this, the new bases undermined their control of the Yellow and East China Seas. Furthermore, the leased territories provided focal points for German and Russian economic expansion into northeast China. The British had to respond. As Assistant Undersecretary. Francis Bertie, responsible for the Far Eastern Department in the Foreign Office, noted, "If we desire to have some counter poise to the preponderance of Russian and German influence at Peking [Beijing], we must have some point of advantage in the north."[14] It was well understood in Britain that naval power and presence were crucial tools of influence. A base offered both the material backing necessary to exercise naval power and ensured a visual expression of British naval strength would be in theater consistently. For this reason, the British government pushed hard to be allowed to establish a naval base in northeast China. In March 1898 London ordered the commander in chief, China Station, to dispatch a force to the waters around Port Arthur that would be comfortably superior to the Russian forces in the region.[15] This statement was designed to coerce the Chinese into agreeing to Britain's leasing a base and to deter any Russian attempt to interfere. The move proved successful, and it was agreed that the British would lease the port of Weihaiwei, which had been seized by the Japanese three years previously and was due to be returned to China. The port provided a northern base for the ships on the British China Station and helped counterbalance the growth of Russian and German strength in the region.

From the perspective of the European powers, these developments largely canceled each other out. The leasing of Weihaiwei and the regular visits of the Royal Navy to these waters reasserted the position of the British as the principal maritime power in the region. Russia's growing naval strength in East Asia, when combined with its military forces, caused concerns in London. However, this was part of a much wider Russian challenge, and it was accepted that only so much could be achieved through shaping maritime geography. Others could not afford to be so phlegmatic. The increasing incursion of European powers into northeast China was the source of considerable concern in Tokyo. There was a clear sense that these powers were taking advantage of the Japanese victory over China while depriving Japan of the spoils. It was only with great reluctance that Japan had given up Weihaiwei, and although the British appeared to be the least threatening of the powers, it was clear that the country had been left out of the imperial game. From 1895 to 1898, the geography of the region had shifted significantly to Japan's disadvantage, and consequently it was necessary for Japan to look to other measures to restore the balance.[16] One of these measures was a focus on home bases. In the reforms of 1889, the Imperial Navy created the Maizuru Naval District, centered on the port of Maizuru. Over the following years its strategic location meant considerable efforts were made to improve its docking facilities and develop its arsenal. Maizuru was Japan's home response to the wider game of strategic basing in northeast Asia, albeit one that did little to remove the frustration at the country's treatment by the European powers.

Basing was the most dynamic means through which the imperial competitors sought to shape maritime geography in this period. However, there were certain underlying principles that remained very important. The most significant of these was an acceptance of the interconnectedness of oceans. The problem of Asia was widely seen as being the most dangerous area of imperial competition at the time, and much attention was focused on the region, including this scramble for bases. However, the size of naval forces deployed in the region remained relatively small. Ultimately it was believed that if it ever came to blows, the fate of the region would be determined by actions in European waters, not East Asian ones. In his review of Mahan's writings on the problem of Asia, Reginald Custance, British director of naval intelligence from March 1899 to November 1902, focused on this aspect. He noted that Mahan "emphasises the view, that I have long held, that it is vital for us to maintain our communications with the East via the Mediterranean."[17] The Mediterranean was likely to be the primary naval theater in any European war and was the location of the Royal Navy's premier fleet. Success in this theater would then flow on across the globe, releasing ships to quash any isolated opposition in more remote regions, such as East Asia.

NAVAL POWER AND DIPLOMATIC INFLUENCE

Through the development of the base at Weihaiwei and Britain's continued strong position in the crucial European theaters, British authorities had considerable success in using strategic maritime geography to limit the challenge from other imperial competitors. In the longer term, however, the fundamental threat posed by Russia to Britain's position in East Asia remained. The nature of Russian land power proved extremely difficult for the British to contend with, and there was a perception that Russian influence in the region was growing. Even in the maritime sphere there were problems. Although the Russian navy as a whole still remained far smaller than the Royal Navy, its forces in the Pacific were expanding rapidly. Financial concerns, in part brought on by the massive expenditure on the Boer War, meant that Britain was unwilling to increase naval construction to match the Russians.

Yet this was not a mere question of material capabilities. In a direct conflict between Britain and Russia, the potential difference in military capabilities would have continued to be manageable. However, the British faced greater diplomatic issues. Russia had a long-standing alliance with France, and although the primary focus of this was to ensure security in Europe, it still posed difficulties.

France and Russia were the second and third naval powers, respectively, and together their fleets could potentially rival the Royal Navy. More prosaically, if a conflict with Russia were to occur, Britain would remain deeply concerned about France, even if Paris did not directly intervene. This would then limit the naval forces Britain could safely transfer out of European waters. Put simply, the Franco-Russian alliance was sufficiently strong to impose major checks on Britain's ability to exercise power in East Asia, and barring a massive increase in naval expenditure, there was no easy solution.

Britain was not the only power feeling a little uneasy about the strategic situation. Japan had surprised many contemporary observers with its victory over the Chinese, and its officials believed that this had earned them a seat at the table of major powers in the region. The Triple Intervention and resultant failure of Japan to secure a position in the scramble for bases had proved a salutary lesson. The European powers would not accept Japan unless they were forced to do so, and while the Japanese were more than willing to take a belligerent line, they had little hope if facing a coalition of more than one power. As such, they needed an insurance policy, someone to keep the ring while Japan reasserted its position in the region.

It was this combination of factors that led to the signing of the Anglo-Japanese alliance agreement in 1902.[18] In many respects, the alliance seemed an unlikely combination, connecting the famously isolationist Britain with the newest arrival in the concert of major powers. However, when viewed from a different perspective, it makes more sense. The alliance was primarily a naval agreement between two maritime powers bound by their opposition to the major land power, Russia. The terms of the agreement stated that Britain or Japan would be obliged to come to the assistance of its ally if the ally were attacked by two or more other powers. The aim of this was to limit the likelihood of either Britain or Japan having to face a combination of powers. From a British perspective, this was primarily an alliance for deterrence. The agreement would ensure that Britain would either face Russia alone or would face the combination of France and Russia in alliance with Japan. In either situation, Britain could ensure naval supremacy in East Asia and beyond. It was believed that this very public insurance policy would deter the Russians from attempting to further challenge Britain's position in the region.

Unlike Britain, Japan was not a status quo power, and thus the alliance had rather different implications. The agreement removed the threat that Japan would be isolated and left facing a combination of European powers, as it had in 1895. This provided the safety net that Japan required to more forcefully challenge growing Russian political and economic influence in Korea and northeast China. It would be incorrect to say that the alliance led directly to the outbreak of the Russo-Japanese War, but it did facilitate Tokyo's demands being pressed in a far more forceful manner. As such, from the perspective of the Japanese, this was an alliance that bolstered Japan's status and implicitly recognized their ambitions, thus freeing them to challenge the status quo.

The British were well aware that the signing of the alliance made war between Russia and Japan more likely, but they did not necessarily see this as a problem. The British prime minister, Arthur Balfour, noted in 1903, "It must be remembered that though Russia's resources in men are unlimited, her resources in money are not, and if she chooses to squander both her naval and her financial strength in this extreme corner of the world, she is rendering herself impotent everywhere else."[19] He concluded positively and declared that "my belief is that a war between those two countries would render Russia innocuous for some little time to come."[20] Thus, the prospect of a war in the Far East would actually improve the security situation of the British Empire across the globe by distracting its primary rival.

LIMITED WAR IN THE AGE OF IMPERIAL COMPETITION

This volume focuses on the use of naval power as a tool of policy in peacetime as opposed to war, and so I am going to pass over the actual events of the Russo-Japanese War (1904–5) and instead focus on how its impacts reshaped the region and the role of naval power within it. At Port Arthur, and then in the Battle of Tsushima, the Japanese overcame distinct numerical inferiority to destroy both the Russian Pacific Fleet and Baltic Fleet. These two victories would effectively remove Russia as a naval power. On land, the Japanese successes had been less startling but equally effective. They had pushed the Russians back out of most of Manchuria and secured Japan's political hold over Korea. Of equal importance, the Japanese victories had undermined the perception of Russia as *the* great land power whose advance into the region was inexorable.

The scale of Russia's losses in terms of matériel and military power was substantial, but arguably more significant was the economic and political damage. The war virtually bankrupted the Russian government and sparked a wave of protests that left the country on the brink of revolution. These factors combined to largely remove Russia from the strategic equation, resulting in an extremely benign political situation in East Asia for Japan and its ally Britain. As the ramifications of the conflict spread to Europe, the situation became even more favorable. During the Russo-Japanese War, the British were very concerned that the conflict might escalate, particularly drawing in France as a result of their alliance with Russia. However, following the end of the conflict France very rapidly moved from being a potential enemy to a close friend. The ramifications of the new Russian weakness were soon apparent in Europe, and France suddenly felt very exposed to German strength, with little hope of support from St. Petersburg. This new security situation at home saw France move much closer to Britain, and this further strengthened the position of the Anglo-Japanese alliance in East Asia.

Five years previously, Mahan had suggested that maritime powers could successfully manage to hold back the spread of the great land power, Russia, and in doing so resolve much of the problem of Asia. The Battles of Mukden and Tsushima proved him to be correct. The use of military power, backed by superior naval forces, to attack the extremities of Russian territory was exactly what Mahan had suggested. The war had confirmed the crucial importance of the maritime sphere in the control of East Asia. The naval strength of the Japanese had provided security against any direct attack on their homeland and had allowed them to exploit the flexibility and capacity of maritime communications.[21] It was not without reason that it was the defeat of the Russian navy at Tsushima that finally brought the czar to the peace table. If the broad outline of the war did not shock many Western observers, then the identity of the victor did. Mahan had suggested that such a conflict might be fought by Britain or perhaps even a grand coalition of maritime powers. That the Japanese managed to do this alone, with nothing more than the safety net offered by the Anglo-Japanese alliance, proved to be a profound shock to the Western nations.

The Japanese victory over Russia was not merely the victory of a small power over a far larger one—it was also the victory of an Asian state over a Western great power. Despite a widespread distrust of Russia, Japanese success was viewed with considerable concern across much of the globe. Discussion of a "yellow peril" was widespread, and fear of further Japanese expansion was soon noticeable around the Pacific Rim, from Australia to California. One area where this type of reaction was notably absent was in the Royal Navy's response to the conflict. On signing the Anglo-Japanese alliance agreement in 1902, the Admiralty had to address the issue of who would command a joint fleet in the event of war. The British acknowledged that, in the short term at least, Japanese forces might represent the major component of any such fleet. Despite this, the first naval lord, Lord Walter Kerr, bluntly stated that "if the two Fleets act together it is desirable that the English admiral should be held to be senior and given local rank as necessary."[22] Following early Japanese victories, the British naval attaché wrote back to London suggesting that the evidence of the war meant that "I am very certain now that the time has come when we may, with the utmost confidence, entrust our ships to the control of a Japanese admiral, when we would sacrifice sentiment and tradition for the sake of the increased efficiency of concerted action."[23] The Admiralty immediately agreed. This represented the most tangible aspect of a wider shift within the Anglo-Japanese alliance.[24] Britain was still undeniably the senior partner, but the relationship between the two powers had become far more balanced.

A NEW NAVAL DIPLOMACY FOR NEW CHALLENGES

The outcome of the Russo-Japanese War represented a huge victory for both parties in the Anglo-Japanese alliance. Japan had successfully established itself as the leading power in Korea and northeast China and had removed the Russian threat, which at times had appeared almost existential. The war also erased the pain of the Triple Intervention and established Japan as a major power whose interests could no longer be ignored. In many respects Britain had benefited even more, certainly in light of its very limited contribution. The rivalry with Russia had been the primary strategic concern in London for over thirty years, and East Asia was only one part of this larger struggle. The Russo-Japanese War ensured that Russia would be unable to threaten British interests anywhere in the world in the foreseeable future. This promised a benign outlook for imperial security that most Victorian statesmen could only have dreamt of. Britain's position as the dominant power in the Indo-Pacific looked more assured than ever. Best of all, this had been achieved without having to fire a shot or even spend a penny.

In East Asia the new maritime strategic geography looked exceptionally favorable to the Anglo-Japanese alliance, with the Russians removed from the Liaodong Peninsula and lacking a naval base south of Vladivostok. The balance of power at sea looked, if anything, even more favorable, with the destruction of the Russian fleet and the altered position of the French ensuring there were no meaningful threats in the region.

This success was impressive, but it brought its own problems. The Anglo-Japanese alliance had always been a slightly unusual pairing but had worked because of the shared strategic interests and complementary aims of the two states. The most important of these interests was a fear of Russia and a desire to restrict any further expansion of Russian power in the region. The most important aims were for Britain to retain global naval dominance and for Japan to secure its place among the world's top powers. In this respect, the alliance had proved effective—in fact, too effective. By destroying Russian power in East Asia and removing the Russian threat for the immediate future, the Russo-Japanese War also destroyed the bedrock of the alliance. Over the course of the decade until the outbreak of World War I, the alliance was forced to evolve to consider the new strategic circumstances. It increasingly became a tool to tie together states on divergent political paths.

Naval diplomacy had always been an essential part of the wider Anglo-Japanese relationship, and this continued following the conclusion of the Russo-Japanese War. In October 1905, within a month of peace being signed, the ships of the Royal Navy's China Squadron made a formal visit to Japan. There were great celebrations in Yokohama, and the commander in chief of

China Station, Adm. Sir Gerard Noel, and his captains traveled to Tokyo for an audience with the emperor. At a formal reception the Japanese navy minister, Adm. Baron Yamamoto Gonbee, spoke of the close connection between the navies and the extent to which the Japanese had learned from the British. He went on to note, "I hope and trust that relationships between us will continue to be as intimate as they have been in the past, and even more so, if such indeed could be possible."[25]

This represented the high point of Anglo-Japanese relations, as over the course of the following years there were increasing points of tension. The destruction of the Russian threat had removed a key aspect of the problem of Asia; however, its root cause—namely, the power vacuum in China—remained. Mahan believed that this could be managed by maritime powers, whose interests were broadly aligned around commerce. He suggested that such powers would not be interested in subjugation of the region, merely access to it, and that their forces "resting on the sea, can only serve to frustrate attempts to exclude themselves."[26] There was some truth in this classical interpretation of the relative strength of maritime alliances over those between territorially focused powers. However, the reality of the situation was more complex, and neither Britain nor Japan fully embraced this evenhanded ideal of unfettered access for all. This was further exacerbated by the impetus the war gave to those, particularly in the Japanese army, who saw the nation's future lying as an Asian land power as opposed to a maritime empire.[27] Without the unifying power of an external rival, Britain and Japan began to drift apart, and their positions as the two leading powers in the region began to see them viewing each other more as rivals than allies.

The Anglo-Japanese alliance increasingly shifted in the period after 1905 to become focused on managing these points of tension and, perhaps ironically, on preventing a naval rivalry developing between the two powers. At a time when Britain was facing a growing threat from Germany, anything that could be done to prevent a new naval arms race in East Asia was very positive. The British dominions, notably Australia, New Zealand, and Canada, were deeply concerned about the growth of Japanese power and hoped for a more robust response from London, including abandoning the alliance. However, as the foreign secretary, Sir Edward Grey, explained to Dominion leaders in 1911, if Britain were to abandon the alliance, "not only would the strategic situation be altered immediately by our having to count the Japanese fleet as it now exists as possible enemies, but Japan would at once set to work to build a fleet more powerful than she would have [done] if the alliance did not exist."[28] Thus, the naval diplomacy shifted from being about exerting power and deterring other states to instead being focused on tying two potential rivals together. Neither Britain nor Japan wanted to be drawn into a costly arms race, and a decision by either party to pull out would be seen as a statement of aggression. The alliance continued, offering a useful framework to restrain any specific tensions; however, it could not prevent the two nations from gradually drifting apart.

Part of what held this alliance together was a clear appreciation of the strength of the other side. It may seem misplaced to talk of deterrence within an alliance structure, but an understanding of the relative strength on both sides acted as a check on those seeking to bring the quiet rivalry into the open. Using modern political science parlance, "reassurance" of each other's strength helped restrain any centrifugal forces. Eventually, however, the strategic realities created by the alliance began to undermine this very process. In mid-1905, following the Japanese success at Tsushima, the Admiralty recalled the British battleships from the China Station. Strategically, the logic of the decision was sound. The Anglo-Japanese alliance had an overwhelming preponderance of forces in the region, and there was no need for the British to station capital ships in Far Eastern waters. The specific decision was also driven by the increasing pressure to focus ships in European waters in the face of the growing German threat. This meant that from 1905 to 1913, there were no major British or imperial fleet units east of Suez.

This decision was a clear signal of the continued strategic value of the alliance to Britain and of the growing influence of Japan as a regional power. However, it is wrong to view this as a "recalling the legions" moment or suggest that it signaled an end of British dominance of East Asian waters. The massive naval construction program mounted in Britain from 1909 was a clear statement of the power of Britannia, and there was a widespread realization that maritime security in East Asia ultimately depended on the balance of power in Europe. This did not stop Admiral Noel from bemoaning that the removal of his battleships was "truly a Little Englander policy reducing our show of naval power abroad."[29] Whether he realized it or not, Noel had struck upon the key issue with this particular policy. While the removal of British capital ships from the region did not directly imperil the interests of the British or indeed undermine their dominance of the region, it did reduce their show of force. The absence of a strong naval presence in East Asia undermined British naval diplomacy. The heavy reliance on the Japanese navy for the control of regional waters appeared to signal a weakness in British commitment to the region. In turn, this fed Japanese perceptions of their own strength and position, something that would become more apparent from 1914 onward.

The absence of tangible signs of British naval supremacy also fed fears in the dominions that they were being abandoned by London in the face of the "yellow peril." It was this fear that prompted the feverish reaction to the visit of the Great White Fleet to Sydney in 1908, as Australians looked to America for the first time as a possible source of security. The perception and the reality of naval power in East Asia were very different in this period. The British fleet was vastly superior to anything the Japanese, or any other power for that matter, could put to sea. However, this force was focused on European waters and never ventured out to East Asia. The interconnectedness of oceans may have been understood by naval officers and policymakers but not by the public at large. The British failed to appreciate that it was not merely the reality of naval power that mattered. It was a failure of perception and not reality that undermined Britain's position in the region in the years after the Russo-Japanese War.

CONCLUSION

Over the course of the decade from 1895 to 1905, Britain and Japan successfully used coercion, deterrence, diplomacy, and—where appropriate—limited conflict to manage the maritime geography and strategic situation in East Asia. In doing so they defeated the major manifestation of the problem of Asia—namely, the interference of Russian continentalist aspirations in the region. These efforts were fundamentally grounded in naval power. It provided both sword and shield, facilitating the intervention of the maritime powers where and when they chose and protecting their interests against similar actions by others. However, its influence extended well beyond these purely military functions and was intertwined with other tools of national power. Throughout this period, naval force had a symbiotic relationship with diplomacy. It proved an effective "stick" to deter and coerce, while more positive engagement was the bedrock of the Anglo-Japanese alliance both before and after 1905. At the same time, diplomacy helped to support naval power through basing and other efforts to shape the maritime geography of the region. The success of these efforts would ensure the dominance of the region by maritime powers for the next forty years until Russia, as the Soviet Union, returned as a major force in East Asian affairs. Ironically, the management of the power of the Soviet Union would far more closely replicate Mahan's predictions in *The Problem of Asia* than did the situation in his own lifetime. It was only after 1945 that a "maritime" coalition of Britain, Germany, Japan, and the United States came together to restrain the influence of the power dominating the Eurasian heartland.

The Anglo-Japanese alliance was, in many respects, extraordinarily successful and demonstrated the value of alliance building to maritime powers. Mahan was correct to suggest that the nature of the seas as a "great commons" and the focus of maritime powers on commercial access to territory, rather than direct control over it, made it easier to establish stable common ground for such alliances. This was a key aspect of what enabled the alliance to work despite Britain being largely a status quo power and Japan being a revisionist one.

The Russo-Japanese War removed the Russian threat in the region and reasserted the dominance of maritime powers. In and of itself, this should not have proved problematic to a maritime alliance such as that between Britain and Japan. However, the reality was different. The war had ended Russian incursion into the region but did not address the root cause of the problem of Asia—namely, the power vacuum in China, which was drawing in imperial competitors. Over the years after 1905, and especially from 1915 onward, there developed a competition between the maritime powers for control of the region. Despite Mahan's suggestions otherwise, even maritime powers in an era of imperial competition were invariably seeking an advantage. British dominance at sea was no longer unchallengeable. Its weakness, both perceived and real, led its rivals, notably Japan and the United States, to seek to expand their own influence in the region. This dynamic of rivalry between the three major maritime powers, once again driven by the power vacuum in China, would be the key driver in international relations in East Asia over the following three decades.

NOTES

1. Alfred T. Mahan, *The Problem of Asia and Its Effect upon International Politics* (London: Little, Brown, 1900).
2. Mahan, *Problem of Asia*, 96; see also 34, 124. Mahan's conception of the problem of Asia was broader and encompassed much of the Asian landmass. However, the issues in East Asia were widely regarded as being the most pressing, and it is to these that Mahan regularly returns.
3. Mahan, v.
4. Mahan, 25, 27.
5. Mahan, 36–46.
6. Gerald Graham, *The Politics of Naval Supremacy: Studies in British Maritime Ascendency* (Cambridge: Cambridge University Press, 1965), 105.
7. Rebecca Matzke, *Deterrence through Strength: British Naval Power and Foreign Policy under Pax Britannica* (Lincoln: University of Nebraska Press, 2011), 142.
8. The provision of good order at sea was an enduring task of the Royal Navy. However, in this period it was primarily seen as a domestic-facing task, facilitating the secure flow of British trade. The discussion of it as a common good only really developed from the later stages of World War I onward.
9. S. M. C. Paine, *The Sino-Japanese War of 1894–1895: Perceptions, Power, and Primacy* (Cambridge: Cambridge University Press, 2003).
10. T. G. Otte, *The China Question: Great Power Rivalry and British Isolation, 1894–1905* (Oxford: Oxford University Press, 2007).
11. Nicholas Papastratigakis, *Russian Imperialism and Naval Power: Military Strategy and the Build-Up to the Russo-Japanese War* (London: I. B. Tauris, 2011).
12. P. K. Kemp, *The Fisher Papers*, vol. 1 (London: Navy Records Society, 1960), 161.

13. Terrell Gottschall, *By Order of the Kaiser: Otto von Diederichs and the Rise of the Imperial German Navy, 1865–1902* (Annapolis, MD: Naval Institute Press, 2003), 136–80.

14. Bertie memorandum, March 14, 1898, quoted in *British Documents on the Origins of the War*, vol. 1, ed. G. P. Gooch and H. Temperley (London: HM Stationery Office, 1927), 17.

15. Ian Nish, "The Royal Navy and the Taking of Weihaiwei, 1898–1905," *Mariners Mirror* 54, no. 1 (1968), https://doi.org/10.1080/00253359.1968.10659417.

16. Urs Matthias Zachmann, "Guarding the Gates of Our East Asia: Japanese Reactions to the Far Eastern Crisis as a Prelude to the War," in *Rethinking the Russo-Japanese War, 1904–05*, vol. 1, ed. Rotem Kowner (Folkstone, UK: Global Orient, 2007).

17. "The Problem of Asia: Articles by Capt. A. T. Mahan," Custance minute, June 5, 1900, ADM 1/7462, National Archives (UK).

18. Ian Nish, *The Anglo-Japanese Alliance: The Diplomacy of Two Island Empires, 1894–1907*, 2nd ed. (London: Athlone Press, 1985).

19. Balfour to Selborne, December 29, 1903, Add Ms 4707, British Library.

20. Balfour to Selborne, December 29, 1903.

21. In both his official history of the war and his war college lectures, Julian Corbett emphasises the extent to which the Japanese fought a "British" war. See Julian Corbett, *Maritime Operations in the Russo-Japanese War 1904–1905* (Annapolis, MD: Naval Institute Press, 1994), and "Lecture Notes: Russo-Japanese War," Corbett Papers, box 2, Liddell Hart Centre for Military Archives.

22. "Memorandum on Joint Action," Kerr minute, June 19, 1902, ADM 116/1231, National Archives (UK).

23. "Remarks on Arrangements for Concerted Action by the Allied Fleets in Time of War," May 27, 1904, ADM 116/1231, National Archives (UK).

24. For a broader discussion, see Richard Dunley, "'The Warrior Has Always Shewed Himself Greater than His Weapons': The Royal Navy's Interpretation of the Russo-Japanese War 1904–5," *War and Society* 34, no. 4 (2015), https://doi.org/10.1080/07292473.2015.1128655.

25. "Minister of Marine (Ad'l Baron Yamamoto) Speech at Tokio Naval Club," October 1905, NOE/15/A/1, National Maritime Museum (UK).

26. Mahan, *Problem of Asia*, 122–23, 133–34.

27. Ian Nish, "The Clash of Two Continental Empires: The Land War Reconsidered," in Kowner, *Rethinking the Russo-Japanese War*, 66.

28. Committee of Imperial Defence meeting, May 26, 1911, CAB 38/18/40, 111, National Archives (UK).

29. Noel to Satow, June 28, 1905, PRO 30/33/9/23, National Archives (UK).

9

The Far East between the World Wars

Daniel Moran

This chapter is concerned with the international history of the Far East from the end of World War I to the onset of World War II, with particular reference to American policy in the region. It is a familiar story and a sobering one. The aim here is not to retell it but to interrogate some of its major episodes in light of the central themes of this volume: great-power competition in a region where maritime geography has exerted a powerful influence on the formulation of strategy, the use of force, and the pursuit of deterrence.

In the interwar period, the outstanding feature of Asian maritime geography was the insular position of Japan. Scholars sometimes propose that, in defiance of its geography, Japan's strategic outlook resembled that of a continental state, to the extent that it was concerned with the direct control of territory rather than with the rationing of strategic and economic access among an array of allies, partners, and rivals—the central concern of maritime strategy.[1] It is a fair point, provided it is not taken to imply some kind of elementary misunderstanding on the part of the Japanese. Japan's position in this period resembled that of England at the time of Agincourt (1415), a battle fought to advance what proved to be untenable territorial claims against a continental opponent of superior natural strength. Japan may have hoped for something more like the Battle of Plassey (1757), at which a few hundred British soldiers led an army of local allies to victory over the forces of the Mughal Empire, thereby securing the East India Company's control of Bengal and eventually of the subcontinent as a whole. However, conditions in China, the only possible place for such a cascading triumph, were nothing like what had prevailed in India two centuries before. Japan's policy of imperial expansion was finally undone by the dawning realization of this inimical fact.

It was easy enough to imagine that the warlords who seized control in China following the collapse of the Qing Dynasty (1911) bore some structural resemblance to the local rulers whose co-optation underpinned the Raj. Yet there was no grassroots opposition to the British in India comparable to that presented by Chinese nationalism, nor was there any organized force capable of mobilizing it against outsiders. As much as anything, it is the mass politics of the twentieth century that disabled the tried-and-true methods of divide-and-rule that the Western powers had perfected and on which the Japanese expected to rely. Japan's proclamation in 1940 of a "co-prosperity sphere," in which all Asians were supposed to have a share, marked Tokyo's belated recognition that times had changed. By then, the Japanese army was fully engaged in China, a commitment for which no form of maritime pressure could have substituted and from which there could be no retreat.

Japan's insular geography mattered less because of the leverage it afforded than because it made Japan vulnerable to pressure from other maritime states. The traditional tools of maritime strategy constitute a virtuous circle: seaborne trade, the naval power that trade supports (and that navies protect), and the political relationships that arise from and help to sustain them. Such tools would doubtless have meant a great deal to Japan had it succeeded in bringing China fully into its orbit. While that enterprise was underway, however, the characteristic instruments of sea power were of greater value to Japan's opponents. This is especially true for the United States, which emerged in this period as Japan's main rival for influence in Asia.

Eight times zones of saltwater separate the United States from Asia. Any American attempt to drive political outcomes there requires that this vast sea space be mastered. The true proportions of this challenge were poorly grasped in a period when American thinking about war at sea was dominated by the requirements of hemispheric defense. Thoughtful sailors may have deprecated such an outlook, but it corresponded to what American politics was prepared to tolerate. Among the color-coded war plans produced by the US Navy between the world wars, the only one that envisioned major operations outside the Western Hemisphere was Plan Orange. "Orange" meant Japan.[2]

America's implied willingness to go out of its way to fight the Japanese was not an expression of aggressive intent. It merely recognized Japan's relative weakness. No one seriously imagined that a Japanese fleet would present itself for destruction in American waters. Regardless, the aim of US policy in Asia was always to reduce the risk of war there, which is why naval arms control was so integral to its policy. That policy's principal instrument was not naval power but trade. Trade was also the main American interest in Asia. This convergence of ends and means is worth pondering.

It is common for modern industrial nations to identify trade as a vital interest—a high bar if "vital" is taken at anything like its literal, life-and-death meaning. Nevertheless, the claim can sometimes be true. It was arguably true for Japan, indisputably so if one considers the resource requirements of its increasingly militarized foreign policy. It was not true for the United States. Trade has always made up a relatively small share of American national income compared to other advanced economies. In the interwar period, the total value of imports and exports together peaked in 1929 at about 10 percent of US gross domestic product and declined thereafter. Less than a quarter of that total was accounted for by trade with Asia.[3] Japanese planners admired the American economy not for its global reach but for its self-sufficiency. That self-sufficiency explains why trade could be employed so unreservedly as a means of diplomatic coercion. Pacific trade meant far more to the Japanese than it did to the Americans.

It is wrong, however, to imagine that the United States went to war on the far side of the world for what were no more than exiguous material interests. After all, those interests might have been equally well served by rapprochement with Japan. Such a course would certainly have made sense to American businessmen, who tended to regard the modernity of Japanese institutions as a model for the Far East generally. Yet American statesmen saw larger issues at stake. If trade was the foundation of American interest in Asia, Asia itself was the arena for the unfolding of a distinctive American vision of international order that became known as the Open Door.

The phase describes a policy based on two diplomatic notes the United States circulated around the time of the Boxer Rebellion in China (1899–1900), the crux of imperial competition before World War I. The notes were intended to avert a scramble for fresh economic or territorial concessions at Chinese expense. China's long decline had by then reached the point where its disintegration and partition were real possibilities. All the imperial powers were wary of such an outcome. By way of reinforcing their common interest in preserving the Qing Dynasty, the United States proposed that they all agree to allow each other access on equal terms to trade within their "spheres of influence or interest" and that they all respect the "territorial and administrative entity" to which China had by then been reduced.[4]

It is in the policy of the Open Door that the roots of America's opposition to Japanese expansionism were struck. American statesmen came to regard it as synonymous with American political identity and as a matter of public morality. The Open Door was a strategic, rather than a merely mercantile, conception. It envisioned a comprehensively new basis for international relations, immediately so in Asia but globally in the long run. It opened onto a political space in which the frictions of imperial competition would be replaced by the smooth operation of international commerce and investment. In economic terms, the Open Door did not seek anything more than the kind of stability that bankers and businessmen have always craved. It was not a policy to promote what is now called "development" or to ameliorate relations between the imperial powers and their colonial subjects. It did not promote free trade or economic competition as such—the United States was (as it still is) relatively protectionist compared to its major trading partners. But it most certainly did aim to dismantle zones of economic privilege and to put an end to the militarized rivalries that grew up around them. The policy's proponents took for granted that American capital, industry, and know-how would thrive in such a peaceable, fair, and orderly environment and that the world would be better off for it. Who could possibly object?

THE WASHINGTON SYSTEM

The Open Door notes were circulated to Britain, Russia, Germany, France, Italy, and Japan. And it turned out that none of them did object, since they all recognized that the American proposals were sufficiently elastic to accommodate a variety of interpretations. Japan welcomed the US initiative because it had especially good reason to fear China's going to pieces. In 1911 China actually did go to pieces, however, and once that had happened, it made sense from Tokyo's perspective to reconsider ideas like the Open Door, which had been overtaken by events. In 1917 Japan succeeded in obtaining acknowledgment from the United States that Japan's "territorial propinquity" to China gave it "special interests" there, particularly in regions adjacent to Japanese possessions.[5] Two years later, at the Paris Peace Conference, the United States was obliged to accept Japan's seizure of the formerly German leased territory on the Shandong Peninsula on the grounds that the Chinese government had agreed to it in exchange for a loan. From Tokyo's perspective, such arrangements were no more than a realistic response to the chaos unleashed by the Chinese Revolution on one hand and the world war on the other.

The United States nevertheless remained convinced that the Open Door could provide the scaffolding for a new order in Asia, and at the end of 1921 it convened an international conference in Washington to make sure that it did. America's position in the world was by then far different from what it had been twenty years before. Its loans had sustained the winning side throughout the Great War, and its belligerency had decided the outcome in the end. The United States felt it had earned the opportunity to make its case for a new approach to international relations, and the place to do it turned out to be Asia.

The Asian framing of the Open Door was partly owed to the fact that it was an inherently maritime conception, a seemingly natural extension of the hallowed principle of *mare liberum*. Asia was a region where great-power interests were overwhelmingly defined by the requirements of seaborne trade. Then as now, political order in Asia was crucially dependent on good order at sea. The image of the Open Door was all about access and movement of a kind that had become unimaginable in Europe, a hive of revolutionary agitation, nationalist resentment, and revanchist obstruction from which the United States recoiled. Its efforts to isolate itself from the Old World's tribulations have been much criticized in retrospect, but they should not be overstated. The United States remained economically engaged in Europe, if only because so many governments there owed it money. Nevertheless, American policy in Europe was narrowly, and defensively, conceived. In the Far East, conditions were different. Viewed from Washington, Asia was one long coastline, which meant that American economic clout could be backed up, at least in principle, by directly relevant naval power. The 1921–22 Washington Conference would underline this connection, albeit in the inverted form of a demand for a limitation of naval armaments in lieu of an arms race.

The conference is best known for having produced the Washington Naval ("Five-Power") Treaty limiting the construction of capital ships by the United States, Britain, France, Italy, and Japan. This was a signal achievement in itself, arising from an American initiative that it might well have pursued for reasons of economy alone. But even so, naval arms control was an instrumental matter relative to the main issue at stake, which was to establish new rules of the road in the Far East. To that end, two further treaties (plus a number of ancillary agreements) were concluded. It is to these that one must look to see the meaning of the whole exercise.

The Four-Power Treaty bound the United States, the United Kingdom, France, and Japan to respect the territorial status quo in the Pacific and to consult collectively on "any question" that threatened to provoke controversy. The Nine-Power Treaty added Italy, Belgium, the Netherlands, Portugal, and China to these four. All accepted that the Open Door would serve as the basis for their relations in Asia. China promised not to concede economic privileges to anyone in contravention of the treaty's principles of fair and equal access. All the others, having thus far tied China's hands, agreed to respect its independence and integrity.

These anodyne declarations were thought necessary in no small part because of Japan's conduct in the war that had just ended, during which it had taken advantage of disarray in China and distraction in Europe to seek far-reaching concessions for itself. Most of the so-called Twenty-One Demands that Japan presented to the Chinese in January 1915 were unexceptional, relative to the imperial practices of the recent past.[6] But some went too far in infringing the rights of other powers, a fact of which the Japanese themselves were perfectly aware and from which they retreated in the face of Anglo-American outrage. Viewed in this light, the Washington treaties were something like an act of contrition for Japan, for which the naval treaty was the absolution.

The logic here has been obscured by the apostles of Japanese militarism, which stoked public resentment over Japan's acceptance of a lower limit on naval construction than those allowed to Britain and the United States. This was a concession, true enough, but one that was more than offset by the treaty's prohibition of new military construction in the western Pacific, an arrangement that guaranteed Japan's regional preeminence, so long as the treaty's other provisions were observed. The real prize, in any case, was the treaty itself, to which the presumptive alternative was an arms race that Japan could not seriously have contested. Viewed in the stark light of realpolitik, no one benefited more from the Washington treaties than Japan, which made concessions on matters of principle (plus the leasehold on Shandong, which reverted to China at America's insistence) in return for down-to-earth material benefits that would have been otherwise unobtainable.

For the United States, on the other hand, the principle was the very thing that mattered. There is reason to doubt the Americans would actually have built the navy they traded away at Washington. Its origins lay in Woodrow Wilson's efforts to position himself as a mediator during the war in Europe, a task that he concluded would be eased if the United States possessed a navy "second to none." The "Big Navy Bill" passed in August 1916 was a first step, but when the United States entered the war eight months later, it turned out that its naval forces had little to do beyond blockade duty. The naval arms race that preceded the outbreak of the war had also demonstrated how expensive capital ships could be, even for a country as rich as the United States. It was well recognized that the voters who had installed the Republican Warren G. Harding in Wilson's place would be disinclined to pay such bills in the future.

The crystallization of American economic might in the form of a powerful navy, however notional, was nonetheless an important step, by way of suggesting that US policy in Asia did not rule out the use of force. Yet the fact remains that the American navy looming over the horizon at the Washington Conference did not actually materialize until the Far East was already in flames. This raises the natural question of whether the deterrent value of America's latent economic strength was undermined by its commitment to disarmament.

It is difficult to see how a naval arms race in the Far East would have created conditions more conducive to American interests than those created by what became known as the Washington system. Given that America's undoubted military potential ultimately proved insufficient to keep the peace, one can only speculate as to what level of real-world preparations might have tipped the balance more firmly against war—always assuming the preparations were not destabilizing in themselves. In the circumstances, naval forces were the only kind that would have mattered, and even in the best case the strategic leverage of sea power tends to be slow to develop and cumulative in nature. As it was, the Japanese did not underestimate American power. They knew that in going to war against the United States, time would not be on their side. It made no difference.

Regardless, there is no question that in the moment, the Washington Naval Treaty served its larger purpose, which was to provide the leverage necessary to elevate the Open Door from diplomatic expedient to legal principle, publicly codified in a multilateral treaty signed by all the victors in the Great War. For the Americans, the Washington Conference was only superficially an exercise in realpolitik. Its real aim was to advance the establishment of new norms of international behavior, a process that had stalled in Europe but might still proceed in the Far East. The Open Door was supposed to provide ballast for a new order still in the making, along the lines of the neutralization of Belgium, which had helped to stabilize great-power relations in post-Napoleonic Europe. And then later on, when all appeared lost, the violation of that neutrality had rallied world opinion against the aggressor.

THE CONQUEST OF MANCHURIA

No one regarded Japan as an aggressor in the 1920s. It was to all appearances a respected member of the coalition that had won the Great War and an important partner in the reconstruction of global order. If the German emperor Wilhelm II had been brought to trial for war crimes, as many hoped he would, one of his judges would have been Japanese. But appearances can be deceiving.

The consultative requirements of the Washington system did not include any binding military or political commitments. Its architects regarded such arrangements as part of the discredited legacy of prewar politics. The Four-Power Treaty had specifically abrogated the Anglo-Japanese alliance first concluded in 1902, a connection esteemed by the Japanese as marking their country's entry into the ranks of states that counted in world affairs. Japan's sense of unaccustomed isolation in the wake of Washington was heightened a few years later when the United States passed legislation excluding Japanese immigrants from its soil. This action was not thought to bear on security arrangements in the Far East, but it touched on a matter of great symbolic significance in Tokyo: the refusal of the other powers, first at the Paris Peace Conference and again at Washington, to declare that racial discrimination could have no bearing on foreign policy. Chinese immigration to the United States had been forbidden since 1882. In the years since, Japan had tried to appease American sensitivities by discouraging the migration of its citizens to the New World. That Japanese immigrants should nevertheless be viewed in the same light as the Chinese was both shocking and instructive to the Japanese. Japan regarded itself as a paid-up member of a global elite, whose relations the Open Door was supposed to smooth. It was disconcerting to consider that Japan might be on the wrong side of the door. Events would soon reinforce this new understanding.

There was nothing in the Washington treaties that directly addressed conditions in China, which had reached something like maximum entropy at the time of the conference. The Chinese government that had been represented there—and which had been treated with ill-concealed disdain by the other participants—was based on a coalition of northern military factions ("warlords") revolving around the Qing capital of Beijing. In 1928 this government was overthrown by the Nationalist Revolutionary Army of the Kuomintang (KMT), based in the south and led by Chiang Kai-shek. Chiang was determined that the territory of the new Chinese republic would coincide with that of the old Chinese empire. In 1927 Japan's prime minister, Baron Tanaka Giichi, met with Chiang on the eve of his victory. He offered Japan's support and promised not to interfere in Chinese affairs. In return, it was to be understood that Chiang's efforts would focus on consolidating control in central China while accepting the status quo in Inner Mongolia and China's northeast provinces, called Manchuria in English, where Japan had substantial investments dating back to the previous century.

Japan had conceded Chinese sovereignty over its prerevolutionary territory at Washington, but in common with other powers (including the United States), it had continued to maintain a military presence in China to protect its property and citizens. In 1927 and again in 1928, Japanese forces in Shandong clashed in bloody fashion with those of the advancing KMT. These early incidents were patched up, but they were an ill harbinger. They convinced Chiang that Japan was an obstacle to China's reconstruction, despite Japan's protestations that, like the other powers, it just wanted good order in a region where it had an undeniable material stake. The fighting in Shandong also marked the first time Japanese army units deployed in China demonstrated their willingness to act without consulting the government in Tokyo. It would not be the last.

In practice, Chiang's writ never ran smoothly in the north. He made his capital in Nanjing for that very reason. Nevertheless, the KMT's claim to rule all of China was broadly accepted internationally. Tokyo briefly imagined that it might continue to hold sway in the north via its warlord clients, but the most important of these was killed by Japanese officers who had come to doubt his loyalty. The murdered man's son and successor then turned against his father's erstwhile sponsors and concluded a pact with Chiang, which brought Manchuria under the KMT's banner, if not fully under its control.

Alongside Japan, the other power with an interest in Manchuria was the Soviet Union. In the second half of the nineteenth century, Russia had taken advantage of Chinese weakness to expand its territory to the Pacific coast below Siberia, with a view to acquiring a warm-water port there. In the west a similar project, aimed at prizing the Turkish straits from the hands of the Ottoman Empire, had been thwarted by opposition from Britain and France. In the Far East, the opponent had been Japan, whose unexpected victory in the Russo-Japanese War (1904–5) had proven it was a power to be reckoned with in Northeast Asia. Afterward Japan and Russia had contrived a modus vivendi whereby Russian interests prevailed in northern Manchuria and Japanese interests prevailed in the south.

This arrangement was still in place when the KMT was establishing itself in charge of the newborn Chinese republic. The Soviets had supported the KMT's struggle against warlordism, a policy that both Lenin and Stalin regarded as consistent with the advance of revolution in Asia. The KMT was nonetheless a nationalist party, however, and its legitimacy rested on its promise to eliminate foreign influence in China, Soviet influence included. The most important Soviet infrastructure in Manchuria was the Chinese Eastern Railroad (CER), which dramatically shortened the Trans-Siberian Railway's connection to the Pacific at Vladivostok. In 1919, in a fit of revolutionary enthusiasm, the new Bolshevik regime had considered turning the CER over to China for free, by way of wiping away all vestiges of the imperial past. Exfoliating chaos in both China and Russia had allowed this thought to fall into abeyance, however, and when Chinese troops arrived to claim the CER in 1929, they were attacked and repulsed by Red Army units deployed to protect it.

Sporadic fighting persisted for months and involved upward of ten Soviet divisions and scores of military aircraft. Needless to say, the new government in Nanjing was wholly unprepared for such opposition. Suitably chastened, it was glad to settle for shared control of the CER, as had been normal in the past. In Tokyo, where any sign of rising Soviet ambition was cause for concern, there were more than a few who were prepared to accept the Soviet action with good grace, as a reminder of the merits of the status quo. Those who saw things this way favored a pacifying strategy in China. They preferred to husband the nation's resources in order to apply them to the further modernization of the Japanese economy and state, on which Japan's ability to hold its own among the other powers depended. The Washington system may have fallen short of Japanese hopes and wounded Japanese pride, but it still provided a frame of reference that prioritized relations among the powerful states with whom Japan wished to be included. Manchuria was a colonial territory, and viewed through the Open Door the region should have been managed so as to keep turmoil to a minimum.

To the commanders of Japan's Kwantung army, however, the spectacle of a victorious Soviet army a few hundred miles away was a matter of serious alarm.[7] Although it was apparent that the Red Army was not yet a match for the Japanese, there was every reason to suppose that it might be one day. Rather than wait upon unwelcome events, some Japanese officers took the occasion of ill-conceived revolutionary agitation by Chinese communists to conduct minor false-flag sabotage against a Japanese rail line outside Mukden. The aim and effect were to force the hand of their own government, which concluded that it had no choice but to acquiesce in the outright conquest of Manchuria. Six months of fighting ensued, and in February 1932 the new state of Manchuria, called Manchukuo, was proclaimed. Its status as a Japanese puppet was obvious.

It goes without saying that this violation of the Open Door did not rally world opinion against the aggressor. Manchuria was not Belgium. Nothing that had been agreed to at the Washington Conference obliged anyone to avenge its violation in what became known as the Mukden Incident. There was no real dispute as to the rights and wrongs of the matter. Although Japan sought to portray its actions in China as a defensive response to intractable instability, the outcome left no doubt that Japan had diverged from the path others had imagined for it. Britain reacted by accelerating its long-planned fortification of Singapore, five thousand miles away. The French, well established in Indochina, were privately pleased to see Japan's energies engaged elsewhere. Mussolini's Italy, fresh from its conquest of Abyssinia, was more than ready to see things Japan's way.

The American position was especially awkward. The League of Nations had been purpose-built to moderate conflicts among its members, which included both China and Japan. The United States was not a member, however, and it did not wish to act in any way that suggested it might be drifting toward involvement in the "collective security" the League embodied. It settled for refusing to recognize any agreements that limited commercial freedom in Asia, while trusting that the burdens of Japan's revived colonialism would eventually become too onerous to bear. This was known as the Stimson Doctrine, named for Herbert Hoover's secretary of state, Henry L. Stimson, ostensibly because Hoover himself was too preoccupied with domestic affairs to get involved. In the meantime, Japan remained America's largest trading partner in Asia. As for the League itself, it could hardly have acted in the Far East without American backing. It convened a commission to investigate what had happened in Manchuria, but by the time grounds for condemnation were worked out, Japan had decided to resign its membership.

All of these events occurred against the background of the Great Depression that followed the collapse of the American stock market in 1929. Its outstanding features internationally were declining commodity prices, competitive currency devaluations, and a rising tide of beggar-thy-neighbor protectionism.

The Open Door offered no remedy to such difficulties. It promised the great powers equal access to colonial producers and consumers, not to each other's. In Japan this dispiriting context encouraged the extreme attitudes exhibited by its army officers. It helped make their case in favor of direct control of markets and resources and against civilian leaders who continued to prattle on about the redemptive powers of overseas trade. In Tokyo it had come to seem obvious that new and stronger measures were required. The creation of Manchukuo was one such measure.

Elsewhere economic stringency enforced strategic caution. The one exception might have been the Soviet Union, the major power least exposed to the perturbation of global markets and the only one that could have put an army in northeast China without prolonged preparation. Soviet soldiers and civilians in Manchuria had been manhandled (though not attacked) by the rampaging Japanese, who had also demanded control of the CER to transport their army. But Soviet military readiness was still in a parlous state, and Stalin preferred to play it safe. He offered the Japanese a nonaggression pact and sold the CER to them outright. But these were gestures. Everyone knew that war between the Soviet Union and Japan was just a matter of time.

THE PACIFIC WAR

In July 1937 local contingents of Japanese and Chinese troops clashed at the Marco Polo Bridge outside Beijing. Such episodes had become common after the Japanese seized Manchuria. Once established there, they had sporadically pressed their advantage south, using similar clashes to extract limited concessions, upon which the next round of clashes and concessions would be built. Recognizing that his army was as yet no match for Japan's, Chiang had sought to bide his time before confronting the Japanese. But a jarring confrontation with his own officers at the end of 1936 persuaded him that more determined resistance was necessary—a necessity made less dire, in Chiang's mind, by the thought that serious violence in China proper might inspire great-power intervention on his behalf.

The Open Door was supposed to facilitate, rather than to discourage, Western penetration of China, and its success ensured a diverse and extensive Western presence there. When Japan slammed the door shut in the northeast, Westerners throughout China became something like hostages—not to Japan but to fortune. Chiang understood the significance of this. Thus, the fighting at the Marco Polo Bridge was not followed by the usual horse trading. Instead, violence escalated throughout northern and central China. In the process, Chiang's fears about the quality of his army proved well founded. By year's end, Nanjing itself was in Japanese hands. Chiang's government retreated to the remote vastness of Chongqing, upstream from the famously rugged Three Gorges of the Yangtze River. There it awaited meaningful assistance from abroad.

It did not occur. In October 1937, as Japanese troops were completing their conquest of Shanghai, President Franklin Roosevelt took the occasion of a bridge dedication in Chicago to decry an "epidemic of world lawlessness," against which he called for an international "quarantine."[8] Roosevelt's remarks did not mention Japan, and on their face they did not go beyond the Hoover administration's carefully measured response to the conquest of Manchuria. It is only in retrospect that Roosevelt's speech can be seen as marking a change of policy, away from pro forma disapproval toward the calculated application of economic pressure. To the extent that the Open Door admitted anything like coercion, this was it.

The degree of deliberate calculation surrounding the American sanctions regime that followed should not be overstated. The ratcheting-up of Japanese inconvenience, beginning with a "moral embargo" on aircraft parts (July 1938), through industrial equipment (June 1940) and aviation fuel (July 1940), to scrap iron (September 1940) and finally petroleum (July 1941), was intended to apply pressure without provoking a crisis. Most of the waypoints that guided these actions were found in Europe. Serious sanctions against Japan required the abrogation of the Treaty of Commerce and Navigation that had been concluded in 1911, but it was still in force when Wuhan fell in October 1938, after which the hard fighting in China began to diminish. The treaty was only denounced eight months later, in line with Britain's abandonment of appeasement toward Germany following the dismemberment of Czechoslovakia. The sterner measures against Japan that began in the summer of 1940 were justified, in political terms, by the fall of France, as was the Two-Ocean Navy Act that accompanied them.

Needless to say, the goal of all this was to avoid war in the Far East, the more so given the far more dangerous crisis unfolding in Europe. War came anyway, and some share of that unwanted result must be put down to American complacency. As US economic measures against Japan grew more severe, its confidence also grew that Tokyo would capitulate in the end, whereas on the Japanese side every demonstration of its vulnerability became an incentive to resistance.

American confidence fed on itself. In what proved to be its final dose of economic pressure, the United States chose to freeze Japanese dollar assets rather than embargo Tokyo's purchases of American oil. It did so because it feared that an oil embargo would cause Japan to attack the Dutch East Indies. An asset freeze was supposed to allow control without provocation. Nevertheless, once it became apparent that the chosen measure had produced a de facto oil embargo anyway, there was no thought of retracing steps that had originally been rejected as leading to war. America's final offer required Japan's complete withdrawal from China in return for little more than its money back and a promise of new trade negotiations, whose terms were unspecified. The Japanese regarded this as an ultimatum, and it is difficult to disagree.

That the Japanese chose war for themselves is also true, however. Japan's predatory conduct toward its neighbors throughout the period this chapter has been considering was rooted in institutional failure and cultural atavism, both of which were reinforced by the ascendancy of Japan's armed forces as the final arbiters of national life. These considerations reach beyond the frame of this discussion, but they should be recorded by way of emphasizing that no simple form of "deterrence failure" can account for the Pacific War. Japanese leaders in and out of uniform dreaded the idea of war with the United States, whose power they understood. But in circumstances in which honor demanded defiance, they were able to persuade themselves that American power was configured so as to provide just sufficient hope of deliverance.

The overdetermined character of Japan's defeat in the war that followed has shadowed the diplomacy that preceded it by lending Japanese conduct a misleadingly suicidal character. It can obscure the fact that the naval power that was supposed to be the final guarantee of the American sanctions regime was still on the drawing board or under construction in 1941. That fact, amplified by the vast defensive glacis of the Pacific, made it possible for the Japanese to imagine that dramatic initial success might alter the regional balance in their favor, sufficiently so to make the full deployment of American power prohibitively expensive in human terms.

America's subsequent eagerness to involve the Soviets in war against Japan, and its reluctance to contemplate the casualties entailed by an invasion of Japan itself, are indirect evidence that a strategy designed to raise the cost of American engagement in the Far East was not absurd. Its plausibility was reinforced by conditions in Europe, which Tokyo correctly judged to be America's strategic priority. The Japanese were also more aware than the Americans of British weakness in the Pacific, a fact the United States fully appreciated only after it found itself alone there with Japan in 1942. Taken together, these considerations caused a window of opportunity to appear before Japanese eyes. It was an illusion, but it was not insane.

Not the least irony of America's engagement in the Far East was that although it failed to avert war as such, it ruled out the war everyone expected: a rematch in Manchuria between Russia and Japan. The Soviet Union was the preferred adversary of the Japanese army even after bruising border clashes at Lake Khasan (1938) and Khalkhin Gol (1939) had demonstrated the improving power of the Red Army. Thereafter high politics got in the way of coming to grips. Japan had aligned with Germany against the Soviets via the Anti-Comintern

Pact (1936) but then saw fit to reconcile with Moscow following the conclusion of the Molotov-Ribbentrop Pact three years later. It might have regained normal bearings with the onset of Operation Barbarossa in June 1941, but by then Japan's logistical dependence on the United States was becoming apparent. Yet the fact remains that it was only the de facto oil embargo that brought an end to preparations for war with Russia.

Given that neither the Red Army nor the US Navy was able to deter Japan, it is tempting to suppose that their combination might have done the trick; an army close at hand could close the window of opportunity propped open by the maritime geography of the western Pacific. The thought cannot be dismissed out of hand. It is encouraged by the diplomatic prehistory of World War II in Europe, which turned on the last-minute inability of the Soviets and the Western democracies to reach agreement, thereby prompting Stalin's turn to Hitler instead. In the Far East, however, the prospects for a combination against Japan were if anything even more remote. Although the United States normalized relations with the Soviet Union in 1933, Roosevelt personally rebuffed Soviet overtures for cooperation against Japan—the main benefit the Soviets were seeking from the Americans. The president told Moscow's newly accredited ambassador, Maxim Litvinov, that, for the United States, bilateral and even multilateral obligations were beyond the pale. Only unilateral action was possible.[9]

CONCLUSION

This council of despair, coming from a committed internationalist like Roosevelt, is the final legacy of the Open Door, a policy that was supposed to require no defense because it contemplated no obligations beyond the ostensibly universal rationality of the marketplace. If we recall the three pillars of maritime strategy mentioned earlier—trade, naval power, and political relationships—it will be apparent that the Open Door was concerned with, and rested upon, only the first of these. The Washington system may have invoked the latent military might of the United States, but it did so by transmuting it into financial pressure, in the form of an arms race that Japan was able to avoid by making political concessions. The element of bluff is apparent in retrospect, however: had that arms race actually been run, its strategic purpose would have seemed awfully mysterious to Americans—though not, of course, to the Japanese.

American isolationists always suspected the Open Door of being a stalking horse for the entangling alliances Thomas Jefferson had denounced, but this was a misunderstanding. Its true pedigree was not Wilsonian internationalism but the American exceptionalism of John Adams's Model Treaty (1776).

The founders liked to think the American republic could hold the world at bay politically while drawing it close economically. World War II dashed whatever was left of this fantasy. Afterward the United States would emerge as the architect and guardian of a postwar global order based on military strength, multilateral obligations, and robust international institutions. The Open Door was conceived as a way of avoiding the burdens and commitments these things entail. It led nowhere.

NOTES

1. See for instance, S. C. M. Payne, *The Japanese Empire: Grand Strategy from the Meiji Restoration to the Pacific War* (Cambridge: Cambridge University Press, 2017), 77–109.
2. Two other plans existed for lesser operations in Asia. Plan Yellow envisioned the dispatch of an American contingent to China, similar to the one sent to help suppress the Boxer Rebellion in 1899. Plan Brown contemplated rebellion in the Philippines.
3. For gross domestic product data, see the Federal Reserve Bank of St. Louis, "Percentage Shares of Gross Domestic Product: Annual," https://fred.stlouisfed.org/release/tables?rid=53&eid=41187&od=1929-01-01#. For the geographic distribution of American trade, see R. M. Boeckel, *Foreign Trade of the United States*, Editorial Research Reports, vol. 4 (Washington, DC: CQ Press, 1930).
4. Quoted passages are from the first note (November 13, 1899), in US Department of State, *Foreign Relations of the United States: 1899* (Washington, DC: US Government Printing Office, 1901), 138–39. The second note (July 3, 1900) is in US Department of State, *Foreign Relations of the United States: 1902* (Washington, DC: US Government Printing Office, 1903), 299.
5. From the exchange of diplomatic notes known as the Lansing-Ishi Agreement (November 2, 1917), US Department of State, *Foreign Relations of the United States: 1926* (Washington, DC: US Government Printing Office, 1927), 264–65. The reference to "possessions" presumably includes Korea, which Japan colonized in 1910, and Taiwan, ceded to Japan by China in 1895. English-language maps of Japan in this period often included Taiwan and the Ryukyu Islands, though not Korea, as Japanese territory. The precedent to which Japan looked in pressing its claim that geography created special interests was the Monroe Doctrine, endorsed (at American insistence) by the Charter of the League of Nations (1919) as exemplifying a "regional understanding . . . for securing the maintenance of peace." "The Covenant of the League of Nations," Yale Law School, accessed August 8, 2020, https://avalon.law.yale.edu/20th_century/leagcov.asp.
6. US Department of State, *Foreign Relations of the United States: 1924* (Washington, DC: US Government Printing Office, 1925), 93–95.
7. The Kwantung army was an army group created to secure the leasehold Japan obtained on the Liaodong Peninsula following the First Sino-Japanese War (1894–95). Its responsibilities later expanded in line with Japanese policy. Its expeditionary role made it the most prestigious unit in the Japanese army and an especially attractive posting to officers who favored a militarized imperial policy.

8. Douglas Lurton, comp., *Roosevelt's Foreign Policy, 1933–1941: Franklin D. Roosevelt's Unedited Speeches and Messages* (New York: W. Funk, 1942), 129–32.

9. Maxim Litvinov to the People's Commissariat for Foreign Affairs, November 17, 1933, quoted in Jonathan Haslam, *The Soviet Union and the Threat from the East, 1933–41: Moscow, Tokyo, and the Prelude to the Pacific War* (Pittsburgh: University of Pittsburgh Press, 1992), 34.

10

Superpower Rivalry and the Strategic Balance in the Cold War

Kevin Rowlands

To many people, the Cold War's geographic center of gravity was always far from Asia and the Indian and Pacific Oceans on the other side of the world in Europe and the North Atlantic. In military terms, the major blocs were the North Atlantic Treaty Organization (NATO) and the Warsaw Pact, their very names indicative of which regions were deemed important to the belligerents. Of course, there is no doubt that the global nature of the Cold War meant that the outlying areas felt the impact of the confrontation and were subject to significant influence and interference from the major protagonists, but rarely were they pivotal to the outcome. If not exactly an afterthought, they were certainly secondary to the principal theater of operations. It is easy to argue that the Cold War, in essence, only served to confirm the geographic determinism of Halford Mackinder and Nicholas J. Spykman.

THE INDO-PACIFIC AT THE PERIPHERY OR THE CENTER?

However, accepting such a reading of the period without further question is shortsighted. The superpowers, the United States and the Soviet Union, did engage heavily in the Indo-Pacific. Through their own strategic competition, they shaped the regional order; through their diplomacy, coercion, and deterrence, they shaped the regional security dynamics. In return those regional dynamics then helped to shape the global geostrategic context. The Indo-Pacific is clearly a maritime-centric region, and an analysis of the strategic balance, international law, resource exploitation, and technological development in the maritime environment can go some way to explain its significance before and during the Cold War. It can also help to explain what came next, including the maritime competition between the United States and the People's Republic of China, but that is a subject for later chapters.

While there are inevitably differences of opinion, this chapter adopts the generally accepted view that the Cold War started around 1946 and ended around 1990. The timescale is long—almost half a century—the topic is huge and varied, and this chapter cannot fully examine every element. Instead it considers four general themes that perhaps encapsulate both the period and the region. One curious point is that these themes are overlapping and, at times, even contradictory. Many readers may disagree with one or all of them. There is no simplicity, no explicit right and wrong, in any attempt to understand the rivalry and the strategic balance between the superpowers during the Cold War. What follows is just one interpretation.

The first theme is that superpower rivalry in the Indo-Pacific acted as a restraint, a constraint, or dampener on conflict in the region. Of course, this assertion can be easily contested. However, without the presence, sponsorship, deterrence, and political and military underwriting of Indo-Pacific governments during the Cold War, the region could well have been beset with kinetic inter- and intrastate conflict on a far greater scale than it was. The brutal history of the region, particularly in Northeast Asia in the unfettered century before the Cold War, illustrates the point. The second theme is that superpower rivalry spurred a desire for self-organization in the so-called third world. Those countries that did not fit or did not want to fit readily into one or other of the major blocs tried to go it alone, while others joined Western-sponsored regional organizations or Eastern groupings of communist actors. The third theme is that superpower rivalry acted as a catalyst for proxy action. The same American and Soviet competition and engagement that put a brake on all-out war and facilitated cooperation and regional partnership also set the conditions for a series of bloody and damaging conflicts of a lesser scale and intensity. The superpowers used these conflicts to further their own ideologies on the world stage and their own domestic agendas at home. The proxy wars in Korea and Vietnam are the obvious Asian examples, but there are more. The final theme, which leads to the conclusion, is that superpower rivalry more broadly facilitated economic development and a growing focus on the Indo-Pacific as a region of opportunity; this is a theme that continues into the present day. For example, Japan and South Korea were able to focus their efforts not on military power but on becoming economic powerhouses largely because their security had been taken out of their own hands, and the "tiger economies" of Southeast Asia grew out of a stable, if precarious, balance of power.

SUPERPOWER RIVALRY AS A CONSTRAINT ON CONFLICT

It is worth considering some of the driving forces of the Cold War rivalry in the Indo-Pacific. Though the Soviet Union was generally and rightly regarded as a European power, it is useful to visualize in map form its vast Asian territory, which it inherited from Russia's land gains during its eastward expansion in the nineteenth century. Around 20 percent of the Soviet population was Asian, and the Soviet Pacific coastline ran close to China, Korea, and Japan.[1] In 1949 the Chinese Communist Party's victory over the Kuomintang (the Chinese Nationalist Party) gave birth to the People's Republic of China (PRC), and soon afterward China and the Soviet Union signed the Sino-Soviet Treaty of Friendship, which guaranteed military assistance to the PRC in the event of an attack by Japan or, crucially, by any other state that might directly or indirectly support Japan. This clearly included the United States.[2] By the early 1950s there was a united communist bloc in East Asia (on paper at least), which presented a clear challenge to American interests and Western capitalism there. Despite this, the relationship between Mao Zedong and Joseph Stalin was never particularly warm, and Washington may well have readily and consistently misinterpreted the true degree of trust between the two.[3] Broad alignment of political ideology does not necessarily mean an instant disregard for differences in culture and history, something that the West would have better understood had it more regularly taken a look in the mirror.

After World War II both superpowers shared an anticolonialist outlook, but they differed in how far and how aggressively they would go to realize their vision. Initially the Union of Soviet Socialist Republics (USSR) championed anticolonialism through communist revolution, with insurgencies rife in Indochina, Malaya, and the Philippines. In contrast, the United States adopted a semipassive, antirevolutionary posture and was content to see the European powers return to and then continue to oversee their Asian possessions. In macro terms, this meant that much of the Indo-Pacific was a mix of insurgency and colonial forms of governments. At the very least, there was a democratic deficit, with an undercurrent of discontent after years of war and "occupation" by one extra-regional state or another.

On the other side of the ideological divide, things were happening too. Because of its successes in World War II, its naval and air power, its nuclear arsenal, its system of alliances, and its cultural soft power, the United States was the strongest actor in the Pacific theater.[4] At the same time, Britain remained a strong presence in the Indian Ocean basin and retained close ties with the Indian subcontinent, the Persian Gulf, numerous island states, and much of East Africa. However, from the end of the war onward, the United States and

Soviet Union were embroiled in an ideological battle that dominated global politics and demonized any adversaries in the collective psyche. In America in the 1950s, McCarthyism and the Second Red Scare gained momentum, and many politicians and citizens alike were convinced that communism was rapidly spreading throughout the world. First posited by President Harry S. Truman and then given even greater prominence under President Dwight D. Eisenhower, the domino theory became a credible notion. In the United States, the likelihood of Asian countries falling into communist hands was taken very seriously. The San Francisco Peace Treaty, which established peaceful relations between the Allied Powers and Japan and welcomed the latter back into the international community, would not be signed until 1951. Many considered Japan, with its long history of militarism and its more recent history of regional dominance, to be critical to Indo-Pacific security.[5] The scars of World War II ran deep, however. From the former Allies' perspective, Germany and Japan had to be kept down. Keeping Japan pliant was a key regional objective, and its territory remained under American occupation. On the global stage, Moscow's aim was to spread communism, whereas Washington's principal strategic policy was to contain it. These goals were put into practice in part by forward deployment of each country's naval and military forces, both in Europe and in Asia. For instance, the US Navy's Seventh Fleet, in its various guises, was a very visible signal of American commitment to the region and was based first in China, then in the Philippines, and then in Japan. Over the years since World War II, the scale of the US Navy's presence waxed and waned, reducing in the détente of the 1970s and then rebounding in the 1980s as President Ronald Reagan's maritime strategy took shape and transformed the Navy's forward presence from concept to real capability at sea. Simultaneously, the Soviet Union maintained and then grew its Pacific Fleet at Vladivostok, though it took twenty years after the end of World War II for it to really make its presence felt beyond East Asia and into the Indian Ocean.

However, despite the superpower strategies (and perhaps a degree of wishful thinking), forward deployment, treaties, pacts, alliance management, and containment did not keep the political map of the world in stasis. The frictions at the boundaries between the two major political systems inevitably resulted in local conflict. The calculus that the other side would not countenance war was tested time and again and proven wrong—but not entirely. For example, the United Kingdom's Joint Intelligence Committee's assessment in the 1950s was that China would not risk a conflict with the United Nations in Korea because it could inevitably lead to a major war with the West.[6] Of course, history tells a different story, one that could have resulted in the use of nuclear weapons, but fortunately that outcome was averted. It is not the purpose of this chapter to engage in counterfactual debate, but it is worth considering that the maintenance of the global strategic balance between the United States and the Soviet Union during the Cold War meant that the powder keg of regional security in the Indo-Pacific did not explode, or at least it did not explode as much as perhaps it might have. The superpowers themselves expected that their opposed interests would generate crises, but the very recognition of this encouraged them both to deescalate and to manage those crises when they did occur.[7] There can also be little doubt that nuclear deterrence played a part in the strategic calculus, first manifest by the American monopoly on atomic weapons with its nuclear umbrella over Japan and other regional allies, by the Soviet Union after 1949, and then from the 1960s onward by China.[8] A third world war was in no one's interest, and the superpower standoff, though terrifying in its potential, did enable Indo-Pacific states to support nonproliferation and pursue nonnuclear postures.[9]

Notwithstanding communist and anticolonial insurgencies, the Chinese Civil War, and the PRC's ongoing pressure on the breakaway Republic of China in Taiwan, there was relative passivity on the part of the PRC during the Cold War on long-standing territorial disputes. For example, the PRC's aggressive East and South China Sea claims were largely put on hold, arguably in a mutual desire to maintain the strategic balance of power in the region while its focus was elsewhere. For instance, the eleven-dash line first appeared on maps in 1947 as Chiang Kai-shek's Kuomintang sought to assert its authority and was later redrawn as nine dashes by the PRC, but there was no real momentum behind Chinese physical dominance in those seas and few physical interactions with other countries in the region until after the end of the Cold War. And then, of course, momentum gathered quickly.

Both Washington and Moscow faced the possibility of hot conflict several times during the Cold War, but these events were generally in the West. The division of Germany, and of Berlin in particular, brought the center of gravity of superpower confrontation firmly into the European theater. Later the Cuban Missile Crisis focused attention farther into the Western Hemisphere, at the edge of the continental United States.[10] Where armed conflict did take place in the Indo-Pacific, it attracted extraregional participation with the superpowers even facing off against each other at times, but it remained predominantly intraregional in nature. Ultimately the wars in East and Southeast Asia did not turn global, which, after the horrors of the first half of the twentieth century, was no mean feat.

SUPERPOWER RIVALRY AS A DRIVER TO ORGANIZE THE THIRD WORLD

At the outset of the Cold War, the two superpowers were essentially novices in international diplomacy.[11] However, countries had to choose whether to side with American-led capitalism or Soviet-led communism, although many did try to forge an independent path. It is interesting to consider why an international organization in the Indo-Pacific never really took hold in the same way that NATO did in Western Europe and North America or the Warsaw Pact did in Eastern Europe. In September 1954 the United States, France, the United Kingdom, New Zealand, Australia, the Philippines, Thailand, and Pakistan formed the Southeast Asia Treaty Organization (SEATO). Western-sponsored and Western-led, SEATO was meant to prevent communism from gaining ground in the region. More important, it was imposed from the outside and not self-initiated. Despite its name, only two Southeast Asian countries became members, and even those did not join through any sense of altruism. The Philippines joined in part because of its close ties with the United States and in part out of concern over its own communist insurgency. Thailand joined after the PRC established the Dai Autonomous Prefecture in Yunnan Province in southern China. The Dai are ethnically related to the Thai and Lao peoples, and Thailand became troubled by the prospect of Chinese communist–sponsored subversion on its own soil. Though this may appear somewhat paranoid in today's world, it is worth remembering the atmosphere of distrust and suspicion that pervaded international relations early in the Cold War. Of course, Thailand had never been colonized by Western powers and cherished its independence, while the rest of the region was less troubled by the threat of communism than it was about its own neutrality and efforts to bring European imperialism to an end. Finally, under the terms of the Geneva Accords of 1954, which were signed after the fall of French Indochina, Vietnam, Cambodia, and Laos were prevented from joining any international military alliance, though they were included as observers. Meanwhile, Washington believed Southeast Asia to be a crucial frontier in the fight against communist expansion, and so it consequently viewed SEATO as an essential element of its global Cold War policy of containment.

Although SEATO maintained no military forces of its own, the organization hosted joint military exercises for member states each year. One was Exercise Sea Horse in May 1965. The ten-day sortie involved thirty-one warships and 130 aircraft from member states and tested the ability of SEATO navies to escort a convoy across the South China Sea. Beginning in Manila, the convoy sailed over two thousand miles to Bangkok, which sent a clear message of SEATO capability and intent to the observing communist bloc.[12] As the communist threat appeared to change from one of outright attack to one of internal subversion, SEATO worked to strengthen the economic foundations and living standards of the Southeast Asian states. It sponsored a variety of meetings and exhibitions on cultural, religious, and historical topics, and the non-Asian members sponsored fellowships for Asian scholars. According to the US Department of State's Office of the Historian, SEATO was also vitally important to the American rationale for the Vietnam War.[13] The United States used the organization as part of its justification for refusing to go forward with elections in 1956 that were intended to reunify Vietnam, and as the conflict unfolded the inclusion of Vietnam as a territory under SEATO protection gave the United States its legal framework for continued involvement.[14]

Unlike NATO, SEATO had no mechanism for obtaining intelligence or deploying military forces, so the potential for collective action was limited. Because it had only three Asian members, it faced charges of being a new form of Western colonialism. By the early 1970s its purpose had run its course, and members began to withdraw. Neither Pakistan nor France supported the US war in Vietnam, and when the war ended with an American withdrawal in 1975, the most prominent remaining reason for SEATO's existence disappeared. SEATO formally disbanded in 1977.[15]

A more Asian-focused organization made up of regional members was the Association of Southeast Asian Nations (ASEAN). Another organization born out of the fear of communism, ASEAN was established by Indonesia, Malaysia, the Philippines, Singapore, and Thailand in 1967. The members signed the Treaty of Amity and Cooperation in Southeast Asia in 1976, emphasizing mutual respect and noninterference in other countries' affairs. In the following years ASEAN grew and incorporated the former Indochina states of Laos, Vietnam, and Cambodia after the end of the Cold War, and it prioritized economic integration and free trade.[16] ASEAN became more successful than SEATO in part because its emphasis was on trade and not physical security in its early years and for being semisynonymous with the tiger economies of some of its members.

At a time when the "first world" referred to American-led liberal democracies with capitalist economies and the "second world" meant the Soviet-led communist bloc, the superpowers intervened in the nonaligned third world to prove the universal applicability of their ideologies. The newly independent states of the Indo-Pacific were "fertile ground" for their competition.[17] After years of introspection and a focus on Europe, the Soviet Union "rediscovered" the third world around 1955–60, and after the death of Stalin Moscow's policy turned away from armed intervention to government-to-government cooperation, particularly with socialist regimes.[18] Under Nikita Khrushchev in the late 1950s and early 1960s, the Soviet Union tried to follow a path of peaceful coexistence with the West. During that time it sought to enhance its position in the third world through the prestige of showcasing its relative economic success and technological advancements through such endeavors as its space program.[19] It did not follow the Western example of creating or encouraging international and regional bodies. Although they each used different tactics and techniques, the superpowers both gained followers and admirers throughout the Indo-Pacific (and other regions of the world) in countries that consolidated their ideological and political leadership for a time, even if they did not significantly expand it.

International security organizations were not the preserve of the super-powers, however. As Britain continued its drawdown from the Indo-Pacific, it sought ways to maintain some influence and to signal its commitment to the region and its former colonies. Along with Australia, New Zealand, Singapore, and Malaysia, it formed the Five Power Defence Arrangements (FPDA). The FPDA was, and still is, an arrangement (not a pact), with the participants agree-ing to consult with each other in the event of aggression against the two smaller Southeast Asian members.[20] What it did do, however, was ensure regular pres-ence of non-American Western militaries in the region, the continuation of defense cooperation through naval, land, and air exercises, and the maintenance of a common outlook without direct, colonial oversight.

Not all countries saw the world in the same way. However, the history of nonalignment as a soft-balancing mechanism is relevant to superpower rivalry in the Indo-Pacific. In the 1950s, faced with the intense Cold War superpower enmity, India's first prime minister, Jawaharlal Nehru, took the lead in organiz-ing Asian and African states. The Non-Aligned Movement and, before it, the 1955 Afro-Asian Conference in Bandung, Indonesia, are examples of materi-ally weaker states using institutional cooperation and diplomacy to balance the influence of the great powers.

Nonalignment was a movement, not an international organization, and it attempted to delegitimize the threatening behavior of the two superpowers and, to some extent, that of the waning colonial powers, such as Britain, France, and the Netherlands, in the area of interest of this chapter. There were declarations on nuclear testing and nonproliferation, which helped to bring about the Partial Test Ban Treaty, several nuclear weapons–free zones, and the Nuclear Non-Proliferation Treaty.[21] In 1971 the Non-Aligned Movement also engineered the passage of Resolution 2832 through the United Nations General Assembly, declaring the Indian Ocean to be a zone of peace.[22] The point here is that this groundswell of action for stability was brought about by nation-states with oth-erwise little in common, apart from their shared determination to stand apart from superpower competition. Competition and cooperation found a way to coexist, at least in the Indo-Pacific.

SUPERPOWER RIVALRY AS A CATALYST FOR PROXY ACTION

Alongside the domino theory (discussed earlier), some Cold War commenta-tors put forward a different perspective on superpower rivalry in the form of the power vacuum theory. In simple terms, it proposed that if one side left a gap, or vacuum, the other side would naturally seek to fill it. Power vacuum theory in the Indo-Pacific was perhaps best summed up in the words of an Indian scholar of the time, Professor K. P. Misra, who observed that, first, if one power failed to act in any given scenario, it would be put in a disadvantageous position relative to the other, so it would always be compelled to do something.[23] Second, Misra found that littoral countries needed some kind of guardian to protect them because they did not have the wherewithal for unilateral defense.[24] Third, he discovered that major powers could use their military might to act as arbiters of disputes, and so they did, and, fourth, that these outside powers wanted to use their position to gain domestic influence within Indo-Pacific littoral states and use it to their own advantage.[25]

Whether or not the zero-sum, realist power vacuum theory was or was not correct, its principal tenets did strike a chord with the superpowers and were manifest through their physical actions. At sea, the US Navy established a naval base at Subic Bay in the Philippines and later another at Diego Garcia in the British Indian Ocean Territory—in addition to its ongoing presence in Japan. After Britain, one of the dominant colonial powers in the region, made clear its intention to withdraw from east of Suez in the late 1960s, Soviet naval activity in the Indian Ocean increased substantially because the US Navy was distracted by the war in Vietnam and its presence waned. However, the threat to Western interests posed by the Soviet Pacific fleet was generally considered to be less than that posed in more pressing parts of the world by the Northern, Baltic, and Black Sea Fleets.[26] Crucially, both sides maintained a degree of maritime freedom of maneuver, and the Soviet presence continued to grow over time. Similarly, after the end of the Vietnam War, the operating tempo of the US Navy in the Indian Ocean rose by about 20 percent relative to what it had been before the conflict, with its principal aim being to limit growing Soviet influence in the region.[27] Similarly, after the US withdrawal from Vietnam, the Soviet navy quickly established an operating base in Cam Ranh Bay because it had the opportunity to do so, and by the mid-1970s the Soviet Navy's total number of days at sea in the Indian Ocean outnumbered that of the US Navy.[28]

Of course, it is simple to extrapolate the power vacuum theory beyond the end of the Cold War to the Chinese and Japanese influence, which increased onward as US and Soviet influence waned.[29] Yet during the Cold War, as the West was helping to organize bodies such as SEATO and the FPDA—partly in a response to the threat of communist expansion and insurgency—a series of regimes did come to power in the third world espousing Marxist ideology, often with Soviet or Soviet-proxy assistance. In turn, these led to Western-supported anti-Marxist resistance movements. The two spheres of influence were almost mirror images of each other, each supporting governments that were friendly to their cause and each supporting opposition groups hostile to the other's camp. A late–Cold War RAND Corporation report looked into anti-Marxist resistance within communist states and noted the West was not slow to capitalize on the discontent there.[30]

It should be no surprise that both superpowers used their proxies, either in government or opposition, to further their own interests. The wars in Korea and Indochina are well-known examples of proxy conflict, but it is worth briefly mentioning a couple of maritime examples of proxy action that took place to demonstrate the range and different scales of interaction that occurred. The first is a renowned cause célèbre of an action by a weaker proxy actor directly against one of the superpowers. The second is an encounter between medium-sized powers, each with a loose proxy role, taking place while the superpowers maneuvered on the periphery of the conflict.

The celebrated case of USS *Pueblo* took place between the United States and North Korea in 1968.[31] Early that year, the *Pueblo*, an intelligence-gathering ship, was on patrol in the East Sea off the coast of North Korea when its presence became known to North Korea. On January 23 a North Korean patrol boat approached the *Pueblo* at high speed, ordered it to heave to, and threatened to open fire if it did not comply. Within the hour, three more patrol vessels had joined the first, and two North Korean MiG-21 fighter aircraft were overflying the area. The *Pueblo* attempted to depart from the scene but could not outrun the faster North Korean vessels. After the North Koreans fired shots, the *Pueblo*'s commanding officer surrendered his ship and followed the patrol boats into the port of Wonsan. The North Koreans held the crew for almost a year before releasing them.

The *Pueblo* incident was ostensibly an altercation between North Korea and the United States. However, to fully appreciate the situation, the wider context must be understood. At the time of the incident, Pyongyang was experiencing difficult and complex relationships with both the USSR and China, and the United States was giving unquestioning support to South Korea. In his classic Cold War work, John Lewis Gaddis (without direct reference to the *Pueblo* incident itself) discusses the Soviet–North Korean relationship and concludes that Moscow disliked the North Korean regime, but it could not let it fail for fear of a perceived American "victory" in the region.[32] For its part, China (North Korea's long-standing if, at times, reluctant ally) played no direct physical role but was mindful of its own influence within the communist world and provided tacit support to Pyongyang.[33]

There was an underlying assumption at the time in Washington that all incidents, wherever they occurred, were connected with the broader Cold War and must, therefore, be orchestrated by Moscow. It would have been incomprehensible for US decision-makers in Washington to think that North Korea could have acted alone against the United States.[34] Recently released contemporary testimony shows that the US House Armed Services Committee was briefed that it was "reasonable to assume . . . that the documentation captured from the *Pueblo* has been turned over to the Soviets and possibly the CHICOMS [Chinese Communists]."[35] It was a tactical action in a high-stakes game.

The *Pueblo* incident demonstrates the importance of strategic calculation by the superpowers and how, sometimes, they could get it wrong. The American assumption was that despite Cold War rhetoric, surveillance vessels operating on the high seas would not be directly interfered with by the other side. This was a convention that had evolved between the United States, the USSR, and their allies, and any violation would obviously upset the strategic balance.[36] After the *Pueblo* incident, the US Navy had to reassess its policy of sailing surveillance ships unescorted near hostile waters and found the cost of providing protection prohibitive. By mid-1969, the US chief of naval operations, Adm. Thomas H. Moorer, recommended decommissioning all "spy ships"; within six months, they had been removed from service.[37] During and after the incident there was significant naval maneuvering and posturing by the various stakeholders. In late January 1968 the US Navy deployed three aircraft carriers to the Sea of Japan, and in February 1968 the Soviet Union deployed cruisers and destroyers to the same area.[38] It was a tense period, but in the end little of substance changed, even if one of the superpowers had lost face.

Just a few years later, in 1971, the third war between India and Pakistan since their independence from Britain erupted. At the time, though it was nominally a leading light of the Non-Aligned Movement, India was supported and equipped by the Soviet Union, and Pakistan sat largely in the Western camp. East Pakistan, which became Bangladesh also in 1971, sought independence from the dominant provinces in West Pakistan. Seeing an opportunity, India began to provide support, including active military support, to the separatists. As part of its strategy, India entered into the Indo-Soviet Treaty of Peace, Friendship, and Cooperation, which included an element of mutual assistance should the other be threatened. From the Indian perspective, the treaty acted as a deterrent to a direct Pakistani attack while India worked overtly and covertly to divide East Pakistan from West Pakistan.

However, Pakistan was undeterred and launched an air attack against Indian targets in December 1971. Land, sea, and air engagements followed in and around the subcontinent. Success went India's way, however, and its army and air force rapidly converged on Dhaka, the capital of East Pakistan, and the city fell to Bangladeshi separatists less than two weeks after the conflict began. The Indian navy simultaneously blockaded East Pakistan and launched Operation Trident, a missile-boat attack on the port city of Karachi in West Pakistan. A number of Pakistani warships were hit and sunk, including PNS *Khyber* and PNS *Muhafiz*. Trident was swiftly followed by Operation

Python, which included further attacks on Pakistani shipping and infrastructure ashore.[39]

As the combatants fought, their Soviet and American supporters moved into position. The Soviets extended a small, routine naval detachment in the Indian Ocean and reinforced it with submarines and cruisers with sufficient firepower to be formidable as an anticarrier task group. Meanwhile, the US Navy formed Task Force 74 around the aircraft carrier USS *Enterprise* to protect "US interests" in the region and moved it from Southeast Asia. The former colonial power, Britain, had already sent the light fleet carrier HMS *Albion* to the Bay of Bengal off East Pakistan. Soviet attention, which had originally been on the British deployment, switched to the American. The subsequent maneuvering sent multiple messages among the superpowers, the former colonial power, and India and Pakistan. The United States was "tilting" against India but would not intervene directly, Britain was trying to preserve its legacy, and the USSR was monitoring and attempting to ensure no further escalation.[40] The coercive diplomacy between and by the superpowers as their proxies pursued their own objectives may or may not have influenced the ultimate outcome with regard to Bangladeshi independence and Indo-Pakistani relations, but it did help cement allegiances there and elsewhere in the decade to follow. Although proxy action can be direct or indirect, it is always complicated.

SUPERPOWER RIVALRY AS A STIMULUS OF ECONOMIC OPPORTUNITY

Finally, one must consider how over the decades of the Cold War, the Indo-Pacific gained prominence on the world stage, particularly as a region for economic opportunity. It would be wrong to assert that commercial growth in the region was solely due to superpower rivalry; it is also important to consider how it was facilitated by the political, diplomatic, and military architecture in the region. As has already been noted, Japan's remarkable economic achievements after World War II were in part due to its cultural abandonment of militarism and the underwriting of its security by the United States. Similarly, Asian city-states and pseudo-city-states, such as Singapore and Hong Kong, thrived, as did South Korea once the war on that peninsula had come to a practical, if not legal, conclusion. Kaname Akamatsu's "flying geese model" of economic and technological development, in which the successes of the lead economy are passed to the second and third economies as it continues to evolve and innovate, was devised with the Indo-Pacific region in mind, and it was underpinned by the relative stability of the Cold War.[41] In the second half of the Cold War, Japan forged ahead, and ASEAN flourished, providing a homegrown economic community that continues to this day. Importantly for this maritime-centric region, the United Nations Convention on the Law of the Sea (UNCLOS) brought together over 150 countries in a fourteen-year endeavor to codify the rules for the use of the oceans.[42] A secure and stable environment is a prerequisite for sustainable development in this or any other part of the world.

Four decades of toe-to-toe competition with the United States had left the Soviet economy stagnating, and in a speech in Vladivostok in July 1986, Mikhail Gorbachev set out the Soviet Union's claims to be a major Pacific power.[43] This was at a time when the USSR was deeply embroiled in Afghanistan at great cost in blood and treasure. The thrust of the speech was about lifting the collective gaze from Europe and Central Asia and realizing the economic opportunities to be found in the relatively untapped resources of the Soviet Far East. To help the shift, Gorbachev urged a different dynamic in the maritime domain. He wanted US and Soviet naval reductions in some areas, though not wholesale in the east, and he wanted greater cooperation and collaboration in the region. At the time of Gorbachev's speech, the USSR was already busy establishing fishery agreements with Pacific island nations such as Kiribati and Vanuatu, but there was a long-term sticking point with Japan. Four of the larger northern Kuril Islands, historically administered by Japan, had been under Soviet occupation since the end of World War II, and the territorial dispute precluded large-scale trade and economic cooperation between Tokyo and Moscow, trade that Gorbachev was keen to address and that the United States was ambivalent about (for obvious reasons). At the same time, communist Vietnam was still occupying Cambodia/Kampuchea after its overthrow of the Khmer Rouge regime some eight years earlier in 1979.[44] The region was living with uncomfortable stability, and the communist bloc was suffering from what today might be called strategic overreach. Given what was going on in the world at the time and what was starting to happen in the Soviet Union, Gorbachev's Vladivostok speech was indicative of a strategic shift to the east—and a bold one. The Soviet Pacific Fleet had already grown by 80 percent from 1970 to 1985 and had become the largest of the four Soviet fleets.[45]

The fall of the Soviet Union and the end of the Cold War could have been another tipping point for the Indo-Pacific. However, despite a glimmer of revolution in China, the region managed the change peacefully on the whole. That stability continued through the 1990s into the early twenty-first century, and it has become widely recognized that the Indian and Pacific Oceans demonstrate the enduring importance of the sea as a resource, not least as a means of transportation, a facilitator of trade, and as a source of natural resources.[46] In such a region, territorial sovereignty matters, and it is no surprise that the provisions of UNCLOS are so important there. However, toward the end of the Cold War, after détente in the 1970s and perestroika in the 1980s, the already prosperous region took off more broadly, and the maritime space in particular opened up to increasing use and exploitation. The superpowers, previously active bystanders, became more active participants in the economic life of the region because they were left with little choice but to do so.

CONCLUSION

Long before President Barack Obama's pivot to Asia, in October 1985 President Ronald Reagan described the Pacific as the ocean where "the future of the world lies."[47] Though the US Navy's Seventh Fleet was still dominant and the full extent of the Soviet military buildup in the region was difficult to gauge, the Defense Secretary Caspar Weinberger asserted that the Soviets were adding enormously to naval and air strength in the region and deploying the most modern surface vessels, submarines, and aircraft.[48]

By the mid-1980s both superpowers had come to realize that the Indo-Pacific region was of vital importance and that they had to be involved there. There had been no change to the four themes highlighted above: superpower rivalry reinforced by nuclear deterrence and active alliance management was still keeping regional conflict more or less in check; there remained a plethora of international and regional organizations maneuvering around each other; proxy action was still prominent, though perhaps more so in South America, Africa, and Central Asia than in the maritime states of the Indo-Pacific; and the economic potential of the region was clear. However, neither side felt that it could afford to ignore the Indo-Pacific or cede advantage there to the other. Power vacuum theory was at play.

The superpowers competed for primacy during the Cold War, and the rivalry over ideology, politics, and military prowess in a global context was more often than not fairly evenhanded. However, once the true extent of the failing Soviet economy became known, any economic rivalry could only result in victory for the capitalist bloc. The superpowers pivoted to the Indo-Pacific far earlier than the received wisdom of today would have us believe, and they did so for good and understandable reasons. The East and South China Seas were resource rich, the Japanese economic miracle showed no signs of slowing, the South Korean rise seemed unstoppable, the ASEAN states were flourishing, and as restrictions were gradually relaxed, huge markets were opening up to trade in China and India. And, of course, by the mid-1980s, the security of the region appeared stable. The Indo-Pacific states could see the shift themselves too, and in this essentially maritime region the modernization of Asian naval forces grew in line with increasing "economic clout and political confidence."[49]

It is not known what would have happened had the Soviet Union not collapsed, but it is worth considering how the regional security and economic dynamics might have evolved differently. However, that is for another time and for a different book. What is known is that by the end of the Cold War, the Indo-Pacific was no longer a global backwater, and the world's strategic center of gravity had moved inexorably eastward.

NOTES

1. Donald S. Zagoria, "Soviet-American Rivalry in Asia," *Proceedings of the Academy of Political Science* 36, no. 1 (1986): 105, https://doi.org/10.2307/1174015.
2. Sheila Miyoshi Jager, *Brothers at War: The Unending Conflict in Korea* (New York: Norton, 2013), 317.
3. Steven M. Goldstein, "Chinese Perspectives on the Origins of the Korean War: An Assessment at Sixty," *International Journal of Korean Studies* 14, no. 2 (2010): 62.
4. Zagoria, "Soviet-American Rivalry in Asia," 105.
5. Arthur H. Mitchell, *Understanding the Korean War: The Participants, the Tactics, and the Course of Conflict* (Jefferson, NC: McFarland, 2013), 37.
6. Richard Aldrich, Rory Cormac, and Michael Goodman, *Spying on the World: The Declassified Documents of the Joint Intelligence Committee, 1936–2013* (Edinburgh: Edinburgh University Press, 2014), 169–70.
7. Avery Goldstein, "First Things First: The Pressing Danger of Crisis Instability in US-China Relations," *International Security* 37, no. 4 (2013): 58, https://doi.org/10.1162/ISEC_a_00114.
8. "Atomic Diplomacy," US Department of State, Office of the Historian, accessed May 25, 2020, https://history.state.gov/milestones/1945-1952/atomic.
9. Kotani Tetsuo, "Presence and Credibility: Homeporting the USS *Midway* at Yokosuka," *Journal of American–East Asian Relations* 15 (2008): 52, https://doi.org/10.1163/187656108793645798.
10. Tetsuo, "Presence and Credibility."
11. Karen A. Feste, *Expanding the Frontiers: Superpower Intervention in the Cold War* (Westport, CT: Praeger, 1994), 174.
12. Jesus M. Vargas, *SEATO Report, 1964–1965* (Washington, DC: Central Intelligence Agency, 1965), 9.
13. "Southeast Asia Treaty Organization (SEATO), 1954," US Department of State, Office of the Historian, accessed November 5, 2020, https://history.state.gov/milestones/1953-1960/seato.
14. "Southeast Asia Treaty Organization."
15. "Southeast Asia Treaty Organization."
16. Eleanor Albert and Lindsay Maizland, "What Is ASEAN?," Council on Foreign Relations, December 20, 2019, https://www.cfr.org/backgrounder/what-asean.
17. Odd Arne Westad, *The Global Cold War: Third World Interventions and the Making of Our Times* (Cambridge: Cambridge University Press, 2007), 4.
18. Westad, *Global Cold War*, 66–67.
19. David MacKenzie, *From Messianism to Collapse: Soviet Foreign Policy, 1917–1991* (Fort Worth, TX: Harcourt Brace, 1994), 170–72.
20. James A. Russell, "The Indian Ocean," in *Maritime Strategy and Global Order: Markets, Resources, Security*, ed. Daniel Moran and James A. Russell (Washington, DC: Georgetown University Press, 2016), 188–89.

21. T. V. Paul, "How India Will React to the Rise of China: The Soft-Balancing Strategy Reconsidered," War on the Rocks, September 17, 2018, https://warontherocks.com /2018/09/india-and-the-rise-of-china-soft-balancing-strategy-reconsidered/.

22. Russell, "Indian Ocean," 189.

23. Howard M. Hensel, "Superpower Interests and Naval Missions in the Indian Ocean," *US Naval War College Review* 38, no. 1 (1985): 63–64.

24. Hensel, "Superpower Interests."

25. Hensel.

26. Bernard D. Cole, *Asian Maritime Strategies: Navigating Troubled Waters* (Annapolis, MD: Naval Institute Press, 2013), 29.

27. James Cable, *Navies in Violent Peace* (Basingstoke, UK: Macmillan, 1989), 68.

28. John Hattendorf, ed., *US Naval Strategy in the 1970s*, Newport Paper no. 30 (Newport, RI: Naval War College Press, 2006), 6.

29. Colin McInnes and Mark Rolls, eds., *Post–Cold War Security Issues in the Asia-Pacific Region* (Ilford, UK: Frank Cass, 1994), 4.

30. Alex Alexiev, *Marxism and Resistance in the Third World: Cause and Effect*, R-3639 (Santa Monica, CA: RAND Corp., 1989).

31. For example, see Mitchell B. Lerner, *The* Pueblo *Incident: A Spy Ship and the Failure of American Foreign Policy* (Lawrence: University Press of Kansas, 2002), and, more recently, Jack Cheevers, *Act of War: Lyndon Johnson, North Korea, and the Capture of the Spy Ship* Pueblo (New York: Penguin, 2013). Comments on the *Pueblo* incident also appear in works discussing wider naval diplomacy, such as Bradford Dismukes and James M. McConnell, eds., *Soviet Naval Diplomacy* (Oxford: Elsevier Science, 1979), 119–23; and in books on Cold War sea power, such as David F. Winkler, *Cold War at Sea* (Annapolis, MD: Naval Institute Press, 2000), 37, 58–62. A more detailed reassessment of the *Pueblo* incident and its relevance to today, see Kevin Rowlands, *Naval Diplomacy in the 21st Century* (Abingdon, UK: Routledge, 2019).

32. John Lewis Gaddis, *The Cold War* (London: Penguin, 2005), 130–31.

33. Relations between the Chinese Communist Party and the Communist Party of the Soviet Union had been strained for some years, and Sino-Russian competition from 1965 to 1969 centered on their relative influence in communist countries. See S. J. Ball, *The Cold War: In International History, 1947–1991* (London: Arnold, 1998), 138.

34. Lerner, Pueblo *Incident*, 99–100, 137; Giseong Lee, "US Coercive Diplomacy towards North Korea" (PhD diss., University of Aberdeen, 2009), 105; Dismukes and McConnell, *Soviet Naval Diplomacy*, 119.

35. US House Armed Services Committee, *Memorandum for the Record on the Secret* Pueblo *Hearings of the House Committee on Armed Services*, DOCID 4121701 (Washington, DC: US House Armed Services Committee, 1969).

36. James Cable, *Gunboat Diplomacy Political Applications of Limited Naval Force*, 3rd ed. (Basingstoke, UK: Macmillan, 1994), 26.

37. Winkler, *Cold War at Sea*, 37.

38. Cable, *Gunboat Diplomacy*, 196.

39. "Indo-Pakistan War of 1971," Global Security, accessed February 20, 2020, https:// www.globalsecurity.org/military/world/war/indo-pak_1971.htm.

40. Dismukes and McConnell, *Soviet Naval Diplomacy*, 178–92.

41. For a contemporary review of the flying geese model, see Terutomo Ozawa, "The (Japan-Born) 'Flying-Geese' Theory of Economic Development Revisited and Reformulated from a Structuralist Perspective," *Global Policy* 2, no. 2 (2011): 272–85.

42. "UNCLOS Overview," United Nations Division for Ocean Affairs and the Law of the Sea, accessed May 25, 2020, https://www.un.org/depts/los/convention _agreements/convention_overview_convention.htm.

43. Amitav Acharya, "The Asia-Pacific Region: Cockpit for Superpower Rivalry," *World Today* 43, no. 8/9 (August/September 1987): 155–58.

44. Acharya, "Asia-Pacific Region."

45. Harry Anderson and Kim Willenson, "A Pacific Power Play: Moscow's Naval Buildup Worries US Allies in Asia," *Newsweek*, May 20, 1985, 42.

46. Geoffrey Till, *Seapower: A Guide for the Twenty-First Century*, 2nd ed. (Abingdon, UK: Routledge, 2009), 322.

47. Kathy Koch, *Dawn of the Pacific Era* (Washington, DC: CQ Press, 2020).

48. Kenneth G. Weiss, "The Naval Dimension of the Sino-Soviet Rivalry," *Naval War College Review* 38, no. 1 (1985): 37–38.

49. Geoffrey Till, *Asia's Naval Expansion: An Arms Race in the Making?* (Abingdon, UK: Routledge, 2012), 32.

PART III

Naval Power and Contemporary Security in the Indo-Pacific

11

Northeast Asia

Ian Bowers

In Northeast Asia, the question of maritime geography's influence on interstate interaction is particularly pertinent. The region is now witnessing a dramatic contemporary buildup in net sea and naval power, which is resulting in increasing strategic uncertainty and raising the stakes of contentious interactions at sea.[1] Importantly, with the notable exception of the Korean Peninsula, the major actors in the region do not share land borders but rather seas, which makes the maritime theater a dominant feature in regional security strategies. These two facts force one to consider the connection between the seas of Northeast Asia, the development of national strategies, and the future of regional stability. The importance of understanding this connection should not be underestimated. Maritime strategies and state interactions at sea only matter inasmuch as how they impact events on land.[2] Naval writers have long noted the importance of maritime geography in determining how states develop and deploy their sea power.[3] However, few extant works examine how the sea as a dominant operational theater influences state interaction on a strategic level.[4]

As defined in this chapter, Northeast Asia encompasses China, North and South Korea, Japan, and the Russian Far East. Therefore, the Yellow Sea and its gulfs, the Bohai Sea, the Korea Bay, the Sea of Japan, and the Sea of Okhotsk are included in the analysis.[5] This theater is rife with potential maritime strategic tinderboxes, including disputed islands, nuclear bastions, and contested littoral waters.

This chapter demonstrates that theaters like Northeast Asia that are dominated by maritime geography require unique strategic and operational calculations. Core considerations, such as strategic stability, the nature and operationalization of deterrence, escalation dynamics, and even alliance formation, are fundamentally informed by the relationship between the sea and the land in Northeast Asia. This relationship is dynamic in that the strategic importance of the sea continuously shifts as operational and strategic priorities change in national capitals across the region. Importantly, although changes in geography occur over eons, technological advances can quickly alter how geography and the sea affect operational and strategic planning.

What follows is a discussion of the core characteristics that underpin how the sea and maritime geography shape the wider strategic environment in Northeast Asia. The chapter then turns to how the sea informs specific regional security relationships and by extension national security strategies. Finally, it concludes by using these relationships to elicit how the sea and maritime geography influence key strategic interactions between states.

THE CHARACTERISTICS OF THE
NORTHEAST ASIAN MARITIME THEATER

The operational and strategic characteristics of the sea are fundamentally different from those of land. Primarily, there are few true barriers to be protected or crossed, and outside of territorial waters the sea is difficult if not impossible to permanently control. Instead, the oceans are a commons wherein both friendly and competitive civilian and military actors can operate freely beside each other. However, as with all theaters, Northeast Asia has specific and intertwined geographic, legal, technological, operational, and economic conditions that frame how states develop and operationalize their national security strategies.

First and foremost, the Northeast Asian maritime theater is defined by its narrowness. A narrow sea is a body of water "that can be controlled from both of its sides and some sea areas."[6] In Northeast Asia, the Yellow Sea, the Sea of Japan, and the Sea of Okhotsk are all narrow seas. In such waters, the relative importance of the tools of sea power changes. While naval vessels remain crucial to military operations at sea, the influence of land-based assets, such as aircraft, sensors, and missiles, increases. Therefore, in contrast with some of the other theaters described in this volume, capabilities on land play a critical role in determining strategic outcomes at sea.

Given the military sophistication of most actors in the region, the waters of Northeast Asia are now a difficult place for any navy, no matter how strong, to secure even temporary sea control. Naval vessels operating in the region lose the advantage of being able to disappear into the vast expanses of the open ocean. Proximity to the shore exposes naval vessels to a potent array of sea-denial capabilities, including shore- and air-launched missiles and short-range but highly effective diesel submarines. The airspace above narrow seas can also be hotly contested by land-based aircraft, reducing the ability of naval aviation to perform key operational tasks such as intelligence, surveillance, and reconnaissance as well as antisubmarine warfare. The compressed size of the operational theater also increases the potential for the heavy and debilitating use of electronic warfare, which can disrupt weapon and command-and-control systems. As Milan Vego states, naval combat operations in narrow seas are characterized by "frequent and drastic" alterations in the "tactical and operational situation."[7]

This operational picture in Northeast Asia is further complicated by the proliferation of conventional short-range ballistic missiles and cruise missiles that can now render previously secure or defendable areas vulnerable to attack. Due to this combination of narrow seas and the proliferation of missile technology, naval bases in the region are no longer safe harbors to withdraw to but are rather areas of potential vulnerability. China, South Korea, and North Korea all possess large arsenals of weapons, and the potential strategic consequences of this cannot be overestimated. For example, studies of Chinese missile capabilities demonstrate that extant missile defenses would be inadequate to protect US and Japanese facilities on the Japanese archipelago. This would expose US Navy and Japan Maritime Self-Defense Force (JMSDF) platforms to attack before they could leave harbor, thereby undermining the core infrastructure that has supported US dominion in the region since the end of World War II.[8]

Narrow seas may also strain regional strategic, political, and economic interactions as they can complicate the setting of maritime boundaries under the regime of the United Nations Convention on the Law of the Sea. Geographic proximity requires political compromise for the permanent delimitation of maritime boundaries. This is particularly true when states are less than four hundred kilometers apart, which results in overlapping exclusive economic zones (EEZs).[9] Such compromise can be difficult to achieve, given competing nationalist narratives, domestic interests, and fears over potential economic loss or strategic vulnerability. In Northeast Asia narrow seas influence the intensity of maritime territorial disputes, which makes the drawing of baselines, the delimitation of EEZs and continental shelves, and the agreement of territorial waters complex and sometimes deadly issues.[10]

The narrowness of the region's waters exposes maritime trade to greater risks. Interruptions to sea lines of communication (SLOCs) in the Yellow Sea or Sea of Japan as a result of instability at sea would have a significant impact on regional economic growth. Northeast Asia is one of the world's most important maritime trading regions. China, Japan, and South Korea are three of the world's top five exporters. The vast majority of the goods they export and the raw materials needed to sustain their economies are transported by sea. Sustained strategic tension or even conflict in the confined spaces of Northeast

Asia would limit the ability of merchant vessels to use the sea safely by disrupting the secure use of SLOCs, thereby restricting free access to ports and raising maritime insurance rates. Therefore, maritime security and the need to minimize or contain damaging interactions at sea continuously inform wider national security strategies in the region.

The permanent and massive presence of the United States is another unique characteristic of the Northeast Asia maritime theater. Although it is a third party, the United States, as the most sophisticated and strongest sea power in the theater, is indivisible from regional strategic dynamics. It maintains substantial naval, air, and land facilities in both Japan and South Korea. These forward bases are vital to a US grand strategy seeking to both maintain a regional balance of power in the face of China's rise and ensure Washington's interests in the Indo-Pacific region are met.[11] While the United States does not take a position on competing territorial disputes, since 2020 it has explicitly stated that China's claims to offshore resources in the South China Sea are illegal.[12] Moreover, the US political, military, and economic capabilities influence how its allies develop strategies and capabilities to manage their security needs. Consequently, policy preferences in Washington, in combination with US military power, play a substantial role in determining regional deterrence and alliance dynamics.

For both China and Russia, specific maritime areas are intrinsic components in their strategic security architectures. In these cases, maritime geostrategy is linked with nuclear-deterrent reliability to inform regional security interactions. For example, the Bohai Sea is vital to Chinese interests. Chinese strategists have long recognized the vulnerability of Beijing due to its proximity to the Bohai Sea and therefore recognized the importance of defending it.[13] However, in the nuclear era the Bohai Sea has taken on an added strategic dimension. Although China's fleet of *Jin*-class nuclear-powered ballistic missile submarines (SSBNs), which form the heart of Beijing's at-sea nuclear second-strike capability, operate out of Hainan Island in the South China Sea, the Bohai Sea plays a vital role in Beijing's nuclear posture. The Bohai shipyard is where China constructs the majority of its nuclear-powered submarines. Therefore, securing this manufacturing infrastructure and unimpeded access to the Bohai Sea is vital to maintaining China's strategic deterrent. Consequently, ensuring dominance in the Yellow Sea and being able to counter a US, South Korean, or even North Korean presence are key considerations in Chinese defense planning.[14] For Russia the Sea of Okhotsk is a bastion for its Pacific SSBN fleet. Therefore, a primary strategic goal for Russian forces operating in the Pacific is ensuring the sea's security. This geostrategic imperative is a key determinant in Russia's broader strategic approach to Japan. It directly impacts not only the resolution of the Kuril Islands dispute but also how Moscow views the potential threat arising from the US-Japanese alliance.

The final important characteristic of the Northeast Asian maritime environment is the relative balance of military and sea power. Unlike other theaters considered in this volume, all the actors in this region possess credible and sustainable military capabilities. In conventional and nuclear capabilities, both the United States and China are the dominant regional military powers. The United States maintains a credible capacity to project power in the region through a combination of forward-deployed forces, treaties with allies, and the capacity to surge reinforcements into the region if required. Currently within the Indo-Pacific area of responsibility, the United States has approximately two thousand aircraft, two hundred vessels, and over 370,000 personnel deployed.[15] Through an unprecedented level of investment in military modernization, China is rapidly becoming a regional peer competitor to the United States. China's naval, missile, and air forces are now the largest in Northeast Asia and are characterized by a growing level of doctrinal and technological sophistication.[16] Although considerably weaker than the militaries of either the United States or China, both the Japanese and South Korean military forces have undergone and continue to undergo substantial force improvements.[17] Both countries are leveraging their access to US military platforms and their advanced economic and indigenous technological capacity to procure equipment such as F-35 aircraft as well as new and advanced submarines, missile technology, and nascent power-projection capabilities. While neither country has the capacity to match the growth of Chinese sea power, each possesses a potent array of capabilities that could inflict substantial damage should conflict break out in the region. Moreover, their close operational coordination with the United States under bilateral alliance agreements bolsters their warfighting capacity and, by extension, their deterrent credibility. While lacking in some areas in the Pacific, Russia still maintains powerful capabilities, particularly in submarines, electronic warfare, and missile technologies.[18] North Korea is an outlier in that its level of sea power is weaker than that of the other states in the region. However, its ability to inflict existential damage on South Korea across the demilitarized zone (DMZ) using conventional and nonconventional weapons creates a unique deterrent effect at sea by holding the region at risk of destabilization should another state use coercive force against it.

THE SEA AND REGIONAL SECURITY INTERACTIONS

The chapter now turns to four regional security relationships that are characterized by ongoing maritime boundary or territorial disputes linked to key strategic considerations: China–South Korea, South Korea–Japan, Russia-Japan, South Korea–North Korea. The chapter uses these relationships to assess how maritime geography and the operational realities of the sea affect how these states interact.

China–South Korea

The seemingly inexorable rise of Chinese sea power arguably exposes South Korea to greater potential risk than any other state in East Asia. Separated by only the Yellow Sea, South Korea shares the same waters as China, and this ensures that Seoul will always be vulnerable to the policy predilections and coercive potential of its larger neighbor. Despite this vulnerability, South Korea's economy is dependent on China.[19] This ensures that the contemporary maritime relationship between both countries is dominated by commercial traffic across the Yellow Sea.[20]

Illegal Chinese fishing in South Korean waters is the most prominent source of maritime tension between the two countries. Due to the narrowness of the Yellow Sea, both countries claim overlapping EEZs, and consequently there has yet to be a definitive delimitation of the boundary. Nonetheless, in 2001 a bilateral fishery agreement came into effect that set out shared and exclusive fishing grounds and was designed to create stability at sea and mitigate potential conflict between fishing fleets. However, illegal Chinese fishing in South Korean waters has persisted in spite of the agreement, and there have been significant and sustained clashes between South Korean coast guard vessels and Chinese trawlers.[21] These clashes have resulted in sunk vessels and the deaths of both South Korean coast guard officers and Chinese fishermen. Moreover, the clashes have forced the South Korean government to enact robust rules of engagement to counter aggressive Chinese behavior.

China and South Korea also disagree over the status of the waters surrounding Ieodo (also known as Socotra Rock), a submerged rock to the south of the Korean Peninsula that sits in an area where South Korean and Chinese EEZ claims overlap.[22] South Korea has tacit possession of Ieodo because it built a research station atop the rock in 2003. While not a territorial dispute per se, it does have many of the characteristics of one. South Korean coast guard and naval vessels regularly patrol the waters surrounding Ieodo, both to indicate control and to counter periodic increases in Chinese presence operations around it.[23]

These points of contention at sea between Beijing and Seoul do create strategic and operational problems, particularly for policymakers in South Korea, who are forced by domestic and economic pressures to respond strongly to China's actions. However, despite the occasional escalation to violence or increase in political rhetoric, incidents at sea are broadly contained and have been kept separate from the wider strategic and economic relationship between Seoul and Beijing. Maritime clashes have yet to severely strain or alter China–South Korea relations in the same way as Chinese actions have with other claimant countries and strategic actors in the South China or East China Seas.[24]

The setting aside of such issues in the wider South Korea–China relationship is in stark contrast with the deployment of a Terminal High Altitude Area Defense missile defense battery to the peninsula in 2016, which resulted in sustained, targeted economic punishment by China.[25] Beijing likely viewed the potential long-term strategic implications of such a deployment as a core challenge to its security, whereas existing problems at sea between the two countries do not reach such a threshold. For South Korea, a similar calculation is in evidence, the one exception being the presence of Chinese fishing vessels in the sensitive Han River Estuary. This is a violation of the Korean Armistice Agreement, and following a strong policing presence by South Korean forces and United Nations Command and high-level political involvement, China has seemingly reined in its fishing fleet's activities in that immediate area.[26]

Of course, China's capacity to dominate its smaller neighbor at sea has, in part, driven the modernization of the Republic of Korea Navy (ROKN). Although the South Korean military primarily focuses on threats from North Korea, it also seeks sufficient capabilities, such as advanced submarines, to asymmetrically deter China from the use of overt, coercive force and to protect South Korean interests at sea. As an example, shortly after China expanded its air defense identification zone in 2013, and in a public demonstration that it would not stand still in the face of Chinese coercive activities in the region, South Korea confirmed the procurement of three new Aegis destroyers.[27]

It should also be noted that China's development of sea power has now given it the capacity to deny the free use of its littoral waters in wartime. This would fundamentally impact the strategic and operational picture should conflict break out on the Korean Peninsula. In stark contrast with the Korean War, wherein the US and allied forces enjoyed unimpeded access to the waters around the peninsula, Beijing's ability to contest control of the Yellow Sea would make it difficult for any US or allied task force to project power from the waters west of the Korean Peninsula.

South Korea–Japan

Animosity and distrust are embedded in the political and strategic narratives of both Japan and South Korea. The continued tension between both countries has its source in the conflicting historical narratives initially arising from Japan's occupation of the Korean Peninsula in the early twentieth century and their sometimes divergent strategic interests in Northeast Asia. However, the sea is an underappreciated element, both driving and alleviating tensions between the two countries.

The status of Dok-do (known in Japan as the Takeshima Islands; also called the Liancourt Rocks) is one of the main sources of South Korea–Japanese animosity. South Korea controls the small islets, and although they are of little strategic value, they could play a role in determining the ultimate delineation of both countries' EEZs in the Sea of Japan.[28] They are also of substantial political and ideational value for both Seoul and Tokyo.[29] Political tensions erupt periodically over the islands, with flare-ups usually occurring around the time of South Korea's biannual military exercises in the area or when Japanese government documents highlight Tokyo's claim to the islands.

Except for South Korea's military exercises around Dok-do / the Takeshima Islands, there is little to suggest that the contested claims directly affect wider strategic and operational dynamics between Japan and South Korea. Both sides are developed countries with advanced militaries and are close allies of the United States. Although it maintains a contingent of police on the islets, South Korea does not maintain military forces there. Instead, South Korean coast guard and naval vessels perform occasional patrols in the surrounding waters.[30] This combination of factors is enough to maintain control of the features, despite their contested nature, without generating significant operational tension at sea. Indeed, regardless of political tension, good order at sea is largely sustained in the Sea of Japan. Despite the lack of an agreed-upon delineation of an EEZ, fishing is regulated through a well-observed agreement, and both countries have agreed on the boundaries through the strategically important Korea Strait. However, this does not mean that there are no incidents between the two militaries. For instance, in 2018 Japan accused a ROKN destroyer of locking on to a nearby Japanese P-1 maritime patrol aircraft with its fire-control radar.[31] South Korea refuted the allegation, but the incident further soured already difficult political relations between both countries.

The sea plays a role in determining the extent to which the political rivalry drives military and naval modernization. Because Japan and South Korea are divided by the sea, maritime geography reduces areas of potential tension that might occur if they shared a land border. From a strategic perspective, the sea and the difficulty of projecting power across it reduces the threat perception on both sides. Neither South Korea nor Japan needs to procure capabilities to counter each other directly; instead, they can leverage the inherent mobility and ambiguity of naval forces. Naval vessels procured to counter China or North Korea can also be used by both Seoul and Tokyo to provide deterrence or the public/political pretense of a deterrent posture within their context of the South Korea–Japan dynamic, even if conflict is highly unlikely.

Indeed, the political conflict and strategic distrust between the two countries have sometimes been offset at sea. The maritime arena has allowed, when political or strategic circumstances require, South Korea and Japan to carry out joint exercises and even coordinate operationally outside of the public eye. This avoids difficult political or public blowback that could have occurred if such activities occurred on land. For example, mutual strategic and alliance interests resulted a number of joint naval exercises led by the United States that focused on missile defense, antisubmarine warfare, and information sharing.[32] Also, following China's 2013 announcement of an expanded air defense identification zone, the ROKN and the JMSDF carried out a coordinated search-and-rescue exercise in international waters and airspace covered by the new zone.[33]

Russia-Japan

The disputed Kuril Islands frame the contemporary strategic relationship between Russia and Japan. Running from the tip of the Kamchatka Peninsula down to the northern part of Hokkaido, the islands bind the Sea of Okhotsk. Japan disputes Russia's control over the four southernmost islands, which sit closest to the Japanese archipelago. Russia's control over the entire chain provides it with a natural strategic barrier on its eastern flank. Conceptually at least, this allows Russia to apply a so-called bastion defense to the Sea of Okhotsk by using the islands as bases of deployment for high-technology denial capabilities, such as antiship and antiair missiles, and as barriers to access for intruding vessels and aircraft.[34] Moreover, Russia's nuclear submarines attached to its Pacific Fleet operate out of the Rybachiy Submarine Base on the east coast of the Kamchatka Peninsula.[35] At the northern end of the Kuril Islands, this base is central to Russia's strategic deterrent. Four *Borei*-class SSBNs, Russia's newest class of ballistic missile submarines, are now attached to the Pacific Fleet, and the easy access to the Sea of Okhotsk provides them with safer waters from which to conduct deterrent patrols. Any weakening of control over the entire island chain could endanger Russia's operational and strategic approach in the Pacific.

Former Japanese prime minister Abe Shinzo made repeated efforts to engage Russia and negotiate the return of the four disputed islands in the chain.[36] Their potential economic value and the need to relieve some of the strategic pressure that Japan's self-defense forces face can explain this pursuit. Dealing with China's operations in the East China Sea, North Korea's continued nuclear program, and Russia's presence proximate to Hokkaido is overstretching Japan's self-defense forces. Solving the Kuril Islands dispute would relieve some of this pressure.[37]

However, Russia has rebuffed Japan's attempts to regain the islands. Their strategic importance explains Moscow's reluctance to give up this territory. Not only would Russia lose control over certain access points to the Sea of Okhotsk— it would also risk having US military capabilities (or Japanese systems networked to US ones) deployed closer to Russian territory.[38] Indeed, even as Tokyo has engaged Moscow, the Russian military continues to reinforce its presence on the islands by deploying Bastion and Bal coastal missile defense systems, Tor-M2U antiair missile batteries, Ka-52K attack helicopters, and even advanced Su-35 fighter aircraft on Iturup Island.[39] In the case of the islands, the demands of at-sea nuclear deterrence and assurance that Russian forces can control their own narrow seas drive broader long-term interactions on a political level.[40]

North Korea–South Korea

Unlike the other dynamics described in this chapter, the dominant and existential nature of the enduring standoff across the DMZ means that the sea around the Korean Peninsula is subsidiary to the land theater. However, this does not mean that sea has no strategic or operational utility; rather, what occurs on it is directly related to events on land. For both North and South Korea, the sea presents not only strategic and operational opportunities; it is also a source of substantial vulnerability.

The Northern Limit Line (NLL), the de facto maritime border between both countries, is the main area of operational interaction between North and South Korea. The NLL is the maritime extension of the military demarcation line that divides the two Koreas on the peninsula and uniquely has taken on many of the characteristics of a land boundary. The ROKN and the South Korean coast guard must maintain a permanent presence along the NLL to deter North Korean civilian and military vessels from crossing it. This is particularly important, given North Korea's focus on maintaining a substantial force of minisubmarines and high-speed amphibious craft designed either to covertly insert special forces along the South Korean coast or to quickly land invasion forces in strategically important islands and areas close to the DMZ.[41] In ideal circumstances the ROKN must have the operational capacity to quickly reinforce its ships at sea and maintain escalation dominance in order to reinforce deterrence.

Pyongyang has successfully used this operational picture to its advantage and has leveraged its relatively weak naval forces to signal its intentions, resolve, capabilities, and displeasure with Seoul. Since the end of the Korean War, naval clashes along the NLL have resulted in some significant casualties. The costliest of the incidents was the 2010 sinking of the South Korean warship *Cheonan* by a North Korean submarine when forty-six ROKN sailors died.[42] Nonetheless, this and other acts at sea neither resulted in military retaliation nor escalated in the land theater.[43] Essentially events at sea, no matter how deadly, have not yet proven important enough for South Korea or the United States to trigger full-scale war on land. Consequently, the sea so far has proven to be a useful, nonescalatory environment for North Korean provocations.

While the sea may be a strategically useful arena for North Korea, it is also a source of great vulnerability. The weakness of its naval and air forces gives it a limited capacity to deny either South Korea or the United States the ability to use the sea as a medium to project power. Geography ensures that its naval forces are divided, and North Korea has demonstrated a limited capacity to develop or integrate modern capabilities into its sea power architecture.

During the Korean War the United States and allied militaries used the sea to great strategic and tactical effect. It is likely that in a future war the United States would again seek to project power from the sea. Indeed, the South Koreans have noted this vulnerability and are developing a potent from-the-sea strike capability, arming nearly all new vessels with the capacity to launch land-attack missiles and building an increasingly capable amphibious component.[44] Although North Korea has attempted to hedge against this weakness by investing in sea-denial forces and posturing for a short, sharp war, any protracted conflict would leave its eastern flank, and possibly its western, heavily exposed.

On the South Korean side, the sea has long been a source of economic and military strength but also of potential weakness. As long as South Korea is a geostrategic island, the sea is a lifeline for its export-driven economy and is equally important as the primary method for receiving US reinforcements in case of war. Consequently, maintaining stability at sea and open SLOCs is crucial for South Korean security. Importantly, although the ROKN is now superior to its North Korean counterpart at sea, the proximity of key South Korean ports, such as Busan, to North Korea renders it vulnerable to Pyongyang's growing arsenal of short-range ballistic missiles. In this case, technology is mitigating the protection that distance once provided key strategic locations.

Indeed, North Korean technological advances are opening a new strategic front at sea. By pursuing a submarine-launched ballistic missile capability, North Korea is elevating the strategic importance of the sea. This will force South Korea and the United States to develop and deploy capabilities to counter North Korean ballistic missile submarines and has already resulted in South Korea deploying a conventional submarine capable of launching ballistic missiles.[45] These developments will alter the calculations of escalation and deterrence that currently characterizes the littorals around the peninsula and potentially make engagements at sea more closely related to strategic stability on land.

IMPLICATIONS OF A MARITIME THEATER

There is no one explanation for the interaction between the sea, interstate security relations, and national security strategies. Each relationship described above has different dynamics that are affected by the relative balance of power, the stability and security of maritime interests, and the proximity of maritime interests to core national strategic, political, and economic interests. Nevertheless, several findings can be derived from these relationships.

As defined in this chapter, the seas of Northeast Asia are more stable than the East or South China Seas. Although maritime disputes and strategic tension are found throughout the region, contentious activity at sea over issues such as illegal fishing have largely been confined to the operational level and have not affected wider interstate interactions on political, strategic, or economic levels.

Maritime territorial disputes, particularly Dok-do and the Kuril Islands, have for different reasons impacted interstate relations. In the case of the former, the disputed islands are one element among several causes of poor South Korea–Japan political relations. However, it is the nationalist and ideational elements of the dispute rather than its influence on boundary delimitation at sea that maintain the islands in national strategic narratives. In the case of the latter, the Kurils play a vital strategic role for Russia, and therefore the dispute directly affects Moscow-Tokyo relations as long as Japan views dispute resolution in its favor as an important policy goal.

The level of conflict stability can be further attributed to the reality that narrow seas, in combination with military technological advances, have vastly increased the vulnerability of naval forces operating in the region. Importantly, all states—except for North Korea—have the financial and technological capacities to operationalize such capabilities. Therefore, the threshold for the use of force at sea is high because the potential of incurring material, economic, and reputational costs on land as a result of using force at sea largely outweighs the possible strategic benefits. The one exception is the Korean Peninsula. Due to the militarized and disputed land border, the stakes of action there are lower at sea than they are on land. Therefore, the sea is sometimes preferred as an arena for coercive actions because there is a smaller possibility of escalation leading to all-out war than on land.

These escalation dynamics in Northeast Asia reveal important lessons about deterrence at sea. As there are normally few red lines or triggering points in a maritime domain, general deterrence is the dominant form of deterrence.[46] States throughout Northeast Asia need to possess sufficient sea power to prevent or discourage the transition to war. Although China possesses substantially greater net capabilities than either Japan or South Korea, both smaller states operate, or are developing, sufficient assets to impose damage should Beijing decide to use coercive force or transition to war. Even in the South Korea–Japan dynamic, the former, despite the remote possibility of conflict, views the possession forces capable of balancing the larger state as important for general deterrence.

Northeast Asia does have a number of specific places where immediate deterrence is observable. In these areas, deterrence strategies are easier to articulate and observe. North and South Korea's enduring standoff across the

NLL is a unique example of immediate deterrence at sea, whereby forces are deployed to prevent specific unwanted actions. Similarly, if less pressing, the deployment of South Korean police on Dok-do and Russian military capabilities on the Kuril Islands each serve as an indicator of control and therefore act as a political and strategic deterrent by raising the cost of any coercive attempt to regain possession.

It is notable that in Northeast Asia, China has yet to operationalize an explicitly hybrid strategy as it has done in the East and South China Seas.[47] The objectives of such a strategy would be less clear in the region, given that Beijing's goal in both the East and South China Seas is to gain some level of control over resource exploitation and ease the projection of its power into Southeast Asia.[48] China's proximity in Northeast Asian waters ensures that it is capable of projecting power without the need to resort to hybridity. Additionally, in terms of resource exploitation, legal and political conditions make such a strategy more complex to operationalize. An examination of the South Korea–China dynamic shows a hybrid approach is not in evidence. China's fisheries agreement with South Korea, while lacking in dispute-resolution measures, reduces China's room to exploit ambiguities in international law, thereby making it more difficult to justify state-sanctioned illegal fishing activities. Instead, the Chinese fishing fleet operates openly and illegally, either without sanction or with tacit permission from Chinese authorities. South Korea's advanced naval and maritime law-enforcement capabilities allow it to enact a deterrent posture that can sometimes counter but not prevent such an approach, and as this chapter has pointed out, Beijing has not responded to these robust countermeasures with the opprobrium seen in other theaters.

The sea also affects how states work together to ensure mutual security interests. Alliance dynamics at sea are different from those on land. As events at sea do not have the level of permanence as those on land, often alliance responses are not triggered, despite enemy behavior. This can lead to uncertainty over commitment within alliances, as is evidenced in the North Korea–South Korea dynamic. Unlike the US Army on the peninsula, the US Navy does not maintain a permanent presence along the NLL. Future North Korean actions along this maritime border would likely not result in US casualties, thereby potentially undermining the kind of trip-wire effect that is operationalized when allied troops are deployed in areas of danger on land.

Additionally, the sea can enable the development of an operational relationship. Former rivals China and Russia both share a land border, but it is at sea and in the airspace above it that the two countries are making their presence felt in Northeast Asia.[49] The maritime arena allows for periodic yet effective cooperation between the two states through joint exercises and even patrols, thereby facilitating both states' desire to reshape the international order without overt or formalized alliance structures.

   Finally, the sea also ensures that neither South Korea nor Japan are fully incentivized to overcome their long-standing historical antipathy. The sea reduces the incentive for an alliance, as Japan would be unable to fully assist South Korea in any land war on the Korean Peninsula and thereby lessens Tokyo's coercive potential. In this vein, the sea magnifies the effects of Japan's peaceful constitution. In areas where cooperation would be possible and even desirable, such as assisting US forces, existing bilateral alliance arrangements would ensure that US assets, particularly those operating off the coast of the Korean Peninsula, would be protected regardless of South Korea–Japan relations. Additionally, operations such as mine warfare and antisubmarine warfare against North Korea would also be conducted regardless of any alliance, as it is in Japan's interests to ensure its near seas are secure in any conflict.

CONCLUSION

Northeast Asia is a complex strategic environment. Multiple state actors all vie to maintain or advance their own security interests in a space with few borders and, importantly, little to conquer. Instead, the military, paramilitary, and civilian assets of each state operate alongside each other in the same, increasingly crowded space. It is with this fundamental reality in mind that we can begin to understand the nature of strategic stability in Northeast Asia. The connection of the sea with maritime geostrategy, the requirements of economic stability, strong deterrent postures, and strategic interests ensure, as this chapter argues, a level of stability not seen in other regions. The strategic stakes in the waters of Northeast Asia have not yet proven significant enough for any actor to upset fundamentally this delicate balance. Although dominated by China, the regional buildup of sea power can assist in maintaining equilibrium in the region because general deterrent postures gain credibility from the combination of advanced technology and the uncertainty of combat in narrow seas. The one area of exception is the Korean Peninsula, the world's most militarized continental theater and arguably the primary source of instability in the region. However, maritime clashes between North and South Korea have yet to escalate to the point that the armistice has broken down on land. Should events on land become unstable, the maritime domain would become rife with tension as multiple actors would seek to attain control of or deny the use of the sea. This speaks to the fundamental relationship between the land and the sea. In Northeast Asia, it is on land where the strategic stakes are high enough to result in conflict on the water.

NOTES

1. Sea power is defined as the total capacity of a state to use the sea. It has military and civilian components and includes navies, coast guards, and merchant marines. Naval power is the military element of sea power.

2. Julian S. Corbett, *Principles of Maritime Strategy* (New York: Dover, 2004), 14.

3. See Alfred Thayer Mahan, *The Influence of Sea Power upon History, 1660–1783* (New York: Dover, 1987), chap. 1; Geoffrey Sloan and Colin S. Gray, "Why Geopolitics?," in *Geopolitics, Geography, and Strategy*, ed. Colin S. Gray and Geoffrey Sloan (Oxford: Routledge, 2013), 2–3; Geoffrey Till, *Seapower: A Guide for the Twenty-First Century*, 2nd ed. (Oxford: Routledge, 2009), 88–96.

4. Some notable exceptions include Robert S. Ross, "The Geography of Peace: East Asia in the Twenty-First Century," *International Security* 23, no. 4 (Spring 1999): 81–118, https://doi.org/10.1162/isec.23.4.81; and Øystein Tunsjø, *The Return of Bipolarity in World Politics: China, the United States and Geostructural Realism* (New York: Columbia University Press, 2018), 126–49.

5. The Sea of Japan is also named the East Sea.

6. Milan Vego, *Naval Operations in Narrow Seas*, 2nd ed. (Oxford: Frank Cass, 2003), 7.

7. Vego, *Naval Operations*, 12.

8. Ashley Townshend, Brendan Thomas-Noone, and Matilda Steward, *Averting Crisis: American Strategy, Military Spending, and Collective Defence in the Indo-Pacific* (Sydney: United States Studies Centre, 2019), 18.

9. Suk Kyoon Kim, "Understanding Maritime Disputes in Northeast Asia: Issues and Nature," *International Journal of Marine and Coastal Law* 23 (2008): 213–47, https://doi.org/10.1163/092735208X272210.

10. Min Gyo Koo, *Island Disputes and Maritime Regime Building in East Asia: Between a Rock and a Hard Place* (London: Springer, 2009), 168.

11. Robert Ross, "US Grand Strategy, the Rise of China, and US National Security Strategy for East Asia," *Strategic Studies Quarterly* 7, no. 2 (Summer 2013): 25.

12. Gregory B. Poling, "How Significant Is the New U.S. South China Sea Policy?," Center for Strategic and International Studies, July 14, 2020, https://www.csis.org/analysis/how-significant-new-us-south-china-sea-policy.

13. Ronald C. Po, *The Blue Frontier: Maritime Vision and Power in the Qing Empire* (Cambridge: Cambridge University Press, 2018), 99–100.

14. James R. Holmes and Toshi Yoshihara, *Chinese Naval Strategy in the 21st Century: The Turn to Mahan* (Oxford: Routledge, 2008), 67–68.

15. US Department of Defense, *The Department of Defense Indo-Pacific Strategy Report: Preparedness, Partnerships and Promoting a Networked Region* (Washington, DC: US Department of Defense, 2019), 19.

16. Office of the Secretary of Defense, *Annual Report to Congress: Military and Security Developments Involving the People's Republic of China 2020* (Washington, DC: US Department of Defense, 2020), 38–48; Eric Heginbotham et al., *US-China Military Scorecard: Forces, Geography, and the Evolving Balance of Power, 1996–2017*, RR-392-AF (Santa Monica, CA: RAND Corp., 2015), 21–22.

17. See Eric Heginbotham and Richard J. Samuels, "Active Denial: Redesigning Japan's Response to China's Military Challenge," *International Security* 42, no. 4 (Spring

2018): 128–69, https://doi.org/10.1162/isec_a_00313; Bryan Harris, "South Korea Plans Blue-Water Naval Fleet," *Financial Times*, October 19, 2018.

18. See Keith Crane, Olga Oliker, and Brian Nichiporuk, *Trends in Russia's Armed Forces: An Overview of Budgets and Capabilities*, RR-2573-A (Santa Monica, CA: RAND Corp., 2019), 39–45; and Office of Naval Intelligence, *The Russian Navy: A Historic Transition* (Washington, DC: US Department of the Navy, 2015), 15.

19. Kyle Ferrier, "Just How Dependent Is South Korea on Trade with China?," Korea Economic Institute of America, accessed February 4, 2020, http://keia.org/just-how-dependent-south-korea-trade-china.

20. By 2012, 57 percent of China's and 70 percent of South Korea's trade came via the Yellow Sea. Michael A. McDevitt and Catherine K. Lea, "East China and Yellow Seas Overview Essay," in *The Long Littoral Project: East China and Yellow Sea; A Maritime Perspective on Indo-Pacific Security*, ed. Michael A. McDevitt et al. (Alexandria, VA: Center for Naval Analyses, 2012), 4.

21. Suk Kyoon Kim, *Maritime Disputes in Northeast Asia: Regional Challenges and Cooperation* (Boston: Brill Nijhoff, 2017), 141–44.

22. Also known as Socotra Rock.

23. Liu Zhen, "South Korea Deploys New Coastguard Ship to Watch Waters around Disputed Islet," *South China Morning Post*, June 23, 2016.

24. For an overview of Chinese actions in the South China and East China Seas, see Ronald O'Rourke, *US-China Strategic Competition in South and East China Sea: Background and Issues for Congress*, R42784 (Washington, DC: Congressional Research Service, 2019).

25. Ketian Vivian Zhang, "Chinese Non-military Coercion: Tactics and Rationale," Brookings Institution, January 22, 2019, https://www.brookings.edu/articles/chinese-non-military-coercion-tactics-and-rationale/.

26. Ju-min Park, "South Korea, U.N. Command Join Patrols to Halt Illegal Chinese Fishing," Reuters, June 10, 2016, https://www.reuters.com/article/us-southkorea-china-fishing-idUSKCN0YW0QI.

27. Eun-jung Kim, "S. Korea to Build Three More Aegis Destroyers," Yonhap News Agency, December 10, 2013, https://en.yna.co.kr/view/AEN20131210001651315.

28. Jon M. Van Dyke, "Legal Issues Related to Sovereignty over Dokdo and Its Maritime Boundary," *Ocean Development and International Law* 38, no. 1/2 (2007): 157–224, https://doi.org/10.1080/00908320601071504.

29. Dong-Joon Park and Danielle Chubb, "South Korean and Japan: Disputes over the Dokdo/Takeshima Islands," East Asia Forum, August 17, 2011, https://www.eastasiaforum.org/2011/08/17/south-korea-and-japan-disputes-over-the-dokdo-takeshima-islands/.

30. Sukjoon Yoon, "Establishing a Maritime Security Joint-Force Partnership between the Republic of Korea Navy and the Korea Coast Guard," in *Grey and White Hulls: An International Analysis of the Navy-Coastguard Nexus*, ed. Ian Bowers and Swee Lean Collin Koh (Singapore: Palgrave Macmillan, 2019), 60.

31. Ankit Panda, "Japan, South Korea in Row over Alleged Radar-Lock Incident," *The Diplomat*, December 26, 2018, https://thediplomat.com/2018/12/japan-south-korea-in-row-over-alleged-radar-lock-incident/.

32. US Seventh Fleet Public Affairs, "USN ROKN JMSDF Conduct Anti-submarine Warfare Exercises," US Navy, April 4, 2017, https://www.public.navy.mil/surfor/ddg85/Pages/USN-ROKN-JMSDF-conduct-anti-submarine-warfare-exercise-.aspx.

33. Samuel Mun, "Destined to Cooperate: Japan-South Korea Naval Relations," *The Diplomat*, February 5, 2014, https://thediplomat.com/2014/02/destined-to-cooperate-japan-south-korea-naval-relations/.

34. For an analysis of the difficulties Russia faces in fully applying a bastion strategy, see Robert Dalsjø, Christopher Berglund, and Michael Jonsson, *Bursting the Bubble: Russian A2/AD in the Baltic Sea Region; Capabilities, Countermeasures, and Implications* (Stockholm: Swedish Defence Research Agency, 2019).

35. Hans M. Kristensen, "Russia Pacific Fleet Prepares for Arrival of New Missile Submarines," Federation of American Scientists (blog), September 14, 2014, https://fas.org/blogs/security/2015/09/pacificfleet/.

36. James D. J. Brown, "Shinzo Abe's Russia Policy Risks Embarrassment for Japan," *Nikkei Asian Review*, September 10, 2019, https://asia.nikkei.com/Opinion/Shinzo-Abe-s-Russia-policy-risks-embarrassment-for-Japan.

37. For more on this approach, see Bjørn Elias Mikalsen Grønning, "The Japan-China-Russia Triangle and Security in North East Asia," in *Sino Russian Relations in the 21st Century*, ed. Jo Inge Bekkevold and Bobo Lo, 243–66 (London: Palgrave Macmillan, 2019).

38. "Abe Tells Putin No US Bases to Be Allowed on Returned Islands," *Asahi Shimbun*, November 16, 2018.

39. "Russia Plans to Beef Up Missile Defense on Northern Kurils, Close to Islands Claimed to Japan," *Japan Times*, September 3, 2019; Franz-Stefan Gady, "Russia Is Building Military Barracks on Disputed Kuril Islands," *The Diplomat*, December 19, 2018, https://thediplomat.com/2018/12/russia-is-building-military-barracks-on-disputed-kuril-islands/.

40. The number of Russian troops and weapon systems on the Kuril Islands likely has been reduced as a result of the February 2022 Russian invasion of Ukraine.

41. Joseph Bermudez, "North Korean Special Operations Forces: Hovercraft Bases (Part IV)," Beyond Parallel, March 5, 2018, https://beyondparallel.csis.org/north-korean-special-operations-forces-hovercraft-bases-part-iv/.

42. The NLL is the seaward extension of the DMZ. North Korea has yet to formally accept the maritime boundary in its current form. See Terence Roehrig, "North Korea and the Northern Limit Line," *North Korean Review* 5, no. 1 (Spring 2009): 8–22, https://doi.org/10.3172/nkr.5.1.8.

43. Christian Le Mière, *Maritime Diplomacy in the 21st Century: Drivers and Challenges* (Oxford: Routledge, 2014), 74.

44. Ridzwan Rahmat, "Crouching Tiger: South Korea Modernises amid Shifting Security Dynamics," *Jane's Navy International* 9 (2008): 28–32.

45. Sukjoon Yoon, "Expanding the ROKN's Capabilities to Deal with the SLBM Threat from North Korea," *Naval War College Review* 70, no. 2 (2017), article 4.

46. General deterrence is aimed at preventing crises or threats of force from occurring. Immediate deterrence is a response to a potential and specific threat. Paul K. Huth, "Deterrence and International Conflict: Empirical Findings and Theoretical Debates," *Annual Review of Political Science* 2, no. 25 (1999): 27, https://doi.org/10.1146/annurev.polisci.2.1.25.

47. I use Alessio Patalano's definition of hybrid strategy: one that "mobilises military, constabulary and paramilitary means in coordinated fashion, using political and legal rhetoric to justify them and to prevent or inhibit responses in pursuit of geostrategic objectives." Alessio Patalano, "When Strategy Is 'Hybrid' and Not 'Grey':

Reviewing Chinese Military and Constabulary Coercion at Sea," *Pacific Review* 31, no. 6 (2018): 813, https://doi.org/10.1080/09512748.2018.1513546.

48. Patalano, "When Strategy Is 'Hybrid.'"

49. Testuo Kotani, "China and Russia in the Western Pacific: Implications for Japan and the United States," National Bureau of Asian Research Maritime Awareness Project, April 18, 2019, https://www.nbr.org/publication/china-and-russia-in-the -western-pacific-implications-for-japan-and-the-united-states/.

12

East and South China Seas

Alessio Patalano and Julie Marionneau

Within the wider Indo-Pacific region, the East and South China Seas (ESCS) bear much of the weight concerning the risk of regional instability. In these theaters, the operational lines separating missions to perform constabulary activities, such as law enforcement, and those pertaining to national defense, diplomacy, and power projection have blurred. Of course, some security issues continue to have a more pronounced constabulary or military nature. Yet it is operationally increasingly difficult to separate activities aimed at advancing national claims in maritime disputes from those aimed at altering the region's military balance. This challenge raises crucial questions. How can states assess the intentions behind specific maritime activities? How can they prevent or, if needed, contrast coercive activities of a constabulary nature without risking military escalation or war? What is the difference between constabulary and military coercive operations? Do these differences matter to regional stability and security?

This chapter addresses the above questions. In so doing, it engages with a fundamental problem underwriting the stability of the ESCS regional maritime security complex—that is, the link between localized territorial disputes and broader structural military competition. To illustrate its case, the chapter focuses on two case studies: the Sino-Japanese territorial dispute in the East China Sea (ECS) over the Japanese-administered Senkaku Islands and the dispute over the ownership of the Spratly Islands in the South China Sea (SCS). The former are claimed by the People's Republic of China (PRC) and the Republic of China (hereafter Taiwan) under the name "Diaoyu," and the latter dispute involves China, Taiwan, Vietnam, the Philippines, and Malaysia. Both cases encompass one type of maritime dispute in the ESCS that focuses on the sovereignty of islands and island features. The other type of maritime dispute concerns maritime boundary delimitations and the setting of the extent of national exclusive economic zones (EEZs). The nature of the different sovereign and delimitation disputes is beyond the scope of this chapter. However, the focus on sovereign disputes allows this chapter to illustrate how and why similar claims may have different impacts on stability issues. Similarly, the chapter focuses on Chinese behavior in both disputes to ensure analytical consistency across the two cases. This also means that the chapter does not engage with other claimants' perspectives on the sovereign disputes directly.

The chapter builds on the volume's overall theme of the centrality of naval matters in Indo-Pacific security to argue that in the ESCS Chinese behavior shows how territorial disputes link local dynamics to both regional stability and international maritime order. In particular, the chapter argues that three sets of issues define the correlation between the operational conduct in the management of territorial disputes and Indo-Pacific security: how operational conduct affects the relationship among the claimant parties, how such conduct affects the broader international maritime order as enshrined in the United Nations Convention for the Law of the Sea (UNCLOS), and how it informs the altering of the regional power balance. In making its case, this chapter departs significantly from the existing literature on "gray zone" activities—which share a similar analytical focus in conflict and contestation conducted under the threshold of war—but is less concerned with explaining the wider international impact of specific disputes. In this respect, the chapter also places the study of Chinese behavior in both disputes at the center of the analysis.

With these parameters in mind, the cases examined in this chapter suggest that Chinese activities in the ESCS challenge the notion of a revisionism that is limited in nature. These activities bring about a fundamental challenge to the international order. Specifically, the chapter indicates how, regardless of whether one agrees on the scope of Chinese revisionism, Beijing's practice of coercion sets a problematic precedent for the maritime order that crucially weakens its core normative principles and regional power balance.[1] In this respect, the chapter endeavors to establish a link between the military implications of Chinese operational conduct in the ESCS and the wider literature on the phenomenon of legal revisionism at sea as part of the wider debate about lawfare.[2]

The chapter is divided into three sections. The first explores the notion of a maritime order and the nature of maritime activities from the perspective of their primary delivery platform, the warship, to set the overall framework. The second and third sections explore the two specific cases before offering a few final observations.

THE FRAGILE STABILITY OF THE MARITIME ORDER

Reflecting on politicians' frequent references to a "rules-based international order," informed observers have recently noted that the reality is much more fragmented than often assumed. In international politics, it would be more appropriate to speak of multiple systems that regulate economic, political, and diplomatic relations.[3] Some academics take these criticisms even further and suggest that there is little in the international order to suggest that it is in fact "orderly."[4] In the maritime context, the former assertion seems to hold true, the latter less so. This is because since 1994 UNCLOS has provided the legal framework setting expectations and standards for the pursuit of maritime governance and order, as Clive Schofield and Peter Alan Dutton have explained in previous chapters. As a result, the maritime domain has a specific rules-based order, with principles defining rights and duties for those who aspire to use the sea. Thus, it is fair to suggest that the system is decidedly orderly in ambitions and nature, though the aspirations of drafters of the convention have been harder to find full practical implementation.

How so? Scholars have noted that the emergence of UNCLOS as a comprehensive framework for the sea has favored the rise of greater consciousness among states about the need for "good order." In turn, this has led to the development of new ideas about how to address in a transnational fashion risks and challenges to maritime governance, from crimes at sea and piracy to overfishing, with greater emphasis on multilateral action.[5] The new requirements for maritime governance have acted as a call for more collaborative and cooperative behaviors. The existence of a widely agreed-upon framework has, however, not meant that disputes over boundary delimitations and territorial sovereignty have disappeared. Indeed, as the process that led to the convention was still unfolding, the aptly named Cod War between the United Kingdom and Iceland proved just how the prospect of greater rights at sea meant that states were willing to fight to secure access to primary resources.[6] The coming into force of UNCLOS did not change that. Rather, it provided new legal ammunition to maximize claims, especially in resource-rich areas. Indeed, the former British first sea lord Adm. Sir Philip Jones recently remarked that some 57 percent of the world's maritime boundaries remain unsettled.[7] He added,

> In a world of dwindling natural resources, 12-mile territorial waters limits, and even more so 200 nautical mile Economic Exclusion zones though the provisions of the United Nations Convention on the Law of the Sea, are of enormous value for coastal states' energy, mining, fishing, and telecommunications industries.

It is perhaps no wonder then that where disagreement exists between states as to where these boundaries should be drawn, resolution often reaches far beyond legal complexity and grey zone activity may well be used as a form of coercion to reinforce maritime claims.[8]

The potential for instability emerging from overlapping claims to territorial waters and EEZs is made more complicated by the balance between coastal states' rights and duties and those that all states enjoy on the high seas. This raises issues in relation to freedom of navigation and overflight in basins like the ESCS where claims such as the controversial Chinese "nine-dash line" significantly affect them. Article 58 of UNCLOS offers a good example of the problem. It supports the proposition that the drafters' ambition was not to "territorialize" the world's oceans or to restrict long-standing freedoms of navigation and overflight by extending coastal states' rights over continental shelves and the management of fish stocks.[9] Article 58 of the convention reads as follows:

(1). In the exclusive economic zone, all States, whether coastal or landlocked, enjoy, subject to the relevant provisions of this Convention, the freedoms referred to in article 87 of navigation and overflight and of the laying of submarine cables and pipelines, and other internationally lawful uses of the sea related to these freedoms, such as those associated with the operation of ships, aircraft and submarine cables and pipelines, and compatible with the other provisions of this Convention.

(2). Articles 88 to 115 and other pertinent rules of international law apply to the exclusive economic zone in so far as they are not incompatible with this Part.

(3). In exercising their rights and performing their duties under this Convention in the exclusive economic zone, States shall have due regard to the rights and duties of the coastal State and shall comply with the laws and regulations adopted by the coastal State in accordance with the provisions of this Convention and other rules of international law in so far as they are not incompatible with this Part.

The article's opening paragraph makes clear that all states enjoy the freedoms in EEZs referred to in Article 87 on freedom on the high seas. In the third paragraph, however, the article adds that in enjoying the freedoms listed in Article 87, states have to give due regard to the rights and duties of coastal states under the provisions of the convention. As some scholars have noted, the drafters' decision to use in Article 56 the term "sovereign rights" instead of "sovereignty" in reference to EEZs was meant to distinguish them from territorial waters in which coastal states enjoy the much broader authority.[10] Still, a tension remained between coastal states rights and those of other states, especially in the EEZs.

This tension has potentially significant repercussions on restrictions on shipping and, crucially, military activities. In the 2019 US Department of Defense *Annual Freedom of Navigation Report*, Chinese maritime claims in the ESCS are described to affect "rights, freedoms, and uses of the sea and airspace guaranteed to all nations by international law" as follows.[11] In the ECS, the Chinese decision to adopt an air defense identification zone in 2013 introduced restrictions to aircraft flying without the intent to enter national space that are misaligned with practices relevant to AIDZs elsewhere. In the SCS, questions are raised by the Chinese application of straight baselines around the Paracel Islands, by prior permission for innocent passage of foreign military vessels through the territorial seas of both the Paracel and Spratly Islands, by the application of territorial sea and airspace around features that are not entitled in the Spratly Islands, and by the exercise of security jurisdiction over contiguous zones. In both theaters, similar issues exist with the exercise of jurisdiction over airspace above the EEZs and the limitations of survey activity by foreign entities in the EEZs.[12] Some restrictions, notably on military maritime data collection, rest in part on the interpretation of these activities as forms of "maritime scientific research," which coastal states have rights to regulate.[13] Others, especially those related to the status of various features in the Spratly and Paracel Islands examined by the arbitral tribunal convened in the case brought by the Philippines against China to the Permanent Court of Arbitration, are regarded as incompatible with international law, as formally expressed also by other countries such as the United Kingdom and Australia.[14]

The imposition of restrictions on military activities creates, in turn, an additional risk of strategic instability in that it directly affects the use of the sea for the projection of national power and influence. In the ESCS this is certainly true for the United States, which relies heavily on unfettered access to both basins to exert a dominant role in the Indo-Pacific. It is no less true for countries like China that are seeking to gain greater capacity to project their own power and influence and see, as a result, the benefits of restricting American maneuver. This question speaks to an instrumental capacity that powerful coastal states such as China possess to mobilize UNCLOS to affect the military balance of a specific regional space. In particular, in the ESCS the PRC seems to have tried to achieve this in three ways: by seeking to expand the radius of its own military and paramilitary activities in the name of exercising its maritime claims, by drawing resources of other state actors away from the conduct of other missions to meet the challenge of excessive maritime claims, and by testing the credibility and resolve of leading powers, most notably the United States, through the exercise of coercion vis-à-vis other claimant states, with specific attention to those with established security ties with the United States.

For all these reasons the organizational distinction that exists in some states between maritime law-enforcement agencies and navies to separate constabulary and military missions does not necessarily facilitate greater maritime stability. As a major 2019 study of the navy–coast guard nexus concluded, the operational divide between services is becoming increasingly less focused on a distinction between civilian and military activities, with greater emphasis being placed on the need to adapt capabilities and organizations to meet specific geopolitical circumstances.[15] This is particularly the case in regions with persistent maritime disputes and geostrategic tensions like the ESCS.[16] These conclusions invite another observation concerning the link between capabilities and maritime stability. Major naval platforms, such as aircraft carriers, may have more ways to implement coercive action than a frigate, a corvette, or a maritime patrol aircraft, but this does not mean that smaller vessels—including coast guard cutters or even militia fishing boats—cannot achieve a variety of objectives, including coercion, through their missions. Missions of this kind are not the exclusive prerogative of large, capable naval forces. The versatility of maritime assets means that in some circumstances small vessels can, in fact, be preferable. This is particularly true if the operation's intended aim is to deliver effect while carrying a sense of restraint and/or to limit counteractions.[17]

THE ECS: CONSTABULARY COERCION
AS A CHALLENGE TO THE MARITIME ORDER

In the ECS the case of the territorial dispute over the Japanese-controlled Senkaku Islands is a fitting example of a maritime dispute with detrimental effect on the stability of the maritime order but relatively limited media attention. In part, this is due to the fact that informed observers regard this dispute as a local affair over a small group of island features of little strategic and economic value, but it is politically significant to China-Japan relations.[18] Yet how the dispute is managed matters greatly because, as a wargame recently indicated, escalatory behavior around the Senkaku Islands takes one step closer the risk of war between Asia's two largest economies and the most consequential US ally in the Indo-Pacific.[19] In turn, every successful coercive step China takes in undermining the status quo around the Senkakus is a direct challenge to the credibility of the US-Japan alliance and, crucially, to the principles enshrined in UNCLOS about the peaceful resolution of disputes.[20] In this case, the predominant use of constabulary assets also offers specific highlights on the link between law enforcement and regional stability.

Chinese plans for the basic tactical action of using maritime law-enforcement vessels to intrude into the territorial waters around the Senkaku Islands date back to 2006 and were first put into action in December 2008.[21] In June 2005 a collision occurred between a Japanese patrol vessel and a Taiwanese ship and prompted authorities in Beijing to decide to step up its maritime activities around the islands. Subsequently Chinese law-enforcement vessels entered the territorial waters only sporadically, in August 2011 and again in March and July 2012. It is likely that another collision in September 2010, this time involving a Chinese trawler and a Japanese coast guard cutter, contributed to China's decision to deploy assets again. As Japanese authorities considered the option of pressing charges against the Chinese trawler's captain, a serious political stand-off between Tokyo and Beijing ensued in the following months.[22]

The Japanese authorities released the Chinese captain eventually, but in September 2012 a new set of circumstances led to a more significant change in Chinese strategy. In response to the Japanese government's purchase of three of the eight Senkaku Islands from their private owner, authorities in Beijing abandoned the logic of occasional incursions and started deploying assets inside the territorial waters on a regular basis. The goal of this new approach was not just to challenge Japanese statements about control of the islands. It was also to prove that such statements could not possibly be true, by normalizing the Chinese law-enforcement presence inside the islands' territorial waters. In particular, as politicians in Tokyo continued to deny the existence of a territorial dispute (a denial that continues to the present day) and President Barack Obama eventually reaffirmed that Japan held administrative control over the islands, presence was an indispensable first step to corroborating Beijing's claims.[23]

A regular presence requires the ability to sustain incursions into the territorial waters over time. To that end, Chinese maritime law-enforcement agencies underwent a considerable transformation. In 2013 Beijing announced a partial fusion of five organizations, and in 2018 it set in motion the significant organizational change to integrate the new Chinese coast guard under the command of the People's Armed Police.[24]

These developments were not merely aimed at addressing presence requirements in the ECS. They were also part of the growing significance of the Chinese Communist Party's ambition to transform China into a maritime power; becoming a maritime power is inherent to the achievement of the "China Dream." Still, as of 2019 these reforms meant a considerable increase in hulls and firepower to conduct patrols. The Chinese coast guard boasts today more than 500,000 aggregated tons, as opposed to the Japanese coast guard's 150,000, and has been taking delivery of much-improved oceangoing vessels, with a considerable number of them deployed in the ECS. This was now a fleet that could do more than just presence.[25]

On Sunday, July 5, 2020, the Chinese strategy changed again. On that day, two Chinese coast guard vessels set a new milestone. They exited the islands' territorial waters after sailing for some thirty-nine hours and twenty-three minutes. This marked the longest time Chinese surface assets had ever spent inside the waters' twelve-nautical-mile limit. This was no mere "incursion." It was, as Chinese reports would have it, a full-fledged law-enforcement patrol of sovereign waters. This deployment was not an isolated event. It followed a similar extended foray of more than thirty hours completed just two days earlier. Combined, these two activities represented the longest time Chinese vessels have ever spent continuously operating inside the Senkakus' territorial waters since September 2012.[26]

If presence had been one preliminary condition to validate Chinese claims, the exercise of sovereign law-enforcement rights in territorial waters was a subsequent vital step to sustain Beijing's legal claims and political narrative. This is why the length of these incursions represents a potentially important novelty in operational behavior. If the "routinization" of deployments distinguished the first step of China's challenge to the status quo, these new extended deployments marked the beginning of a genuine exercise of control. During the second extended stay, the ships reportedly operated at some four to six nautical miles off the islands on average, coming as close as within two and a half nautical miles from the shoreline.[27] The ships also sought to approach Japanese fishing boats at least on one occasion—an act that is consistent with the attempt at exercising law-enforcement rights—which prompted the Japanese coast guard to deploy its own assets to counter the Chinese actions.

How does one know that these two events are symptomatic of a new phase? One important indicator is the more continuous presence in the islands' contiguous zone. Since January 2020, Chinese vessels have in fact been spotted in waters around the islands for more than one hundred days without interruption.[28] This represents the longest streak since the Japanese government acquired the islands in 2012. Such a continuous presence reinforces the Chinese ability to project a capacity to patrol inside the territorial waters when needed. It seems no coincidence that the relative reduction of number of vessels spotted inside the territorial waters in the last months of 2020 has occurred against a stark climb in number of vessels spotted in the contiguous zone. Higher continuity in presence in the contiguous zone allows for more prompt deployments inside the territorial waters to engage with foreign fishing boats. In fact, following a case that occurred early in May 2020, Chinese spokespersons pointed out that Chinese vessels "tracked and monitored" a Japanese boat illegally fishing inside the territorial waters.[29] According to a report in the Japanese press, the crews of the Chinese vessels asked the Japanese fishing boat to leave the area and eventually "resolutely responded to the illegal interference of the Japanese coast guard."[30]

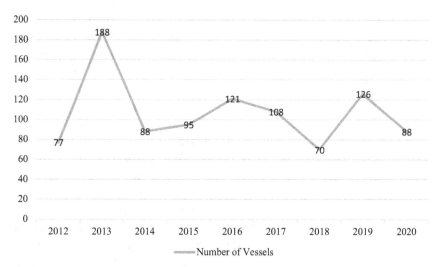

FIGURE 12.1. Number of Chinese vessels identified inside the contiguous zone around the Senkaku/Diaoyu Islands.

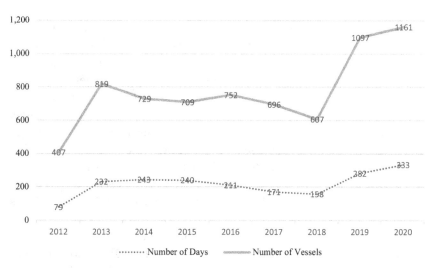

FIGURE 12.2. Number of Chinese vessels identified inside the territorial waters around the Senkaku/Diaoyu Islands.

Official Japanese figures indicate that this year's pattern of deployments and operational conduct are looking like the beginning of a new normal rather than an exception (see figures 12.1 and 12.2). In 2019 Chinese vessels entered the contiguous zone around the Senkakus 1,097 times and spent a total of 282 days, which far exceeded previous highest data of 819 times for 232 days collected in 2013.[31] Crucially, this sharp increase had not gone unnoticed by leaders of Japan's ruling party, the Liberal Democratic Party (LDP). In December 2019 the LDP General Council's chair, Shunichi Suzuki, specifically raised the party's concerns about Chinese maritime activities, something that the LDP expected Prime Minister Shinzo Abe to consider as the government prepared for Xi Jinping's official visit the following spring.[32] Eventually Xi's visit was postponed due to the COVID-19 pandemic, but the LDP's concerns over Chinese behavior in the ECS have not eased. Despite warnings that many Chinese fishing boats might enter the Senkakus' territorial waters in August and September 2020, little noticeable Chinese fishing activity occurred, which suggests that indeed the Chinese primary objective is to establish its law-enforcement capacity rather than to offer the opportunity to Japanese authorities to exercise theirs.

Where to go from here? In 2018 the celebration of the fortieth anniversary of the 1978 Treaty of Peace and Friendship was cause for optimism since the Japanese government sought to engage with China on political dialogue and economic cooperation—including the decision to resume discussions on maritime crisis management.[33] There were fewer incursions around the islands, Shinzo Abe became the first Japanese prime minister to visit China in seven years, and Tokyo and Beijing agreed to a maritime and air communication mechanism to improve crisis prevention in the ECS. Fast-forward to June 2020, when optimism seemed all but vanished. The Japanese defense white paper suggested as much. In the report, the nature of the Chinese challenge to Japanese security—especially to the Senkaku Islands—was presented in the strongest terms yet. Chinese authorities were in fact described as "relentlessly" pressing their claims to the islands with ever-increasing levels of maritime activities undermining the "status quo."[34] Former Japanese defense minister Taro Kono recently added to this by making it clear that further intensification of activities would not preclude the intervention of Japanese military assets.[35] In response to Japanese concerns, the commander of US Forces Japan has stated that the United States would help monitor the situation.[36]

The challenge to Japanese control is real, and what has happened since 2012 suggests that a return to a status quo ante is likely. This is why the Senkaku Islands matter to the stability of the ECS and the broader maritime order. Actions aimed at changing and challenging the islands' status quo through coercion and force affect the stability of the international maritime order. China's use of constabulary coercion to advance a territorial claim sets a precedent in the management of contested maritime spaces that fundamentally undermines the international maritime rules-based order as a whole. What happens around the Senkakus can be replicated elsewhere, not least across the Strait of Taiwan or in the disputes in the SCS or the Eastern Mediterranean. Similarly, since the Senkaku Islands are close to American bases in Japan—exposing them directly to the effects of military escalation—an increased risk of armed conflict would inevitably put the alliance to its most critical test.

THE SCS: CHALLENGING POWER BALANCE, WEAKENING MILITARY STABILITY

If the case of the ECS dispute over the Senkakus links first and foremost issues of constabulary nature to the stability of maritime order, the case of the SCS dispute over the Spratly Islands highlights the strategic relevance of territorial disputes to military stability. In July 2020 US secretary of state Mike Pompeo provided the most recent reminder of such a link when he released a statement that denounced in the strongest terms yet the unlawful nature of Chinese claims in the SCS, notably concerning the Spratly Islands.[37] The statement drew on the 2016 award by the Arbitral Tribunal to point out that the PRC could not assert a maritime claim vis-à-vis the Philippines in areas that the tribunal had found to be in the Philippine EEZ. It also rejected Chinese claims beyond territorial waters derived from claims in the Spratly Islands and claims to (or derived from) the James Shoal.[38] Although the statement did not amount to a change of legal position of the United States, it did come at a time of increased political and economic tensions between Beijing and Washington and was regarded by informed observers as a way to set the tone for a more systematic challenge to a Chinese behavior perceived as increasingly assertive well beyond the pursuit of maritime claims.[39]

This should come as no surprise. Since 2012, when Chinese vessels seized control of the Philippine-controlled Scarborough Shoal, Beijing's behavior in the management of the SCS maritime disputes has steadily increased in the typology and variety of coercive activities in a fashion that is consistent with activities conducted in the ECS. What sets the case of the Spratly Islands apart, and to a similar extent the Paracels, is the specific pursuit of a form of coercion, which, because of its scale and magnitude, seems to serve military objectives more than mere maritime claims. In 2015 the commander of the US Pacific Fleet, Adm. Harry Harris, was the first senior American official to remark that the PRC was building a "great wall of sand" with dredges and bulldozers that raised serious questions about Chinese intentions. Speaking at the Australian Strategic Policy Institute, the admiral pointed out how China had already constructed four square kilometers of artificial landmass, a space comparable to Canberra's Black Mountain Nature Reserve.[40]

In the following months, Admiral Harris's comments proved to capture the contours of an ambitious project. In the SCS Beijing was intent in an unprecedented effort at developing artificial offshore structures designed to host shore-based infrastructures for military use. As the artificial-island-building process unveiled its military potential, some informed observers came to regard these remarkable construction projects as passive assertion measures.[41] In some crucial respects, this is an apt description. They are "passive" measures in that once they are in place, they perform their function not as part of a specific response or initiative—their existence is an act of coercion in itself. This has occurred within the context of the island-reclamation and upgrading efforts of seven features China occupies in the Spratly Islands and of an equal number of features in the Paracel Islands.[42]

In the Spratlys, by 2018 China had created a staggering thirteen square kilometers of land to accommodate port facilities, radar stations, airstrips, reinforced hangars, close-in weapon systems, and point-defense systems. These facilities are today considered to be operational and capable of supporting both constabulary and, crucially, sustained military operations. The hangars in the Spratlys are capable of accommodating twenty-four fighter jets and relevant air-refueling and logistical support assets. In this regard, in 2017 commercial aircraft had already conducted the first test flights at Fiery Cross, Subi, and Mischief Reefs.[43] By summer 2020 international analysts were observing how recent satellite and air surveillance had revealed how far the development of these offshore installations had gone.[44] This suggested an intention to permanently populate these outposts and de facto extended Chinese territory—and the military potential that goes with it—across the majority of the SCS. The islands now include large barracks, administrative buildings, hospitals, farming facilities, and even sports complexes.[45] Crucially, in January 2019 the China Academy of Sciences established an oceanographic research center on Mischief Reef to ensure the monitoring of the artificial structures and ensure their sustainability over time.[46] These developments should be considered in light of the fact that the runways and the surrounding facilities on Fiery Cross already correspond to an area roughly the size of Heathrow Airport's, and the enclosed lagoon inside Mischief Reef is the approximately the size of central London from Tower Bridge to Buckingham Palace. This is a remarkably large area that could be easily used to harbor and support a fleet.

The previous observations fundamentally undermine the frequent attempts by the Chinese to claim that they are not "militarizing" the SCS. To put the PRC's reclamation activities in perspective, the scale finds no equal in similar activities by Taiwan, Vietnam, Malaysia, and the Philippines. Indeed, China has "reclaimed 17 times more land in 20 months than the other claimants combined over the past 40 years, accounting for approximately 95% of all reclaimed land in the Spratly Islands."[47] Specifically addressing the potential implications of these artificial outposts, the former director of national intelligence in the United States, James Clapper, noted that once completed they would empower China with a "significant capacity to quickly project substantial offensive military power to the region."[48] A year after his comments in Australia, Admiral Harris further commented that Chinese efforts in this context are "changing the operational landscape" of the SCS.[49] Even the Arbitral Tribunal in the Philippines case against China took care to observe that while the civilian use of the islands may have been a motivation for the "extensive construction activities," it was not "the only" reason.[50]

Indeed, a cursory overview of China's constabulary forces—also known as maritime militias—offers an indication of their use for both the defense of maritime rights and interests and to advance China's military assertion in this theater. The notion of "national defense mobilization for low-intensity maritime rights protection" underwrites the militias' mobilization system.[51] In constabulary activities, militias have contributed to escort assets owned by Chinese corporations for the conduct of scientific exploration and resource exploitation in contested areas as well as to ensure regular and continuous presence. In regard to the former, in 2013 one of the leading militia organizations in the Hainan Province, the Sanya Fugang Fisheries Co. Ltd., provided escorts to the China National Offshore Oil Corporation's (CNOOC) survey vessels near Triton Island. In May 2014 the People's Liberation Army's (PLA's) then Guangzhou Military Region Command supervised People's Armed Forces Maritime Militia units from Guangdong, Guangxi, and Hainan as they escorted a CNOOC HYSY-981 drilling platform to operate in an area in dispute between China and Vietnam.[52] In relation to verifying presence operations, data analysis of the automatic identification system pertaining to vessels operated by the Sansha Maritime Militia established systematic patterns of deployment to the Chinese-controlled Spratly Islands—including Fiery Cross Reef, Mischief Reef, and Subi Reef—as well as at Scarborough Shoal.[53]

In the realm of military coercion, some of the militias' core functions have revolved around providing support to the PLA, from transportation services to search and rescue, resupply, reconnaissance, surveillance, and even combat. Indeed, its expanded use in constabulary operations has not diminished its contribution to military coercion. In terms of intelligence surveillance and reconnaissance, the Hai'an Militia Regiment in Jiangsu Province was documented gathering information during a US naval exercise in 2014 and today fields 119 vessels, all equipped with advanced radar and Beidou satellite navigation system. Militia units regularly conduct harassment and sabotage operations against foreign naval vessels, as in the cases of USNS *Bowditch* (T-AGS 62) and USNS *Impeccable* (T-AGOS-23) and the 2014 case of obstruction of supplies to the Philippine detachment on an outpost at the Second Thomas Shoal.[54]

What, then, is the wider significance of the claim on the Spratly Islands? Security analysts have observed that the islands are a consistent part of Xi Jinping's wider project of "national rejuvenation."[55] It is perhaps no coincidence

that in 2018 two-hundred-ton commemorative megaliths quarried from Taishan stone were erected on each of the three larger Spratlys. Mount Taishan is viewed as the most sacred of China's mountains and emphasizes the importance of the country's projection at the very heart of the SCS.[56] During a visit to the navy's headquarters the previous year, President Xi had in fact directly linked the navy to the nation's goal "of great rejuvenation" since a "strong and modern force" with the ability "to defeat all invading enemies and safeguard China's national sovereignty, security, and development interests" was more important than at any other time in the country's history.[57] This vision had also informed the 2014 defense white paper, the first published since Xi became president, with naval missions set to encompass sea-lanes' defense and overseas interests' security because "the seas and oceans bear on the enduring peace, lasting stability and sustainable development of China."[58] In all, under Xi, the sea has been taking center stage in national policy; within it, the SCS was China's first line of defense and power-projection space—with maritime capabilities ensuring "open seas protection" alongside "offshore defense."[59]

It should come as no surprise, therefore, that Chinese officials have spared no effort to portray comments and actions challenging Chinese military coercion in the SCS as symptomatic of double standards, of aggressive behaviors against China, and indeed of American "hegemonism in disguise."[60] For example, Chinese authorities have been systematically seeking to present activities such as the US Navy freedom-of-navigation operations (FONOPs) in an escalatory light in a way that was inconsistent with their intended scope. In 2015 a Chinese media commentary on US FONOPs blasted "Washington's promotion of maritime militarization and threats of other countries' sovereignty and national security in disguise of navigation freedom" as "against international law."[61] In 2016, shortly after the release of its annual freedom-of-navigation report, Chinese Foreign Ministry spokesperson Hua Chunying commented that these activities showed the American attempt "to dominate maritime order and reflect its logic of hegemony and exceptionalism in its treatment of international law, which it uses when convenient and abandons on unfavorable conditions."[62] Under the Donald J. Trump administration, FONOPs increased in frequency and consistently sought to reinforce the findings of the Arbitral Tribunal by challenging Chinese attempts to normalize its artificial outposts (see table 12.1 and figure 12.3).

CONCLUSION

In the ESCS, maritime disputes present challenges that, if left to fester, are likely to have severe repercussions at the regional and international levels. If we look back to the questions set forth at the beginning of this chapter, the cases examined in the previous pages offer the following final observations.

TABLE 12.1.   Freedom-of-Navigation Operations Conducted by US Military Vessels in the South China Sea, 2015–2020 (publicly disclosed).

27/10/2015	USS *Lassen*	Within 12m, Subi Reef
29/01/2016	USS *Curtis Wilburn*	Within 12 m, Triton Island
10/05/2016	USS *William P. Lawrence*	Within 12m, Fiery Cross Reef
21/10/2016	USS *Decatur*	Straight Baseline Claim, Paracels
24/05/2017	USS *Dewey*	Within 6m, Mischief Reef
02/07/2017	USS *Stethem*	Within 12m, Triton Island
10/08/2017	USS *John S. McCain*	Within 12m, Mischief Reef
10/10/2017	USS *Chafee*	Straight Baseline Claim, Paracels
17/01/2018	USS *Hopper*	Within 12m, Scarborough Shoal
23/03/2018	USS *Mustin*	Within 12m, Mischief Reef
27/05/2018	USS *Higgins*, USS *Antietam*	Within 12m, Lincoln, Tree, Triton, Woody Islands
30/09/2018	USS *Decatur*	Within 12m, Gaven and Johnson Reefs
26/11/2018	USS *Chancellorsville*	Straight Baseline Claim, Paracels
07/01/2019	USS *McCampbell*	Within 12m, Lincoln, Tree, Woody Islands
11/02/2019	USS *Spruance*, USS *Preble*	Within 12m, Mischief Reef
06/05/2019	USS *Chung Hoon*, USS *Preble*	Within 12m, Gaven and Johnson Reefs
19/05/2019	USS *Preble*	Within 12m, Scarborough Shoal
28/08/2019	USS *Wayne E. Meyer*	Within 12m, Fiery Cross and Mischief Reefs
13/09/2019	USS *Wayne E. Meyer*	Straight Baseline Claim, Paracels
20/11/2019	USS *Gabrielle Giffords*	Within 12m, Fiery Cross Reef
21/11/2019	USS *Wayne E. Mayer*	Challenged restrictions on innocent passage, Paracels
25/01/2020	USS *Montgomery*	Challenged restrictions on innocent passage, Spratlys
10/03/2020	USS *McCampbell*	Challenged excessive maritime claims, Paracels
28/04/2020	USS *Barry*	Challenged excessive maritime claims, Paracels
29/04/2020	USS *Bunker Hill*	Within 12m, Gaven Reef
28/05/2020	USS *Mustin*	Within 12m, Woody Island and Pyramid Rock
14/07/2020	USS *Ralph Johnson*	Within 12m, Cuarteron and Fiery Cross Reefs
27/08/2020	USS *Mustin*	Straight Baseline Claim, Paracels
09/10/2020	USS *John S. McCain*	Straight Baseline Claim, Paracels

Data courtesy of Collin Koh, S. Rajaratnam School of International Studies, Singapore.

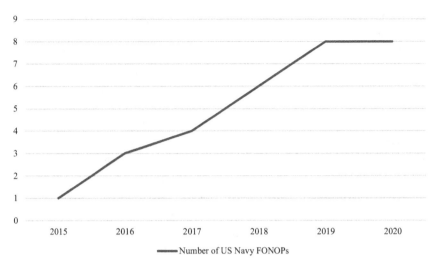

FIGURE 12.3. US freedom-of-navigation operations in the South China Sea, 2015–20 (publicly disclosed).

First, to assess the intent behind activities at sea, it is necessary for policy-makers and scholars to examine capabilities against their wider legal and strategic frameworks. This is particularly true in the context of maritime territorial disputes in which the deployment of law-enforcement and/or paramilitary assets does not necessarily reflect a cautious or restrained intent. On the contrary, Chinese use of coast guard and militia assets seem to indicate clear intent to push for changes in the status quo by making it more difficult for opposing claimants to respond. Similarly, despite Chinese claims to the contrary, the development of artificial outposts in the Spratlys has more to do with Beijing's wider ambition to project military power across the SCS than with attempts at affirming a territorial claim.

What can other actors do to counter this type of coercive behavior? In the ECS, a good place to start is for Japan to review the notion of "control" in territorial waters to frustrate Beijing's constabulary-focused attrition strategy. Exploring options to widen the meaning of "administrative control"—from imposing limits on all fishing, to the building of lighthouses or resuming research activities around the islands or their use as training grounds for the US military—should not be off the table. The idea is to regain the initiative by changing the parameters within which Beijing seeks to normalize its behavior, while keeping the focus within the space of law-enforcement activities. In the SCS the United States has stepped up its own FONOPs to restate freedom of navigation, though Chinese military advances continue. Given the impact of these outposts on the operational landscape in the SCS, greater internationally coordinated responses could be a desirable option, pending an agreement on the type of desired behavioral change from the PRC.

This leads to one final, but no less relevant, observation. The use of constabulary coercion to advance a territorial claim contributes to setting a precedent in the management of contested maritime spaces that fundamentally undermines the international maritime rules-based order as a whole. In the ECS, Sino-Japanese bilateral ties remain affected by such attempts at changing the status quo outside the boundaries of the existing normative framework. It is not difficult to imagine how Chinese behavior might be replicated by other actors with outstanding disputes with similar negative consequences for diplomatic ties. What happens in the ECS can be replicated elsewhere. Similarly, the military buildup of artificial outposts in the Spratly Islands sets a problematic precedent in the instrumental use of maritime disputes to advance a wider strategic ambition to alter the military balance of a given theater. In the SCS such changes have contributed to deteriorating US-China relations and reinforcing respective negative perceptions about the risk of conflict and war between the two actors. In this sense the military balance in the SCS matters internationally and should require broader international responses. Recent initiatives by countries from within the Indo-Pacific, from Japan to Australia, and from without its confines, from France to the United Kingdom and Germany, are a positive indication. Whether these will suffice to maintain a good measure of stability in the ESCS remains to be seen. What is certain is that maritime stability will retain a central role in the final outcome.

NOTES

1. Michael J. Mazarr, *Mastering the Gray Zone: Understanding a Changing Era of Conflict* (Washington, DC: US Army War College Press, 2015), 20–21.
2. Orde F. Kittrie, *Lawfare: Law as a Weapon of War* (Oxford: Oxford University Press, 2016), 161–96. On the broader link between law and instability and conflict, see David Kennedy, *Of War and Law* (Princeton, NJ: Princeton University Press, 2006); and Janina Dill, "Abuse of Law on the Twenty-First Century Battlefield: A Typology of Lawfare," in *Soft War: The Ethics of Unarmed Conflict*, ed. Michael L. Gross and Tamar Meisels, 119–23 (Cambridge: Cambridge University Press, 2017).
3. Malcolm Chalmers, *Which Rules? Why There Is No Single "Rules-Based International System,"* Occasional Paper (London: Royal United Services Institute, 2019), 2–4.
4. Patrick Porter, *The False Promise of Liberal Order: Nostalgia, Delusion, and the Rise of Trump* (Cambridge: Polity Press, 2020).
5. Alessio Patalano, "Naval Warfare," in *Routledge Handbook of Defense Studies*, ed. David J. Galbreath and John R. Deni (London: Routledge, 2018), 200–202. See also

Bruce B. Stubbs and Scott C. Truber, "Towards a New Understanding of Maritime Power," in *The Politics of Maritime Power: A Survey*, ed. Andrew T. H. Tan (London: Routledge, 2011), 3–28.

6. Directorate of Naval Staff Duties, Ministry of Defence (United Kingdom), *The Cod War: Naval Operations off Iceland in Support of British Fishing Industry, 1958– 1976*, BR 1736/57 (London: Her Majesty's Stationery Office, 1990), 1–8, 25–30, 37–54, 95–106.

7. Philip Jones, "Speech at the First Sea Lord's Sea Power Conference 2019," Royal United Services Institute, May 15, 2019, https://rusi.org/annual-conference/first -sea-lords-sea-power-conference/admiral-sir-philip-jones-speech-first-sea.

8. Jones.

9. Ian Townsend-Gault, "The 'Territorialisation' of the Exclusive Economic Zone: A Requiem for the Remnants of the Freedom of the Seas?," in *The Limits of Maritime Jurisdiction*, ed. Clive H. Schofield, Seokwoo Lee, and Moon-Sang Kwon (Leiden: Brill, 2014), 66–67.

10. Raul Pedrozo, "Military Activities in the Exclusive Economic Zone: East Asia Focus," *International Law Studies* 90, no. 1 (2014): 514, 516–17.

11. US Department of Defense, *Annual Freedom of Navigation Report FY 2019* (Washington, DC: US Department of Defense, 2019).

12. US Department of Defense, *Annual Freedom of Navigation Report*, 3–4.

13. Pedrozo, "Military Activities," 524–26.

14. Permanent Mission of the Commonwealth of Australia to the UN, "Declaration No. 20/206 (Chinese Claims in the South China Sea)," July 23, 2020, United Nations, https://www.un.org/depts/los/clcs_new/submissions_files/mys_12_12 _2019/2020_07_23_AUS_NV_UN_001_OLA-2020-00373.pdf; Foreign and Commonwealth Office, "UK Government's Position on Legal Issues Arising in the South China Sea," Ref. DEP2020-0516 House of Commons, 2020, http://data.parliament .uk/DepositedPapers/Files/DEP2020-0516/UK_govt_analysis_of_legal_issues_in _the_South_China_Sea.pdf.

15. Ian Bowers and Swee Lean Collin Koh, eds., *Grey and White Hulls: An International Analysis of the Navy–Coast Guard Nexus* (Singapore: Springer / Palgrave Macmillan, 2019), 272–74.

16. Anguang Zheng, "Integrating the China Coast Guard with the PLA Navy," in Bowers and Koh, *Grey and White Hulls*, 17–36.

17. Christian Le Mière, "Policing the Waves: Maritime Paramilitaries in the Asia-Pacific," *Survival* 53, no. 1 (2011): 133–46, https://doi.org/10.1080/00396338.2011 .555607; Christian Le Mière, "The Return of Gunboat Diplomacy," *Survival* 53, no. 5 (2011): 53–68, https://doi.org/10.1080/00396338.2011.621634; Christian Le Mière, *Maritime Diplomacy in the 21st Century: Drivers and Challenges* (Abingdon: Routledge, 2014), chaps. 2 and 4.

18. Todd Hall, "More Significance Than Value: Explaining Developments in the Sino-Japanese Contest over the Senkaku/Diaoyu Islands," *Texas National Security Review* 2, no. 4 (2019): 11–37, https://doi.org/0.26153/tsw/6668.

19. Michael Peck, "Slaughter in the East China Sea," *Foreign Policy*, August 7, 2020.

20. Shinzo Abe, "Keynote Address at the 13th IISS Security Summit Shangri-La Dialogue," Singapore, May 30, 2014, https://www.mofa.go.jp/fp/nsp/page18e_000087 .html.

21. "China's Patrols around Japan-Held Senkakus Planned Years Earlier, Ex–Coast Guard Chief Says," *Japan Times*, December 30, 2019.
22. Alessio Patalano, "Seapower and Sino-Japanese Relations in the East China Sea," *Asian Affairs* 45, no. 1 (2014): 34–54, https://doi.org/10.1080/03068374.2013.876809.
23. Ryan D. Martinson, "Deciphering China's Armed Intrusion near the Senkaku Islands," *The Diplomat*, January 11, 2016, https://thediplomat.com/2016/01/deciphering-chinas-armed-intrusion-near-the-senkaku/.
24. Tsukasa Hadano, "China Adds Military Might to Coast Guard in Maritime Push," *Nikkei Asia*, June 21, 2020.
25. Joshua Hickey, Andrew S. Erikson, and Henry Holst, "China Maritime Law Enforcement Surface Platforms: Order of Battle, Capabilities, and Trends," in *China's Maritime Gray Zone Operations*, ed. Andrew S. Erickson and Ryan D. Martinson, 108–32 (Annapolis, MD: Naval Institute Press, 2019).
26. "Chinese Ships Sail in Japanese Territorial Waters near Senkakus for 39 Hours: Longest Since 2012," *Japan Times*, July 6, 2020.
27. Brad Lendon and Yoko Wakatsuki, "Japan Says Ships Spend Record Time Violating Its Territorial Waters," CNN News, July 7, 2020, https://edition.cnn.com/2020/07/06/asia/japan-china-island-dispute-intl-hnk-scli/index.html.
28. Tsukasa Hadano and Shotaro Miyasaka, "Chinese Ships Probe Waters around Senkakus for 100th Day," *Nikkei Asia*, July 23, 2020.
29. "Chinese Ships Chase Japanese Fishing Boat near Senkaku Islands," *Nikkei Asia*, May 10, 2020.
30. "China Says Japanese Fishing Boat near Disputed Senkakus Was Illegal," *Japan Times*, May 12, 2020.
31. Alessio Patalano, "What Is China's Strategy in the Senkaku Islands?," War on the Rocks, September 10, 2020, https://warontherocks.com/2020/09/what-is-chinas-strategy-in-the-senkaku-islands/.
32. "Ahead of Xi's Visit, Japan Troubled by Senkaku Incursions," *Nikkei Asia*, December 13, 2019.
33. Takashi Shiraishi, "Shinzo Abe Is Redefining Japan's China Policy for a Generation," *Nikkei Asia*, February 12, 2020, https://asia.nikkei.com/Opinion/Shinzo-Abe-is-redefining-Japan-s-China-policy-for-a-generation.
34. Japan Ministry of Defense [JMOD], *Defense of Japan 2020 Pamphlet* (Tokyo: JMOD, 2020), https://www.mod.go.jp/e/publ/w_paper/wp2020/DOJ2020_Digest_EN.pdf.
35. "Kono Tells China SDF Will Respond to Intrusions around Senkakus," *Asahi Shimbun*, August 5, 2020, http://www.asahi.com/ajw/articles/13609256.
36. Yuri Kageyama, "US Commander Affirms US Support for Japan on China Dispute," *Washington Post*, July 29, 2020.
37. Michael R. Pompeo, "US Position on Maritime Claims in the South China Sea," press release, July 13, 2020, US Department of State, https://www.state.gov/u-s-position-on-maritime-claims-in-the-south-china-sea/.
38. Pompeo, "US Position."
39. Gregory B. Poling, "How Significant Is the New US South China Sea Policy?," CSIS Critical Questions, July 14, 2020, https://www.csis.org/analysis/how-significant-new-us-south-china-sea-policy.

40. Harry B. Harris Jr., "Speech Delivered at Australian Strategic Policy Institute," US Pacific Fleet, March 31, 2015, https://www.cpf.navy.mil/leaders/harry-harris/speeches/2015/03/ASPI-Australia.pdf.

41. Ashley Townshend and Rory Medcalf, *Shifting Waters: China's New Passive Assertiveness in Asian Maritime Security* (Sydney: Lowy Institute for International Policy, 2016), 11–14.

42. "China's Continuing Reclamation in the Paracels," Asia Maritime Transparency Initiative, August 9, 2017, https://amti.csis.org/paracels-beijings-other-buildup/#:~:text=China%20has%20reclaimed%20new%20land,those%20elsewhere%20in%20the%20Paracels.

43. "China's Continuing Reclamation in the Paracels," Asia Maritime Transparency Initiative, August 9, 2017, https://amti.csis.org/paracels-beijings-other-buildup/. See also James E. Fannell, "The 'New Spratly Islands': China's Words and Actions in the South China Sea," *Military Power Review*, no. 1 (2016): 32–33.

44. Alexander Neill, "South China Sea: What's China's Plan for Its 'Great Wall of Sand?'" BBC News, July 14, 2020, https://www.bbc.co.uk/news/world-asia-53344449.

45. Neill, "South China Sea."

46. Neill.

47. US Department of Defense, *The Asia-Pacific Maritime Security Strategy: Achieving US National Security Objectives in a Changing Environment* (Washington, DC: US Department of Defense, 2015), 16.

48. Letter from James Clapper to Sen. John McCain, quoted in "Document: DNI Clapper Assessment of Chinese Militarization, Reclamation in South China Sea," USNI News, March 8, 2016, https://news.usni.org/2016/03/08/document-dni-assessment-of-chinese-militarization-reclamation-in-south-china-sea.

49. Letter from Clapper; David Brunnstrom and Mohammed Arshad, "China Gearing Up for East Asia Dominance: US Commander," Reuters, February 23, 2016, https://www.reuters.com/article/us-southchinasea-usa-missiles-idUSKCN0VX04O.

50. Permanent Court of Arbitration [PCA], *Award by the International Arbitral Tribunal in the Matter of the South China Sea Arbitration between the Republic of the Philippines and the People's Republic of China* (PCA Case No. 2013-19, July 2016), 373.

51. Conor M. Kennedy "Maritime Militia Operations and Trends: Gray Zone Tactics" (paper presented at the conference China's Maritime Gray Zone Operations, China Maritime Studies Institute, Naval War College, Newport, RI, May 2–3, 2017), 110–17. We are grateful to the author for sharing the original draft paper.

52. Ryan D. Martinson, "Shepherds of the South Seas," *Survival* 58, no. 3 (2016): 200–201, https://doi.org/10.1080/00396338.2016.1186987.

53. Kennedy "Maritime Militia Operations and Trends."

54. Andrew S. Erickson, and Conor M. Kennedy, *China's Maritime Militia* (Arlington, VA: Center for Naval Analyses, 2016).

55. International Crisis Group, *Competing Visions of International Order in the South China Sea*, Asia Report no. 315 (Brussels: International Crisis Group, 2021), 4.

56. Neill, "South China Sea."

57. "Xi Calls for 'Strong, Modern' Navy," Xinhua, May 24, 2017, http://www.xinhuanet.com//english/2017-05/24/c_136312062.htm/.

58. Ministry of National Defense (China), *White Paper 2014* (Beijing: Ministry of National Defense, 2014).

59. Caitlin Campbell, "Highlights from China's New Defense White Paper, 'China's Military Strategy,'" *US-China Economic and Security Review Commission Issue Brief*, June 2015.
60. "Commentary: US-Called Freedom of Navigation Is Hegemonism in Disguise," Xinhua, November 19, 2015.
61. "Commentary."
62. "China Dismisses Pentagon Report on Freedom of Navigation," Xinhua, April 27, 2016.

13

The Taiwan Strait

Sheryn Lee

This chapter examines the role of naval power in strategic thinking and operational behavior from the perspective of the two actors facing the Taiwan Strait, the Republic of China (ROC, also known as Taiwan) and the People's Republic of China (PRC). It sets forth a threefold argument. First, the chapter shows how naval power offers an ideal vantage point for understanding the multilayered security dynamics across the strait and the diverse tools used by the ROC and the PRC to prosecute their objectives. Second, the chapter shows the extent to which Taiwan's and China's naval capabilities do not apply purely to the Taiwan Strait; rather, they speak to a broader strategic context in which Taiwan is a key factor in Chinese and American strategies. Third, as a result of the first two points, the chapter argues that the progressive change in the cross-strait military balance increases the risk of conflict in the medium term in a fashion that is consistent with recent senior US military assessments.[1]

China is incrementally changing the cross-strait balance of power in its favor. Its goal is to unify Taiwan and its offshore territories with the mainland by winning the "hearts and minds" of the Taiwanese people and without harming Taiwan's economy, industry, and critical infrastructure. To this end, China's naval power uses capabilities across multiple domains in operations below the threshold of military escalation. While it relies on conventional and nuclear forces at sea to deter US and allied forces from intervening, it also employs its coast guard and maritime militias, lawfare tactics, and disinformation campaigns to pressure Taipei to accept Beijing's sovereignty claim.[2] Knowing that it cannot compete with China's comprehensive military modernization, Taiwan is responding by sharpening the ideological dimension of its political and economic status. Taiwan is important to the United States and its allies as a mature democracy and a market economy with its own standing military. Taiwan's importance to the United States and its allies poses a direct challenge to the PRC's claims to having legitimate authority over Taiwan. However, in the event that China attempts to invade the island, the ROC's armed forces are enhancing their asymmetric capabilities to impose risks and costs on the People's Liberation Army (PLA).

A forceful unification of mainland China and Taiwan and its archipelago would give China considerable freedom for its naval activities in its "first island chain" while also denying access to others. A Taiwan controlled by the Chinese Communist Party (CCP) would mean China could press a stronger claim to the East China Sea, as mainland China would subsume the ROC's territorial sea, air defense identification zone (ADIZ), exclusive economic zone, and claims to the Senkaku/Diaoyu Islands. This would particularly leave Japan's sea-lanes vulnerable and further complicate the US ability to support forward-deployed forces in southwest Japan and defend its key Northeast Asian ally. The control of Taiwan and its territories would also allow China to project power with greater ease into its "second island chain" through to Southeast Asia.[3] Taiwan is the largest landmass between Japan and the Philippines, and it controls Pratas Island at the northern tip of the South China Sea along a major sea route between the Indian and Pacific Oceans and the largest natural island, Taiping, in the Spratly Islands. Thus, the PLA would no longer have obstructed access to the Pacific Ocean, and it would more easily be capable of conducting sea-denial operations.

The geostrategic significance of Taiwan as an "unsinkable aircraft carrier" and the offshore islands it controls has not changed since the Cold War. While the risk of conflict over Taiwan in the short term remains low, the mid- to long-term situation is becoming less stable. The unconventional and ideological ways with which Beijing and Taipei are now prosecuting their respective objectives is increasing the complexity and number of actors involved in the maritime operating theater of the Taiwan Strait. Taiwan's actions to further embed itself into what the United States and its partners and allies call the "liberal" or "rules-based" order poses a question of how far Washington would go to protect an Indo-Pacific democracy from China's authoritarian reach. And China's gray-zone operations against Taiwan further tests the credibility of US extended deterrence and the willingness of regional countries, in particular Japan and Australia, to support another democracy.

CHINA'S NAVAL POWER

The PLA-Navy has become a significant force within China's near-seas region, and it will likely achieve its aim of challenging the US Navy's ability to intervene in a Taiwan Strait contingency in the next five to ten years. Any less than this show of strength as the region's preeminent military power would undermine President Xi Jinping's and the CCP's mandate to unify its claimed sovereign territories. Allowing Taiwan to remain independent weakens the validity of Beijing's claim as Taiwan's legal authority and the credibility of China's territorial claims in the East and South China Seas. To this end, Xi considers unifying China's claimed territories with the mainland an "unswerving historical task" for the party.[4] "To oppose and contain 'Taiwan independence'" is ranked third in a list of national defense priorities in China's 2019 *Defense White Paper*, and Beijing has stated that Taiwan is the "main strategic direction" of its military planning.[5]

The PLA's military modernization thus focuses on the enhancement of a range of naval capabilities, including amphibious assault.[6] In the event of a forceful unification, the PLA needs such capabilities to land on Taiwan and its offshore islands and fight a limited war around China's maritime periphery by 2035.[7] To this end, many of the PLA's amphibious assault ships, with displacements of thirty-five thousand tons and space for thirty helicopters, will enter service in 2021–22. Additionally, more guided-missile destroyers, landing helicopter docks, and missiles to strike Taiwan in the early stages of conflict are being fielded or constructed.[8] Such enhancements aim to reduce traditional weaknesses in PLA capabilities, including antisubmarine warfare, long-range targeting, at-sea resupply, combat experience, and limited overseas bases and support facilities.[9]

Taking Taiwan would also mean the PLA would subsume the ROC's control over its offshore islands and its claims in the East and China Seas. Thus, the PLA also has to maintain the capability to enforce the CCP's long-term presence on nearby islands or island groups: Matsu, Jinmen, Penghu, Senkaku/Diaoyu, Pratas, and Taiping.[10] To control such a large maritime domain, the PLA's naval modernization effort aims to achieve, first, a greater degree of maritime control over the blue-water areas in the East China Sea. To achieve this priority, from 2016 to 2020 China launched more than eighty warships, surpassing the US Navy in numbers and tonnage of surface combatants.[11] The increasing qualitative capabilities of these ships meet robust requirements for sea- and airlift, advanced maritime-domain awareness, and intelligence, surveillance, and reconnaissance.

China's naval power is also a critical pillar in the PLA's antiaccess/areadenial operations that aim to deter US intervention in a conflict over Taiwan in China's near-seas region or, failing that, delay the arrival or reduce the effectiveness of intervening allied forces. To support this development, Beijing is reducing the military's weaknesses in joint and combined operations and reorganized the PLA into five regional theater commands in 2016.[12] Specifically, the Eastern

Theater Command, which handles Taiwanese contingencies, is now home to a large number of air, ground, amphibious, and special operations forces units and the largest concentration of PLA vessels, the East Sea Fleet. The area also hosts long-range surface-to-air missiles, intermediate-range missiles, long-range strike aircraft, and a fleet of nuclear ballistic missile submarines, which are capable of targeting allied naval forces and bases.[13]

In tandem, the PLA is developing an over-the-horizon capability that aims by 2025 to deprive Taiwan and the United States of early warning of an attack. Two radar stations have already been built in the center and north of China (Hubei and Inner Mongolia). Such a capability could track targets from three thousand kilometers, including US carrier groups, stealth F-35 fighter jets launched from southwest Japan, and movements of allied forward-deployed forces in Japan and South Korea.[14] More radars are likely planned for southern China, which could complicate US and allied movements to Taiwan and the islands of Pratas and Taiping via the South China Sea.

However, taking Taiwan by unilateral force is China's worst-case scenario. Doing so would be quite difficult (as is discussed in the second section), and it would damage the industry and critical infrastructure that Beijing needs. Because Beijing asserts that the Taiwan issue is a domestic one, its assertion of naval power in the strait first aims to demonstrate that Taiwan falls under China's sovereignty. Military showmanship is often timed to display Beijing's displeasure with the ROC government and to deter Taiwan's "independent separatist forces" from "provocative" actions.[15] China's military activities are also often accompanied by lawfare, state-sponsored activities, and disinformation campaigns. The messages, usually from the PLA's Strategic Support Force, flood Taiwan's social media to sow doubt about the ROC armed forces' abilities and undermine public trust in the central government.[16] This pattern of pressure began with Taiwan's democratization and the 1995–96 Taiwan Strait Crisis. A visit to Cornell University by the then Taiwan president Lee Teng-hui precipitated a dramatic escalation between China and Taiwan as the PLA conducted war games, live-fire exercises, and missile tests in Taiwan's vicinity. Additional tests included a large-scale amphibious landing near the Matsu Islands off the Fujian coast several months later, intended to intimidate Taiwan before its first direct presidential election, chasten Lee, and deter the ROC from declaring independence.[17] This prompted the United States to send two aircraft carrier battle groups to the strait.

In 2005 the PLA conducted a large multiservice exercise to practice an invasion scenario in response to the referendum proposed by the then Taiwan president Chen Shui-bian for Taiwan to join the United Nations. In tandem, Beijing enacted its Anti-Secession Law, whose Article 8 authorized the use of "non-peaceful and necessary" means to unify Taiwan with China.[18]

Additionally, after the election of President Tsai Ing-wen in 2016, the PLA began to conduct regular circumnavigation flights around Taiwan, which included fighter aircraft, intelligence and early warning aircraft, and strategic bombers.[19] After Tsai's election, China's first aircraft carrier battle group, led by the *Liaoning*, began transits of the Taiwan Strait. Ahead of Tsai's reelection campaign, China's second carrier group, headed by the *Shandong*, sailed through the strait in an effort to intimidate Taiwan's voters.

Apart from China's major cross-domain exercises, it maintains a regular schedule of entering Taiwan's maritime area and airspace using gray-zone operations. Such activities also aim to normalize China's presence in the Taiwan Strait. For instance, in 2021 the PLA flew a record number of more than eighty aircraft into Taiwan's ADIZ.[20] Beijing will likely rely more on these types of operations to tip in its favor the risks and costs of unification with Taiwan. Such activities—termed by a PLA general as a "cabbage strategy"—surround Taiwan with so many vessels that the "island is thus wrapped layer and layer like a cabbage," with the PLA-Navy remaining in overwatch.[21] To normalize these activities, domestic legislation was passed in 2021 authorizing China's coast guard to use lethal force on foreign ships operating in China's claimed waters and in the airspace above these waters as well as to destroy other countries' structures on China's claimed islands.[22] Beijing also enacted amendments to expand its 1983 maritime enforcement law beyond China's coastal waters to "sea areas under the jurisdiction of the People's Republic of China."[23] These laws collectively assert China's right to impose restrictions via the legitimate use of force on the navigation and overflight of foreign actors in the Taiwan Strait and in the East and South China Seas. Currently in the Taiwan Strait, China's coast guard ships, maritime militia ships, and fishing vessels, which are often armed and crewed by militiamen disguised as fishermen, are more regularly and extensively deployed than its navy in sovereignty-assertion operations.[24] Moreover, since 2020 China has actively deployed state-sponsored sand dredgers and sand-transportation vessels to swarm the Matsu Islands.[25]

TAIWAN'S NAVAL POWER

The primary aim of Taiwan's naval power is to deter China from a unilateral attempt at unification—and the likelihood of this scenario will continue to increase as China's perception of the strength of its capabilities vis-à-vis Taiwan and the United States grows.[26] The PLA's rapid military modernization has led to Taipei and Washington's realization that Taiwan's military is unable to win a conventional war or war of attrition.[27] While Taiwan's people are firmly resistant to unification with the mainland, the ability to deter this scenario solely by the ROC armed forces is continuing to weaken. The PLA's modernization of standoff capabilities is undermining Taiwan's capabilities in fighters, surface-to-air missiles, and early warning and surveillance. Taiwan's ability to deny PLA ships access to the strait is also decreasing, as its fast attack craft and onshore launchers are vulnerable to China's missiles and air strikes.[28] PLA and state-sponsored activities in the Taiwan Strait are also exhausting Taiwan's personnel and platforms, as the ROC's armed forces and coast guard are often engaged in round-the-clock patrols, fatiguing officers and shortening the lifespans of ships and associated air support.[29]

Due to the PLA's gains in overcoming its weaknesses in amphibious assault, airborne, and over-the-horizon capabilities, in the next ten to fifteen years Taiwan may not be able to rely on the advantages conferred by its terrain, weather, and extreme geography. Currently, Taiwan's main island is surrounded by approximately one hundred smaller islands that defend the coastline with emplacements of missiles, rockets, and artillery guns.[30] There are only thirteen small beaches and approximately six ports suitable for an amphibious landing, and these choke points are bordered by densely populated cities and natural granite cliffs that have a military-controlled tunnel and bunker system. The weather could also deprive any would-be invasion of strategic surprise and tempo—there is extreme fog in February to March, typhoons from May to September, high winds and gales in January to March, and strong tidal currents from June to September. Thus, a PLA amphibious assault in the short- to medium-term could only be feasible in April or October because the logistics of ferrying a large force across the strait multiple times would require predictable weather.[31]

This led to Taipei formulating its Overall Defense Concept in the 2010s. It states that Taiwan should focus its limited resources on the development of asymmetric capabilities to impose large costs on a PLA attempt at unilateral unification.[32] Due to Taipei's assertion that it will not "turn to adventurism" and that China is the aggressor,[33] its armed forces are thus focused on second-strike capabilities, the protection of its outer islands, and defense of Taiwan's coastline and airspace. The *2021 Quadrennial Defense Review* states that the ROC armed forces must now aim to "resist the enemy on the opposite shore, attack it at sea, destroy it in the littoral area, and annihilate it on the beachhead." In 2021 the ROC navy fielded its first indigenous "carrier killer" corvette, equipped with antiair and antiship capabilities, to patrol Taiwan's northeast coastline where China's vessels frequent.[34] To support this territorial defense capability, Taipei is developing an indigenous submarine capability, and the first of eight are to be commissioned by 2025. Taipei also aims to deploy unmanned submersibles and sea mines to complicate China's approach to Taiwan's coast and its offshore islands.[35] In tandem, Taiwan's coast guard has enhanced its vessels—based on US Coast Guard cutter designs—to withstand hostile ramming and shouldering action by China's maritime militias. The largest of these vessels also have room for antiship missiles.[36]

Taipei's *2019 National Defense Report* also states that Taiwan is developing advanced command, control, communications, computers, intelligence, surveillance, and reconnaissance (C4ISR) and intelligence support to counter China's early warning and amphibious assault capability development. Taiwan's military will also increase the number of light and fast vessels and develop long-range and antiship weapons and portable air defense missiles to exploit the vulnerabilities in the logistical and civilian support of a PLA amphibious assault.[37] In 2021 Taiwan's government authorized an additional $9 billion to fund indigenous development of surface combatants, and the air force announced it would upgrade its bases and runways.[38] To address the problems of maintaining a professional defense reserve, by 2022 Taiwan will launch the All-Out Defense Mobilization Agency to oversee mobilization. Members of the agency will receive training in the United States to support Taiwan's objective that its reserve forces remain a reliable supplement for the armed forces.[39]

In the face of increasing pressure from China's qualitative military modernization, the United States is also increasing its overt commitments to safeguarding Taiwan.[40] Washington views this as fulfilling its 1979 Taiwan Relations Act commitment to "maintain peace and stability in the Western Pacific" by providing Taiwan with "such defense articles and defense services in such quantity as may be necessary to enable Taiwan to maintain a sufficient self-defense capacity."[41] Recent arms sales suggest that the Pentagon is increasingly concerned about Taiwan's ability to defend itself in light of Beijing's military enhancements.[42] The types of systems the United States has sold to Taiwan have shifted from relatively expensive platforms that strive for air and sea control over the strait, such as F-16 fighters and Patriot surface-to-air missile systems, to cheaper asymmetric platforms that increase the risks and costs of Beijing's power projection. For instance, due to the limited places where amphibious landings could take place, the United States has sold Taiwan drones, smart mines, precision-guided munitions, and coastal missile defense systems.[43] These systems can be camouflaged and dispersed across Taiwan's coastline to disrupt an amphibious landing.[44]

US-Taiwan cooperation to develop the ROC armed forces' and coast guard's qualitative capabilities also has increased support, which the Pentagon states is "commensurate with the threat from China" and its "efforts to intimidate and pressure Taiwan."[45] Spurred by China's comprehensive military modernization aimed at deterring US intervention, assertions of US naval power in the Taiwan Strait have become more frequent. Such displays aim to show the credibility of US extended deterrence over Taiwan and that the US Navy remains committed to freedom of navigation in the Taiwan Strait and the East and South China

Seas. Since the end of 2018, reported US transits through the Taiwan Strait have averaged one per month.[46] Regular joint and combined exercises (Exercise Balance Tamper) by US Army Special Forces and US Navy SEALs and Taiwan's air force and special operations forces in Taiwan's mountainous regions are now publicized, and amphibious training and speedboat infiltration exercises involving the US Marine Corps and Taiwan's marines have been ongoing since 2020.[47] In 2017 the annual Luhou (Marine Roar) program was reestablished, in which ROC marines receive a month of joint operations training in Guam, including urban warfare and amphibious and airborne assault. The US-Taiwan commitment to coast guard cooperation also includes basic information sharing, and reportedly the US and Taiwan coast guards completed their first joint exercise near Hualien in 2021.[48] This agreement likely also covers Taiwan's efforts to defend the islands of Taiping and Pratas, which are administered by the ROC's coast guard administration.

More important, President Tsai has sharpened the ideological argument for defending Taiwan. Tsai's administration has made deliberate and incremental steps to embed Taiwan in the US-led "liberal order" or "rules-based order," so that bolstering Taiwan's military is widely viewed within Taiwan and by the region as supporting an Indo-Pacific democracy that opposes authoritarian control. In 2021 Tsai wrote, "If Taiwan were to fall, the consequences would be catastrophic for regional peace and the democratic alliance system. It would signal that in today's global contest of values, authoritarianism has the upper hand over democracy."[49]

To this end, Taipei's soft-power promotion of its democratic and market economy is a critical part to its military strength. In particular, Taiwan is emphasizing the importance of maintaining its leading role in innovation and advanced technologies, particularly semiconductors. Maintaining Taiwan's democracy and independence would be critical to continuing fair, stable, and open access to such technologies in global supply chains. The Taiwan Semiconductor Manufacturing Company controls 50 percent of the market, and many of the key machines and chemicals used to make chips come from Japan, the United States, and Europe.[50] Should a unification occur on Beijing's terms, it would disrupt not just global trade but also would likely give China greater political and economic leverage over the global supply of critical technologies.

Consequently, Taiwan has emphasized its role as a frontline democratic state that is willing to share its burden of the defense of the US-led Indo-Pacific order. Furthermore, as is discussed in the next section, Taipei is emphasizing its geostrategic significance to Japan, the United States, Southeast Asia, and the South Pacific to demonstrate the negative implications of Taiwan under mainland China's control.

BEYOND THE TAIWAN STRAIT

The heightened debate about when and how China will invade Taiwan assumes the best-case scenario for China in terms of a docile Taiwan that waits for American intervention. However, this is based on the assumption that US forward-deployed forces, Japan, and maritime Southeast Asia are also not preparing for a contingency involving Taiwan and its offshore territories. Conceptualizing naval power in the Taiwan Strait also means considering allied forces and bases in the East and South China Seas.

Forces based in southwestern Japan, which would play a major role in a Taiwan contingency, bolster US forces in Taiwan. Moreover, Tokyo now has a toughened outlook on China's activities in the Taiwan Strait and the East China Sea. Japan's island groupings of Yaeyama and Miyako connect Okinawa to Taiwan, and Taiwan's military-controlled offshore island of Pengjiayu is just 140 kilometers from the Senkaku/Diaoyu Islands.[51] For the PLA to have unconstrained access to the Indo-Pacific, it would need to control Pengjiayu Island, the Senkaku/Diaoyu Islands, and the Miyako Strait between Miyako and Okinawa. Supporting this, a former deputy director general of Japan's National Security Secretariat stated, "A Taiwan contingency is a Japan contingency," as Japan's Sakishima Islands, which include Yonaguni Island, Iriomote Island, the Miyako Islands, Ishigaki Island, and the Senkaku/Diaoyu Islands, would be physically involved in any attempt at unilateral unification by Beijing.[52] Furthermore, with the 2014 affirmation by the then president Barack Obama that the Senkaku/Diaoyu Islands are covered by Article 5 of the US-Japan alliance treaty,[53] any unilateral steps by China to take administrative control of those islands would likely lead to Tokyo invoking US assistance.

Japan's ADIZ neighbor Taiwan and its vessels are dependent for supply and communication on those East China Sea sea-lanes that are close to Taiwan. Should China occupy Taiwan, Japan would be outflanked, and its own southwestern island chain, including the US forces deployed there, would be left vulnerable.[54] Thus, in 2021 Japanese authorities asked their US counterparts to share US plans for defending Taiwan. US officials responded that the eventual aim would be for the United States and Japan to "write a single integrated plan for a Taiwan contingency."[55] Tokyo would thus likely view a Taiwan invasion contingency as a survival-threatening situation via the "collective self-defense" interpretation of Japan's constitution. This would allow US forces to launch combat operations from Japanese soil, and Japan could add its naval, amphibious, and associated air capabilities to US forces to defend Taiwan.[56]

The defense of the Taiwan-controlled islands of Pratas and Taiping also has implications for maritime Southeast Asia. Should China control the air and maritime domains of these territories, it could more aggressively deny the

United States and its allies and partners access to the South China Sea and ports and bases in Southeast Asia. This would include Singapore's Changi and Sembawang naval bases and the Philippines' Basa and Palawan air bases. A CCP-controlled Pratas and Taiping means the PLA would hold two of the largest airstrips in the South China Sea and could actively assert China's claims against the Philippines, Vietnam, Malaysia, and Brunei. Moreover, the lack of natural barriers and the geographical distance from Taiwan's main island means they are particularly vulnerable to China's activities. China's militarization of its South China Sea islands, regular air incursions by China's fighter jets, and military surveillance drones into Taiwan's ADIZ over Pratas Island, as well as Beijing's mock invasion plans of the island, have led Taiwan to enhance the defense of both Pratas and Taiping Islands.[57]

While small, Pratas Island is strategically close to the Philippines and within Hong Kong's airspace, and as the only link between Taiwan and Taiping, it is ideally situated to give Taipei early warning support in a possible attack on Taiwan's southwest coast. Pratas Island also lies on the strategic waterway of Bashi Channel, which connects the South China Sea to the western Pacific Ocean. This is a principal entryway for PLA nuclear submarines and for US naval transits between Taiwan and the Philippines. Since 2020 Taiwan has bolstered Pratas Island's defense by hosting a garrison of five hundred ROC marines trained by the US military to defend against air landings and assault. Currently being upgraded, Pratas Island's fifteen-hundred-meter airstrip can host C-130 Hercules cargo planes and could provide a base for antisubmarine warfare in any attempt to blockade or attack Taiwan's southern ports, in particular Kaohsiung.[58]

A senior Taiwanese legislator stated that if Pratas Island were to be captured or blockaded, the ROC army, special operations forces, and marines have a joint battle plan to mount a counterattack by sea and air from Taiping Island.[59] In 2021 Taiwan's coast guard stated it would also fortify the defenses around Pratas and schedule two rounds of live-fire exercises there. The defense of Pratas and Taiping was further bolstered by the deployment of 292 Kestrel antiarmor rockets to defend them against hostile landings.[60] Furthermore, the recently renovated twelve-hundred-meter airstrip on Taiping could accommodate Taiwan's F-16 fighter aircraft and C-130 transport planes and potentially host P-3 maritime patrol craft. The latter could give Taiwan the largest maritime surveillance range in the South China Sea, with a radius of approximately twenty-five hundred kilometers.[61] Taiwan has also invested in a port on Taiping capable of handling deep-draft naval vessels. To enhance Taiping's ability to provide early warning of an attack, Taiwan has reportedly built advanced intelligence, surveillance, and reconnaissance capabilities to monitor Subi Reef and the major north-south sea-lane through the South China Sea.[62]

The midterm outlook for the waterways that connect Taiwan to the East and South China Seas is that they will be more crowded and contested and an area where no country enjoys assured freedom of movement. Should China control Pratas Island and Taiping Island, it would change the South China Sea military balance. The islands would support the PLA's sustained military presence in the littoral seas. Moreover, should the PLA also control the Senkaku/Diaoyu Islands, the PLA could project power out to Guam. While the PLA is making progress on capabilities for such scenarios, doing so would be difficult considering the US forward-deployed presence in Japan, Singapore, and the Philippines as well as the enhanced assistance Washington is providing Taipei to bolster its coastal defense and islands.[63]

CONCLUSION

An investigation of how naval power informs Chinese and Taiwanese strategies suggests the following three conclusions. First, should China feel emboldened by a perception that the military balance is in its favor—particularly its naval forces vis-à-vis those of the United States—it could be tempted to unilaterally unify Taiwan and its offshore territories with the mainland. Moreover, Beijing likely believes that Washington is politically unwilling to incur the same level of military casualties that China is over Taiwan.[64] An analysis of the enhancement of China's naval capabilities suggests that its aim remains to address the Taiwan situation militarily, whether by the use or the threat of the use of force. Chinese preparations to achieve this goal, however, entail a great degree of control over China's near-sea region and the denial of access to the United States and its partners and allies.

Second, the pursuit of stronger capabilities to address Taiwan contingencies is making the operational conditions in the Taiwan Strait more complicated. While US naval capability remains qualitatively superior to China's, China's modernization efforts are addressing deficiencies in its navy, coast guard, and maritime militia, including ship design, material quality, doctrine, C4ISR, manpower, training, and equipment.[65] Consistent with this objective, China is also enhancing its capabilities in gray-zone operations, lawfare, and the disinformation domain. Taiwan is responding by focusing on asymmetric capabilities to ensure that any unilateral unification attempts will be bloody and costly. It is also strengthening its ideological place in the US-led order in the Indo-Pacific and seeking partnerships with those countries that are increasingly wary of China's military might.

Finally, the situation of the Taiwan Strait is changing in a way that it will no longer be a contingency concerning just China, Taiwan, and the United States as Taiwan's security guarantor. Indeed, it is drawing in forces from beyond the strait. In particular, Japan and maritime Southeast Asian countries that near Taiwan and its islands—areas where China aims to establish sea control—are considering the long-term impacts on their own security. Such a contingency where conventional and unconventional power is used to prosecute China's and Taiwan's objectives has led to a less stable and more militarized maritime theater. Beijing's aggressive military showmanship is leading Taipei to provide for its own defense regardless of Beijing's reactions, and heightened allied responses to reduce Taiwan's vulnerabilities are increasing China's motivation to unilaterally control Taiwan and its offshore islands.

NOTES

1. Mallory Shelbourne, "Davidson: China Could Try to Take Control of Taiwan in 'Next Six Years,'" USNI News, March 9, 2021, https://news.usni.org/2021/03/09/davidson-china-could-try-to-take-control-of-taiwan-in-next-six-years.
2. Robert S. Ross, "Navigating the Taiwan Strait: Deterrence, Escalation Dominance, and US-China Relations," *International Security* 27, no. 2 (Fall 2002): 50.
3. Andrew S. Erickson and Joel Wuthnow, "Why Islands Still Matter," *National Interest*, February 5, 2016, https://nationalinterest.org/feature/why-islands-still-matter-asia-15121.
4. "Xi Rallies Party for 'Unstoppable' Pursuit to National Rejuvenation as CCP Celebrates Centenary," National People's Congress of the People's Republic of China, July 2, 2021, http://www.npc.gov.cn/englishnpc/c23934/202107/6ff93d39da7548fbae37cbed01184c34.shtml.
5. State Council Information Office (PRC), *Defense White Paper* (Beijing: State Council Information Office, 2019), quoted in Office of the Secretary of Defense, *Military and Security Developments Involving the People's Republic of China 2020* (Washington, DC: US Department of Defense), 25.
6. US-China Economic and Security Review Commission [USCC], "China's Growing Power Projection and Expeditionary Capabilities," in *2020 Annual Report to Congress of the US-China Economic and Security Review Commission* (Washington, DC: US Government Publishing Office, 2020), 389.
7. USCC, "China's Growing Power," 391.
8. USCC, 395.
9. Ronald O'Rourke, *China Naval Modernization: Implications for US Navy Capabilities: Background and Issues for Congress*, CRS Report no. RL33153 (Washington, DC: Congressional Research Service, 2021), 4.
10. US-China Economic and Security Review Commission, "Taiwan," in *2020 Annual Report to Congress of the US-China Economic and Security Review Commission* (Washington, DC: US Government Publishing Office, 2020), 459.
11. O'Rourke, *China Naval Modernization*, 23.
12. Bates Gill and Adam Ni, "China's Sweeping Military Reforms: Implications for Australia," *Security Challenges* 15, no. 1 (2019): 33–34.

13. Peter Wood, "Snapshot: China's Eastern Theater Command," Jamestown Foundation, *China Brief* 17, no. 4 (March 2017): 1–6.
14. "Project 2319 Tianbo (Skywave): Over-the-Horizon Backscatter Radar (OTH-B)," Global Security, July 16, 2019, https://www.globalsecurity.org/wmd/world/china/oth-b.htm.
15. This is language used by China's policymakers to describe Taiwan. For instance, see Matthew Impelli, "China Furious over US Senator's' Trip to Taiwan, Says It Could Embolden Separatist Forces," *Newsweek*, June 7, 2021.
16. Scott W. Harold, Nathan Beauchamp-Mastafaga, and Jeffrey W. Hornung, *Chinese Disinformation Efforts on Social Media*, RR-4373/3-AF (Santa Monica, CA: RAND Corp., 2021), 4.
17. Andrew Scobell, "Show of Force: Chinese Soldiers, Statesmen, and the 1995–1996 Taiwan Straits Crisis," *Political Science Quarterly* 115, no. 2 (2000): 241, https://doi.org/10.2307/2657901.
18. Kerry Dumbaugh, "Taiwan: Overall Developments and Policy Issues in the 109th Congress," CRS Report no. RL33520 (Washington, DC: Congressional Research Service, 2008), 1.
19. Nathan Beauchamp-Mustafaga, Derek Grossman, and Logan Ma, "Chinese Bomber Flights around Taiwan: What Does It Mean?," War on the Rocks, September 13, 2017, https://warontherocks.com/2017/09/chinese-bomber-flights-around-taiwan-for-what-purpose/.
20. Chris Buckley and Amy Qin, "In Surge of Military Flights, China Tests and Warns Taiwan," *New York Times*, October 14, 2021.
21. Maj. Gen. Zhang Zhaozhong, television interview, May 2013, quoted in Jeff Himmelman, "A Game of Shark and Minnow," *New York Times Magazine*, October 27, 2013.
22. Nguyen Thanh Trung, "How China's Coast Guard Law Has Changed the Regional Security Structure," CSIS Asia Maritime Transparency Initiative, April 12, 2021, https://amti.csis.org/how-chinas-coast-guard-law-has-changed-the-regional-security-structure/.
23. Amber Wang, "South China Sea: China Demands Foreign Vessels Report before Entering 'Its Territorial Waters,'" *South China Morning Post*, August 30, 2021, quoted in Ronald O'Rourke, *US-China Strategic Competition in South and East China Seas*, CRS Report no. R42784 (Washington, DC: Congressional Research Service, 2021), 15.
24. Yimou Lee, "Taiwan's New Coast Guard Flagship to Counter China's 'Grey Zone' Threat," Reuters, April 29, 2021, https://www.reuters.com/article/us-taiwan-security-idUSKBN2CG0AV; O'Rourke, *US-China Strategic Competition*, 11.
25. Yimou Lee, "China's Latest Weapon against Taiwan: The Sand Dredger," Reuters, February 5, 2021, https://graphics.reuters.com/TAIWAN-CHINA/SECURITY/jbyvrnzerve/.
26. Oriana Skylar Mastro, "The Taiwan Temptation: Why Beijing Might Resort to Force," *Foreign Affairs* (July/August 2021), https://www.foreignaffairs.com/articles/china/2021-06-03/china-taiwan-war-temptation.
27. Ministry of National Defense (ROC), *2021 Quadrennial Defense Review* (Taipei: Ministry of National Defense, 2021), 19.
28. Shang-su Wu, "Taiwan's Security: An Intertwined Knot," *Indo-Pacific Perspectives* (March 2021): 20.

29. See, for instance, Wu Su-wei and Jake Chung, "PLA Helicopters Testing Taiwan's Military: Experts," *Taipei Times*, August 29, 2021.
30. Ian Easton, *Hostile Harbors: Taiwan's Ports and PLA Invasion Plans* (Arlington, VA: Project 2049 Institute, 2021), 4.
31. Tanner Greer, "Taiwan Can Win a War with China," *Foreign Policy*, September 25, 2018.
32. Mark Episkopos, "Is Taiwan's New Defense Strategy Enough to Protect Them from a Chinese Invasion?," *National Interest*, May 21, 2021.
33. Tsai Ing-wen, "Taiwan and the Fight for Democracy: A Force for Good in the Changing International Order," *Foreign Affairs* (November/December 2021).
34. Yu Nakamura and Tsukasa Hadano, "Taiwan Navy Launches 'Carrier Killer' with 28 Missiles," *Nikkei Asia*, September 10, 2021, https://asia.nikkei.com/Politics/Taiwan-Navy-launches-carrier-killer-with-28-missiles.
35. "Taiwan's Submarine Building Program," *IISS Strategic Comments* 27, no. 1 (2021): i–ii.
36. Tso-Juei Hsu, "Taiwan Coast Guard Receives Its First *Chiayi*-Class Large Patrol Vessel," *Naval News*, April 30, 2021.
37. Ministry of National Defence (ROC), *2019 National Defense Report* (Taipei: Ministry of National Defense, 2019), 76; Mike Yeo, "Taiwan Is Spending an Extra $9B on Its Defense: Here's What the Money Will Buy," *Defense News*, October 7, 2021, https://www.defensenews.com/global/asia-pacific/2021/10/07/taiwan-is-spending-an-extra-9b-on-its-defense-heres-what-the-money-will-buy/.
38. Liam Gibson, "Taiwan Plans US$9 Billion Boost in Arms Spending in Response to 'Severe Threat' from China," *Taiwan News*, September 16, 2021, https://www.taiwannews.com.tw/en/news/4288910.
39. "New Agency to Oversee Mobilization of Reserves," *Taipei Times*, April 21, 2021, https://www.taipeitimes.com/News/taiwan/archives/2021/04/21/2003756078.
40. Meia Nouwens and Henry Boyd, "Analysis: Taiwan in the Pentagon Report's Spotlight," *IISS Military Balance+*, September 11, 2020, database, accessed October 5, 2021.
41. "H.R. 2479–96th Congress (1979–1980)," Congress.gov, https://www.congress.gov/bill/96th-congress/house-bill/2479.
42. Tara Copp, "'We Will Not Flinch': Austin Promises US Will Continue to Bolster Taiwan's Self-Defense," *Defense One*, July 27, 2021, https://www.defenseone.com/policy/2021/07/we-will-not-flinch-austin-promises-us-will-continue-bolster-taiwans-self-defense/184058/.
43. Ben Blanchard, "Timeline: US Arms Sales to Taiwan in 2020 Total $5 Billion amid China Tensions," Reuters, December 8, 2020, https://www.reuters.com/article/us-taiwan-security-usa-timeline-idUSKBN28I0BF.
44. Sidharth Kaushal, "US Weapons Sales to Taiwan: Upholding the Porcupine Strategy," RUSI Commentary, December 8, 2020, https://rusi.org/explore-our-research/publications/commentary/us-weapons-sales-taiwan-upholding-porcupine-strategy.
45. John King Fairbank, *China: A New History* (Cambridge, MA: Belknap Press of Harvard University Press, 2006), quoted in Demetri Sevastopulo, "US Special Forces Secretly Train Taiwan's Military," *Financial Times*, October 8, 2021, https://www.ft.com/content/46794116-7355-4669-b947-ce32bc5aff1a.

46. Collin Koh, "Reported US Navy Taiwan Straits Transits," Twitter, October 16, 2021, https://twitter.com/CollinSLKoh/status/1449544818833563648/photo/1.
47. Joseph Trevithick, "Army Releases Ultra Rare Video Showing Green Berets Training in Taiwan," The Drive, June 29, 2020, https://www.thedrive.com/the-war-zone/34474/army-releases-ultra-rare-video-showing-green-berets-training-in-taiwan.
48. Yu Tai-lang and Kayleigh Madjar, "Coast Guard Denies It Held Joint Drill with US," Taipei Times, August 11, 2021, https://www.taipeitimes.com/News/taiwan/archives/2021/08/11/2003762423.
49. Tsai, "Taiwan and the Fight for Democracy."
50. See Fiona H. C. Fan, "It's Time for the World to Help Step out of China's Shadow," Sydney Morning Herald, October 10, 2021.
51. Masahiro Akiyama, "Geopolitical Considerations of the Senkaku Islands," Sasakawa Peace Foundation Review of Island Studies, August 7, 2013, https://www.spf.org/islandstudies/research/a00007.html.
52. Nobukatsu Kanehara, "Complete Deterrence in Japan and the United States to Prevent Taiwan's Emergency: New Policies Such as Strengthening Defense Are Needed," Nippon.com, May 13, 2021, https://www.nippon.com/ja/in-depth/a07402/?cx_recs_click=true.
53. Mark E. Manyin, The Senkakus (Diaoyu/Diaoyutai Dispute): US Treaty Obligations, CRS Report RL42761 (Washington, DC: Congressional Research Service, 2021), summary.
54. Nancy Bernkopf Tucker and Bonnie Glaser, "Should the United States Abandon Taiwan?," Washington Quarterly 34, no. 4 (2011): 32, https://doi.org/10.1080/0163660X.2011.609128.
55. David Axe, "It's Getting More Likely the Japanese Would Fight for Taiwan," Forbes, July 2, 2021, https://www.forbes.com/sites/davidaxe/2021/07/02/its-getting-more-and-more-likely-japanese-troops-would-fight-for-taiwan/?sh=721081463a4c.
56. See Ministry of Defense, 2021 Defense of Japan (Tokyo: Ministry of Defense, 2021), 235–36; Government of Japan, "Three New Conditions" in Japan's Legislation for Peace and Security: Seamless Responses for Peace and Security of Japan and the International Community (Tokyo: Government of Japan, 2015).
57. "China to Conduct Major Military Drill Simulating Seizure of Taiwan-Held Island," Japan Times, May 14, 2020.
58. Felix K. Chang, "China's New Pressure on Taiwan in the South China Sea," Foreign Policy Research Institute, November 16, 2020, https://www.fpri.org/article/2020/11/chinas-new-pressure-on-taiwan-in-the-south-china-sea/.
59. Keoni Everington, "Taiwan's Marine 'Iron Force' Sent to Dongsha Islands ahead of PLA Invasion Drill," Taiwan News, August 5, 2020, https://www.taiwannews.com.tw/en/news/3980811.
60. George Liao, "Taiwan Deploys 292 Kestrel Anti-armor Rockets to the South China Sea," Taiwan News, April 7, 2021.
61. "Airpower in the South China Sea," Asia Maritime Transparency Initiative, July 29, 2015, https://amti.csis.org/airstrips-scs/.
62. Ankit Panda, "South China Sea: What's Taiwan Building on Itu Aba?," The Diplomat, September 21, 2016, https://thediplomat.com/2016/09/south-china-sea-whats-taiwan-building-on-itu-aba/.
63. Stephen Biddle and Ivan Oelrich, "Future Warfare in the Western Pacific: Chinese Antiaccess/Area Denial, US AirSea Battle, and Command of the Commons in East

Asia," *International Security* 41, no. 1 (Summer 2016): 13–14, https://doi.org/10 .1162/ISEC_a_00249.

64. Chris Buckley and Steven Lee Myers, "'Starting a Fire': US and China Enter Dangerous Territory over Taiwan," *New York Times*, October 15, 2021.

65. O'Rourke, *China Naval Modernization*, 2–3.

14

The South Pacific

James Goldrick

This chapter argues that the South Pacific is indeed a theater of strategic competition, a contest being conducted in several different ways. However, although there are military elements to the great maritime game that is being played out in the region, these are and will almost certainly remain secondary, not only to what are primarily diplomatic and economic rivalries but also to managing the increasingly serious consequences of climate change. This will mean that although conflict remains possible, competition will be leavened by cooperation, and the balance between the two depends on both regional and external influences.

UNDERSTANDING THE ENVIRONMENT

There are two key factors inherent to any geostrategic consideration of the South Pacific region that together combine to create a natural mismatch between resources and capacity, which affects practically every aspect of activity. The first is distance. It is as far from the western edge of the three-part nation of Kiribati to its eastern edge as Los Angeles is from New York. Conversely, the second factor is the minuscule size of the region's population by global standards. Kiribati has fewer than 120,000 people, more than half of whom live on Tarawa, and the entire population of Oceania is less than four million.[1] This does not include the key exception of Papua New Guinea (PNG), which has a rapidly growing population of more than seven million, which will nearly double by 2050 given current trends.[2] Although PNG has its own set of problems, most of which—however severe they may become—are likely to play out within that country rather than outside it.

Both the region's factors of distance and population size contribute to its unique strategic geography. Its sea lines of communication are critical to the small countries within it, as well as to New Zealand and Australia, but they have no such significance for the great powers. Any major conflict between China and the United States would be fought much farther north; diverting forces into the South Pacific might distract the great-power opponent but would be unlikely to justify the investment of such forces. Naval power is currently employed as a contribution to maritime security and will likely be employed so in the foreseeable future. This role is less familiar to the US Navy with its legal restrictions and the usual delegation of such work to the US Coast Guard, but it is customary for other nations. Thus, even though there are increasing uncertainties about the emerging role of China and its exercise of naval power in the South Pacific, it is likely that strategic competition will remain focused on maritime security.

The region and the Pacific Island countries (PICs) have traditionally been supported by the Quadrilateral Defence Coordination Group—Australia, France, New Zealand, and the United States—with the United Kingdom remaining moderately active as a postcolonial power (it retains the Pitcairn Islands as its sole Pacific overseas territory). Japan is also present as a long-term and leading provider of aid. Cooperation among the quadrilateral powers has long extended to coordinating maritime surveillance and response activities. All the actors, the United States included, face major challenges in finding the necessary resources to cope with the required scale of effort over the vast areas, with a premium on avoiding duplication. This includes close engagement with the Pacific Islands Forum Fisheries Agency (FFA). The FFA conducts four major multilateral operations a year. A typical example of such operations is Operation Rai Balang 2019, during which participants assessed 14.1 million square kilometers over a twelve-day period in March 2019.[3] Such work exemplifies the nature of most military activity in the region over the past seventy years.

What has not been undertaken for surveying, research, or remediation—particularly, for example, mines and other unexploded ordnance left over from World War II—has thus very largely been in the constabulary role and direct assistance to local authorities. This focus has also been apparent in efforts to build capacity, as several of the PICs do not in fact have military forces at all; their maritime enforcement is handled by police forces. Some long-standing maritime aid programs have been successful and are in the process of renewal. For instance, Australia initiated the Pacific Patrol Boat Program in 1983, which has resulted in the presentation of twenty-two patrol boats to twelve nations from 1985 to 1997. Both New Zealand and the United States have provided support to member nations within the program. In addition to regular refits, the program included the allocation of key technical and management personnel to help keep the boats running, a step that contributed very substantially to its long-term success. Australia recently initiated a follow-on program in the form of the Pacific Maritime Security Program (PMSP). In addition to a separate regional maritime aerial surveillance program, the PMSP is due to gift nineteen new construction boats to twelve Pacific countries by 2023. The fifth unit to be completed was handed over to the Solomons in November 2019. After delivery, these larger boats will continue to be supported by in-country technical and operational staff from both Australia and New Zealand.[4]

REFOCUSING ON THE REGION

The continuing patrol boat programs have been something of an exception in terms of the priority given them by the powers responsible for them. The United States and Australia have never stopped their regional support efforts, but it is true that the South Pacific had a relatively low priority for many years, particularly after the 2003 invasion of Iraq and the consequent draw on resources for the Middle East. For Australia, one of the key areas of reduced activity was its own naval and air presence, drawn off by a combination of Middle East deployments and Australia's own difficulties with illegal maritime arrivals via its northwestern approaches. That diversion of military effort was accompanied by a reduction in senior political engagement. New Zealand never drew down in the same way, but it did not have the resources to cover the gap.

In the past two years, Australia has been in something of a catch-up mode—its current efforts have even been formally designated as its "step up" in the region. Although the present government continues the mantra of its previous term—that the renewed Australian emphasis on the South Pacific is not about countering China—it is difficult to draw any other conclusion from the urgency of the effort and the scale on which it is being conducted. That the prime minister, Scott Morrison, visited the Solomon Islands in 2019 is indicative of the importance attached to the step up.[5] Ironically, not only Australia's but the collective attitude and approach of the Pacific powers to the new strategic challenge posed by China is probably best summed up by France's president Emmanuel Macron on a visit to New Caledonia in May 2018:

> In this part of the globe China is building its hegemony—it's not a question of raising fears but to look at the reality. China has to be a partner for this region. Its strategy of new Silk Road and its ambitions in the Pacific—we have to work with China to intensify exchanges and use the opportunities.

But if we don't organise ourselves, it will soon be a hegemony which will reduce our liberties, our opportunities which we will suffer.[6]

Acceptance of the reality that China will be an actor within the South Pacific no matter what others think is inherent in this approach. Thus, the questions are, What will China do and for what reasons, and How should the traditional powers respond?

CHINA IN THE SOUTH PACIFIC

China's goals for the region certainly have a security element but should be viewed largely in the context of its regional and global efforts to achieve influence—intensified by the situation of Taiwan—and secure economic benefits. The small South Pacific nations have been targets of the competition between Taiwan and the People's Republic of China (PRC) for diplomatic recognition over many years. They are relatively easy targets for money politics that range from extremely generous national aid programs to schemes that are practically direct bribes for individual politicians. National efforts have also become closely linked to individual Taiwanese or Chinese businesses buying access to timber and other natural resources, exacerbating existing problems of corruption in several countries. This mix of "checkbook diplomacy" and predatory business practices has long been criticized by the other Pacific powers. With six nations (Kiribati, the Marshall Islands, Nauru, Palau, the Solomon Islands, and Tuvalu) recognizing Taiwan and the remainder siding with the PRC, the situation has reached something of a modus vivendi in recent years, and Taiwan seems to be managing matters in a more responsible way. However, the election of a new Taiwanese president, Tsai Ing-wen, in 2016 saw the resurgence of direct competition when China sought to undermine Taiwan's claims to be a sovereign power. The mainland's efforts bore fruit in September 2019 when, in quick succession, the Solomons and Kiribati turned away from Taiwan (at a cost to China of approximately $500 billion in aid to the Solomons alone). The Taiwanese government would have received only some comfort from Tuvalu's strong statement of commitment to its diplomatic ties with Taiwan in November 2019.[7] Arguably, it has been the unwelcome side effects of this clash that have drawn most attention to the scale on which China can and does now operate in the region.

Outside the competition with Taiwan, China's efforts have generally had an economic focus. This has included seeking access to resources on land, in PNG and the Solomons in particular, but also access to the fish stocks of the region. Most of the economically viable fisheries lie within exclusive economic zones rather than in the high seas, and this requires permission to fish from the nation-states involved or results in illegal fishing issues if permission is not obtained. The expansion of China's distant water fisheries and the collapse of fish stocks closer to mainland Asia have also increased its interest in the potential of the Pacific deepwater fisheries.

CHINA AS A MILITARY PRESENCE IN THE SOUTH PACIFIC

China's military intentions for the region are uncertain and are likely to remain limited. Its most prominent naval presence has been in the form of a hospital ship, the *Daishan Dao*, designated as the "Peace Ark." In 2018 it treated some twenty thousand patients in PNG, Vanuatu, Fiji, and Tonga.[8] However, the PRC has long had a pattern of deployments for missile tracking and recovery—dating back to what was probably the first major oceanic group deployment of the People's Liberation Army–Navy (PLAN) in the vicinity of Fiji in 1980.[9] This pattern may now extend to intelligence gathering for other purposes. The arrival of the tracking ship *Yuanwang 7* in Suva, Fiji, in June 2018 when the Australian amphibious ship *Adelaide* was berthed there occasioned some comment.[10] In reality, however, *Yuanwang 7* had been a regular visitor to Suva,[11] and it is undeniable that the levels of long-term activity for this tracking role alone mean that a permanent South Pacific base and fueling facility would be very convenient for China. Such a facility would need to be combined with a substantial airhead and port facilities for it to be worthwhile. China's most clearly "naval" actions in the region to date have been the deployment of a single *Dongdiao*-class intelligence gatherer into the Coral Sea in 2017 and another in 2019 to monitor the biennial US-Australian Exercise Talisman Sabre.[12] Ironically, both intelligence ships operated within Australia's exclusive economic zone, in clear breach of China's declared interpretation of the 1982 Law of the Sea. Moreover, in 2019 the ships passed through Australian territorial waters without giving prior notification— something China demands of foreign warships in its own waters.

There is certainly evidence of much-increased levels of oceanographic and hydrographic activity by Chinese government vessels. These recently came into prominence with the analysis of various data sources, which indicated that the Chinese had been conducting operations in areas that were most likely to provide information concerning the underwater conditions in the eastern approaches to the key American naval base at Guam as well as to the area between Guam and Manus Island.[13] In behaviors like this, China seems to be following the example of the Soviet Union's extensive oceanic research efforts of the 1960s to the 1980s and for probably the same mix of reasons. Knowledge of the seabed and the water mass has both potential commercial and military benefits. China is extremely interested in both fisheries and deep seabed mining, and its submarines are operating ever farther afield. Gaining detailed knowledge of the approaches to the major American naval base on Guam would be a high priority for the PLAN.

The prospect of China establishing a naval base in the region has confirmed both the worries of the traditional powers and the sensitivities of the PICs. The Australian prime minister, Malcolm Turnbull, was publicly concerned about reports in 2018 that Vanuatu was discussing with the PRC the possibility of such a base. This followed the completion of a three-hundred-meter wharf, capable of berthing very large ships, on Espiritu Santo, Vanuatu. China denied the suggestion of the base. Additionally, the suggestion evoked a furious response from Vanuatu's foreign minister, Ralph Regenvanu, who not only denied that there was any truth to the story but, significantly, also said, "I would hope the upsurge in the paranoia about China in Australia is not used to destroy or denigrate the good relationship Vanuatu has with Australia."[14] That Vanuatu was prepared to favor China in other ways had become apparent with its June 2016 statement of support for China's South China Sea claim to "historical" rights. Despite China's denials, the potential for a Chinese base in the region continued to be a concern. At the Shangri-La Dialogue in Singapore in June 2019, the secretary of Australia's Department of Foreign Affairs and Trade, Frances Adamson, reiterated Australia's view that "any foreign base in the region would not be welcome. We would strongly condemn and oppose that."[15]

There have been suggestions that China may want to establish a naval presence in the South Pacific to threaten communications between the United States and the Antipodes (Australia and New Zealand). Even a small facility to support its continuing space-tracking program could easily be viewed as the thin end of the wedge for such a more extensive project. However, as suggested previously, a sustained commitment of capable combat forces to the region would require substantial efforts by the PLAN and could only come at the expense of higher strategic priorities. Furthermore, it would send a signal of Chinese expansionism that could not be cast in the same light (as friendly and innocuous) as the base at Djibouti or the naval deployments in the Indian Ocean, which would further undermine not only its present fractious relationship with Australia and New Zealand but also alienate most of the Pacific Island nations—not to mention the United States.

It is much more likely than any increase in Chinese maritime presence would be in the form of Chinese coast guard cutters, ostensibly to protect and regulate the operations of Chinese fishing fleets licensed to operate in the region. Yet even this could prove a two-edged sword if the PICs came to believe that Chinese interventions were reducing their ability to control their own fish stocks and the local management of their fisheries as a whole.

THE PACIFIC ISLAND COUNTRIES AND
CHINA: OPPORTUNITY AND THREAT

The regional response to China has been arguably as opportunistic as much of China's own efforts are opportunist. Vanuatu may not be an exception. Apart from the attractiveness of Chinese aid and gifts, long-term resentments (conscious and unconscious) of the historical dominance in the region by so many former colonial powers, as well as not always unjustified continuing objections to being treated as junior partners rather than equals, has made many PICs open to Chinese approaches—at least until they have had direct experience of the results.

Nevertheless, there are emerging opportunities for China still. One of the central concerns of the Pacific Island nations and a potential lever for their relationship with the great powers is climate change. Many of the low-lying islands feel threatened by the prospect of sea-level rise, which carries the potential not only for temporary, and eventually permanent, inundation but also for contamination of existing freshwater sources and salination of what is already very limited arable land. The "climate wars" in Australia and the Liberal-National Coalition government's ambivalence on carbon-emission reductions and renewable energy have become a source of constant (although not unreasonable) complaint by the PICs. The United States has also been the subject of direct criticism. The attitude of the Donald J. Trump administration to climate change is viewed with distaste by the PICs. In 2017, after the American withdrawal from the Paris Agreement, Tuvalu went as far as to suspend cooperation with the United States until the latter changes its policy.[16] This fundamental divergence on such a critical—indeed existential—problem could well become a lever for China to draw the PICs toward it.

There are other potential sources of trouble in the South Pacific region. It is arguable that the nations have not completed their full transition to postcolonial states. Although the latest referendum in New Caledonia (a French territory) rejected independence, the result was both closer than expected and more closely aligned with ethnic divisions than hoped. With further plebiscites possible in 2020 and 2022, New Caledonia's continuance as part of overseas France cannot be assumed.[17] Moreover, the strategic alignment of any independent New Caledonian state that may result cannot be assumed either, regardless of how expert the French have been in managing analogous situations in Africa. Bougainville's late 2019 referendum on greater autonomy or full independence from PNG came down overwhelmingly (more than 97 percent) in favor of outright independence. However, the PNG government is not bound to abide by the vote, which must be ratified by the national parliament. Given Bougainville's importance as a source of natural resources, PNG may well be unwilling to let the island go, which could result in a return to unrest and violence.[18] Maintaining a balance between PNG and Bougainville may prove very difficult for all the Pacific powers.

Certainly, a righteous attitude toward internal problems in the region has not always had the results Australia or its partners have wanted. For example, Australia's sanctions against Fiji (lifted in 2014) had several consequences that have become object lessons. Australia cut military ties after the 2006 Fijian coup that brought the current prime minister, Frank Bainimarama, to power; it was understandable but created a vacuum into which China attempted to move. Since 2014 Australia and New Zealand have restored a number of training and infrastructure programs, but there is an awareness that there is a generation of Fijian military personnel who have no personal experience of working with either nation's defense forces.[19]

One initiative by Australia that does seem to have succeeded is the Coral Sea Cable Project. Commenced in 2018, it involves the deployment of a forty-seven-hundred-kilometer undersea fiber-optic cable from Australia, with branches to PNG and the Solomons as well as internal links to islands within the latter's archipelago.[20] Completed in December 2019, the system is jointly owned by PNG and the Solomons. Australia took on the coordination and the lion's share of the cost of this key project as a deliberate effort to exclude Chinese interests from an infrastructure project of considerable significance.

THE PROSPECTS FOR BALANCING CHINA

In the case of the Coral Sea Cable Project, Australia seems to have adopted an approach that benefits but does not burden the two Pacific states concerned. Yet the ease with which the traditional Pacific powers can and have miscued on several other issues suggests ironically that China's goals may not, in the end, be easily gained—unless the Chinese learn lessons more quickly and thoroughly than the other major powers. Although China has achieved a number of opportunistic successes in developing closer relationships in the South Pacific, particularly with Fiji, its lack of "emotional intelligence" in external affairs has caused repeated offense, most recently at the 2018 Pacific Island Forum in Nauru and at the Asia-Pacific Economic Cooperation assembly in PNG in 2019. On both occasions, heavy-handed tactics by Chinese officials proved extremely counterproductive. The visit of Vice Premier Hu Chunhua to Samoa in October 2019 to sign a number of trade agreements ahead of the China–Pacific Island Countries Economic Development and Cooperation Forum suggested that China had realized that a much more emollient approach was required.[21] Nevertheless, Chinese officials have much to learn about managing relationships in a region where the personal can quickly become national.

Furthermore, although the PICs regard some of the warnings from Australia and other countries about the pitfalls of Chinese largesse as patronizing, there is increasing awareness of the consequences of falling into a Chinese debt trap. For instance, when Tonga's loans from China totaled approximately one third of its gross domestic product by 2018, China proved unwilling to forgive the debt. That Sri Lanka had been forced to hand over its new container port to China on an extended lease as partial payment for an unmanageable debt should have seemed ominous to Tonga at least; yet Tonga signed the loans.[22] An Australian exposé in November 2019 of China's dubious financial practices in the Solomons and other island states was a straw in the wind of increasing regional awareness of the problem.[23] A Chinese attempt the previous September to secure a seventy-five-year lease on the island of Tulagi in the Solomons from its provincial government was overturned by national authorities, albeit only after international protests (and many local ones).[24]

China's fishing fleets may be another vulnerability. Illegal and unregulated fishing continues to deplete the fish stocks and the potential revenue of many of the PICs, and it is likely that Chinese vessels are deeply implicated. Although the reporting by agencies such as the FFA tries to avoid naming any particular national groups, it is clear that there are serious problems with the underreporting of catches by licensed fishing vessels.[25] The multinational South Pacific Regional Fisheries Management Organisation recently held that China was not in compliance with its efforts to combat illegal fishing—a significant step, especially given that China is one of the fourteen member nations of the organization.[26] At the start of 2020, China gave some publicity to its revision of fishing laws to allow blacklisting of fishing enterprises acting illegally in distant waters.[27]

China may have been tone-deaf in another way. The Chinese Communist Party's assertions that the Chinese diaspora owes loyalty not only to China's national culture but also to the Chinese nation and its political system can only exacerbate the existing tensions between the Melanesian and Polynesian first peoples of the PICs and the readily racially identifiable Chinese communities dominating much of the commercial sector in many nations—and to which there have been many additions in recent years. The 2006 anti-Chinese riots in the Solomons were at least partly a response to the racism and cultural insensitivity of the new arrivals, something acknowledged by the Chinese government.[28]

RESPONDING TO CHINA

The management of the coronavirus pandemic has been both a key challenge and an opportunity since 2020.[29] The speed with which Australia and New Zealand developed their own "bubble" for travel between the two nations and then incorporated the PICs may be critical to the health of the future relationship—and the extent to which China remains a secondary influence.

Some recent initiatives have clearly been intended to get a step ahead of the Chinese. For instance, the European Union has promised the region increased priority, as has Canada. Additionally, Japan has moved to increase its aid to the South Pacific, targeting Vanuatu in particular, while also extending its diplomatic presence across the region. Even more pointed is the recent decision by Australia, with the help of the United States, to fund the redevelopment of the naval facilities on Manus Island.[30] Although a patrol boat base was left available to PNG upon independence in 1975, it had effectively become moribund. The redeveloped joint facility will extend earlier plans to upgrade the base's wharf to accommodate PNG's new PMSP boats. Furthermore, the Australian government has indicated that it is possible that Royal Australian Navy units would be based at Manus, and the inclusion of the United States in the arrangement suggests that American units will also become regular users of the facility. Nevertheless, the scale of the modernization suggests that the renovated base will remain basic, configured for the support of patrol boats but only as a forward-operating base for larger ships. What the result will be remained uncertain in early 2019, although the first stage of the AU$42 million project was completed in August 2019.[31]

Another example of direct competition between Australia and China was the redevelopment of the Fijian military base in Nadi. Australia's offer, which was described as "more holistic" by the Fijians, included training support as well as building work and was accepted in September 2018 ahead of China's bid.[32] On the other hand, in December 2018 China handed over a hydrographic and oceanographic research catamaran to the Fijian navy. A team of eighteen PLAN personnel also provided four months of training to thirty-five Fijian personnel; most of the training was in Fiji and directly related to the operation of the ship.[33] The training was completed in March 2019 and marked by the declaration by Fiji's minister of defense, Inia Seruiratu, of the "growing enhanced relationship" between the two countries.[34]

CONCLUSION

These experiences confirm that the future relationship of the traditional powers with China in the region should not be treated only as a zero-sum game. The PICs will look to their own self-interests, just as Fiji has done and as Vanuatu and the Solomons, among others, appear to be doing. A key message from the PICs is that they have no desire to become involved in any kind of military strategic competition, and it is possible that this consensus may act as a key restraint on any individual PIC government overreaching in the China relationship. Furthermore, although military elements will continue to have a place in the inevitable competition, success in limiting China's influence on constructive measures will depend much more on solving, or at least managing, some of the region's chronic problems.

In this regard, initiatives such as the stated intent of the United States to establish an information-fusion center for the region need not only to be coordinated with efforts such as Australia's plan for a Pacific fusion center but also to be careful to avoid the appearance of a military focus.[35] The PICs will welcome any measures that assist them in controlling their maritime zones, but they will be understandably reluctant to become involved in anything that suggests militarization of the region.

Managing sea-level rise may be one of the major challenges of the next two decades, and managing the relationships with the PICs may be a central part of any power's strategic equation in the South Pacific. The problem is not really one of mass migration, given the limited numbers of people involved. Some PICs, notably Kiribati, have already been hedging, through the purchase of land in higher-elevation islands. Several PICs have more people living in New Zealand and Australia than remain in their own nations. Nevertheless, achieving free access to employment in Australia is one of the primary requests of PICs that do not enjoy entry privileges to the United States, like some of the northern island groups do, or that countries such as Niue have to New Zealand. Although the most obvious pressures will be on Australia, all the supporting powers will need to look at both direct and indirect support of the PICs. This will include making provision for the continuing economic and other rights of the original inhabitants to the maritime domains of already submerged (and thus unoccupied) islands—as well as to the new mechanisms that will be required for their management. New Zealand has become the first country to create a visa category specifically based on displacement as a result of sea-level change.[36]

China can and should play a part in all this; however, the realities of geography, history, and continuing social and cultural connections mean that the lead must come from Australia and New Zealand, supported by the United States and France. Japan and the European Union will be important partners—as may Canada, with its new emphasis on aid to the PICs. Only if the quadrilateral powers mismanage the challenge is China likely to have the opportunity to take a dominant role in the South Pacific.

The future of naval power in this equation is relatively straightforward. It will largely be one involving patrol craft and not battle groups. The traditional powers will continue to focus on supporting the maritime security of the island states through a combination of capacity-building and operational endeavors. The forms and levels of their naval deployments are unlikely to change unless

China radically alters its current approach and seeks to develop a substantial permanent naval presence. Within such a maritime security focus, however, the extent to which cooperation or competition between the quadrilateral powers and China will dominate is much less clear. This, too, may depend much more on external factors than the key drivers of regional need. Finally, it will also depend on whether China can restrain itself from employing its own maritime security units in ways that are seen to act against the interests of the small island nations of the South Pacific.

NOTES

1. Excludes Australia, PNG, and New Zealand. "Oceania Population 2020," World Population Review, https://worldpopulationreview.com/continents/oceania-population/.
2. Stewart Firth, *Instability in the Pacific Islands: A Status Report* (Sydney: Lowy Institute, 2018), https://www.lowyinstitute.org/sites/default/files/documents/Firth _Instability%20in%20the%20Pacific%20Islands_A%20status%20report_WEB.pdf.
3. Pacific Islands Forum Fisheries Agency, "First FFA-Led Monitoring, Control, and Surveillance Operation for the Year: Operation Rai Belang 2019 Ends on a High Note," press release, April 10, 2019, https://www.ffa.int/node/2247.
4. Department of Defence (Australia) "Pacific Maritime Security Program," in *Department of Defence Annual Report, 2017–2018* (Canberra: Department of Defence, 2018), 15, https://www.defence.gov.au/annualreports/17-18/Downloads /DAR_2017-18_Complete.pdf.
5. Lisa Martin, "Scott Morrison to Sell Pacific 'Step Up' on Solomons Visit as Pressure Builds Up over Climate," *The Guardian*, May 27, 2019, https://www.theguardian .com/australia-news/2019/may/27/scott-morrison-expected-to-get-a-whack-on -climate-change-on-solomons-visit.
6. Dateline Pacific, "Macron Wants a Balance against China in the Pacific," RNZ, May 7, 2018, https://www.rnz.co.nz/international/programmes/datelinepacific /audio/2018643812/macron-wants-a-balance-against-china-in-the-pacific.
7. Yimou Lee, "Tuvalu Rejects China Offer to Build Islands and Retains Ties with Taiwan," Reuters, November 21, 2019, https://www.reuters.com/article/us-taiwan -diplomacy-tuvalu/tuvalu-rejects-china-offer-to-build-islands-and-retains-ties -with-taiwan-idUSKBN1XV0H8.
8. Atmakuri Lakshmi Archana and Minjiang Li, "Geopolitical Objectives Fuel China's Peace Ark," East Asia Forum, November 13, 2018, https://www.eastasiaforum .org/2018/10/13/geopolitical-objectives-fuel-chinas-peace-ark/.
9. "Chinese Test Success: Naval Ships See Missile Re-entry," *Canberra Times*, May 19, 1980.
10. "Australia Suspicious of Chinese Vessel in Suva: RNZ Pacific, June 13, 2018, https://www.rnz.co.nz/international/pacific-news/359490/australia-suspicious-of -chinese-vessel-in-suva.
11. Nacanieli Tuilaveka, "PRC Research Vessel Refuels, Restocks after 100 Days at Sea," *Fuji Sun*, April 25, 2018, http://fijisun.com.fj/2018/04/25/prc-research-vessel -refuels-restocks-after-100-days-at-sea/.

12. Euan Graham, "China's Naval Surveillance off Australia: Good News and Bad," *The Interpreter*, July 24, 2017, https://www.lowyinstitute.org/the-interpreter/china-s -naval-surveillance-australia-good-news-and-bad.

13. Andrew Greene, "Chinese Surveillance near PNG Expanding as Australia and US Begin Manus Island Naval Upgrades," ABC News Australia, April 21, 2019, https://www.abc.net.au/news/2019-04-21/china-increases-surveillance-near-png /11028192.

14. "Vanuatu Denies It Will Host China Military Base," BBC News, April 10, 2018, https://www.bbc.com/news/world-australia-43707975.

15. Graeme Dobell, "South Pacific Security at Shangri-La," *The Strategist*, June 5, 2019, https://www.aspistrategist.org.au/south-pacific-security-at-shangri-la/.

16. Grant Wyeth, "For Pacific Island States Climate Change Is an Existential Threat," *The Diplomat*, June 5, 2017, https://thediplomat.com/2017/06/for-pacific-island -states-climate-change-is-an-existential-threat/.

17. Denise Fisher, "New Caledonia Votes to Stay with France This Time, but Independence Supporters Take Heart," *The Conversation*, November 5, 2018, https:// theconversation.com/new-caledonia-votes-to-stay-with-france-this-time-but -independence-supporters-take-heart-106329.

18. Kate Lyons, "Bougainville Referendum: Region Votes Overwhelmingly for Independence from Papua New Guinea," *The Guardian*, December 11, 2019, https:// www.theguardian.com/world/2019/dec/11/bougainville-referendum-region -votes-overwhelmingly-for-independence-from-papua-new-guinea.

19. "#KYR: Fiji—The Vuvale Partnership," The Cove, September 21, 2021, https://cove .army.gov.au/article/kyr-fiji-vuvale-partnership.

20. "About the Project," Australian Aid, accessed June 23, 2020, https://www.coralsea cablesystem.com.au/about/.

21. Liam Fox and Michael Walsh, "China Inks Several New Deals with Samoa ahead of Pacific Island Economic Forum in Apia," ABC News Australia, October 21, 2019, https://www.abc.net.au/news/2019-10-21/china-and-samoa-ink-deals-ahead-of -pacific-island-economic-forum/11622096.

22. Charlotte Greenfield and Jonathan Barrett, "Tonga PM Fears Asset Seizures as Pacific Debts to China Mount," Reuters, August 16, 2018, https://www.reuters .com/article/us-pacific-debt-tonga-graphic/tonga-pm-fears-asset-seizures-as -pacific-debts-to-china-mount-idUSKBN1L10KM.

23. "China's 'Soft Invasion' of South Pacific," *60 Minutes*, November 17, 2019, https:// www.news.com.au/entertainment/tv/current-affairs/60-minutes-investigates -chinas-growing-influence-in-the-south-pacific/news-story/d855ee6982de6eea 5c60327893dc1008.

24. AFP in Honiara, "Solomons' Government Vetoes Chinese Attempt to Lease an Island," *The Guardian*, October 26, 2019, https://www.theguardian.com/world /2019/oct/25/solomons-government-vetoes-chinese-attempt-to-lease-an-island.

25. MRAG Asia Pacific, *Towards the Quantification of Illegal, Unreported, and Unregulated (IUU) Fishing in the Pacific Islands Region* (Toowong, Australia: MRAG Asia Pacific, 2016), 24.

26. "World's Largest Fish Factory Vessel Stays on IUU List," Maritime Executive, May 2, 2019, https://www.maritime-executive.com/article/world-s-largest-fish-factory -vessel-stays-on-iuu-list.

27. Zhang Chun, "China Targets Distant-Water Criminals with New Fisheries Law," *China Dialogue Ocean*, January 21, 2020, https://chinadialogueocean.net/12714 -china-fisheries-law-distant-water-fishing/.
28. Firth, *Instability in the Pacific Islands*, 8.
29. Natalie Whiring, "Could Australia Expand Its Proposed Coronavirus Travel Bubble to the Pacific Islands? Here's What You Need to Know," ABC News Australia, May 20, 2020, https://www.abc.net.au/news/2020-05-20/coronavirus-pacific -islands-tourism-plan-nz-fiji-travel-bubble/12259532.
30. Stephen Dziedzic, "US to Partner with Australia, Papua New Guinea on Manus Naval Base," ABC News Australia, November 17, 2018, https://www.abc.net.au /news/2018-11-17/us-to-partner-with-australia-and-png-on-manus-island-naval -base/10507658.
31. AAP, "Australia–Papua New Guinea Naval Base Deal Goes Ahead," SBS News, November 1, 2018; AAP, "First Stage of Manus Naval Base Opens," *Canberra Times*, August 24, 2019.
32. "Australian Offer over Fiji Base Beats China's," RNZ Pacific, September 13, 2018, https://www.rnz.co.nz/international/pacific-news/366386/australian-offer-over -fiji-base-beats-china-s.
33. Shirika Shalini, "*Kacau* to Enhance Service Delivery," *Fiji Sun*, December 26, 2018, https://fijisun.com.fj/2018/12/26/kacau-to-enhance-service-delivery/.
34. Swashna Chand, "Minister Seruiratu Praises Fiji-China Navy Ties," *Fiji Sun*, March 21, 2019, https://fijisun.com.fj/2019/03/21/468340/.
35. Blake Herzinger, "US Plans in the Pacific Islands Could Undermine Australia's Efforts," *The Strategist*, June 12, 2019, https://www.aspistrategist.org.au/us-plans -in-the-pacific-islands-could-undermine-australias-efforts/.
36. Matt Young, "Pacific Island Nations Urge World Leaders to Act as Islands Expected to Sink," News.com.au, November 15, 2017, https://www.news.com.au /technology/environment/pacific-island-nations-urge-world-leaders-to-act-as -islands-expected-to-sink/news-story/9416ac1726d1f8d02a1ae435924e364f.

15

The Indian Ocean

The Rise of the US-India Partnership?

Abhijit Singh and James J. Wirtz

Over the past two decades, a transformation in geopolitical realities has spurred a new strategic convergence between the United States and India. Having spent much of the Cold War as estranged democracies, the two countries today are close partners sharing common values and an array of core interests.[1] New Delhi and Washington cooperate on a range of complex security challenges—from terrorism and weapon proliferation to global governance, climate change, trade, and disaster relief.[2] Their partnership continues to grow stronger, despite changing administrations and their respective domestic political distractions.

For many, maritime security has been the "best performing area" of the bilateral relationship between New Delhi and Washington, and other observers have noted that "no area of United States–India cooperation holds more promise than maritime cooperation."[3] Indeed, year after year since the early 2000s, India-US maritime ties have grown, which is leading not only to greater policy convergence but also to growing naval cooperation across the Indo-Pacific region. Apart from their shared vision on maritime security issues, the two navies of the two nations have upgraded their bilateral maritime security partnership and have been collaborating to build regional partner capacity as well as to improve the security environment in the Indian Ocean region (IOR).[4]

The emergence of this maritime partnership has not been without speed bumps. There has been anxiety in some sections of India's strategic community over the consequences of closer military alignment with the United States and occasional grumbling in Washington about the details of technology transfers and weapon sales.[5] A US freedom-of-navigation patrol off India's Lakshadweep Island in the Arabian Sea in April 2021 caused disquiet in New Delhi, with some Indian observers calling the move "an act of impropriety."[6] A new strategic grouping of Australia, the United Kingdom, and the United States called AUKUS, seemingly intended to transfer US nuclear submarine technology to Australia, has also raised apprehensions in Indian strategic circles over the possible marginalization of the Quadrilateral Security Dialogue (Quad) grouping, which comprises India, Japan, Australia, and the United States (and is not to be confused with the Quadrilateral Defence Coordination Group mentioned in chapter 14).[7]

Yet the consensus in New Delhi has largely been that the benefits of cooperation with the United States in the maritime domain far outweigh the costs, and policymakers in Washington have also been keen to identify new ways of intensifying collaboration, especially with India, in the IOR.[8] This chapter explores the prospects for greater bilateral naval synergy in littoral Asia through a scrutiny of the maturing India-US maritime partnership. It argues that China's rapidly rising presence and assertiveness in the Indian Ocean creates an imperative for the United States and India to consult more closely on matters of regional security. As New Delhi and Washington expand their engagement in the Indian Ocean, their collaboration could mature into active cooperation across the wider Asian littorals.

India-US maritime activities also highlight several issues central to this volume's objectives. They illustrate how both Washington and New Delhi view maritime *cooperation* as an instrument of statecraft that conveys a message greater than the military importance of combined naval operations per se. This collaboration also is shaped by geography in the sense that it is strongest when it comes to the key challenges facing both nations in the IOR; it diminishes in intensity when one considers issues and potential operations outside the region. Indeed, one is left to wonder if the India-US maritime partnership will act as a catalyst and further strengthen strategic collaboration between the two states or fail when it encounters issues that defy simple solutions. Will two maritime powers continue to find it easier to enhance their collaboration than more common partnerships between land and maritime nations?

This chapter unfolds in four parts. First, we evaluate Indian and US security challenges in the IOR and the individual perspectives of the two countries regarding maritime security. Then we assess the bilateral maritime relationship and outline both opportunities and obstacles to greater engagement. Often Indian and US maritime interests broadly overlap, but they occasionally diverge, sometimes based on substantive disagreements but mostly owing to misperceptions and misunderstandings of the other's maritime posture. Next we examine the prospects of an India-US nautical alliance—a compact between maritime powers that aims to achieve common objectives in a broader space. In this section, we look at the unique characteristics of maritime alliances that might shape a deeper engagement. The chapter concludes by offering several observations about the practical extent of a joint endeavor in the commons and what such a partnership might realistically achieve.

INDIA'S MARITIME CHALLENGES

From the Indian perspective, the Indian Ocean littoral is the core security space in the Indo-Pacific region and a sphere of Indian interest.[9] Since Prime Minister Narendra Modi assumed office in 2014, India has been on a quest to reclaim influence in the neighborhood.[10] In March 2015 Modi articulated a five-pronged vision regarding the future of the Indian Ocean, key elements of which envisage "collective action and cooperation" in the commons. The vision is called Security and Growth for All in the Region, the acronym of which is SAGAR, meaning "the sea" in Hindi.[11] Since its release, New Delhi has expanded its political engagement with Sri Lanka, Seychelles, Maldives, and Mauritius, and it has been improving maritime security cooperation, assisting with hydrographic surveys, and raising the frequency of naval and coast guard patrols.[12] India's capacity-building initiatives provide surveillance aircraft and patrol boats to the small island states and build maritime infrastructure, including radar and communication facilities.[13] India has paid particular attention to improving maritime domain awareness. An information-fusion center in Gurgaon now regularly exchanges information with littoral states. Furthermore, the Indian navy's P-8I surveillance aircraft, along with naval and coast guard vessels, conduct regular patrols within the large exclusive economic zones belonging to Mauritius and Seychelles to deter drug trafficking and illegal fishing, among other things.[14]

The IOR embodies a complex set of issues and a large number of actors. The region has seen greater naval deployments from a host of regional and extraregional players, some of whom have friendly relations with New Delhi.[15] What worries Indian policymakers and security watchers is China's growing economic and military footprint, which many say poses a threat to Indian influence and geopolitical leverage in the neighborhood.[16] For many Indian analysts, China's antipiracy activities suggest growing strategic ambitions in the Indian Ocean.[17] The People's Liberation Army–Navy (PLAN) activities in the Indian Ocean, especially submarine visits to Sri Lanka and Pakistan and China's attempts to establish logistics bases like the one in Djibouti, seem consistent with a broader Chinese quest for geopolitical influence in oceanic littorals.[18] The growing complexity and scope of the Chinese submarine deployments is an indication that PLAN commanders are keen to study the operating environment of the Indian Ocean. Chinese submarines have been spending unusually long periods exploring the southern Asian littorals. These cruises give PLAN commanders the opportunity to gain familiarity with the regional shipping patterns, fine-tune standard operating procedures, and gather vital hydrological and bathymetric data.[19]

India's political leaders also worry about PLAN warship deployments in the western Indian Ocean. China has been leveraging antipiracy task force deployments to maintain a naval presence and to secure geopolitical leverage in the East African and West Asian littorals. The PLAN escort forces' frequent regional port visits and exercises with littoral navies has helped burnish China's global image and provide important soft-power benefits in a region that is not a traditional sphere of Chinese influence.[20] Adm. Arun Prakash, a former Indian naval chief, notes that the shift in China's maritime focus from "offshore waters defense" to "open seas protection," mandated by the Chinese 2015 white paper on national defense, signals the PLAN's intent to move beyond the notional "first island chain" barrier and to sail into the blue waters of the Indo-Pacific.[21] With the PLAN having inaugurated its first Indian Ocean base in Djibouti and invested in strategically located ports, such as Gwadar in Pakistan and Hambantota in Sri Lanka, Prakash surmises that it is now well positioned to project power, exercise sea control, and even mount expeditionary operations on India's doorstep.[22] Not coincidentally, Sri Lanka, Pakistan, Bangladesh, and Maldives have been expanding their own nautical engagement with the Chinese navy. Nontraditional security threats in the neighborhood also continue to be a strong driver of India's maritime security strategy. Since the attacks in Mumbai on November 26, 2011, terrorism has been a key area of focus for India's security agencies; their primary concern has been to prevent another Mumbai-like terrorist attack from the sea.[23] India's long coastline and the proximity of terrorist organization bases make this mission a daunting proposition. Whether it is driven by certain extremist groups or part of a larger strategic investment by regional actors, terrorism is a significant security issue for India and one that is not likely to abate for some time.

Another important area of security focus for the Indian navy is humanitarian assistance and disaster relief. Building on its 2004 tsunami experience of undertaking humanitarian assistance and disaster-relief operations in the regional seas, the Indian navy has been a "first responder" during many humanitarian crises in the IOR.[24] This includes a major evacuation effort in Yemen, providing supplies during a drinking water crisis in Maldives, and relief efforts in Sri Lanka and Bangladesh. The navy's biennial Milan exercises at Port Blair (on South Andaman Island) have given special attention to relief and rescue operations and noncombatant evacuation drills as well as prompted growing participation by regional maritime forces.[25]

Meanwhile, coastal security continues to be a source of concern. Despite improvements in littoral security over the past decade, India's coastal states have struggled to institute effective littoral security measures.[26] The Indian navy and coast guard have had to pitch in, which leaves them with fewer resources and less energy for international partnerships. Adding to the navy's workload, it has had to take on the role of a "net-security provider" in the neighborhood.[27] Besides contributing to the counterpiracy initiative off the coast of Somalia, the Indian navy has been a leading player in constabulary and benign security tasks, in particular combating illegal fishing, drug smuggling, and human trafficking in the Bay of Bengal. Still, a paucity of assets and limited operational capacity has forced the Indian navy to seek partners willing to invest resources in joint security endeavors.

Indian observers worry about the influence of external powers in the Indian Ocean but realize their impact could be salutary, in some cases at least. For instance, with its base at Diego Garcia, the United States seems well positioned to assist in the creation of greater security capacity in littoral South Asia. India's security planners also favor greater engagement with the United Kingdom and France, whose bases in Réunion and Mayotte have the potential to expand India's naval reach into the southwestern Indian Ocean. New Delhi has been quick to consolidate its maritime partnership with France by signing logistics agreements and improving joint maritime surveillance in the Indian Ocean.[28] Recent reports suggest that from the first quarter of 2020, the Indian navy has been deploying a maritime patrol aircraft to Réunion Island regularly.[29]

Yet it remains unclear to New Delhi how its maritime partners, in particular Washington, would respond if China achieves a position of dominance in the Indian Ocean. Following the India-China clash in eastern Ladakh in June 2020, many in New Delhi anticipate an aggressive Chinese naval strategy in the eastern Indian Ocean. Furthermore, Indian observers believe that China seeks a permanent presence in the IOR in the form of operational bases, though not all of India's partners share that assessment. David Brewster, an Australian maritime expert, avers that China may not in fact challenge Indian or US interests in the IOR immediately. Instead he suggests that the PLAN will exert dominance incrementally, following strategies drawn from the Chinese game of Go, which would complicate India's security calculus.[30] A 2020 report by the US Naval War College also states that despite a significant enlargement of presence in the Indian Ocean, the PLAN's capacity for maritime power projection remains limited.[31] A key task for Indian experts, then, is to estimate the commitment of India's partners in preserving stability and responding to the slow increase in Chinese capability and influence across the IOR.

THE US PERSPECTIVE

From the US perspective, the growing PLAN presence in the IOR, its slow development of port facilities and privileges in the region, and its obvious interest in courting additional political favors among the capitals along the Indian Ocean littorals are all sources of concern. Under the "Belt and Road Initiative" in Beijing's discourse, these projects hark back to earlier days when the Silk Road was the main commercial route between East and West.[32] In today's parlance, the "road" is formed by maritime communications and suggests that Beijing is working on its own independent trade routes, not only through the IOR but also across the Indo-Pacific region. This commercial activity and even modest PLAN activity in the IOR does not necessarily threaten US interests in a significant way, but it does portend a threatening and unsafe future. An increasing PLAN presence in the IOR threatens to siphon off US maritime assets from the western Pacific, opening a new theater for competition or even conflict. In contrast, the US Navy has traditionally treated the IOR as a relatively permissive environment.

As Washington directs its attention toward the Indo-Pacific and assumes more responsibilities in the region, some fear it might create "a potential mismatch between US policy objectives and the structure of American naval power."[33] Given the Indian Ocean's numerous sea-lanes and choke points, the United States needs partners to share the burden of security. Nevertheless, Washington should be careful. On one hand, US policymakers need to guard against overcommitting forces in the Indian Ocean; on the other, undercommitment might force regional states to "bandwagon" with Beijing.[34] Therefore, for the United States, the central task is to forge meaningful partnerships with credible partners, and India is undoubtedly one.

Unlike previous administrations, the Donald J. Trump administration was visibly committed to boosting India's capability and role in the IOR. In 2017 the administration embraced the objective of creating conditions for a free and open Indo-Pacific region, which was largely seen as a strategy to counter growing Chinese influence in South and East Asia. A critical element of the Free and Open Indo-Pacific (FOIP) initiative was to bring India more into play through an integrated approach to the IOR involving the United States, Australia, and Japan. In 2018 Deputy Assistant Secretary of State Alex Wong explains how the FOIP recognized India's role in the IOR: "India is a nation that is invested in a free and open order. It is democracy. It is a nation that can bookend and anchor the free and open order in the Indo-Pacific region, and it's our policy to ensure that India does play that role, does become over time a more influential player in the region."[35]

From Washington's perspective, a strategic maritime partnership with New Delhi continues to be seen as an ideal "economy of force" initiative because it co-opts a capable and trustworthy partner in the mission of securing the commons. Instead of deploying to the Indian Ocean US naval forces, which have been traditionally split between the Atlantic and the Pacific, Washington could team up with New Delhi in ways that strengthen the Indian navy's ability to protect its back against Chinese aggression. The ongoing view from Washington is that the two states could start with low-cost initiatives to bolster situational awareness in littoral South Asia and gradually increase Indian and US capabilities to deal with regional contingencies. Given the rapid pace of events in the world today, it would not be surprising if operational or logistical cooperation between the Indian and US navies begins to become a routine matter and not just the stuff of planned exercises or experiments.

From the US perspective, another security problem in the IOR is the threat of Iran's closure of the Strait of Hormuz.[36] In response to the Trump administration's imposition of sanctions in April 2019, Tehran renewed its threat to close the strait, the world's busiest transit lane for seaborne oil shipments.[37] Although the United States does not expect India to contribute to the security effort in the Persian Gulf—given New Delhi's traditionally cordial ties with Tehran—it seems clear to many in Washington that there will always be limits to how much the United States and India can cooperate in the western Indian Ocean.

Despite substantial contributions to security in the Indian Ocean—especially in counterpiracy and humanitarian assistance—there is a sense that US policymakers believe the IOR's problems can be managed with the existing naval posture of the US Navy's Fifth and Seventh Fleets' areas of responsibility. American military leaders remain focused on the China challenge in the East and South China Seas.[38] Despite the fact that the Joe Biden administration has not emphasized the India-US relationship during its two years in office, nothing has occurred to diminish Washington's high expectations concerning bilateral maritime cooperation with India and India's growing role in the IOR.

INDIA-US MARITIME COOPERATION

Even given the rapid pace at which US-India ties have evolved, the maritime relationship stands out for special mention. Consistent with their global strategic partnership and a new framework for defense cooperation, the two sides have steadfastly raised the level of their maritime engagement. Three developments have allowed this to happen. First, the strategic conceptualization of the wider Indo-Pacific region has expanded India's "mental" map. A decade after Shinzo Abe, the Japanese prime minister, spoke of the "confluence of the Indian Ocean and the Pacific" in a speech delivered at the Indian parliament,[39] India's policy elite have come to accept the idea of an integrated Asian littoral. Abe's idea of "a dynamic of the Pacific and the Indian Oceans as seas of freedom and of prosperity" resonates in current Indian strategic thinking, and the concept of "a broader Asia" has begun to take on a distinct form.[40] US strategists, too, have embraced the concept of the "Indo-Pacific" and are beginning to look beyond their traditional focus on the western Pacific. The Trump administration's FOIP concept mirrored this new thinking.

The second development has been the growing convergence of the United States' and India's maritime security interests in the Indo-Pacific region. As early as 2004, the Indian maritime doctrine recognized "the shift in global maritime focus from the Atlantic-Pacific combine to the Pacific-Indian Ocean."[41] The United States recognized this formulation in 2010 when former secretary of state Hillary Clinton spoke in Honolulu. She commented about "expanding our work with the Indian Navy in the Pacific because we understand how important the Indo-Pacific basin is to global trade and commerce."[42] In November 2017 President Trump announced the FOIP strategy, and Prime Minister Modi outlined India's vision of the concept during his Shangri-La address in June 2018.[43]

For India the Indo-Pacific region fits squarely within its "Act East" policy.[44] New Delhi's actions in settling maritime disputes with Bangladesh peacefully and greater rapprochement with Sri Lanka are signs of its intention to reduce the potential for conflict in the region. India is also keen on emerging as a net security provider in the IOR—an aspiration that is detailed in its latest maritime strategy document, released in 2016.[45] India has considerably enhanced its security and military assistance, disaster support, and relief operations to various island states, such as Mauritius and Seychelles, and in the Bay of Bengal generally.

For the United States, the IOR is critical to maintaining its preeminent position in Asian affairs. The South China Sea is the locus of maritime trade and energy supplies, and the Strait of Malacca forms the choke point for transit routes in the IOR. The United States must also maintain a strong maritime presence to enforce its security commitments to Taiwan, Japan, and South Korea as well as to other partners in the region. US maritime cooperation with India constitutes an "economy of force effort"; engagement with India could create synergies to increase available capabilities in the IOR while freeing up US forces for other contingencies in the western Pacific. Recent PLA advances in the field of hypersonic weapons have raised the military and political salience in Washington and beyond of the looming challenges faced by the US Navy in the western Pacific.[46]

The third development is China's expanding maritime actions in the western Pacific, specifically the South China Sea, and its regular forays into the Indian Ocean. Ever since the Taiwan Strait crisis of 1996, Chinese strategy has emphasized building its maritime capacity to limit the ability of the United States to project power into the South China Sea.[47] Part of these efforts have included attempted interference with US operations along the first island chain and acquisition of air, naval, and missile capabilities to project power out to the second island chain. From here, China intends to establish a permanent naval presence in the Indian Ocean. Already it has strategically acquired ports from Colombo to Djibouti, which allows it to extend and maintain extensive maritime operations in the region.

EXPLORING INDO-PACIFIC SYNERGIES

The India-US maritime relationship has been riding a crest of enthusiasm since the signing of the 2015 joint strategic vision document and renewed a ten-year defense framework agreement in June 2015.[48] In May 2016 the two sides held their first maritime security dialogue and followed it up with the logistics support memorandum of understanding (MOU), a crucial agreement that allows the Indian navy and the US Navy to access logistics on a reciprocal basis.[49] In September 2018 New Delhi and Washington signed the Communications Compatibility and Security Agreement (COMCASA) during their first 2+2 Ministerial Dialogue in New Delhi.[50] In October 2020 India and the United States inked the Basic Exchange and Cooperation Agreement for Geo-Spatial Cooperation (BECA), the last of four foundational pacts allowing India access to US expertise on geospatial intelligence, which will potentially increase the accuracy of Indian cruise missiles, ballistic missiles, and drones.[51]

This operational synergy is matched by advances in maritime defense trade. By November 2022, the Indian navy had received six (of twenty-four) US-made MH-60R Seahawk maritime helicopters—widely seen by Indian analysts as a "game-changer" asset.[52] The Indian navy had also taken delivery of twelve Boeing P-8I Poseidon maritime patrol aircraft making the Indian fleet second in size only to the US Navy in terms of operating this advanced aircraft.

Washington's recognition of India as a major defense partner has further elevated the latter's status as an actor of increasing strategic importance, raising Indian hopes for high-tech defense sales.[53] The Indian navy's induction in November 2020 of two Sea Guardian drones, unarmed version of the deadly Predator series—on lease from the United States—is seen as a welcome portent. India has also announced plans to buy thirty armed unmanned aerial vehicles from the United States to boost its sea and land defenses.[54]

In a boost for maritime security cooperation, Washington has announced its willingness to partner with India in developing drone swarms and other high-technology military surveillance equipment aimed reportedly at tracking Chinese naval activity in the Indian Ocean.[55] Meanwhile a bilateral "white shipping" data-sharing arrangement promises to enhance maritime domain awareness, even as the two navies have expanded their maritime patrol aircraft exercises involving P-8As and P-8Is.[56] For its part, India has expressed support for US observer status in the Indian Ocean Naval Symposium, even in the face of opposition by Iran, which chaired the forum between 2019 and 2021.[57]

The most encouraging development in the US-India maritime partnership has been the growing scope and complexity of the annual Malabar naval exercises, with an overt focus on antisubmarine warfare.[58] An abiding symbol of warming strategic ties between New Delhi, Washington, and Tokyo (Japan has been a permanent exercise partner with India since 2015), the Malabar exercises have been expanded to include Australia. Since November 2020 the Royal Australian Navy has participated in two successive editions of the Malabar exercises, held in the Bay of Bengal and the western Pacific. The exercises have featured some of the most advanced platforms in the four navies, including aircraft carriers, guided missile cruisers, destroyers, submarines, and Poseidon P-8A/8I aircraft. In recent years, the drills have featured high-end interactions, with special emphasis on carrier strike group activities, maritime patrol and reconnaissance, surface warfare, explosive ordnance disposal, and helicopter operations.[59] In an operational sense, the Malabar exercises demonstrate that the Indian and US navies are already working effectively together and with the other Quad partners to shape security dynamics in the IOR.

DIFFERENCES IN STRATEGIC POSTURES

Although Washington and New Delhi are eager to increase their naval cooperation to guarantee the security of maritime communications in the IOR, their interests begin to diverge when one considers the wider Indo-Pacific region. For all its newfound zeal for Pacific operations, New Delhi has been less than enthusiastic in joining the wider US security projects in the East. Despite proposals from Washington to jointly protect shared spaces, India has studiously refrained from displaying naval vigor in the western Pacific.[60] Although India's political leadership has been happy to support US-India cooperation in the Indian Ocean, the diplomatic establishment has resisted the idea of joint patrols in the South China Sea. India's rejection of Australia's request to participate in the Malabar exercises (wholeheartedly supported by the United States) has also revealed differences in New Delhi's and Washington's approaches to regional maritime security.[61] The Trump administration's FOIP initiative envisioned a future of growing Japanese, Australian, US, and Indian naval cooperation, a vision that is a few steps outside of New Delhi's comfort zone.

Indian observers also have noted the Biden administration's relative indifference to the maritime geopolitics of South Asia. The administration's preoccupation with challenges in Southeast and East Asia leaves little bandwidth for India's concerns in its near littorals. These concerns include China's growing footprint in Sri Lanka, Bangladesh, and Myanmar; the Indian navy's inability to track Chinese submarines in the Bay of Bengal; and the strengthening China-Pakistan nexus in the Arabian Sea.[62]

New Delhi realizes that Washington's real equities reside in the western Pacific, which explains why senior US officials expect the Indian navy to play a larger security role beyond New Delhi's traditional areas of concern. Nevertheless, the ongoing US trade war with China and Washington's reliance on Chinese leaders to help solve vexing problems such as North Korea leads many in New Delhi to believe that US leverage in shaping Beijing's strategic choices in the Indian Ocean is fairly limited.

Indian analysts also complain that the Indian navy's cooperation with the United States is confined to the eastern half of the Indo-Pacific region.[63] At the western end of the Indo-Pacific, where India's real security and economic interests lie, maritime cooperation with the United States remains limited. Although New Delhi announced in 2018 that it would be appointing a military attaché to the US Naval Forces Central Command in Bahrain,[64] the move appears more symbolic than substantive. Even on the critical issue of China's naval presence in the Indian Ocean, Indian and US perspectives do not fully align. For India's strategic observers, the PLAN's activities in the IOR—particularly the PLAN submarine presence in South Asia—raises the worrisome prospect of a Chinese takeover of India's geopolitical space. American policymakers empathize with this view but believe Indian projections of Beijing's strategic domination of the Indian Ocean are significantly overblown. It is China's aggression in the Pacific Ocean, they suggest, that is the real threat.

Some in India believe that the partnership with the United States in the western Indian Ocean has been feeble because of US sensitivity to Pakistani concerns, more so in the wake of events in Afghanistan. Although the dynamics in US-Pakistan relations have been changing, Washington has kept its relationship with Islamabad on even keel. That means there will always be limits to the US Navy's cooperation with the Indian navy in the Arabian Sea. But critics in Washington blame New Delhi for the slow pace of progress on the maritime front. The fact that the foundational agreements were delayed, embroiled in Indian domestic politics with talk in New Delhi of exploitation and second-class status, does little to raise American hopes for closer US-India maritime relations.

The bilateral dynamic is further complicated by AUKUS and the British and American efforts to provide Australia with nuclear submarine technology. Indian practitioners say the pact could lead to a crowding of nuclear attack submarines in the eastern Indian Ocean, causing an erosion of India's regional primacy.[65] Regrettably, an Indian plan to develop a fleet of nuclear attack submarines has elicited no help from the United States, which seems willing to share its nuclear submarine technology with only the United Kingdom and Australia. For Indian observers, AUKUS raises the possibility of Australia deploying nuclear submarines in the eastern Indian Ocean well before India positions its own, which would lead to an attenuation of the Indian navy's "net-security provider" status.

For their part, US scholars see little possibility that India's more militarized continental approach vis-à-vis China would ever be complemented by an assertive Indian posture at sea.[66] Even though the Indian navy remains focused on countering its Chinese counterpart, especially so in the wake of events on the India-China border, New Delhi is still reluctant to project military power in the eastern Indian Ocean.

To observers in the United States, it seems unlikely that maritime factors will be a significant driver of India's strategic policymaking. The fact that the Indian army still dominates Indian military planning and that its navy faces persistent problems in acquiring advanced equipment to operate in the Indian Ocean suggests a continuing limited ability to partner with the United States in the region.[67] The enthusiastic advocacy by India's naval leadership, amplified in the Indian press and think-tank community, must then be taken with a grain of salt. The fact that the Indian navy enjoys a relatively free hand when it comes to operations with maritime partners does not necessarily transfer into political leverage when it comes to overall defense policies in New Delhi. Oddly, the US Navy enjoys more pull back in Washington, given the Mahanian focus of US foreign and defense policy, but it, too, can also get out ahead of both Democratic and Republican policymakers.

US policymakers also have concerns about India's continuing dependence on Russian weaponry and platforms. Although New Delhi has sought to diversify risk by forging partnerships with multiple external partners, the Indian military's heavy dependence on foreign imports from Russia serves only to dampen the US-India relationship. For many in Washington, India's inability to break away from Russia is a significant impediment to the development of strategic ties.[68]

Yet a majority of US strategic experts believe that a stronger military relationship with India is a viable proposition. Observers posit that the Indo-Pacific framework inherently places India "at the heart, rather than as an appendage to a concept of Asia focused on East Asia."[69] Moreover, observers such as Alyssa Ayres posit US strategic policymaking cannot ignore "a country on the brink of becoming the most populous in the world; a stable democracy with the world's sixth-largest economy, third-largest military by personnel strength, and fifth-largest defense budget; and one with a commitment to rule of law and the liberal international order."[70] For the proponents of stronger US-India maritime ties, it is incumbent on Washington to carve out more space for India and the Indian Ocean in the US Indo-Pacific strategy.

A POSSIBLE MARITIME ALLIANCE

The emergence of an India-US maritime alliance occurs within a broader strategic partnership that reflects several elements. First, various types of realist theory indicate that both India and the United States have a stake in balancing China (as do indeed many other states in South and Southeast Asia). Realists believe that since they are inherently insecure, competitive entities, states nearly always prefer balancing. China's neighbors fear its rise and seek to prevent it from achieving regional hegemony, and joining "an American-led balancing coalition to check China's rise" is a proposition most are willing to seriously consider.[71] The literature also suggests that maritime powers make good allies. If two maritime powers find themselves in an environment wherein a common adversary challenges them, an alliance should be especially easy to form.

Admittedly, an alliance with the United States is neither an obvious or simple choice for India. Given New Delhi's recent differences with Washington in a host of areas—Russia, Iran, Afghanistan, and trade—many Indian policymakers remain skeptical of the idea of an alliance with the United States. Some Indian experts argue that the reason why India rejected American requests for joint India-US naval patrols is the perennial inconstancy of US foreign policy.[72] For others, the "Pakistan question" is still what bedevils the bilateral relationship; there is a worry in Washington that cooperation with India in the IOR would cause New Delhi to shift resources away from its focus on security issues with Islamabad. American analysts say the United States values its partnership with India but would not want maritime cooperation to be held up as evidence that Washington is "tilting" toward India and away from Pakistan. Too much collaboration between Washington and New Delhi also could create panic in Islamabad, which could lead to heightened tensions along the India-Pakistan border or a surge of Chinese aid to and influence in Pakistan.

Luckily, growing maritime cooperation between India and the United States should only have a tangential impact on the balance of land power in South Asia. Admittedly, maritime collaboration and associated material and technological transfers could free up some Indian resources to bolster land forces. Nevertheless, the real growth in New Delhi's maritime capabilities will be concentrated in sea-control and reconnaissance capabilities, not in force projection against land targets. There is a relatively high degree of transparency associated with India-US naval cooperation, which makes it possible to discern that Pakistan is not the motivating factor in this growing maritime relationship.

For a thriving maritime relationship, it would appear both sides need higher levels of strategic empathy. An appreciation by New Delhi that the United States needs partners to assist in preserving strategic access in the wider-Asian littorals would lead to a more purposeful partnership. Furthermore, Washington's quest for innovative solutions to long-standing security challenges in the Indo-Pacific would be well served if partner states developed better capabilities to police the regional commons. The Indian navy could then take the burden from the US Navy in key areas of constabulary and benign security—tasks such as survey salvage, disaster relief, and humanitarian assistance—and burnish its own credentials as the Indian Ocean's principal security provider. The United States could also build on the recently signed logistics support MOU to explore greater Indian participation in the US Navy's worldwide logistical network.

For its part, Washington must recognize the critical inventory gaps that prevent the Indian navy from exerting influence in its near seas.[73] In the absence of submarines, antisubmarine warfare helicopters (only two MH-60Rs have been delivered so far), and critical underwater-detection equipment, the Indian navy is unable to keep track of PLAN subs in littoral South Asia, the primary theater of Indian naval operations. To assist New Delhi in making up for this capability deficit, American defense firms must be more willing to part with proprietary technology (including vital antisubmarine warfare knowledge).[74] Needless to say, a greater commitment to sharing technology to enhance the Indian navy's surveillance and combat prowess would lead to a stronger maritime partnership. In particular, India's naval leadership expects Washington's assistance in augmenting the Indian navy's antisubmarine warfare and underwater surveillance capabilities. Though the United States has offered to transfer naval surveillance drones and multirole helicopters, submarine technology is still off-limits for India.

More crucially Washington needs to address the issue of arbitrary bureaucratic separations that adversely impact the US Navy's ability to cover the Indo-Pacific adequately. Such seams within the US Defense Department's combatant commands have long been a sore issue with India's naval leadership. US Pacific Command's area of responsibility covers the Bay of Bengal countries but ends along the west coast of India. Afghanistan and Pakistan fall under US Central Command's purview, and the islands in the Indian Ocean off the east coast of Africa are within US Africa Command's area of responsibility. Senior Indian naval officers say the artificial divisions impact their coordination with the US Navy in the Arabian Sea and the western Indian Ocean. For their part, American officials and officers recognize that the dividing lines between these areas of responsibility are somewhat arbitrary, but this awareness has not generated sufficient political will or bureaucratic momentum to tackle the reorganization needed to address these boundary issues. One might also add that the "cultural" differences among the competing US combatant commands are probably more apparent to Indian officers than to their American counterparts. After all, the push for maritime cooperation emanates from the US Pacific Command.

TOWARD GREATER SYNERGY IN THE COMMONS

In recent years Washington has moved to harmonize maritime policy with New Delhi. In 2018, in seeming recognition of India's importance in the US Pacific commander's area of responsibility, the United States rechristened Pacific Command as Indo-Pacific Command.[75] The US Navy has also increased its presence in South Asia by carrying out Exercise CARAT (for Cooperation Afloat, Readiness, and Training) with Sri Lanka and Bangladesh among other initiatives. In addition, it is helping with regional maritime security capacity building.[76]

Washington also has been urging New Delhi to play a greater security role in the western Indian Ocean. Trump administration officials' repeated reference to India's critical role in securing the western flank of the Indo-Pacific indicated that the United States is keen to let New Delhi take the lead in Indian Ocean security. It is now up to India to coordinate its deployments with the United States to subtly balance the growing Chinese influence in the region.

The core elements of the India-US defense partnership include the adoption of common platforms and weapon systems as well as shared software and electronic ecosystems, closer cooperation on personnel training, and the convergence of strategic postures and doctrines. These initiatives can realize their full potential only if the two countries enable large-scale data sharing, which would significantly enhance interoperability between their two militaries. With the signing of the COMCASA and New Delhi's stated willingness to consider the remaining foundational agreements, a legal structure for logistical cooperation and transfer of communications-security equipment and geospatial data is likely to soon emerge.

PRESERVING A STRATEGIC "BALANCE OF ANXIETY"

The US-India maritime partnership is critical to preserve a favorable strategic balance in the littorals. Even though Indian observers acknowledge an imbalance in strategic power with China, New Delhi has been slow to recognize the disparity in "strategic anxiety." In recent years, China's expanding footprint in the Bay of Bengal has abated Beijing's Strait of Malacca dilemma as well as expanded its political influence in the Bay of Bengal. As a result, Beijing's sense of security in the region has grown, given its fears of an interdiction of Chinese trade and energy shipments in the strait have faded. By contrast, New Delhi's anxiety levels have surged as its influence and heft in the neighborhood has declined.

Analysts say the trend lines in the India-China military equation are broadly negative. Notwithstanding improvements in New Delhi's defense capabilities, its long-standing superiority over China in the Indian Ocean is at real risk of slipping away.[77] It is incumbent, then, on the United States and India to come together in ways that can reverse not only the anxiety imbalance but also the emerging capability imbalance in the Indian Ocean. The two countries must evolve a joint structure to tackle challenges, one that envisions strategic, policy, and working-level engagement—not only in the western Pacific, where the United States has a sizable military presence, but also in the western Indian Ocean, where inter-action between the Indian and the US navies has been limited.

One way to spur bilateral naval cooperation would be to create an India cell within the US Department of Defense. A dedicated, cross-functional India-planning cell could involve elements from US Indo-Pacific Command, US Central Command, US Africa Command, the Joint Staff, and the deputy chief of naval operations for strategy (N3/5), and it could be monitored by the under-secretary of defense for policy. The cell's remit could include (1) bilateral and multilateral exercises to enhance critical warfighting capabilities, such as anti-submarine warfare and counterterrorism; (2) ways to improve interoperability between the navies; and (3) exploring opportunities to operationalize foun-dational agreements like the logistics support MOU and the COMCASA.[78] Moreover, a combined disaster-relief team could coordinate bilateral disaster-response planning and training across the Indo-Pacific littorals, which could enhance interoperability, help operationalize foundational agreements like the logistics support MOU, and demonstrate to skeptics and adversaries alike what the US and Indian militaries can achieve together.[79]

Also crucial is the need for the two navies to address governance and human-itarian issues in the Asian littorals. India's maritime security strategy outlines the need to combat terrorism, illegal fishing, drug and human trafficking, and marine pollution. Nevertheless, the Indian navy cannot do these tasks without assistance from regional maritime forces. Washington and New Delhi need to deepen their intelligence sharing in ways that would enable a safe and secure environment in the Indian Ocean. The US Navy could allow the Indian navy to leverage American tactical systems, such as the Combined Enterprise Regional Information Exchange, to facilitate the exchange of finished intelligence prod-ucts.[80] An observer nation to the Western Pacific Naval Symposium, India could extend a similar status to the United States at the Indian Ocean Naval Sympo-sium. In turn, Washington could invite the Indian navy to be an observer at the Southeast Asia Cooperation and Training Exercises, which would further integrate the latter into Asia's larger maritime security grid.[81]

Another proposal is to create a "maritime domain awareness" working group that includes Indian and US service personnel.[82] The move would help forge an institutional relationship between the two navies and could in time be expanded to include education and training, codevelopment and acquisition of underwater domain awareness, and joint acoustic processing. With the goal to observe and manage activities in the littorals, the two navies could organize tabletop exercises designed to share capabilities and monitor sea lines of communication in the Indian Ocean.

The bilateral naval interactions would need to be designed in a way to allow both sides to deal with challenges across the conflict spectrum, including the threat of a possible attempt to close key choke points into the Indian Ocean. To address this sort of challenge, the two navies would have to work in a loose coalition of willing states capable of protecting the regional littorals. A collaborative model of maritime security would also provide better opportunities for capacity building, especially in nontraditional security areas such as maritime law-enforcement, humanitarian assistance and disaster-relief operations, search-and-rescue activities, and noncombatant evacuation operations.[83]

To ensure progress, India and the United States would also need to conclude and operationalize foundational agreements, such as the Information Security Arrangement and the Basic Exchange and Cooperation Agreement. The partners should begin discussions on intelligence sharing, with a particular focus on regional issues, under the 2002 General Security of Military Information Agreement. It would be imperative for India and the United States to conduct exercises across the range of maritime security operations, including counterterrorism, counterpiracy, humanitarian assistance, diving and salvage operations, explosive ordnance disposal, and amphibious and submarine rescue exercises.

The United States hopes that India will decisively shape the military balance in Asia. This hope hinges, in large measure, on an effective partnership between the two nations in the Indian Ocean littorals.[84] At a time when there are fears of a decline in US strategic power, an effective India-US alliance in the IOR's sensitive littorals would impact the future strategic trajectory of Asia. Countering China in the Indian Ocean would deny Beijing a panregional sphere of influence while also promoting a vision of a free and open Indo-Pacific shared by Washington and New Delhi. The inability of the two to come together effectively could lead to a failure to uphold a favorable balance of power.

CONCLUSION

Naval leaders in India and the United States acknowledge the historic opportunity that confronts them while recognizing the constraints that politics and personalities may impose on the maritime relationship. Even so, the US-India nautical ties remain on an upward trajectory. Now more than ever, there is a sense of common purpose and a shared destiny as well as a growing belief that South Asia's leading maritime power and the preeminent power in the Indian Ocean will work out a functional pact to protect their interests in the maritime commons. The military benefits engendered by maritime activities are important, but their real power lies in the perception that they are a harbinger of future strategic cooperation.

NOTES

1. Salman Khurshid, "India-US Relations: The Search for a Transformative Moment," Ministry of External Affairs, Government of India, June 24, 2013, https://mea.gov .in/articles-in-foreign-media.htm?dtl/21868/IndiaUS+Relations+The+Search+for +a+Transformative+Moment.
2. K. Alan Kronstadt and Sonia Pinto, *US-India Security Relations: Strategic Issues,* CRS Report no. R42948 (Washington, DC: Congressional Research Service, 2013), 4–7.
3. Vivek Mishra, "India-US Maritime Cooperation: Crossing the Rubicon," *Maritime Affairs* 14, no. 2 (2018): 1, https://doi.org/10.1080/09733159.2018.1562453; Aman Thakker and Arun Sahgal, *US-India Maritime Security Cooperation* (Washington, DC: Center for Strategic and International Studies, 2019), 1.
4. "US Develops Three-Pronged Approach for Maritime Cooperation with India," *Economic Times,* modified July 12, 2018, https://m.economictimes.com/news /defence/us-develops-three-pronged-approach-for-maritime-cooperation-with -india-heres-what-it-includes/articleshow/48576709.cms.
5. Bharat Karnad, "India Is Courting Peril by Aligning Militarily with the United States," Security Wise (blog), June 21, 2018, https://bharatkarnad.com/2018/06/21 /india-is-courting-peril-by-aligning-militarily-with-the-united-states/; Dinakar Peri, "India, US Cooperation on Jet Engines 'Suspended,'" *The Hindu,* October 25, 2019.
6. Arun Prakash, "US 7th Fleet's Patrol in India's EEZ Was an Act of Impropriety," *Indian Express,* April 12, 2021.
7. Bharat Karnad, "True Inflection Point: AUKUS vs. Quad," Security Wise (blog), https://bharatkarnad.com/2021/09/16/true-inflection-point-aukus-vs-quad/.
8. Raja Menon, "The Strategic Imperative," *Indian Express,* April 12, 2016.
9. C. Raja Mohan, "Modi and the Indian Ocean: Restoring India's Sphere of Influence," *ISAS Insights,* no. 277 (March 2015), https://www.files.ethz.ch/isn/189804 /ISAS_Insights_No._277_-_Modi_and_the_Indian_Ocean_20032015163047.pdf.
10. Mohan, "Modi and the Indian Ocean."
11. "Text of the PM's Remarks on the Commissioning of Coast Ship *Barracuda,*" Narendra Modi, March 12, 2015, https://www.narendramodi.in/text-of-the-pms -remarks-on-the-commissioning-of-coast-ship-barracuda-2954.
12. Ian Hall, "India's Clever Alliances with Island States," Interpreter (blog, Lowy Institute), November 5, 2019, https://www.lowyinstitute.org/the-interpreter/india-s -clever-alliances-island-states.
13. Dhruva Jaishankar, *Acting East: India in the Indo-Pacific,* Impact Series (New Delhi: Brookings Institution India Center, 2019).
14. Jaishankar, *Acting East.*
15. Geoffrey Till, "Small Pond, Big Navies: Managing Competition in the Indian Ocean," Observer Research Foundation, February 21, 2017, https://www.orfonline .org/expert-speak/small-pond-big-navies-managing-competition-in-the-indian -ocean/.

16. C. Raja Mohan, *Samudra Manthan: Sino-Indian Rivalry in the Indo-Pacific* (New Delhi: Oxford University Press, 2013), 329. See also Brahma Challeney, "An Oceanic Threat Rises against India," Statecraft and Stagecraft (blog), January 20, 2016, https://chellaney.net/2016/01/20/an-oceanic-threat-rises-against-india/.

17. Brahma Chellaney, "Democracies Must Rally to Curb China's Indian Ocean Ambitions," *Nikkei Asia Review*, October 12, 2017, https://asia.nikkei.com/Politics/Brahma-Chellaney-Democracies-must-rally-to-curb-China-s-Indian-Ocean-ambitions.

18. Abhijit Singh, "China's Military Base in Djibouti: Strategic Implications for India," War on the Rocks, August 21, 2017, https://warontherocks.com/2017/08/chinas-military-base-in-djibouti-strategic-implications-for-india/.

19. Singh, "China's Military Base."

20. Andrew S. Erickson and Austin M. Strange, "China's Blue Soft Power," *Naval War College Review* 68, no. 1 (2015): article 6, 2. See also Zhou Jingnan, "China's Naval Escort Mission Builds Up PLA's Global Image," CGTN, April 21, 2019, https://news.cgtn.com/news/3d3d674e7759544d34457a6333566d54/share_p.html.

21. State Council of the People's Republic of China, *China's Military Strategy* (Beijing: Information Office of the State Council, 2015), http://english.www.gov.cn/archive/white_paper/2015/05/27/content_281475115610833.htm; Arun Prakash, "Abandoned at Sea," *Indian Express*, June 5, 2018.

22. Prakash, "Abandoned at Sea."

23. Abhijit Singh, *India's Coastal Security Paradox*, Special Report no. 52 (New Delhi: Observer Research Foundation, 2017).

24 Abhijit Singh, "The Indian Navy's Humanitarian Impulse," *Mint*, June 14, 2017, https://www.livemint.com/Opinion/5yMHIeapeZianzdanLf9JN/The-Indian-Navys-humanitarian-impulse.html.

25. Singh, "Indian Navy's Humanitarian Impulse."

26. Singh, *India's Coastal Security Paradox*, 19.

27. "Indian Navy: Net Security Provider to Island Nations in IOR," press release, Press Information Bureau, Ministry of Defence (India), October 12, 2011, https://pib.gov.in/newsite/PrintRelease.aspx?relid=76590.

28. Asia News International, "India, France Express Commitment to Freedom of Navigation in Indo-Pacific," *India Today*, August 23, 2019.

29. "India to Deploy Naval Aircraft at France's La Réunion for Joint Surveillance Mission," The Wire, October 27, 2019, https://thewire.in/diplomacy/india-to-deploy-naval-aircraft-at-frances-la-reunion-for-joint-surveillance-mission.

30. David Brewster, "China's New Network of Indian Ocean Bases," Interpreter (blog, Lowy Institute), January 30, 2018, https://www.lowyinstitute.org/the-interpreter/chinas-new-network-indian-ocean-bases.

31. Jeffrey Becker, *Securing China's Lifelines across the Indian Ocean*, China Maritime Report no. 11 (Newport, RI: US Naval War College, 2020).

32. Andrew Chatzky and James McBride, "China's Massive Belt and Road Initiative," Backgrounder, Council of Foreign Research, March 21, 2019, https://www.cfr.org/backgrounder/chinas-massive-belt-and-road-initiative.

33. Toshi Yoshihara, "The US Navy's Indo-Pacific Challenge," *Journal of the Indian Ocean Region* 9, no. 1 (2013): 92, https://doi.org/10.1080/19480881.2013.793914.

34. Harsh V. Pant and Yogesh Joshi, "The American 'Pivot' and the Indian Navy," *Naval War College Review* 68, no. 1 (2015): 51, https://doi.org/10.1057/9781137557728.0005.

35. Congressional Research Service, *The Trump Administration's "Free and Open Indo-Pacific": Issues for Congress*, CRS Report no. R35496 (Washington DC: Congressional Research Service, 2019), 4.
36. Arsalan Shahla and Ladane Nasseri, "Iran Raises Stakes in US Showdown with Threat to Close Hormuz," Bloomberg News, April 22, 2019.
37. The Biden administration withdrew the sanctions in February 2021.
38. Jon Donigan, "IndoPaCom and the Indo-Pacific Fleet: Organizing for Future Conflict," US Naval Institute blog, July 26, 2019, https://blog.usni.org/posts/2019/07/26/indopacom-and-the-indo-pacific-fleet-organizing-for-future-conflict.
39. "'Confluence of Two Seas': Speech by H. E. Mr. Shinzo Abe, Prime Minister of Japan at the Parliament of the Republic of India, Ministry of Foreign Affairs of Japan," August 22, 2007, https://www.mofa.go.jp/region/asia-paci/pmv0708/speech-2.html.
40. Chilamkuri Raja Mohan, "India and Shinzo Abe's Strategic Legacy," Institute of South Asian Studies, National University of Singapore, September 15, 2020, https://www.isas.nus.edu.sg/papers/india-and-shinzo-abes-strategic-legacy/.
41. Integrated Headquarters, *Indian Maritime Doctrine* (New Delhi: Ministry of Defence [Navy], 2004), 91.
42. Hillary Clinton, "America's Engagement in the Asia-Pacific" (presented at Kahala Hotel, Honolulu, October 28, 2010), https://2009-2017.state.gov/secretary/2009 2013clinton/rm/2010/10/150141.htm.
43. "Remarks by President Trump on His Trip to Asia," White House, November 15, 2017, https://www.whitehouse.gov/briefings-statements/remarks-president-trump-trip-asia/; "Prime Minister's Keynote Address at Shangri La Dialogue (June 1, 2018), Ministry of External Affairs, Government of India, June 1, 2018, https://mea.gov.in/Speeches-Statements.htm?dtl/29943/Prime+Ministers+Keynote+Address+at+Shangri+La+Dialogue+June+01+2018.
44. Manish Chand, "Act East: India's ASEAN Journey," Ministry of External Affairs, Government of India, November 10, 2014, https://mea.gov.in/in-focus-article.htm?24216/Act+East+Indias+ASEAN+Journey.
45. Directorate of Strategy, Concepts and Transformation, Integrated Headquarters, Ministry of Defence (Navy), *Ensuring Secure Seas: Indian Maritime Security Strategy* (New Delhi: Ministry of Defence [Navy], Government of India, 2016), 8.
46. Peter Martin, "US General Likens China's Hypersonic Test to a 'Sputnik Moment,'" Bloomberg News, October 27, 2021.
47. M. Taylor Fravel, "Power Shifts and Escalation: Explaining China's Use of Force in Territorial Disputes," *International Security* 32, no. 3 (Winter 2007/2008): 47, https://doi.org/10.1162/isec.2008.32.3.44.
48. "US-India Joint Strategic Vision for the Asia-Pacific and Indian Ocean Region," Ministry of External Affairs, Government of India, January 25, 2015, https://www.mea.gov.in/bilateral-documents.htm?dtl/24728/USIndia_Joint_Strategic_Vision_for_the_AsiaPacific_and_Indian_Ocean_Region.
49. Dinakar Peri, "India, US Hold First Maritime Security Dialogue," *The Hindu*, May 17, 2016; Varghese K. George, "India, US Sign Military logistics pact," *The Hindu*, August 30, 2016.
50. "Indo-US 2+2 Dialogue," press release, Press Information Bureau, Ministry of Defence (India), December 31, 2018, https://pib.gov.in/newsite/printrelease.aspx?relid=186956.

51. "India and the US Sign BECA to Deepen Military Ties Aid China Tensions," *Mint*, October 22, 2020, https://www.livemint.com/news/india/india-us-sign-beca-deal-to-deepen-military-ties-amid-china-tensions-11603787192836.html.

52. Abhinav Dixit, "MH-60R Helicopters: The Game Changer of Indian Ocean," Chanakya Forum, August 19, 2021, https://chanakyaforum.com/mh-60r-helicopters-the-game-changer-of-indian-ocean/.

53. Joe Gould, "US Names India 'Major Defense Partner,'" *Defense News*, June 7, 2016, https://www.defensenews.com/home/2016/06/07/us-names-india-major-defense-partner/.

54. "India to Buy 30 US Predator Drones for $3 BN to Counter China, Pakistan," *Business Standard*, March 11, 2021.

55. Rajat Randit, "India, US to Collaborate on Drone Swarms and Other Military Hi-techs," *Times of India*, October 24, 2019.

56. Franz-Stefan Gady, "India, US Conduct Anti-Submarine Warfare Drill in Indian Ocean," *The Diplomat*, April 16, 2019, https://thediplomat.com/2019/04/india-us-conduct-anti-submarine-warfare-drill-in-indian-ocean/.

57. Manu Pubby, "India Led Initiative to Bring Together Regional Navies Turns 10 with Big Ideas on the Table," *Economic Times*, November 14, 2018.

58. Manu Pubby, "India, US to Focus on Jointly Countering Submarine Operations at Malabar Exercise," *Economic Times*, June 3, 2018.

59. "Malabar 2018: All You Need to Know about the Trilateral Naval Exercise," *Business Standard*, June 15, 2018.

60. Anjana Pasricha, "India Rejects Joint Naval Patrols with US in South China Sea," *VOA News*, March 11, 2016.

61. Suhasini Haidar and Dinakar Peri, "Not Time Yet for Australia's Inclusion in Malabar Naval Games," *The Hindu*, January 22, 2019.

62. Abhijit Singh, "India, Singapore, and Thailand Navy Exercise Is Delhi's Chance to One-up China in Bay of Bengal," Observer Research Foundation, September 21, 2019.

63. Manoj Joshi, "Get Closer, but Not Too Closer," *Economic Times* (blog), November 6, 2018, https://economictimes.indiatimes.com/blogs/et-commentary/get-closer-but-not-too-closer/.

64. Shishir Gupta, "Soon, India Defence Attaché at US Navy Bahrain Command," *Hindustan Times*, March 21, 2019.

65. Abhijit Singh, "India Is Not a Bystander in AUKUS," *The Hindu*, September 25, 2021.

66. Henry I. Hannah, "The Great Game Moves to Sea: Tripolar Competition in the Indian Ocean Region," War on the Rocks, April 1, 2019, https://warontherocks.com/2019/04/the-great-game-moves-to-sea-tripolar-competition-in-the-indian-ocean-region/.

67. Hannah, "Great Game."

68. Harsh V. Pant and Kartik Bommakanti, "India's National Security: Challenges and Dilemmas," *International Affairs* 95, no. 4 (July 2019): 847, https://doi.org/10.1093/ia/iiz053.

69. Alyssa Ayres, "The US Indo-Pacific Strategy Needs More Indian Ocean," Council of Foreign Relations, January 22, 2019, https://www.cfr.org/expert-brief/us-indo-pacific-strategy-needs-more-indian-ocean.

70. Ayres, "US Indo-Pacific Strategy."

71. Jeff M. Smith, "China's Rise and (Under?) Balancing in the Indo-Pacific: Putting Realist Theory to the Test," Heritage Foundation, January 9, 2019, https://www.heritage.org/asia/commentary/chinas-rise-and-under-balancing-the-indo-pacific-putting-realist-theory-the-test.

72. Pramit Pal Chaudhary, "The China Factor in Indian Ocean Policy," in *India and China at Sea: Competition for Naval Dominance in the Indian Ocean*, ed. David Brewster (New Delhi: Oxford University Press, 2018), 68.

73. Rajat Pandit, "Lack of Helicopters Hits Navy's Operational Capabilities against Enemy Submarines," *Times of India*, March 5, 2017.

74. Aditya Kalra and Sanjeev Miglani, "US Defence Firms Want Control over Technology in 'Make in India' Plan," *Mint*, September 19, 2017, https://www.livemint.com/Industry/LyscMTtryJ3ii4gMdJFVmN/US-defence-firms-want-control-over-technology-in-Make-in-In.html.

75. Scott Neuman, "In Military Name Change, US Pacific Command Becomes US Indo-Pacific Command," NPR, May 31, 2018, https://www.npr.org/sections/the two-way/2018/05/31/615722120/in-military-name-change-u-s-pacific-command-becomes-u-s-indo-pacific-command.

76. Amy Forsythe, "US, Sri Lanka Partner for First-Cooperation Afloat Readiness and Training Exercise," US Indo-Pacific Command, October 3, 2017, https://www.pacom.mil/Media/News/News-Article-View/Article/1333340/us-sri-lanka-partner-for-first-cooperation-afloat-readiness-and-training-exerci/.

77. Daniel Kliman, Iskander Rehman, Kristine Lee, and Joshua Fitt, *Imbalance of Power: India's Military Choices in an Era of Strategic Competition with China* (Washington, DC: Center for New American Security, 2019).

78. Samir Saran and Rahul Richard Verma, *Strategic Convergence: The United States and India as Major Defence Partners* (New Delhi: Observer Research Foundation, 2019), 8.

79. Saran and Verma, *Strategic Convergence*.

80. Thakker and Sahgal, *US-India Maritime Security*.

81. Thakker and Sahgal.

82. Thakker and Sahgal.

83. Nilanthi Samaranayake, Michael Connell, and Satu Limaye, *The Future of US-India Naval Relations* (Arlington, VA: Center for Naval Analyses, 2017), v.

84. Kliman et al., *Imbalance of Power*, 69.

Conclusion

Strategy, Order, and Regional Security
in the Indo-Pacific

Alessio Patalano, James A. Russell,
and Catherine L. Grant

Ian Urbina's *The Outlaw Ocean* and Bruce Jones's *To Rule the Waves* stand today as two important examples of the extent to which public debates about how the sea is shaping, testing, and redefining societies as well as how states' management of international affairs and order have changed.[1] Urbina points out, "For all its breathtaking beauty, the ocean is also a dystopian place, home to dark inhumanities. The rule of law . . . is fluid at sea, if it's to be found at all."[2] The sea is, according to Urbina, a paradoxical space from a normative perspective. On one hand, it is an inherent part of human history and civilization—as a wider literature that draws upon a tradition set forth by scholars such as Fernand Braudel and David Abulafia has convincingly shown.[3] On the other, as Urbina's narrative makes clear, it is a place in which assumptions about how international norms and order remain underexplored and untested. This is not entirely surprising since until the late nineteenth century the sea represented a space between destinations.[4] The groundbreaking impact of marine research and discovery changed such an understanding, with the United Nations Convention on the Law of the Sea (UNCLOS) representing an inflection point in a global reconceptualization of the link between the sea and international order and security. Yet the sea remains a space that is "vulnerable and fragile," notably to environmental challenges, one that transcends "the arbitrary borders that mapmakers have applied to the oceans over the centuries."[5]

Jones's book does not approach the sea from the perspective of its importance as a space in which human interactions unfold. Rather, *To Rule the Waves* is set on the oceans as the context in which "the geopolitics of globalization" are reviewed and redefined.[6] It links maritime transport and connectivity to global trade and how, in turn, this has both enabled the rise of the United States to undisputed leadership and underwritten the country's requirement for a global naval posture. Additionally, Jones explores how China's naval rise gauges specific national ambitions linked to the growing stake and influence the country has in maritime connectivity, how this phenomenon affects the United States, and how the impact of climate change on the use of the ocean as a medium of global communication further complicates the ability of the United States to adapt its role as maritime hegemon.[7]

In Jones's narrative, in particular, what becomes apparent is the connection between the sea as a platform for the projection of states' hard power and influence beyond their shores and the extent to which naval power demands defense and security planners to think about military power as a tool of statecraft in international politics in a way that is different from its land, air, and space counterparts. As global supply chains and flow of data continue to depend on sealanes and sea cables, this reality is unlikely to change in the foreseeable future.

When combined, these two books provide the wider boundaries to the public debate informing the themes we have explored in this volume. In the Indo-Pacific, the age of naval power could not be more apparent. Naval power actively contributes to underwrite the shape of regional security from competition to deterrence, from peace to war. In this respect it is not only a key tool of statecraft but it also speaks to issues that encompass concerns from marine resources exploitation to the mitigation of rising sea level. Additionally, it informs how the pursuit of maritime claims relates to strategic balance and operational access. Regardless of how widely or narrowly the confines of the Indo-Pacific are defined, naval forces—including in their wider understanding navies, coast guards, marines, and paramilitaries—are primary tools for stability and risk management and, failing deterrence, war.

In this book, we placed the maritime fabric of this region at the center of our analysis and explored specific national strategies in relation to this environment. In our quest, we were inspired by the ability of authors such as Urbina and Jones to bring maritime matters to a broader public audience. We sought to venture on a similar journey by joining recent calls to expand the research agenda linking naval affairs to security studies. In the introductory essay of a 2020 special issue of the eminent journal *Security Studies*, Jonathan Caverley and Peter Dombrowski made two particularly relevant points. First, they highlighted how we live in a time in international politics in which the "most likely friction points" between leading major powers (the United States and China) are located at sea. Second, precisely because of the first observation, there is a need for naval specialists and security scholars to work together to develop the handrails for a stronger dialogue between the two disciplines of international security and maritime studies.[8]

We share their view. Therefore, we proposed an approach that combined an international relations framework developed for the study of regional security with a strategic studies methodology that accounted for the specificities of a maritime-centric regional space. We did so because while we agree with Caverley and Dombrowski that the Sino-American maritime competition is a major factor in how the Indo-Pacific is reshaping international affairs, we also believe that maritime issues inform regional security more broadly. They encompass issues of material power as well as questions of normative behavior and order. Thus, from a maritime perspective, in the Indo-Pacific issues of competition and cooperation and of capabilities (means) and legitimacy (ways) coexist. Indeed, as the chapters in this volume attest, national strategies—from Japan to South Korea, from Australia to South Pacific islands and India—are designed and implemented to address more than one factor. In a way to create an intellectual dialogue with the *Security Studies* special issue, we tried to place maritime competition within the wider canvass of maritime issues that define regional security. In particular, we focused on the links between competition and good order at sea, especially as the latter may have an impact on the former.

Our task was facilitated by Ian Bowers and Swee Lean Collin Koh, who have made an important contribution to the specific debate over how navies and coast guards interact with each other.[9] They highlighted how national maritime architectures, across the Indo-Pacific and elsewhere, can be very different as a result of national perceptions about security issues and priorities as well as access to technology, institutional arrangements, and political history. Their conclusions reinforce this volume's overall argument about the need to cast a wider net to better understand the role of naval power in Indo-Pacific security. We sought to achieve that in two ways. First, the volume correlated the specific significance of the different national maritime architectures as an expression of specific strategies to the security landscapes in five main operational theaters of the Indo-Pacific: Northeast Asia, the China Seas, the Taiwan Strait, the South Pacific, and the Indian Ocean. Second, we assessed how the security landscape in each basin informs national strategies. States seek to balance capabilities for hard-security concerns that result from competition with other states with the capabilities to address disaster response, constabulary activities, and environmental degradation at sea. This approach allows us to draw four main conclusions that are relevant for future research endeavors.

THE INDO-PACIFIC AS A MARITIME REGIONAL SECURITY COMPLEX

The first overarching observation unfolding from this book concerns the importance of considering the Indo-Pacific as a particular type of regional security complex—in the meaning originally conceptualized by Barry Buzan, Ole Wæver, and Jaap de Wilde.[10] The Indian and Pacific Oceans create the fabric that links coherently the shores of Oman to the Korean Peninsula, through the South Pacific. The uses of the sea as a highway for trade and the movement of goods and resources, as well as a resource in itself, constitute the primary factors informing the region's broader connectivity and coherency. Perhaps in one pertinent example, the naval commitment of countries such as Japan and China to combat piracy—and in the case of Japan monitor potential instability in the Persian Gulf area more broadly—is symptomatic of the wider security link between the western Indian Ocean and the China Seas. This wider maritime framework includes a series of adjacent operational theaters, or basins, in which the specific composition of local issues contribute to inform the complexity of the wider region. In this regard, our findings align with, and further reinforce, Rory Medcalf's work on the Indo-Pacific as a concept that is useful to the study of regional security because it is both sufficiently coherent and inherently flexible.[11]

Within this context, we identified five key "factors of influence'" underwriting the theater-regional nexus. The first focused on the importance of understanding the extent to which a specific theater is essential to major powers' strategic ambitions as a space to exercise sea control and power projection. The second factor is related to the first in that it encompasses strategic deterrence and the use of different theaters for the deployment of nuclear deterrents. The third factor pertains to how actors operating in each theater understand, apply, and implement law of the sea with specific reference to possible diverging interpretations of UNCLOS. This leads to a fourth factor of influence, the presence of resources, which in turn may lead to competition over rights to access and exploit them. The fifth factor is technological innovation. In many ways, the last underwrites the previous in that access to a technological edge in relevant capabilities has a considerable impact on how far state actors can endeavor in a maritime-centric region. These five factors of influence, which draw upon the core uses of the sea for human activities, shape how security issues manifest themselves in the specific security landscapes of the Indo-Pacific as a maritime regional security complex.

The first section of the book explored these key factors of influence in considerable depth. The chapters by Christopher Twomey and Peter Alan Dutton naturally complemented each other. The former highlighted how the sea as a geopolitical space for the projection of power and influence underwrites much of the structural tensions between China and the United States. The latter introduced the idea of "normative resonance" to explain how the geopolitics of naval power today no longer rest just on national "might" that makes right. On the contrary, in the broader Indo-Pacific how one's behavior aligns or conflicts with the dominant normative framework—UNCLOS—is just as important. It is the standard by which actions are accepted or seen as invalid. In part, this helps to better understand how, as Chinese naval might expanded and modernized, states in the region have progressively demanded more American naval presence, not less. Chinese naval power and its uses do not seem to be making headway in terms of their normative resonance. Conversely, regional perceptions seem also to suggest that normative resonance is a two-way street, one in which acceptance of one's naval power is linked also to one's ability to listen and to understand other actors' perceptions of what constitutes acceptable behavior.

Clive Schofield's chapter surgically investigated the nature, composition, and extent of territorial claims and the potential for access and exploitation of resources. His work established a strong link between national sovereign claims and boundary delimitations as manifestations of very "localized" issues and their potential wider regional implications. In many ways, his chapter highlighted how this driver articulates the nexus between domestic dynamics and regional and international security. Schofield's contribution to this volume speaks directly to James A. Russell's chapter on the role of technology in regional stability. In a maritime-centric region, the capacity to access, develop, and sustain advanced technology informs the extent to which actors can develop strategies and pursue capabilities to cover wider canvasses of security options. In this respect, the cases of China and the United States show that technology is not going to provide an answer in and of itself about how to gain the upper hand in war, but it might reinforce patterns of confrontation and, with them, increase the prospect of actual conflagration.

The volume could not explore how every single state actor reacts to the previously mentioned factors of influence. Rather, it sought to articulate how the factors can represent a useful framework to better examine national security strategies. In this respect, we hope others will agree on the utility of applying this framework to examine other state actors and dynamics within the different basins and subtheaters of the Indo-Pacific region.

REGIONAL SECURITY AS MORE THAN MANAGING MAJOR-POWER WAR

The above considerations about the Indo-Pacific as a "maritime regional security complex" lead to a second overarching conclusion. Studies of national strategies and regional security in the Indo-Pacific need to look beyond the current focus on the risks of a clash between fleets of major powers operating in the region. This does not mean that the risk of naval clashes—or worse, the possibility of war—is not real. On the contrary, we do share the view that developments in capabilities—especially China's continued and sustained investments in advanced hard naval power—are particularly problematic. In this respect, we respectfully disagree with David C. Kang's underestimation or, indeed, fundamental lack of appreciation of the qualitative significance that current naval modernization processes, chiefly the transformation of the Chinese military, have on the regional military balance.[12] Nonetheless, in this volume, we sought to highlight how the centrality of the sea to regional security unfolds also from the impact that these issues have on order at sea.

The meaning of order at sea has, in fact, changed over time. One very significant point that emerged in the section focusing on the history of the Indo-Pacific as a wider space for international competition concerns this shift. In particular, this comes across quite clearly in the chapter by Ryan Gingeras, who explored the dynamics of interaction in the premodern Indian Ocean. His conclusions are significant in that they emphasize how hegemonic powers in the Indo-Pacific have had to constantly engage with local actors and forge relationships with them to ensure stability and recognition of their hegemonic status. This chapter created an interesting contrast with the following two chapters, on the Pax Britannica by Richard Dunley and on the interwar period by Daniel Moran. These authors respectively provided clear guidance on how naval power in the Indo-Pacific pertained to the long-standing function of navies as tools to shape foreign and security policy through a hierarchy of power. During the period each author examined, technology played a role in how hegemonic powers sought to assert themselves and maintain "order."

Whether as a primus inter pares—as in the case of Britain—or through formal naval agreements, as during the interwar period until World War II, naval power defined order through the ranking of national strength at sea. This element did not wane during the Cold War. Nonetheless, Kevin Rowlands noted how as the competition for global influence between the Soviet Union and the United States escalated, the Indo-Pacific also became a major space of economic development precisely because of its maritime connectivity. It became a space in which the potential economic opportunities from resources and maritime transport accelerated regional growth and the development of multilateral frameworks. Hard power was essential to maritime stability. By the end of the Cold War, the Indo-Pacific was no longer a space in which material capabilities alone defined regional order and stability. Rights and duties unfolding from the coming into force of UNCLOS, as much as sustained maritime trade, had widened perceptions across the region about the notion of what security meant and opened up new opportunities for cooperation and competition beyond sea control and power projection. Within this process, major powers had to engage local coastal states to gain recognition and legitimize their role and presence—bringing the story to full circle. The contributions in the historical section of this volume trace this transformation across different centuries.

The history of the role of naval power in the Indo-Pacific sets up the context that helps us understand why across the five theaters the very meaning of regional order today varies. In the Indian Ocean, India's growing interest in working with the United States has to be understood within a context of New Delhi's challenging relationship with China. It reflects also the country's own ambitions in the Indian Ocean region with a greater focus on dealing with maritime security issues and an understanding of order that speaks to the need to address transnational challenges such as piracy.

In the China Seas and in Northeast Asia, alliance management and outstanding maritime-sovereignty and boundary-delimitation disputes add to the mix of possible sources of maritime tensions and conflict—and as a result "disorder," or lack of order at least. In particular, in his chapter, Bowers sought to capture through the lenses of how the sea connects the different regional actors to the wider theater's dynamics. One remarkable observation is that although the theater has seen some of the most significant maritime clashes of the past two decades, especially across South Korea's Northern Limit Line, it remains a relatively stable area. Conversely, Alessio Patalano and Julie Marionneau showed how states along the East and South China Seas, most notably China, have mobilized legal narratives to justify military actions intended to alter the theater's military and political balance. Similar considerations apply to Sheryn Lee's chapter on the Taiwan Strait, in which order and stability are inherently linked to military balance and the risk of war. In particular, as this book goes to press, Lee's observations about the link between military instability across the strait and its wider implications for regional stability resonate with the continuous rise of the defense of Taiwan as a policy question in capitals the world over.

This does not mean that regional order in the Indo-Pacific does not encompass concerns over transnational security and governance at sea. In his chapter on the South Pacific, James Goldrick highlighted how island states regard the Sino-American maritime competition, or indeed territorial and strategic issues, as a less pressing issue. Rather, from their perspective, these issues are to be engaged from the perspective of how they can help address what they see as the existential challenges unfolding from the consequences of climate change and environmental degradation. In the space of this volume, it was not possible to fully explore all regional perspectives from the different theaters, especially from actors in Southeast Asia, but there, too, transnational challenges related to climate change and different types of crimes at sea remain nontrifling priorities. Still, in the broader economy of this volume, it is fair to suggest that governance at sea as a positive manifestation of regional order remains somewhat elusive, especially in light of China's gains in the China Seas.

Related to this is the specific issue of nuclear order at sea. As Nicola Leveringhaus's chapter on "nuclear navies" highlighted, the Indo-Pacific is home to the largest number of nuclear-armed states that have not signed the Non-Proliferation Treaty. There remains marked asymmetry in capabilities between established powers such as the United States and emerging naval nuclear powers such as India and China. Conversely, although nuclear-powered ballistic missile submarines are traditionally known for their second-strike role, in the Indo-Pacific efforts to rebalance existing asymmetries are potentially leading them to be integrated into first-strike doctrinal grammars. Again, China represents a specific case in point. When combined with the understanding that nuclear navies in the Indo-Pacific (India's and China's) seem to have little to no communication with each other, these factors raise important questions on nuclear deterrence and escalation and, consequently, on the impact this has on regional stability.

In all, our findings indicate that there is a correlation between regional order and international instability, with risks of instability and war at the regional and localized levels having the potential to create spillover effects. Whether for reasons of maritime and territorial disputes in the China Seas or across the Taiwan Strait, regional order in the Indo-Pacific does not depend purely on the stability at the structural level. It also demands that issues among claimant states be addressed to avoid broader repercussions.

GOVERNANCE AND GOOD ORDER AT SEA AS LESS THAN A PROMISE OF STABILITY

The previous observations about the nature of regional order in the Indo-Pacific lead to a third observation more directly related to matters of maritime governance. The field of research in maritime security that deals specifically with this question has expanded considerably over the past few years. Christian Bueger has been at the forefront of the conceptual debate over what maritime security is and how its meaning changes depending on the stakeholders.[13] One important assumption underpinning much of this literature is the inherent potential for cooperation presented by security challenges related to the maintenance of good order at sea, whether to tackle piracy, smuggling, or indeed illegal unreported and unregulated fishing. Their transnational nature has represented an important opportunity for countries to develop ways to work together to ensure good order at sea, subsequently promoting greater stability. Yet, as the chapters in this volume highlighted, this assumption should not be overstated in the case of the Indo-Pacific.

Indeed, to some extent, in the Indo-Pacific the existence of numerous outstanding sovereignty and boundary-delimitation disputes presents a non-negligible risk to stability, if not a detrimental factor to stronger cooperation. Endeavors to assert maritime "rights and interests" as a way to reinforce claims can be, as the chapter by Patalano and Marionneau focusing on the East and South China Seas attested, damaging to regional stability. At the very least, disputes such as the ones related to the Chinese-claimed nine-dash line in the South China Sea or over the Senkaku/Diaoyu Islands in the East China Sea constitute a persistent source of tension in bilateral and multilateral ties. In a fashion not too dissimilar, the dispute between South Korea and Japan over Dok-do / Takeshima Islands remains a politically thorny issue that not merely adds to a difficult relationship but also undermines broader cooperation between two allies of the United States. In the case of the Northern Limit Line, actual military clashes between forces from the two Koreas occurred before some measure of stability ensued. In all, the emergence of new regimes allowing for governance to become an important question for states to address did not invite greater cooperation. Rather, in the Indo-Pacific, it created the conditions for competition to be taken more firmly in the realm of constabulary and law-enforcement activities.

This relates to another aspect of how frameworks for governance and good order at sea have not fostered an atmosphere leading to stronger stability. As the chapter on the legal dimension of the Indo-Pacific noted, different interpretations of provisions in UNCLOS and their applicability in exclusive economic zones—particularly regarding military activities—also represent a potential source of tension and conflict. This is particularly true in maritime theaters that are of primary importance to states in regard to sea-lanes and freedom of navigation. In the South China Sea, US freedom-of-navigation operations have been symptomatic of differences between the United States and China on this matter, but other countries with important maritime interests—notably France, Japan, and the United Kingdom—have also conducted activities aimed at challenging China's interpretations of legal frameworks. Therefore, while cooperative action is unlikely to defuse tensions or competition in the foreseeable future, it is also very likely that issues of governance and good order at sea are likely to increase their impact on regional security.

COMPETITION AT SEA AS A DRIVER OF COLLECTIVE ACTION

This last observation is pertinent to the fourth conclusion of this volume. Whereas maritime disputes seem to have hampered, particularly during the last decade, greater cooperation on matters of governance and good order at sea, peer-on-peer competition has had somewhat the opposite effect. Whether to ensure that a rules-based maritime order centered on the respect of well-established principles and practices concerning freedom of navigation is not undermined or, indeed, to counter coercive activities, naval partnerships are becoming a regular feature of the Indo-Pacific. These forms of military cooperation, ranging from simple activities aimed at better maritime domain awareness to coordinated multinational task groups, are in no measure a linear process, as shown by Abhijit Singh and James J. Wirtz's chapter on India-US ties in the Indian Ocean. Nonetheless, there is a growing tendency, one led by the United States and its closest partners in the Indo-Pacific (notably Japan and Australia and, to a lesser degree, India), to increase exercises and opportunities for coordinated activities to generate more regular presence, influence, and, as a result, stability. The proliferation of trilateral forms of maritime-centric cooperation, from Australia-Japan–United States to the more recent pact linking Australia, the United Kingdom, and the United States, is leading how the link between order and stability is being redefined.

This drive for more regular multilateral engagement, often featuring the United States or US allies, has thus far produced mixed results. In one sense, these partnerships were predominantly the result of and designed to address Chinese assertiveness. Yet maritime activities have not elicited a change in Chinese behavior. On the contrary, they have been matched by a constantly increasing number of Chinese and multilateral exercises and activities (predominantly with Russia). There is no evidence to suggest that in the absence of initiatives led by the United States or its allies, Chinese activities would not have increased.

Still, the current wave of multinational cooperation is different from the activities of the previous two decades that focused on addressing nontraditional security challenges and raises an important question about what is needed for them to produce effective multinational capabilities if needed. In Europe, organizations such as the North Atlantic Treaty Organization can draw on a considerable apparatus covering command and control, doctrines, and training—all designed to achieve military integration to maximum effect. In the Indo-Pacific, individual state actors have different degrees of interoperability and integration with the United States and increasingly among each other. Trilateral groupings such as the United States, Japan, and Australia, or indeed formations such as the Quad (the United States, India, Japan, and Australia), are a good example of the widening scope of multilateral arrangements based on practical military cooperation to produce specific capability packages. Whether current practices in the Indo-Pacific are sufficient remains an open question, but these trends are likely to create the conditions for greater military convergence with, if not dependence on, the United States.

This does not make issues of maritime governance as part of the regional security complex less relevant. Indeed, as the impact of climate change in the region is unlikely to diminish, there is still an important question about how to address its potentially devastating consequences. In this respect, the concerns across the South Pacific islands are symptomatic of a problem that is felt across the wider Indo-Pacific, and that remains a significant factor in how regional influence is likely to evolve and what demands—especially among small island nations—one will need to address to ensure it. More broadly, regional ambitions over matters of access and exploitation of maritime resources will require stronger frameworks to prevent irreparable damage to the marine ecosystem and more capabilities to ensure their respect. Indeed, taking the question of maritime governance one step further, the management of data flow through underwater sea cables is likely to add a new dimension to the debate over regional order. In this, the centrality of maritime connectivity—in a digital sense—to regional economic prosperity might see a degree of spillover from the current maritime disputes into the cyber realm, with debates over national sovereignty in cyberspace matters similarly affecting matters of regional order and power balance.

In all, the nature of the Indo-Pacific as a security complex places maritime forces in general—including land-based capabilities designed to operate at sea—and navies in a privileged position in maintaining regional security. In this volume, we sought to explain why that is the case and offered a new way to apply a strategic studies approach to engage with its meaning and impact. In so doing, we contextualized issues of national strategy and the relevance of capabilities in relation to specific theaters within the Indo-Pacific, while also offering an explanation as to why they remain interconnected. Our ambition was to unroll the complexity of this region and offer initial answers to articulate a more fruitful conversation closing the gap between separate disciplines. By no means did we set out to provide the ultimate answer to this conversation. On the contrary, we have sought to set a framework to propel the conversation toward new directions. Whether and to what extent our efforts will generate a sea change in the way Indo-Pacific security is debated remains a question that rests beyond the horizon of this volume.

NOTES

1. In her review of Jones's book, Kori Schake emphasizes the crucial importance for elites in the United States in particular to debate naval power in the contemporary world. Kori Schake, "Lost at Sea: The Dangerous Decline of American Naval Power," *Foreign Affairs*, March/April 2022, https://www.foreignaffairs.com/reviews/review-essay/2022-02-22/lost-sea.
2. Ian Urbina, *The Outlaw Ocean: Journeys across the Last Untamed Frontier* (New York: Knopf, 2019), xi.
3. Fernand Braudel, *A History of Civilizations* (New York: Penguin, 1995); David Abulafia, *The Boundless Sea: A Human History of the Oceans* (New York: Oxford University Press, 2019).
4. Michael S. Reidy and Helen M. Rozwadowski, "The Space in Between: Science, Ocean, Empire," *History of Science Society* 105, no. 2 (2014): 338–39, https://doi.org/doi.org/10.1086/676571.

5. Urbina, *Outlaw Ocean*, xi.

6. Bruce D. Jones, *To Rule the Waves: How Control of the World's Oceans Shapes the Fate of the Superpowers* (New York: Scribner, 2021), 7.

7. Jones, *To Rule the Waves*, 303–12.

8. Jonathan D. Caverley and Peter Dombrowski, "Too Important to Be Left to the Admirals: The Need to Study Maritime Great-Power Competition," *Security Studies* 29, no. 4 (2020): 580–81, https://doi.org/10.1080/09636412.2020.1811448.

9. Ian Bowers and Collin Koh Swee Lean, eds., *Grey and White Hulls: An International Analysis of the Navy–Coast Guard Nexus* (London: Palgrave Macmillan, 2019), 271–79.

10. Barry Buzan, Ole Wæver, and Jaap de Wilde, *Security: A New Framework for Analysis* (Boulder, CO: Lynne Rienner, 1998).

11. See, for example, Rory Medcalf, "The Indo-Pacific: What's in a Name?," *American Interest* 9, no. 2 (2013): 58–66, and Rory Medcalf, *Indo-Pacific Empire: China, America, and the Contest for the World's Pivotal Region* (Manchester: Manchester University Press, 2020).

12. For example, see David C. Kang, *East Asia before the West: Five Centuries of Trade and Tribute* (New York: Columbia University Press, 2010); and David C. Kang, "Hierarchy and Legitimacy in International Systems: The Tribute System in Early Modern East Asia," *Security Studies* 19, no. 4 (2010): 591–622, https://doi.org/10.1080/09636412.2010.524079.

13. Christian Bueger, "What Is Maritime Security?," *Marine Policy* 53 (March 2015): 159–64, https://doi.org/10.1016/j.marpol.2014.12.005; Christian Bueger and Timothy Edmunds, "Beyond Seablindness: A New Agenda for Maritime Security Studies," *International Affairs* 93, no. 6 (2017): 1293–1311, https://doi.org/10.1093/ia/iix174.

INDEX

Note: Information in figures and tables is indicated by page numbers in *italics*.

CONTRIBUTORS

IAN BOWERS is an associate professor at the Institute for Military Operations, Centre for Joint Operations, Royal Danish Defence College. His research interests include deterrence, naval operations, Asian security, and the future of warfare. He coedited the volume *Grey and White Hulls: An International Analysis of the Navy-Coastguard Nexus* and he is the author of *The Modernisation of the Republic of Korea Navy: Seapower, Strategy and Politics.*

RICHARD DUNLEY is a lecturer in history in the School of Humanities and Social Sciences, University of New South Wales Canberra, where he specializes in British naval history and strategy before World War II.

PETER ALAN DUTTON is the interim dean of the Center for Naval Warfare Studies at the US Naval War College. He formerly served as director of the China Maritime Studies Institute, a professor of strategic research, and a professor of law. His research focuses on China's maritime expansion, Chinese views of sovereignty and international law, and factors shaping China's rise. A retired US Navy judge advocate and former naval flight officer, he holds a PhD from King's College London, a JD from the College of William & Mary, and an MA from the Naval War College. He is an adjunct professor at the New York University School of Law, a faculty adviser to NYU's U.S.-Asia Law Institute, and an associate in research at Harvard University's Fairbank Center for Chinese Studies.

RYAN GINGERAS is a professor in the Department of National Security Affairs at the Naval Postgraduate School in Monterey, California. He is an expert on Turkish, Balkan, and Middle Eastern History.

REAR ADM. JAMES GOLDRICK, Royal Australian Navy (Ret.), was a naval historian, an analyst of contemporary naval and maritime affairs, and a retired senior officer. He held the position of fellow at the Sea Power Centre–Australia.

He was also an adjunct professor in the School of Humanities and Social Sciences at the University of New South Wales, at the Australian Defence Force Academy, and at the Strategic and Defence Studies Centre of the Australian National University; a member of the Naval Studies Group at the Australian Centre for the Study of Armed Conflict and Society; and a professorial fellow of the Australian National Centre for Ocean Resources and Security at the University of Wollongong. He passed away shortly before the publication of this book.

CATHERINE L. GRANT is a graduate of the international policy master's program at the Monterey Institute of International Studies (Middlebury Institute) and worked for several years as a research associate for the Department of National Security Affairs at the Naval Postgraduate School.

SHERYN LEE is a senior lecturer at the Swedish Defence University. She previously worked for the Office of National Intelligence, Australia's peak intelligence-assessment agency, and as a lecturer at Macquarie University, Sydney. Her work focuses on strategic studies and the foreign and defense policies of Taiwan, Japan, and Australia. Her first book was *Explaining Contemporary Military Modernization: The Myth of Asia's Arms Race.*

NICOLA LEVERINGHAUS is senior lecturer at the Department of War Studies, King's College London. She specializes in the International Relations of Asia, with a focus on China and the security of that region, especially as it relates to nuclear weapons. In September 2016 she joined the Department of War Studies from Sheffield University, where she was a lecturer in international politics.

MAJ. JULIE MARIONNEAU, French Air Force (Ret.), served with distinction in military operations in Afghanistan and Libya as a legal officer and at the French Air Force operational headquarters and the Office of the Prime Minister. She is now head of international affairs at ADS Group , a trade association representing the aerospace, defense, and security industries, and was previously a research fellow at the London-based think tank Policy Exchange.

DANIEL MORAN has been a member of the Naval Postgraduate School's Department of National Security Affairs since 1994. He teaches and writes about the history of war and international relations in Europe and Asia since the nineteenth century.

ALESSIO PATALANO is a professor of war and strategy in East Asia at the Department of War Studies, King's College London, specializing in Japanese naval history and strategy and contemporary maritime issues in East Asia. He is the author of *Post-war Japan as a Sea Power: Imperial Legacy, Wartime Experience and the Making of a Navy* and, with James A. Russell, edited the volume *Naval Innovation and Maritime Strategy.*

VICE ADM. ANN E. RONDEAU, USN (Ret.), is president of the Naval Postgraduate School. Prior to her appointment, Admiral Rondeau served as president of the College of DuPage. Her most recent military position was as the president of the National Defense University. In 1985 she became a White House fellow in the Reagan administration and went on to serve as the deputy commander of US Transportation Command, Pentagon director and chief of staff for the US Navy Staff, commander of Navy Personnel Development Command, commander of Naval Service Training Command, Pacific Fleet Staff chief of staff in Hawaii, commanding officer of Naval Support Activity, and other staff and commanding responsibilities in policy, planning, fleet support, joint logistics, training, and education. Rondeau was the second woman to achieve the three-star rank in the US Navy. Rondeau holds a BA from Eisenhower College, an MA from Georgetown University, and an EdD from Northern Illinois University.

CAPT. KEVIN ROWLANDS, Royal Navy, was awarded a PhD in war studies from King's College London and is the author of *21st Century Gorshkov: The Challenge of Seapower in the Modern Era* and *Naval Diplomacy in the 21st Century: A Model for the Post–Cold War Era.*

JAMES A. RUSSELL serves as associate professor in the Department of National Security Affairs at the Naval Postgraduate School. His previous books include *Military Adaptation in Afghanistan*, edited with Theo Farrell and Frans Osinga and *Innovation, Transformation and War: US Counterinsurgency Operations in Anbar and Ninewa Provinces, Iraq, 2005–2007.* He holds a PhD in war studies from King's College, University of London.

CLIVE SCHOFIELD is a professor and the head of research at the WMU-Sasakawa Global Ocean Institute at the World Maritime University in Malmö, Sweden. He also was previously a professor and past director of research at the Australian Centre for Ocean Resources and Security (ANCORS) at the University of Wollongong and remains a visiting professor with ANCORS. He holds a PhD in geography from the University of Durham and an LLM from the University of British Columbia.

CAPT. ABHIJIT SINGH, Indian Navy (Ret.), is senior fellow and head of the Maritime Policy Initiative at the Observer Research Foundation. A maritime professional with specialist and command experience in frontline Indian naval ships, he has been involved in the writing of India's maritime strategy since 2007. He is a keen commentator on maritime matters and has written extensively on security and governance issues in the Indian Ocean and Pacific Ocean littorals. His articles and commentaries have been published in *Asia Policy*, the *Lowy Interpreter*, the *World Politics Review*, and *The Diplomat*.

CHRISTOPHER TWOMEY received his PhD in political science from the Massachusetts Institute of Technology and joined the faculty of the Naval Postgraduate School in 2004, later serving as associate chair for research and director of the Center for Contemporary Conflict from 2007 to 2009. Today he supports the Office of the Secretary of Defense (Policy) and the State Department on a range of diplomatic engagements across Asia and advises Indo-Pacific Command, Strategic Command, and the Office of Net Assessment. He has been the lead organizer of the US-China Strategic Dialogue, a track 1.5 diplomatic meeting on strategic nuclear issues, since its inception in 2005. He is currently a member of the Institute of International Strategic Studies and a member of the adjunct staff at the RAND Corporation and has consulted for the National Bureau of Asian Research since 2009.

JAMES J. WIRTZ is professor of strategy at the Department of National Security Affairs at the Naval Postgraduate School. He is the author of *Understanding Intelligence Failure: Warning Response and Deterrence* and *The Tet Offensive: Intelligence Failure in War* and coeditor of several books, including (with Jeffrey A. Larsen) *Nuclear Command, Control, and Communications: A Primer on US Systems and Future Challenges* and (with Eliot Cohen, Colin Gray, John Baylis, and Jeannie Johnson) *Strategy in the Contemporary World*.